READINGS IN ANCIENT HISTORY

19608

ILLUSTRATIVE EXTRACTS FROM

THE SOURCES

II. ROME AND THE WEST

BY

WILLIAM STEARNS DAVIS

PROFESSOR OF ANCIENT HISTORY IN THE UNIVERSITY
OF MINNESOTA

WITH AN INTRODUCTION

BY

WILLIS MASON WEST

FORMERLY HEAD OF THE DEPARTMENT OF HISTORY
IN THE UNIVERSITY OF MINNESOTA

——⋯⋯——

ALLYN AND BACON

Boston   New York   Chicago

Norwood Press
J. S. Cushing Co. — Berwick & Smith Co.
Norwood, Mass., U.S.A.

AUTHOR'S PREFACE

THIS book aims to set before students beginning the study of Ancient History a sufficient amount of source material to illustrate the important facts mentioned in every good text-book. There is also a clear intent to give the reader some taste of the notable literary flavor pervading the histories of Greece and Rome. It is a distinct loss of an opportunity to pass from the study (*e.g.*) of the Roman Emperors and to read no typical passages of Tacitus. This compilation has been prepared for constant use along with some standard text-book, and various matters of marked historical importance, as the *Servian Constitution* of Rome, have been deliberately omitted, because most school histories state the fact sufficiently well, and little is added by reproducing the arid statements in Livy. On the other hand, many tales have been included, like the story of *Horatius at the Bridge* or of *Cincinnatus called from the Plow,* which condensed histories may well slight but which afford refreshing illustrations of the ancient life or the ancient viewpoint.

Comparing the compass of this work with the wide extent of available literature, it is evident that a very large number of desirable passages have been perforce omitted. There are practically no quotations from Cicero, because Cicero is a writer many students will earn a passing acquaintance with in the schools; again, certain highly significant passages are omitted, because they are quoted in so many school histories. There are no quotations from many of the poets, because the tragedians and lyricists were, after all, poets and not historians. The compiler has been forced continually to exercise his best judgment. He is entirely aware how fallible that judgment may have been.

To meet the requirements for a work covering the Old Orient and the Early Middle Ages (to 800 A.D.) sections have been added covering these topics, but no attempt has been made to have them so long as the chapters relating strictly to Greece and Rome. Even for the "classical" history itself, far more material came to hand for some periods than for others. Desirable selections for the First Age of Rome are scanty, while again readings on the First Century of the Empire come in bewildering profusion. As a rule, however, those epochs for which one has the most material are, in turn, the best worth studying, and no apology is made for the lack of proportion in the length of some of the chapters.

This volume has been prepared for immature students: it is therefore stripped of the learned notes, citations, references, etc., which are rightly demanded by the erudite. The notes and introductions have a single end in view, — to make the selections comprehensible to readers with little experience in Ancient History problems. Out of consideration for this audience, also, the pages have not been disfigured by frequent indications of omission, where passages of the ancient writer have been stricken out in the interests of brevity. In every case, however, where, to facilitate condensation, words *not* of the original author have been substituted, they are always inclosed in brackets [ ], to guard against misconception.

In compiling a work of this kind a great number of translations have been put under requisition. In many cases these have been diligently compared with the originals, and often such alterations have been made in the wording as to render the present author largely responsible for the form here given. This is entirely the case (except with Plutarch) where the translation appears without being ascribed to any particular translator. The translations from Plutarch may be generally acknowledged here as always being taken from the version of Dryden (revised by Clough). Considerable use has been made, as duly noted, of the familiar Bohn Library translations, but these often offend by their inelegant and overliteral following of the text, and, as a consequence, are most unsatisfactory guides for English readers. In many cases what amounts to a new translation has been prepared. To the various authors and publishers of copyrighted books from which excerpts are taken, who have generously given permission to copy, all thanks are here extended. Specific acknowledgments are due here to the History Department of the University of Pennsylvania for matter taken from their "Historical Reprints"; to Dr. Horace White for excerpts from his "Appian"; to Professor F. W. Kelsey for extracts from his edition of Mau's "Pompeii"; to Professor G. H. Palmer for his "Hymn of Cleanthes"; and to the friends of the late Professor H. B. Foster for the use of his "Cassius Dio."

The dates given in the running headlines are often highly approximate, especially for the earlier periods of history; and should not be memorized without careful comparison with the text and with various standard authorities.

In the preparation of this work the compiler has received generous assistance from many quarters, but particularly from Professor W. M. West of the University of Minnesota, who, besides writing the Introduction, has at all times given most friendly counsel out of a wide, practical experience, and who has afforded active assistance upon the work both during its inception and its final development. Hearty thanks are also due to Mr. Richard A. Newhall, formerly Assistant in History in the University of Minnesota, who

went over the entire manuscript most faithfully, checking
up all important references and otherwise making it useful
to historical students.

W. S. D.

THE UNIVERSITY OF MINNESOTA,
    MINNEAPOLIS, MINNESOTA,
        December, 1912.

INTRODUCTION

DR. DAVIS has placed high school teachers of history under an obligation which they will be quick to recognize. This book takes rank by itself. There are excellent "source books" in Greek and Roman history adapted to their own valuable work. But this is not a source book, in the usual sense. Fitly, it calls itself *Readings*. It unfolds a panorama of ancient life — etched, drawn, painted, caricatured, by contemporaries. No great phase of that life is neglected, and I take this opportunity to testify my special delight in the attractive presentation of two important epochs often slighted, — the Hellenic World after Alexander and the Roman Imperial World. It was a happy adaptation of workman to work that persuaded Dr. Davis to this task. His instinct for dramatic story and striking situation, and his faultless literary sense, have never, I believe, served better use. The boy or girl who once gets hold on the volume is sure to breathe in more of the atmosphere of the ancient world than from any possible study of a conventional textbook. Indeed, the *Readings* will lend needed light and color to any text-book. In my judgment, a high school class in Ancient History should have this book, not merely in the library for occasional reference, but constantly in the hands of each student. If that is arranged, most other "library work" *may*, perhaps, be omitted by a first-year class without serious loss, providing the following year in Modern History is so planned as to put emphasis on library reference. Not all varieties of historical training can be given with equal stress in one year — certainly not in a first

year. This volume makes it possible to do the most desirable things for that year more easily and more effectively
than ever before.

Now as to some of those things and how to do them. I
hesitate to speak as a dogmatic pedagogue; but this is just
the matter on which I am particularly requested to speak in
this Introduction. Concrete details depend largely upon
the articulation with the regular text-book, and must vary
with the text used. I must confine myself to a few general
principles.

1. The volume is not designed for "hard" study, to be
tested scrupulously by minute questioning: it is meant for
reading. At the same time, it is planned so that, with a
little thought by the teacher, it may be a daily companion
to any standard text in Ancient History. Readings should
usually be assigned for a group of days ahead (two days to
five), to allow for variation in arrangement between this
book and the text; and students should then be expected —
and helped — to go back at the proper times from passages
in the text to the appropriate passages in the *Readings*.
They should be taught to look for and to utilize Dr. Davis's
suggestions at the head of each "number" as to the most
essential things to look for in the extract. And almost
daily, while the correct habit is forming, the teacher will
find opportunity to ask, "What further light on this do you
find in the *Readings*?" "Did you get that idea from your
text-book or from a 'contemporary' authority?" "Does
the passage from Tacitus in the *Readings* support or
weaken this statement of your text?" Such practice should
be continued and varied until the student instinctively turns
from text to *Readings* and back again, supplementing each
by the other, in his consideration of each topic.

2. Now and then a suitable passage (not too long) may
even be used in the way more peculiar to "source books"
proper, for painstaking and exhaustive study, to establish

conclusions in advance of the text, or to disclose evidence for positions there taken. For this purpose, the teacher may need at first to dictate searching questions. For a few typical documents Dr. Davis has supplied such questions; but the selection of documents to be used in this way will necessarily vary with the text-book. Now and then the class may be required to write questions upon a document; and, still better, a student may prepare himself to question the class orally — first, of course, *communicating to the instructor the points he intends to bring out.*

3. When the survey of an important period or topic has been completed (Greek life in the days of Pericles, for instance), it will sometimes be well to spend a day or more in re-reading the *Readings,* with a class exercise to bring out points found there and not previously dwelt upon.

4. The historical introductions by Dr. Davis should, of course, be compared carefully with the corresponding matter in the regular text; and any divergences of opinion will afford convenient occasion for reference to larger standard authorities by an individual or by the class.

5. The student should certainly acquire some discriminating sense as to why one source differs from another in historical value or reliability. He can appreciate easily why (*e.g.*) Vol. II, § 63 (contemporary statement) is better authority for the facts it recites than is Vol. II, § 13, which has *tradition* or *recollection* merely for the facts it states. And such discrimination is susceptible of considerable development. Moreover, it is quite possible for the student to comprehend that even where a contemporary's judgment is erroneous as to *fact,* it is still often a historical fact *itself* of great significance. In this connection, to all cautions by Dr. Davis in his introductions against taking an opinion as an infallible authority — merely because it is contemporary and old — the teacher will need to add frequent reminder as to the partisan or personal or class bias of many of the

writers quoted. It may be driven slowly into the everyday consciousness of the class that Homeric bards sang to chieftains for largess, and were glad to gratify such auditors by raising a laugh at the expense of the annoying Thersites, who, in real life, may that day have bested the chief in the Assembly; that Aristophanes and Juvenal were ancient "muckrakers," with far less zeal for accurate statement than have their successors who trouble our society in the monthly magazines; that Cicero was a complacent and delightful old "standpatter," and Tacitus a preacher who heightened the virtues of other peoples in order to darken the vices of his own land; that most professed historians were more eager for a good story than for scientific accuracy; and that, during all time, democracy has had its history written chiefly by its enemies — since literature has belonged so largely to the aristocrats.

6. I close with a suggestion, hardly needed, of perhaps the finest use of the volume. A true teacher ought to find in every class *some* students before whom these extracts may be dropped as delectable bait, to lure them on to high enjoyment of Plutarch and the *Odyssey* and Marcus Aurelius in their entirety.

WILLIS MASON WEST.

December, 1912.

CONTENTS

CHAPTER I

The First Roman Age

CHAPTER II

The Growth of the Republic

CONTENTS xiii

CHAPTER V

The Founding of the Roman Empire

CHAPTER VI

The Deeds of the Emperors

CHAPTER VII

Public and Private Life under the Empire

CHAPTER VIII

Philosophical and Religious Life in the Last Pagan Centuries

CONTENTS

CONTENTS

CHAPTER X

The Dying Empire and the German Invaders

CHAPTER XI

The Early Middle Ages and Charlemagne

ROME AND THE WEST

ROME AND THE WEST

CHAPTER I

THE FIRST ROMAN AGE

The transition from Greece to Rome reflects itself in our literary sources ; our narratives of Greek history are vivid, personal, abounding in illuminating detail ; the annals of early Rome are bare and formal, telling of events rather than of individuals. Even where it seems as if enlightening personalia are given, they may be justly suspected of being the fabrications of late historians trained to imitate Greek literary models. The first age of Rome never immortalized itself in anything like the Homeric poems or the delightful tales of Herodotus ; instead we have Grecianized legends, none too faithfully reproduced by the uncritical Livy. There is not a single personality in all Roman history who stands out for us with a clear-cut individuality — whom in short we can say we comprehend as we comprehend Themistocles or Pericles ; until we come at last to Scipio the Elder. . Nevertheless, we are not without interesting memorials of the period of the early Roman Republic or even of the period of the Kings. Thanks to the inherent conservatism of the Latin genius we find in the literature of later ages legal and religious formulæ which manifestly have been handed down in unbroken tradition from very early times (*e.g.* The Song of the Arval Brethren ; The Form of Declaring War, etc.) ; and such memorials as these aid us not a little to understand the institutions and modes of thought of the cold, unpoetic, practical, patriotic, and wholly effective folk of central Italy who were to build an empire such as the more versatile and æsthetically brilliant Greeks could never create.

Besides certain of these "literary survivals" just mentioned, there are also given one or two of the famous tales from Livy, which, whatever their authenticity, truly illustrate the stern spirit

1

of self-immolation for the common weal which was one of the noblest features of the life of early Rome.

1. DESCRIPTION OF ITALY

Pliny the Elder, " Natural History," book III, chap. 6.   Bohn translation

The natural advantages of the Italian peninsula are here set forth by an enthusiastic Roman writer.   The Italians were — and are — justified in the praise of their country ; it is in every respect the queen of the southern European lands — vastly superior in every way to Spain with its few harbors and uplands and plains ; and again with far greater resources than picturesque but rocky and restricted Greece.   On the whole, it is the most favored land bordering the Mediterranean, if not — area considered — in the entire world.

When we come to Italy, we begin with the Ligures [in the Northwest], after whom we have Etruria, Umbria, Latium, where the mouths of the Tiber are situate, and Rome the "Capital of the World," sixteen miles distant from the Sea.   We then come to the coasts of the Volsci and Campania, and the districts of Picenum, of Lucania and of Bruttium, where Italy extends the farthest in a southerly direction, and projects into the [two] seas with the chain of the Alps,[1] which there forms pretty nearly the shape of a crescent.   Leaving Bruttium we come to the coast of [Magna] Græcia, then the Apuli, Peligni, Sabini, Picentes, Galli, the Umbri, the Tusci, the Venetes [and other peoples].

I am quite aware that I might be justly accused of ingratitude and indolence, were I to describe thus briefly and in so cursory a manner the land which is at once the foster-child and the parent of all lands : chosen by the providence of the Gods to render even heaven itself more glorious, to unite the scattered empires of the earth, to bestow a pol-

---

[1] This, of course, refers to the Apennines.

ish upon men's manners, to unite the discordant and uncouth dialects of so many nations by the powerful ties of one common language, to confer the enjoyments of discourse and of civilization upon mankind, to become, in short, the mother-country of all the nations.

But how shall I begin the task? So vast is the number of celebrated places [no one living can name them all]. So great is the renown [of each spot] I feel myself wholly at a loss. The city of Rome alone, which forms a portion [of Italy], a face well worthy of shoulders so beauteous, how great a book it would take for a due description! And then too [there is] the coast of Campania, just taken by itself, — so blessed with natural charms and riches, that it is evident that when nature formed it, she took a delight in accumulating all her blessings in a single spot — how am I to do justice to this?

Again the climate, with its eternal freshness, and so abounding in health and vitality, the sereneness of the weather so enchanting, the fields so fertile, the hill sides so sunny, the thickets so free from every danger,[1] the groves so cool and shady, the forests with a vegetation so varying and luxuriant, the fruitfulness of the grain, the vines, and the admirable olives, the flocks with fleeces so noble, the bulls with necks so sinewy ; the lakes with one ever coming after another, the numerous rivers and springs which refresh the land on every side with their waters, the numerous [gulfs of] the sea with their havens, and the bosom of the lands opening everywhere to the commerce of the wide world, yes, as it were, eagerly reaching out into the very midst of the waves, for the purpose of aiding — so it seems — the efforts of the Immortals!

At present I omit speaking of its genius, its manners, its men, and the nations whom it has conquered by eloquence and the might of arms. The very Greeks — a folk fond

[1] Presumably from dangerous wild beasts.

mightily of spreading their own praises — have given ample
judgment in favor of Italy, when they named simply a
small part of it " Magna Græcia." But we must be content
in this case, as in our description of the heavens. We must
only touch upon these points, and take notice of merely a
few of its stars.

I may begin by remarking that this land very much re-
sembles in shape an oak-leaf, being much longer than it is
broad ; towards the top it inclines to the left [if one is facing
south], while it terminates in the form of an Amazonian
buckler,[1] in which the central projection is called Cocinthos,
while it sends forth two horns at the end of its crescent-
shaped bays — Leucopetra on the right, and Lacinium on the
left.   It extends in length 1020 miles, if we measure from
the foot of the Alps at Prætoria Augusta through the city of
Rome and Capua to Rhegium, — which is situate on the
shoulder of the Peninsula, just at the bend of the neck as it
were.   The distance is much greater if measured to Lacinium,
but in that case the line, being drawn obliquely, would incline too much to one side.   The breadth [of Italy] is variable ; being 410 miles between the two seas, the Lower
[Tuscan] and the Upper [Adriatic], and the rivers Varus
[by Gaul] and Arsia [by Istria] ; at about the middle and in
the vicinity of the city of Rome, from the spot where the
river Aternus flows into the Adriatic to the mouth of the
Tiber, the distance is 136 miles, and a little less from Cas-
trum-Novum on the Adriatic sea to Alsium on the Tuscan ; —
but at no place does it exceed 200 miles in breadth.   The
circuit of the whole from the Varus to the Arsia is 3059 miles.[2]

As to its distance from the countries that surround it,
Epirus and Illyricum [nearest points toward Greece] are

[1] That is, a shield, whose side was shaped like a kind of crescent.
[2] A good example of how inaccurate the Ancients were in their calculations — and Pliny doubtless used the best available data ; the real
circuit is about 2500 miles.

50 miles distant, Africa is less than 200, as we are informed by Marcus Varro, and Sicily a mile and a half.

2. Roman Rustic Festival

Ovid, "Fasti," book IV, 1. 735 ff.

The following is from an author of the Augustan Age, but the old worship herein described had survived practically unchanged in agricultural districts from very primitive times. We may imagine the men of the age of the Tarquins practicing almost exactly these identical rites.

Shepherd! at the first streak of dawn purify thy well-nourished flocks; first besprinkle them with water, and let a branch sweep clean the ground. Let the folds be decked with leaves and branches, while a trailing wreath covers the gates so gaily adorned. Then make the blue flames to rise from the living sulphur, and the sheep bleat loudly whilst she feels the touch of the smoking sulphur. Burn next the olive-branch, the pine twig, the juniper, — for this is the food which rejoices the country goddess the most. Give also to her an especial share of the feast, and her pail of milk; and when her share has been set aside, then, with milk warm from the cow, make thou thy prayer to. Pales [1] — warder of the woods.

[In this prayer the farmer must beg forgiveness for any unconscious sins against the rustic deities, such as trespassing on their groves, or sheltering his flocks under their altar; then he should beg that disease be averted, and good luck attend his crops, herds, and flocks.]

Thus must thou win the favor of the divinity; and say this prayer four times, turning toward the sunrise, and wash thy hands at the running stream. Then set the rustic bowl

[1] A rustic divinity who figures in early Roman mythology as the especial patron of herdsmen.

upon the table in place of the wine-bowl, and drink ye the snowy milk and dark must, and soon through the heaps of crackling straw leap in swift course with eager limbs.

[All the worshipers then begin to leap through the blazing fires, and even the flocks and herds are driven through, while fierce hilarity reigns.]

3. Part of an Early Latin Farmer's Calendar

Inscription in " Corpus Inscript. Lat.," vol. VI, p. 637

This inscription for the month of May was on a marble cube, on the four sides whereof were indications of the works and festivals for each month. Notice the brief, pithy injunctions, — very suitable for a community of hard-headed, totally unimaginative rustics.

The month of May

Thirty-one days, with the nones falling on the seventh day. The day has fourteen and one half hours. The night has nine and one half hours. The sun is under the sign of Taurus. The month of May is under the protection of Apollo.

The corn is weeded.

The sheep are shorn.

The wool is washed.

The young steers are put under the yoke.

The vetch in the meadows is cut.

The lustration of the crops is made. Sacrifices (ought to be made) to Mercury and to Flora.

4. Song of the Arval Brethren

Old Latin Fragment from Wordsworth's Translation

The "Arval Brethren" were a company of twelve priests, whose main business seems to have been to offer sacrifice for the fertility of the soil. During their solemn festival they executed a sacred dance, and recited the hymn here given.　This hymn is in such primitive Latin that its correct translation is in some points disputed; but it continued to be recited centuries after the priests had almost forgotten its meaning.　Compare this early *Latin* effort at poetry with the earliest known poetry of the Greeks!

Help us, O Lares, help us, Lares, help us!
　And thou, O Marmar, suffer not
　Fell plague and ruin's rot
　Our folk to devastate.
Be satiate, O fierce Mars, be satiate!
　Leap o'er the threshold!　Halt!　now beat the ground!

　　　　[Above couplet repeated three times.]

Call to your aid the heroes all, call in alternate strain;
　Call, call the heroes all!
Call to your aid the heroes all, call in alternate strain.
Help us, O Marmar, help us!　Marmar, help us!
Leap high in solemn measure; leap and leap again!
　Leap high and leap again!

5.　THE ANCIENT ROMAN FORM OF DECLARING WAR

Livy, " History," book I, chap. 32

Among the very old formulas and usages that survived at Rome down to relatively late times, this method of declaring war holds a notable place.　It was highly needful to observe all the necessary formalities in beginning hostilities, otherwise the angry gods would turn their favor to the enemy.

[Ancus Marcius, the fourth king of Rome, was at once a man of peace and an efficient soldier; and on the outbreak of a war with the Latins he is said to have instituted the customs which later ages of Romans observed in war.]

Inasmuch as Numa had instituted the religious rites for days of peace, Ancus Marcius desired that the ceremonies relating to war might be transmitted by himself to future ages. Accordingly he borrowed from an ancient folk, the Æquicolæ, the form which the [Roman] heralds still observe, when they make public demand for restitution.

The [Roman] envoy when he comes to the frontier of the offending nation, covers his head with a woolen fillet, and says, —

"Hear, O Jupiter, and hear ye lands (of such and such a nation), let Justice hear! I am a public messenger of the Roman people. Justly and religiously I come, and let my words bear credit!" Then he makes his demands, and follows with a solemn appeal to Jupiter. "If I demand unjustly and impiously that these men and goods [in question] be given to me, the herald of the Roman people, then suffer me never to enjoy again my native country!"

These words he repeats when he crosses the frontiers; he says them also to the first man he meets [on the way]; again when he passes the gate; again on entering the [foreigners'] market-place, some few words in the formula being [then] changed. If the persons he demands are not surrendered after thirty days, he declares war, thus: —

"Hear, O Jupiter and thou too Juno, — Romulus also, and all ye celestial, terrestrial, and infernal gods! Give us ear! I call ye to witness that this nation (naming it) is unjust, and has acted contrary to right. And as for us, we will consult thereon with our elders in our homeland, as to how we may obtain our rights."

After that the envoy returns to Rome to report, and the king was wont at once to consult with the Senators in some such words as these,

"Concerning such quarrels as to which the 'pater patratus'[1] of the Roman people has conferred with the pater patratus of the [foreign] people, and with that people themselves, touching what they ought to have surrendered or done, and which things they have not surrendered nor done

---

[1] The head of the Roman heralds (fetiales).

[as they ought]; speak forth," he said to the senator first questioned, "what think you?"

Then the other said, " I think that [our rights] should be demanded by a just and properly declared war, and for that I give my consent and vote."

Next the others were asked in order, and when the majority of those present had reached an agreement, the war was resolved upon.

It was customary for the *fetialis* to carry in his hand a javelin pointed with steel, or burnt at the end and dipped in blood. This he took to the confines of the enemy's country, and in the presence of at least three persons of adult years, he spoke thus, " Forasmuch as the state of the [enemy here named] has offended against the Roman People, the Quirites; and forasmuch as the Roman People the Quirites have ordered that there should be war [with the enemy] and the Senate of the Roman People has duly voted that war should be made upon the enemy [here named]: I acting for the Roman People declare and make actual war upon the enemy!"

So saying he flung the spear within the hostile confines. After this manner restitution was at that time demanded from the Latins [by Ancus Marcius] and war proclaimed; and the usage then established was adopted by posterity.[1]

6. NUMA AND HIS INSTITUTION OF THE VESTALS, ETC.

Plutarch, " Life of Numa," chaps. IX–XIV, XIX, XX

To Numa the traditional second king of Rome (assumed dates 715 to 673 B.C.) later ages attributed many of the religious usages

---

[1] When in later ages the Romans had to wage war with nations beyond the seas, they resorted to a very curious fiction in order to keep this old custom. They transferred a spot of ground near the Circus Flaminius to a prisoner from the unfriendly nation; and on this spot, in front of the Temple of Bellona, they set a column. The land could now be accounted hostile territory, and the spear of the fetialis could be hurled upon it. Another example of Roman literalism.

of the city. We may dismiss Numa as legendary ; but the institutions and customs ascribed to him were not legendary, and survived nearly intact down to the triumph of Christianity, thus
illustrating the essentially conservative character of the Roman
genius. Note that the old Roman religion was almost formalism
incarnate. The relations of god and worshiper are those of creditor and debtor ; the latter must discharge his duty literally, and
in exchange require a due amount of favor. Almost *no* religion
was so deficient in spirituality as that of Rome. It did, however,
put a premium on the scrupulous performance of duty.

The original constitution of the priests, called Pontifices
is ascribed unto Numa, and he himself was, it is said, the
first of them ; and that they have the name of Pontifices
from *potens*, powerful, because they attend the service of
the gods, who have power and command over all. The
most common opinion is the most absurd, which derives this
word from *pons*, and assigns the priests the title of bridge-
makers.[1] The sacrifices performed on the bridge were
amongst the most sacred and ancient, and the keeping and
repairing of the bridge attached, like any other public sacred
office, to the priesthood. It was accounted not simply unlawful, but a positive sacrilege, to pull down the wooden
bridge ; which moreover is said, in obedience to an oracle,
to have been built entirely of timber and fastened with
wooden pins, without nails or cramps of iron. The stone
bridge was built a very long time after, when Æmilius was
quæstor, and they do, indeed, say also that the wooden
bridge was not so old as Numa's time. . . .

The office of Pontifex Maximus, or chief priest, was to declare and interpret the divine law, . . . he not only prescribed
rules for public ceremony, but regulated the sacrifices of
private persons, not suffering them to vary from established

---

[1] Nevertheless this seems the probable origin of the word. The Pontifices are said to have had the making or maintenance of the Sublician
bridge built over the Tiber by Ancus Marcius.

custom, and giving information to every one of what was requisite for purposes of worship or supplication. He was also guardian of the vestal virgins, the institution of whom, and of their perpetual fire, was attributed to Numa, who, perhaps, fancied the charge of pure and uncorrupted flames would be fitly intrusted to chaste and unpolluted persons, or that fire, which consumes, but produces nothing, bears an analogy to the virgin estate.

Some are of opinion that these vestals had no other business than the preservation of this fire; but others conceive that they were keepers of other divine secrets, concealed from all but themselves. Gegania and Verenia, it is recorded, were the names of the first two virgins consecrated and ordained by Numa; Canuleia and Tarpeia succeeded; Servius Tullius afterwards added two, and the number of four has been continued to the present time.

The Term of Service for the Vestals

The statutes prescribed by Numa for the vestals were these: that they should take a vow of virginity for the space of thirty years, the first ten of which they were to spend in learning their duties, the second ten in performing them, and the remaining ten in teaching and instructing others. Thus the whole term being completed, it was lawful for them to marry, and leaving the sacred order, to choose any condition of life that pleased them; but of this permission few, as they say, made use; and in cases where they did so, it was observed that their change was not a happy one, but accompanied ever after with regret and melancholy; so that the greater number, from religious fears and scruples, forbore, and continued to old age and death in the strict observance of a single life.

For this condition he compensated by great privileges and prerogatives; as that they had power to make a will in the lifetime of their father; that they had a free administration of their own affairs without guardian or tutor, which was the privilege of women who were the mothers of three children; when they go abroad, they have the fasces carried before them; and if in their walks they chance to meet a criminal on his way to execution, it saves his life, upon oath being made that the meeting was accidental, and not concerted or of set purpose. Any one who presses upon the chair on which they are carried is put to death.

Punishment of Unfaithful Vestals

If these vestals commit any minor fault, they are punishable by the high-priest only, who scourges the offender, sometimes with her clothes off, in a dark place, with a curtain drawn between; but she that has broken her vow is buried alive near the gate called Collina, where a little mound of earth stands, inside the city, reaching some little distance, called in Latin *agger;* under it a narrow room is constructed, to which a descent is made by stairs; here they prepare a bed, and light a lamp, and leave a small quantity of victuals, such as bread, water, a pail of milk, and some oil; that so that body which had been consecrated and devoted to the most sacred service of religion might not be said to perish by such a death as famine. The culprit herself is put in a litter, which they cover over, and tie her down with cords on it, so that nothing she utters may be heard. They then take her to the forum; all people silently go out of the way as she passes, and such as follow accompany the bier with solemn and speechless sorrow; and, indeed, there is not any spectacle more appalling, nor any day observed by the city with greater appearance of gloom and sadness. When they come to the place of execution, the officers loose the cords, and then the high-priest, lifting his hands to heaven, pronounces certain prayers to himself before the act; then he brings out the

prisoner, being still covered, and placing her upon the
steps that lead down to the cell, turns away his face with
the rest of the priests ; the stairs are drawn up after she
has gone down, and a quantity of earth is heaped up over
the entrance to the cell, so as to prevent it from being
distinguished from the rest of the mound. This is the
punishment of those who break their vow of virginity.

The Priests known as "Salii"

[From Numa's day also were dated twelve sacred targets
of bronze, said to have the virtue of guarding the city from
pestilence.]

The keeping of these targets was committed to the charge
of certain priests, called Salii, who received their name from
that jumping dance which the Salii themselves use, when in
the month of March they carry the sacred targets through
the city ; at which procession they are habited in short frocks
of purple, girt with a broad belt studded with brass; on their
heads they wear a brass helmet, and carry in their hands short
daggers, which they clash every now and then against the
targets.   But the chief thing is the dance itself.   They move
with much grace, performing, in quick time and close order,
various intricate figures, with a great display of strength and
agility.   The targets are not made round, nor like proper
targets, of a complete circumference, but are cut out into a
wavy line, the ends of which are rounded off and turned in
at the thickest part towards each other.

After Numa had in this manner instituted these several
orders of priests, he erected, near the temple of Vesta, what
is called to this day Regia, or king's house, where he spent
the most part of his time, performing divine service, instructing the priests, or conversing with them on sacred subjects.
He had another house upon the Mount Quirinalis, the site of
which they show to this day.   In all public processions and

solemn prayers, criers were sent before to give notice to the people that they should forbear their work, and rest.[1] . . .

The Worship of Janus

[Numa is alleged to have reformed the calendar and named the months.]

January was so called from Janus, and precedence given to it by Numa before March, which was dedicated to the god Mars; because, as I conceive, he wished to take every opportunity of intimating that the arts and studies of peace are to be preferred before those of war. For this Janus, whether in remote antiquity he were a demi-god or a king, was certainly a great lover of civil and social unity, and one who reclaimed men from brutal and savage living; for which reason they figure him with two faces, to represent the two states and conditions out of the one of which he brought mankind, to lead them into the other. His temple at Rome has two gates, which they call the gates of war, because they stand open in the time of war, and shut in the times of peace; of which latter there was very seldom an example, for, as the Roman empire was enlarged and extended, it was so encompassed with barbarous nations and enemies to be resisted, that it was seldom or never at peace. Only in the time of Augustus Cæsar, after he had overcome Antony, this temple was shut; as likewise once before, when Marcus Atilius and Titus Manlius[2] were consuls; but then it was not long before, wars breaking out, the gates were again opened. But, during the reign of Numa, those gates were

[1] Note the extreme formalism of the Roman religion. The people were not bound to stop working on religious holidays; but the priests must not *see* them work. Therefore the crier was sent ahead when the priests passed to warn the people to cease labor just for the moment. The man beheld working by the priest was subject to a fine.

[2] In 235 A.D. shortly after the close of the First Punic War.

never seen open a single day, but continued constantly shut for a space of forty-three years together ; such an entire and universal cessation of war existed.[1]

7. BRUTUS CONDEMNS HIS OWN SONS TO DEATH

Livy, " History," book II, chap. 5

This story is the best illustration of the " old Roman discipline," its unrelenting severity, and its subordination of all private feelings to the demands of public duty.   It is ascribed to the year 509 B.C.

[An unsuccessful plot to restore the Tarquin dynasty was discovered, and some of the most prominent youths of Rome were implicated in it, including the sons of Brutus the Consul, the highest magistrate of the city.]

The traitors were condemned to capital punishment. Their doom was the more memorable, because the duties of the consular office imposed upon [Brutus] the father the task of punishing his own children. He who ought not even to have witnessed their fate, was ordained by fortune to exact their punishment. A number of [other] young men of high rank stood tied to the stake for the requital of their crimes, but the consul's sons attracted the most attention from the spectators : [although exasperation with their treason destroyed much of the popular pity].

The consuls seated themselves in their tribunal. The lictors then, fulfilling their office, stripped the criminals naked, beat them with the rods and smote off their heads. During all this time their father presented a touching sight indeed, in his looks and his whole general manner : for now and again the feelings of a parent, even as he superintended the public execution, would burst forth to plain view.

[1] The reign of Numa was regularly looked back upon as a kind of a Golden Age. It is needless to say that Early Rome never enjoyed this immunity from war.

8. How Horatius held the Bridge

Livy, "History," book II, chaps. 9, 10

The story of "Horatius at the Bridge" and how he saved Rome, when she was in deadly peril from attack by Lars Porsena, lord of the Etruscans, would not be worth reproducing, so familiar is it, were it not for the natural interest in the original narrative as rehearsed by Livy. It is to be feared the historicity of the incident will not bear too close inspection. Its alleged date was 508 B.C.

Porsena, thinking it would be glorious for the Tuscans, if there were a king in Rome, and a king too of their own nation, marched on Rome with a hostile army. Never before did so great terror seize the Senate; — so powerful was Clusium then, and so great the renown of [its King] Porsena.

Not only did they dread their foreign enemies, but even their own citizens; fearing lest the common people, cowed by fear, should receive the Tarquins [supported by Porsena] back into the city, and thus gain peace even at the price of slavery.

Many conciliatory concessions were therefore granted to the Plebeians by the Senate during these times. [The taxes were abated, an effort was made to provide salt at a fair price, and, as a result, it came to pass that good feeling prevailed in Rome, so that] from the highest to the lowest all equally detested the name of "King"; nor did any demagogue in later times gain greater popularity by his intrigues, than did the whole Senate then by its excellent government.

Some parts of Rome were secured [against the foe] by walls; other parts by the barrier of the Tiber; but the Sublician Bridge nearly afforded a passage to the enemy had there not been one man, Horatius Cocles — whom the Fortune of Rome gave for a bulwark that day — who chanced to be posted as a guard on the bridge. When he saw the Janiculum [the hill across the Tiber] carried by a sudden assault, and the enemy charging thence with full onset, while his friends in terror and confusion were actually casting away their arms, he laid hold on them one by one ; and standing out in the way [of the fugitives] he appealed to them in the name of gods and men, and cried out : "Their flight would profit nothing, if they fled their posts. If they once left the bridge behind them, there would soon be more foes on the Palatine hill and the Capitol than on the Janiculum!" He therefore urged and enjoined them "to hew down the bridge, by sword, fire, or any means; and *he* would stand the brunt of the foe, so far as one man might."

Thereat he advanced to the first entrance of the bridge, and faced about, to engage the foe hand to hand, with so surprising a front that he terrified the enemy. But two other Romans, impelled by conscious shame, stood with him, Spurius Lartius and Titus Herminius, men of high birth and of brave renown. With them, Horatius for a little stood back the first onset, and the fiercest brunt of the battle. But now the men hewing down the bridge called on them to retire; and Horatius compelled the others to fly to safety across the scanty part of the bridge still left. Then casting his eyes sternly with threatening mien upon all the Tuscan chiefs, he now challenged them singly, now taunted them all, as "slaves of proud tyrants, and men who cared not for their own freedom, and so were come to crush out the freedom of others!"

For some little time they hesitated, looking one to the other, ere commencing the fight; then mere shame put their host in motion ; they raised their war shout, and from every side hurled in their darts on their lone adversary. But all these darts stuck fast in his shield, and with a firm stand he held the bridge. Then they strove by a single push to thrust him down, but hereupon the crashing noise of the falling bridge, and the cheers of the Romans, checked their fury with a sudden panic.

Thereupon Cocles spoke: "Holy Father Tiber, I pray that thou do receive these my arms, and this thy soldier in thy benignant stream."

All in his armor he sprang down into the river, and while darts showered around him he swam across quite safely to his friends, — the hero of a deed which generations to come will more easily glorify than believe. The state was not ungrateful for his valor. A statue was erected to him in the assembly place [in the Forum] and as much land was given him as he was able to plow around in a single day.

CHAPTER II

THE GROWTH OF THE REPUBLIC

The story of the growth of early Rome is the story of a small city surrounded by a small farming community, rent within by feuds and beset without by hostile neighbors. Rome was obliged to be master of her own house and her own energies before she was able to embark on her great period of conquest. Small and humble as these civic contests and border warfare might seem, they were pregnant with vast accomplishment for the future. In the strife betwixt Patrician and Plebeian were learned those lessons in mutual concession, in the developing of practical political expedients and in the honest submission to an unwelcome fact when the battle had been fairly ended, which were to stand Rome in such good stead when she was summoned to rule the nations. In the petty frontier warfare with Volscian and Etruscan was slowly perfected that military art which was to make the Roman armies the most efficient war machines which, weapons considered, the world has ever witnessed.

Many of the details of this early Republican period are obscure; our records are often dubious and scanty, but the great facts stand patent. In this chapter are given some of the narratives of Livy as to certain capital events, stories that are always picturesque, and which we will gladly try to believe to be true. A typical incident from Plutarch is given, and in addition a couple of excerpts from Polybius illustrative of conditions in Rome when the Republic had fairly embarked on its voyage toward empire.

9. THE SECESSION OF THE PLEBS AND THE FIRST TRIBUNES

Livy, " History," book II, chaps. 23–24 and 32–33

The mutiny of the Plebs and the setting up of the first tribunes form, of course, a cardinal point in the history of the Roman

Republic. But note the essentially *peaceful* character of the resistance; it was a "strike" rather than a revolt, despite bitter and prolonged grievances. A Greek city in like condition would have been rent asunder by armed conflicts, and the defeated party would probably have tasted massacre or, at best, exile. The Roman habit was to obey the law, except when it became intolerable, and then to resist simply enough to redress the immediate wrong, — not to put through a "Reform Program." This willingness to sink private or class wrongs in the public good was one of the secrets of the successes of the Republic.

War with the Volscians was threatening, but the state was also sorely disturbed within itself, the animosity betwixt Senate and people glowing now to white heat, largely on account of the imprisonments for debt. Loud was the complaint that while men were fighting abroad for lands and liberty, they were seized and oppressed at home by their own fellow citizens; and that the "liberty of the people" was more secure in war than in peace. This feeling of discontent increasing of itself was still further aggravated by a case of individual suffering.

A certain aged man thrust himself into the Forum, with all the tokens of his miseries upon him. His clothes were utterly squalid; his very body was shocking, pale and emaciated as it was. His long beard and hair impressed, too, a savage wildness upon his features. Notwithstanding his wretched state he was nevertheless recognized, and it was repeated how he had been a centurion, and, while pitying him, men announced his other distinctions won in the public service, — while he displayed the various scars on his breast, witnesses as they were to honorable battles.

[As the multitude gathered and questioned him he told how,] " while serving in the Sabine War, because he had not merely lost the produce of his little farm through the hostile ravagers, but also because his house had been burned, his goods stolen, his cattle driven away, and too because a

tax had been imposed [on him at that very distressing
time, he had fallen into debt. Then this debt had aggravated. First he had been stripped of his father's and his
grandfather's farm, then of his other property.] Finally
he was seized in person by his creditor, and haled away, not
into mere slavery, but into a regular house of correction
and punishment. He finally displayed his back, all covered
with the marks of the stripes so lately inflicted.

The Outbreak of Rioting

Hearing and seeing this, the people rose in great uproar.
No longer was the tumult in the Forum merely; it spread
all over the city. Those who had been in bonds for debt
and those also at liberty rushed into the streets from all
quarters, begging the protection of the multitude. Everywhere there was a spontaneous banding together and sedition. Down all the streets they ran with clamorous shouting, and so into the Forum. Such of the Senators as they
met there were hustled by the mob to their no slight peril;
nor would the people have stopped short of extreme violence
had not the consuls Publius Servilius and Appius Claudius bestirred themselves hastily to quiet the uproar.

Turning on the consuls, the multitude displayed their
chains and other tokens of misery, and thus taunted the
consuls; then they demanded, with threatenings rather
than as petitioners, that they " assemble the Senate "; while
they posted themselves around the Senate House in a body,
resolved to witness and to control all the public counsels.

[The Senators met in great fear, and the people in turn put
little confidence in their professions, while the consuls lacked
harmony among themselves. In the midst of the peril news came
of an attack by the Volscians. To induce the people to take up
arms, the consul Servilius suspended the rigors of the law. The
foreign peril was thus speedily ended, but simultaneously the oppres-

sion of the debtors began again. The Patricians would yield nothing ; especially Appius Claudius urged a policy of extreme severity.
The only thing that seemed able to prevent a downright revolt was
the keeping of the commons continually in the army, and hence
subject to rigid military discipline. Despite all this, the Patricians
did not yield. At length the sedition came to a head.]

The Plebeians go to the Sacred Mount

At first it was proposed to kill the consuls, in order to
discharge the men from their oath of obedience; but when
it was asserted that no religious obligation could be discharged by a mere crime, on the advice of one Sicinius, *they
retired without any orders from the consuls, to the " Sacred
Mount" beyond the river Anio, three miles from Rome.*

There, without any regular leader, they fortified their
camp with a rampart and a trench, and remained quiet, taking nothing but the food they needed. Thus they kept to
themselves for some days, neither attacked themselves nor
attacking others.

Meantime in the city was panic and mutual fear. The
Plebeians, still in Rome, dreaded the violence of the Senators ;
these in turn dreaded the commons, and were doubtful
whether they wished them to stay [as hostages for the rest]
or to depart. [Everybody questioned how long the mutineers
would remain quiet, and what would happen if a foreign foe
fell upon Rome.]

Menenius Agrippa brings back the Plebeians

Therefore it was determined to send out an ambassador
to the Plebeians, Menenius Agrippa, an eloquent man and
withal acceptable, because he himself was of humble origin.
When he was admitted to the camp, he is said to have related this story. " Once upon a time the parts of the human
body did not agree together, but the various members had
each their own policy ; and it befell that the other parts

were indignant that everything was procured for the belly by their care, while the belly did nothing but enjoy the pleasures they afforded it. So they conspired : — the hands should no more carry food to the mouth, the mouth would not receive it, nor the teeth chew it. But while they wished to subdue the belly by famine, these parts themselves, and the whole body, were reduced to the last degree of emaciation. Thus it became evident that the service of the belly was by no means a slothful one [but that it had a most important purpose].

By comparing thus how similar was the sedition within the body to the resentment of the people against the Senators, he made an impression on the minds of the multitude. A commencement was accordingly made toward a reconciliation, and it was allowed that "the Plebeians should have their own magistrates, with inviolable privileges; and these men should have the right of bringing assistance against the Consuls; nor could any Patrician hold these [Plebeian] offices."

Thus *two tribunes of the Plebeians were created,* Gaius Licinius and Lucius Albinus.

10. How the Plebeians won the Consulship

Livy, "History," book VI, chaps. 34–42

The struggle about the "Sexto-Licinian Laws" (376 to 367 B.C.), described in this passage, was practically the end of the long battle between the Patricians and the Plebeians. It is true, the final capitulation of the Patricians did not come until the "Hortensian Law" of 286 B.C., but from 367 B.C. onward the Romans were in such a position of inner harmony that they could devote most of their energies to the great task of subjugating Italy. Again is to be noticed the methods of merely passive resistance employed by the Plebeian malcontents, and their refraining from those drastic measures which mark the average revolution.

[At this time there was a lull in the civic disturbances:
The Plebeians did not consider the "consular tribuneship"
to which they were nominally eligible to be really within
their power of winning, and the Patricians seemed to have]
recovered possession of an honor which had been seized for
only a few years by the commonalty.   A trifling cause, as
generally happens, had the result of producing a mighty
outcome; and this now intervened to stop the Patricians'
exultation.

[Two daughters of Ambustus, a prominent Patrician,
were married; one to a Plebeian, the other to a Patrician.
The former repined over the superior honors and state of
her sister, whose husband was then consular tribune, and
she complained bitterly to her father.   Ambustus thereupon
promised] " that she should soon see the same honors at her
own house, which she had just seen at her sister's."   He
then proceeded to concert plans with his son-in-law [Gaius
Licinius], and they attached to the undertaking Lucius
Sextius, a young man of great enterprise, who had found
in his non-patrician birth the chief barrier to his ambition.

The Proposals of Sextius and Licinius

There appeared a favorable opportunity for making innovations on account of the immense load of debt; since the
Plebeians could hope for no lightening of the burden unless
their own party gained control of the highest magistracies.
To this end they realized they must exert themselves.
After Gaius Licinius and Lucius Sextius had been elected
tribunes of the Plebs, they proposed laws aimed directly at
the Patricians and for the benefit of the commonalty.   The
proposal as to *debt* was that all interest previously paid
should be deducted from the principal, the remainder to be
paid off in three years by equal installments: the next,
touching the limitation of *land*, was that no one should

possess more than five hundred jugera of land:[1] and the third was that the elections of military tribunes should cease, and that *at least one of the consuls should be chosen from the Plebeians.* These were all matters of vast importance, and such as could not be obtained without a desperate struggle.

The Furious Resistance of the Patricians

So was opened a contest in which were staked all those objects for which men have ever had the keenest desires, — land, money, and public honors. The Patricians were terrified and dismayed. They could find no other remedy [than their old expedient] of winning over the colleagues [of these two tribunes] to oppose their bill.

[The vetoes of the other tribunes prevented the measures from being put to a vote in the assembly, but Sextius retaliated in kind.]

" Well is it," spoke he, " that if it is intended that your protests should possess such power, that by this same weapon [of prohibition] we should protect the people. Come, Sir Patricians, call the assembly to select military tribunes. I will take care that the word VETO, which you hear our colleagues chanting with so much pleasure, shall not prove so very pleasant in turn to you."

Nor were his threats vain. No elections were held, except those of the ædiles and tribunes of the Plebs. Licinius and Sextius were reëlected tribunes, and they did not allow any curule magistrates[2] to be appointed. For *five years* this total absence of the [higher] magistrates continued. The Plebeians, however, continued to reëlect the two [radical]

[1] About 300 acres. This measure seems only to have applied to occupation of the public land (*ager publicus*).

[2] " Curule magistrates " at this time were practically the same thing as Patrician magistrates.

tribunes of the Plebs, and these in turn prevented the election of military tribunes.

[In this crisis a war broke out with Velitræ (a Volscian town), and it was almost impossible to conduct it effectively, owing to the sturdy opposition now of *five* Plebeian tribunes, although at first the two revolutionists had been alone among their ten colleagues.]

The Plebeians are at Last Triumphant

[This opposition and the attitude of the Patricians kept matters for years at a deadlock, even actual foreign warfare being impeded by the tribunes.   During the contest a dictator, Publius Manlius, named a Plebeian, Gaius Licinius, as his master of the horse. At last the resistance of the Patricians broke down.]

The same tribunes Sextius and Licinius were reëlected at length for the tenth time; and they succeeded in passing a law which provided that of "The Board of Ten for attending to Religious Matters" one half should be Plebeians.   This step seemed to open the way to the Consulship.   [Soon after the dictator Camillus returned after defeating the Gauls] and by great struggles his opposition and that of the Senate were overcome.   The elections for consuls were then held in spite of the resistance of the nobles, and Lucius Sextius was elected — *the first consul of Plebeian rank.*

This was not entirely the end of the contest.   The Patricians withheld their consent to the proceedings, and matters were close to a "Secession of the Plebeians," and other direful threats of civic tumult, but through the interference of the dictator matters were compromised, — the Patricians yielded to the Plebeians one consul; and the Plebeians in turn granted to the Patricians that one of the latter should be elected as *praetor* to administer justice in the city.[1]

Harmony being at length restored among the orders, the

---

[1] Virtually he was almost a third consul, although without the same formal honors.

Senate [ordered that magnificent games should be held to celebrate the return of concord.]

11. How Cincinnatus saved a Roman Army

Livy, "History," book III, chaps. 26–29

The following story ascribed to 458 B.C. was one that later ages of Romans delighted to recall as a typical anecdote of the "good old times"; and the lapse of centuries does not make the "Republican simplicity" of Cincinnatus any less delightful. Note that the wars of Rome were still almost neighborhood affairs. The enemies of the Roman Republic, in its first century, were planted a very few miles away; and very gradually did the city by the Tiber cease to have only a mere *Ager* — some farm lands outside the walls and a few villages; and come to possess an *Imperium*, — a wide-stretching domain, with the frontier far distant.

[The Roman army was led out against the Æquians by the consul Minucius, and being unskillfully generalled was presently inclosed by the enemy, who soon held the camp closely besieged. Just before their lines were inclosed, five Roman horsemen escaped through to the city with tidings of the peril. The alarm in Rome was great, and it was resolved to call in Lucius Quintius Cincinnatus to act as dictator in the emergency.]

He [Cincinnatus] the sole hope of the Romans, cultivated a little farm of four jugera[1] across the Tiber. There he was either pushing upon a stake in a ditch, or busy plowing [when the envoys of the Senate came]. After saluting him they bade him put on his toga and listen to the commands of the Senate. He was greatly astonished and — asking repeatedly "if everything was safe?" — called to his wife Racilia, "to bring his toga from the hut." When he had put it on, and wiped off some of his sweat and dust, he presented himself; and the envoys at once congratulated him and saluted him as dictator; next they

[1] About two and a half acres.

summoned him into the city and explained the sore plight
of the army.

[He entered the city with due state, and spent the night
posting guards and making preparations. The next morning he was in the Forum ere daylight, and named Lucius
Tarquitius his master of the horse. Then he ordered] a
suspension of all civil business, ordered all the shops in the
city closed, and forbade any one to attend to any private
affairs. His next command was for every man of military
age to be with his weapons at the Campus Martius ere sun-
down, with five days' provisions and twelve stout stakes,
[while the older men were to be preparing victuals for the
soldiers. Throughout Rome there prevailed the greatest
zeal and bustle.]

When the troops were formed, the dictator marched at
the head of the infantry, and the master of the horse at the
head of the cavalry. In both divisions the orders ran " to
go on the double-quick. The consul and his Romans were
besieged. They had now been shut in three whole days,
and everything might be decided in a moment!" And
the troops, to please their chiefs, were always shouting,
" Hurry, standard-bearer! Follow on, comrade!" At mid-
night they were at Algidum, and halted near the enemy.

[The dictator then reconnoitered and presently] drew the
whole host in a long column around the enemy's camp, and
ordered that on the signal they should all raise the war
shout and thereupon every man throw up a trench before
his position and fix the stakes he had in it. [This was
successfully done, and the besieged Romans took heart at
the shout, saying " Aid was at hand "; whereupon the consul promptly ordered a sortie. The night passed amid
fighting and with terror and confusion for the Æquians.]

At dawn the Æquians were encompassed by the dictator's
barriers, and scarce able to maintain the fight against a
single army; but their lines were now attacked by Cincin-

natus's men also. So they were attacked furiously and continuously from both sides. Then, in their distress, they appealed to the dictator and the consul not to turn the victory into a massacre, but to suffer them to depart without their arms. The consul, however, ordered them "to go to the dictator"; and the latter in his wrath against them, added ignominy to mere defeat. He ordered Gracchus Clœlius, their general, and their other leaders, to be haled before him in fetters, and enjoined that they should evacuate the town of Corbio [but asserted]: "He did not want their blood. They could depart, but at last they must be brought to confess that their nation had been vanquished and crushed; and so they must 'pass under the yoke.'"

The "yoke" is formed of three spears, two whereof are fixed in the ground, and one is tied across between the upper ends. Under this "yoke" the dictator sent the Æquians. Their camp was taken, full of every kind of booty, — for they were sent away naked; — and the dictator distributed the spoil to his own men only [telling the consul's army it was reward enough that they were rescued. But this army, grateful to Cincinnatus for his services, voted him] a golden crown of a pound's weight, and saluted him as their "patron," when they marched forth [from their camp].

[He reëntered Rome in triumph, the spoils and captive chiefs accompanying his procession, amid general rejoicing; and] he laid down his dictatorship on the sixteenth day, although he had received it for six months.

12. The Personal Traits and Characteristics of the Gauls

Ammianus Marcellinus, "History," book XV, chap. 12

The following characterization of the Gauls is by a decidedly late Roman writer (fourth century A.D.), but the description is probably true in many substantial details to the followers of Brennus, who sacked Rome in 390 B.C.   In the description will be noticed certain prominent traits of the less civilized classes of the Celtic peoples of to-day.

Nearly all the Gauls are of a lofty stature, fair and of ruddy complexion ; terrible from the sternness of their eyes, very quarrelsome, and of great pride and insolence.   A whole troop of foreigners would not be able to withstand a single Gaul if he summoned his wife to his assistance.   The woman is usually very strong, and with blue eyes : [sometimes] swelling her neck, gnashing her teeth, and brandishing her huge sallow arms, she begins to strike blows mingled with kicks, as if they were so many darts shot out of a catapult.

The voices of most Gauls are fierce and threatening, whether they are in good humor or angry ; they are all exceedingly careful of cleanliness and neatness, nor in all the country, and especially in Aquitania [in the Southwest] could any man or woman, however poor, be seen either dirty or ragged.   The men of every age are equally inclined to war, and the old men and men in the prime of life answer with equal zeal the call to arms, their bodies being hardened by their cold weather and their constant exercise, so that they are all inclined to despise dangers and terrors.   Nor has any Gaul ever cut off his thumb [for fear of being levied in the army] as men have done in Italy.

The Gauls are fond of wine, and of similar liquors.   And many people of the lower classes, whose senses have been unsettled by continual intoxication, which the saying of Cicero defined to be a kind of voluntary madness, run about in all directions at random : so that there appears to be some point in that saying which is found in Cicero's oration in defense of Fonteius, " that henceforth the Gauls will drink their wine less strong than formerly " — because, it would seem, they thought there was poison in it.

13. THE GEESE OF THE CAPITOL

Livy, "History," book V, chaps. 47–49. Bohn Translation

The story here given of how the Capitol was saved from surprise, and how later the Gauls were ejected from Rome [390 B.C.] is another tale of Livy which is never spoiled by repeating. The incident of the geese is probably in the main historical; but it is very doubtful whether the Gauls were attacked by the dictator Camillus as here described. Probably they retired with their ransom money, and any vengeance with the sword came considerably later.

The Capitol of Rome was meantime in great danger; for the Gauls had remarked the easy ascent [to it] by the rock at the Temple of Carmentis. On a moonlight night, after they had first sent ahead a man unarmed to test the way, by alternately supporting and being supported by one another, and drawing each other up, as the ground required, they gained the summit all in silence. Not merely had they escaped the ken of the sentinels, but even the dogs, sensitive as they are to noises at night, had not been alarmed. But they did not escape the notice of the geese; for these creatures were sacred to Juno, and had been accordingly spared [by the garrison] despite the scarcity of food.

Thus it befell that Marcus Manlius, who had been consul three years earlier, and who was a redoubted warrior, was awakened by their hissing and the clapping of their wings. He snatched his arms, and calling loudly to his fellows, ran to the spot. Here he smote with the boss of his shield a Gaul who had already gained a foothold on the summit, and tumbled him headlong. The fall of this man as he crashed down dashed over those next to him. Manlius also slew certain others who in their alarm had cast aside their weapons and were clinging to the rocks. By this time the rest [of the Romans] had rushed together, and crushed the enemy with darts and stones, so that the whole band, dislodged from their foothold, were hurled down the precipice in general ruin.

At daylight, the soldiers were summoned by the trumpet to attend their [military] tribunes, for the meting out of rewards for merit and demerit. The first to be commended for bravery was Manlius, and he was presented with gifts — not merely by the military tribunes, but by the consent of the soldiers, for they all carried to his house, which was in the citadel, a donation of half a pound of corn and half a pint of wine: a trifling matter enough it seems in the telling, but in the prevailing scarcity a mighty proof of gratitude. The sentinel, however, who was manifestly negligent, was cast down from the rock [to his death] with the approval of all; and from this time forth the guards on both sides were more vigilant.

How the Gauls were driven from Rome

[At length, however, the garrison became weakened by constant watching and by famine, while the Gauls found the ruined site of Rome highly unhealthful and the siege wearisome. Negotiations therefore took place between the leaders on both sides.]

It was agreed between Quintus Sulpicius, a military tribune, and Brennus, the Gallic chief, that a thousand pounds weight of gold[1] should be the ransom of a people so soon to be the veritable rulers of the world. The transaction was humiliating enough; but insult was added. False weights were brought by the Gauls, and when the tribune objected, the insolent Gaul threw in his sword, as an additional weight, while uttering words most intolerable to the Romans. *"Woe to the vanquished!"*

[But at this moment, according to the story, the dictator Camillus appeared with his army, raised from the Roman refugees who had fled to Veii, and he ordered that the gold be withdrawn, while he told the Gauls to get ready for battle.]

[1] If taken literally, about $225,000.

The Gauls were thrown into confusion by this unexpected turn. They seized their arms, and with rage, rather than wisdom, they rushed upon the Romans. But Fortune now had changed; the aid of the gods and of human prudence alike aided the Romans. At the first encounter the Gauls were routed, even as easily as they had formerly won the day at the Allia. After they had fled as far as the eighth milestone on the Gabii road, they were beaten again by Camillus in a second battle. There the slaughter was universal. Their camp was stormed, and not one soul was left to carry away the tale of the defeat.

Having thus recovered his country from the enemy, Camillus returned to the city in triumph, and [the soldiers] styled him, with well-deserved praise, " Romulus," " Father of his Country," and " Second Founder of the City !"

14. THE CENSORSHIP OF APPIUS CLAUDIUS

Livy, " History," book IX, chaps. 29, 30, 33, 34, 36. Bohn Translation

Appius Claudius Cæcus (he became blind in his old age) was censor in 312 B.C. The innovations he wrought during his magistracy may be regarded as part of the general process of leveling the Patricians with the Plebeians. The Claudii, although among the very noblest of the Patrician gentes, were often opposed to their fellow-nobles, and espoused the popular side, — for which they received abundant ill will from the Patricians, as in the present case. The verdict of history, however, is that Appius Claudius was a far-sighted statesman : and that the much-abused ædile Flavius was like unto him.

This censorship of Appius Claudius and Gaius Plautius was noteworthy. The name of Appius Claudius has, however, been held in particular remembrance because he made the great road [called after him the Via Appia], and because he built a water supply for the city. These works he executed alone, for his colleague, overwhelmed with shame, by reason of

the infamous and unworthy choice [the censors] made of
senators, had abdicated his office. But Appius possessed
that inflexible temper which from of old had characterized
his family, and he continued to act as censor all by himself.
[For this clinging to office] he was, by the unrelenting
wrath of the gods, some years later, stricken blind.

[When the new consuls came into office the following
year] they complained in the Assembly, that by the evil
choice of senators [by the censors], the Senate had been
disgraced, and declared "they would pay no attention
to such appointments, which had been made merely to
gratify interest or prejudice." They then at once had the
Senate list called over [when they transacted business] in
the same order which had prevailed before this censorship.

The Strike of the Flute Players [1]

In this year an event occurred which I [Livy] would omit
as trifling if it did not have a certain religious bearing.
The flute players' guild, taking offense because they had
been prohibited by the last censors from holding their
banquets at the Temple of Jupiter, as was their ancient
usage, marched away in a body to Tibur; so that nobody
was left in Rome to play at the sacrifices. [The Senate
sent envoys to Tibur to get the men sent back, and the
Tiburtines, anxious to please the Senate] first urged the
fellows "to return to Rome." When, however, they could
not prevail on them, they practiced an artifice not unsuitable
for the kind of people they had to deal with. On a festival
day they invited the flute players into separate houses, as if
they wanted to add the pleasures of music to their feasts.
There the Tiburtines plied them with wine, of which such

[1] The solemn and matter-of-fact manner in which Livy relates this
highly droll incident is an example of the serious manner in which the
Romans took their history — how unlike the treatment which would have
been given by a Greek, e.g. Herodotus!

fellows are always fond, until they had put them to
sleep.

In this state, all senseless as they were, they threw
them into wagons, and carried them away to Rome. The
flute players knew nothing of the business until, after the
wagons had been left at the Forum, they were awakened by
the daylight, and they found themselves still heavily sick
from their debauch. The people now crowded about them,
and when they had at length promised to stay in Rome,
they were given the privilege of rambling about the city, in
full dress and with their music, every year for a space of
three days.

How Appius Claudius clung to Office

When Appius Claudius was censor and the eighteen
months [legally allowed] for the duration of the censorship
had expired, although his colleague Plautius had already
resigned it, nothing could induce *him* to lay it down. A
certain tribune of the Plebeians, Publius Sempronius, undertook to bring the censor to trial to force him to lay down
his office; and his action was agreeable to every man of
character.[1] [Sempronius vainly argued with Claudius, demanding of him that he obey the law, and not defy the
mandate of a tribune, but Claudius remained obdurate, and
Sempronius at last] ordered the censor to be arrested and
borne off to prison. But though six of the other tribunes
approved of their colleague's doings, three supported Appius
when he appealed to them; and he held the censorship
alone [for the remaining three and a half years to which
he claimed he was entitled] to the great disgust of all
ranks of people.[2]

[1] Livy with his aristocratic sympathies would not consider that Appius's
"popular" partisans came within this category.

[2] This incident illustrates how a Roman magistracy did not technically
expire with a set term, but had to be resigned formally by the incumbent
before the office became really vacant.

The Ædileship of Flavius

In [303 B.C.] Cneius Flavius, the actual grandson of a
freedman, a notary, and a man of decidedly humble origin,
but artful and eloquent, was elected curule ædile.

Against the nobles, who insulted him for his mean beginnings, he contended with much vigor. He published the
rules of proceeding in legal cases, hitherto shut up in the
closets of the pontiffs;[1] and hung them up to public view,
around the Forum, written out on white tablets that all
might know when business could be transacted in the courts.
To the wrath of the nobles, he performed the dedication of
the Temple of Concord,[2] and the *Pontifex Maximus*, Cornelius Barbatus, was compelled, by the popular clamors, to
dictate to him the correct formulas, although he asserted
that "according to ancient usage, no one but a consul or
a commanding general could dedicate a temple."

[Flavius showed his ability to deal with the discourtesy
of the nobles in this incident.] He went on a visit to
his sick colleague; and [at the house] by prearrangement
some young nobles who were sitting there, did not rise on
his entrance; thereupon he ordered his curule chair to be
brought in, and from this honorable seat he surveyed with
satisfaction his enemies as they were tortured with envy.

It was the faction of the lower classes, however, that had
gathered strength during Claudius's censorship, and which
made Flavius ædile. For Claudius was *the first who degraded
the Senate by electing into it the immediate descendants of freedmen*. [He also] distributed the persons of the lowest classes
among the several [35] Roman tribes [as full voters] and
thus he corrupted [to his ends] the popular assemblies.

---

[1] And to be used by the nobles to their own great advantage against the
uninstructed Plebeians.

[2] A ceremony which a Patrician would consider peculiarly reserved to
himself.

As for Flavius, so much indignation did his election excite, that most of the nobles laid aside their gold rings and bracelets [as a sign of mourning.]

[Claudius's arrangement was not accepted as permanent, however. The next censors] Fabius and Decius, to secure concord and to free the elections from the clutches of the lowest classes, purged the rest of the tribes of all the "Forum Rabble," and threw it into four tribes only, called "City Tribes." This arrangement gave general satisfaction.

15. CINEAS AND APPIUS CLAUDIUS CÆCUS

Plutarch, " Life of Pyrrhus," chaps. XVIII-XX

Pyrrhus, king of Epirus (born 318 and died 272 B.C.), was perhaps the ablest general among the galaxy of skillful warriors in the generation of Græco-Macedonians following Alexander. In his campaign to save Tarentum from the Romans, he doubtless hoped to establish a dominion in the West somewhat corresponding to the great Macedonian's conquests in the East. He found, however, the Romans very different enemies from the Persians. His first victory (280 B.C.) cost him so dear that he was fain to send Cineas, his clever and extremely eloquent prime minister, "whose words had won him more cities than his own arms," to try the effects of negotiation.

[The Romans, notwithstanding their first defeat by Pyrrhus at Heracleia,] filled up their legions, and enlisted fresh men with all speed, talking high and boldly of war, which struck Pyrrhus with amazement. He thought it advisable to send first to make an experiment whether they had any inclination to treat, thinking that to take the city and make an absolute conquest was no work for such an army as his was at that time, but to settle a friendship, and bring them to terms, would be highly honorable after his victory. Cineas was dispatched away, and applied himself to several of the great ones, with presents for themselves and their ladies from the king; but not a person would receive any, and answered, as well men as women, that if an agreement were publicly concluded, they also should be ready, for their parts, to express their regard to the king. And Cineas, discoursing with the Senate in the most persuasive and obliging manner in the world, yet was not heard with kindness or inclination, although Pyrrhus offered also to return all the prisoners he had taken in the fight without ransom, and promised his assistance for the conquest of all Italy, asking only their friendship for himself, and security for the Tarentines, and nothing further.

Nevertheless, most were well inclined to a peace, having already received one great defeat, and fearing another from an additional force of the native Italians, now joining with Pyrrhus. At this point Appius Claudius [the former censor], a man of great distinction, but who, because of his great age and loss of sight, had declined the fatigue of public business, after these propositions had been made by the king, hearing a report that the Senate was ready to vote the conditions of peace, could not forbear, but commanding his servants to take him up, was carried in his chair through the forum to the senate house. When he was set down at the door, his sons and sons-in-law took him up in their arms, and, walking close round about him, brought him into the Senate. Out of reverence for so worthy a man, the whole assembly was respectfully silent.

And a little after raising up himself; "I bore," said he, "until this time, the misfortune of my eyes with some impatience, but now while I hear of these dishonorable motions and resolves of yours, destructive to the glory of Rome, it is my affliction, that being already blind, I am not deaf too. —

["You have boasted that you could have defeated Alexander the Great: yet you are about to make peace with this Pyrrhus who was himself but a humble servant to one of

Alexander's life guard.] Do not persuade yourselves that making him your friend is the way to send him back, it is the way rather to bring over other invaders from thence, contemning you as easy to be reduced, if Pyrrhus goes off without punishment for his outrages on you, but, on the contrary, with the reward of having enabled the Tarentines and Samnites to laugh at the Romans."

Cineas is dismissed without a Treaty

When Appius had done, eagerness for the war seized on every man, and Cineas was dismissed with this answer, that when Pyrrhus had withdrawn his forces out of Italy, then, if he pleased, they would treat with him about friendship and alliance, but while he stayed there in arms, they were resolved to prosecute the war against him with all their force, though he should have defeated a thousand Lævinuses.[1] It is said that Cineas, while he was managing this affair, made it his business carefully to inspect the manners of the Romans, and to understand their methods of government, and having conversed with their noblest citizens, he afterwards told Pyrrhus, among other things, that the Senate seemed to him an assembly of kings, and as for the people, he feared lest it might prove that they were fighting with a Lernæan hydra, for the consul had already raised twice as large an army as the former, and there were many times over the same number of Romans able to bear arms.

Fabricius's Dealings with Pyrrhus

Then Caius Fabricius came in embassy from the Romans to treat about the prisoners that were taken, one whom Cineas had reported to be a man of highest consideration among them as an honest man and a good soldier, but extremely poor. Pyrrhus received him with much kindness,

[1] Lævinus commanded the Romans at the lost battle of Heraclea.

and privately would have persuaded him to accept of his gold, not for any evil purpose, but calling it a mark of respect and hospitable kindness.   Upon Fabricius's refusal, he pressed him no further, but the next day, having a mind to discompose him, as he had never seen an elephant before, he commanded one of the largest, completely armed, to be placed behind the hangings, as they were talking together. Which being done, upon a sign given the hanging was drawn aside, and the elephant, raising his trunk over the head of Fabricius, made an horrid and ugly noise.   He, gently turning about and smiling, said to Pyrrhus, "Neither your money yesterday nor this beast to-day make any impression upon me."

At supper, amongst all sorts of things that were discoursed of, but more particularly Greece and the philosophers there, Cineas, by accident, had occasion to speak of Epicurus, and explained the opinions his followers hold about the gods and the commonwealth, and the object of life, placing the chief happiness of man in pleasure, and declining public affairs as an injury and disturbance of a happy life, removing the gods afar off both from kindness or anger, or any concern for us at all, to a life wholly without business and flowing in pleasures.   Before he had done speaking, "O Hercules!" Fabricius cried out to Pyrrhus, "may Pyrrhus and the Samnites entertain themselves with this sort of opinions as long as they are in war with us."   Pyrrhus, admiring the wisdom and gravity of the man, was the more transported with desire of making friendship instead of war with the city, and entreated him, personally, after the peace should be concluded, to accept of living with him as the chief of his ministers and generals.   Fabricius answered quietly, "Sir, this will not be for your advantage, for they who now honor and admire you, when they have had experience of me, will rather choose to be governed by me, than by you."   Such was Fabricius.   And Pyrrhus received his answer without any resentment or tyrannic passion; nay, among his friends he highly commended the great mind of Fabricius, and intrusted the prisoners to him alone, on condition that if the Senate should not vote a peace, after they had conversed with their friends and celebrated the festival of Saturn, they should be remanded. And, accordingly, they were sent back after the holidays; it being decreed pain of death for any that stayed behind.

16. The Training of Roman Nobles in the Best Period of the Republic

Heitland, "Roman Republic," vol. I, p. **184**

The Romans were at their best probably at about the end of the First Punic War (241 B.C.). Their social system was not calculated to produce truly great men; but it was exceedingly well calculated to produce men of very fair ability. What was the strength and what the weakness of the training given young Roman noblemen, is well stated by a recent English writer. Let it be remembered that it was men trained in this manner who finally wore away the genius of Hannibal.

[Amid austere] surroundings the young Roman of good family grew up. Reared in the stern unchallenged discipline of home, he willingly attended his father as he went through the duties and occupations of the day. Thus he learned by actual observation at an impressionable age what things were enjoined or forbidden by ancestral custom. The exact formalities of sacrifices, the dates of festivals, the order of proceedings in the various Assemblies, the competence of the various magistrates, the usages of the law courts, the forms of buying and selling and contracts, the episodes of the registration if a Census was being held, or of the military levy if preparations were on foot for a campaign; these and many other matters would from time to time be present to his eager eyes and ears. He would ask questions and receive explanations, and by the time he was himself of age to begin his public career, he would have acquired a considerable store of experience and precedent.

As he laid aside the games of childhood, his chief sports were running and riding on horseback in the Campus Martius and swimming in the Tiber. With the completion of his sixteenth year he became a man of military age (*juvenis*), liable to be called out for service. From this time onward he remained a servant of the state, first as a soldier, later in a civil capacity. *His ambition was to be a Roman of the Romans*, to excel in representing a type of which he and his comrades were not unreasonably proud. And the nobles of this [best] period, judged from this point of view, were as a rule efficient and sturdy patriots, worthy of the support of the sound Roman people, the farmers of the country side.

In short, the training of the men who led Rome was good and practical within its own narrow range. It served to build up the Roman power at home; it sufficed for the conquest of Italy; [but it broke down when the complicated problems of a great world empire were thrust upon the Republic.]

17. A Learned Greek's Analysis of the Roman Constitution

Polybius, "History," book VI, chap. 1 ff.   Shuckburgh's Translation

About the year 140 B.C. Polybius, a learned Greek, wrote this analysis of the factors in the Roman Constitution, which had enabled the Latins to master the Carthaginians, Greeks, and Asiatics. Polybius had lived long in Italy, and had enjoyed abundant opportunities for observation. His comments possess an extremely high value. He wrote shortly before the period of civil commotions, while the old constitution was still standing outwardly intact, and with only a few internal signs of decay.

As for the Roman constitution it had three elements, each of them possessing sovereign powers, and their respective share of power in the whole state had been regulated with such careful heed to equality and poise, that no one could say surely — not even a native — whether the constitution as a whole were an aristocracy or democracy or despotism. And no wonder; on looking at the power of the Consuls it seems despotic; if on that of the Senate as aristocratic; and if finally one regards the power of the People, it would seem sheer democracy.

The Powers of the Consuls

The Consuls, before leading out the legions, remain in Rome and are chiefs of the [civil] administration. All other magistrates, save the Tribunes, are under them, and take their orders. They introduce foreign ambassadors to the Senate, bring matters requiring deliberation before it, and see to the execution of its decrees. If, again, there are any matters of state which require the authorization of the People, it is their business to see to them, to summon the popular meetings, to bring the proposals before them, and to carry out the decrees of the majority. In the preparations for war also, and in a word in the entire administration of a campaign, they have almost absolute power. They can impose on the allies such levies as they think good; also appoint the military tribunes, make up the roll for soldiers, and select those that are fit. Besides, they have absolute power of inflicting punishment on all who are under their command while on active service; and they have authority to expend as much of the public money as they choose, being accompanied by a quæstor, who is entirely at their orders. A survey of these powers would in fact justify our describing the constitution as despotic, — a clear case of royal govern‌ment.

The Powers of the Senate

[But on the other hand] The Senate has first of all the control of the treasury, and regulates the receipts and disbursements alike; for the Quæstors cannot issue any public money for the various departments of the state, without a decree of the Senate, except for the service of the Consuls. The Senate controls, too, what is by far the largest and most important expenditure, — that, namely, which is made by the censor every *lustrum* [fifth year] for the repair or construction of public buildings; this money cannot be obtained by the censors except by a grant of the Senate. Similarly all crimes committed in Italy, requiring a public investigation, such as treason, conspiracy, poisoning or willful murder, are in the hands of the Senate. Besides, if any individual or state among the Italian allies requires a controversy to be settled, a penalty to be assumed, help or protection to be afforded— all this is in the province of the Senate.

Or again, outside Italy, if it is necessary to send an embassy to reconcile communities at war, or to remind them of their duty, or sometimes to impose requisitions upon them, or receive their submission, or finally to proclaim war against them — all this is the business of the Senate. In like manner the reception to be given to foreign ambassadors in Rome, and the answers to be returned to them, are decided by the Senate. With such business the People have nothing to do. Consequently, if one were staying at Rome when the Consuls were not in town, one would imagine the constitution to be a complete aristocracy, and this has been the idea held by many Greeks, and by many kings as well, from the fact that nearly all the business they had at Rome was settled by the Senate.

The Powers of the Roman People

[After this one naturally asks what part is left for the People, but] they have a part and that a most important one. For the People are the sole fountain of honor and of punishment; and it is by these two things, and these alone, that dynasties, and constitutions, and, in a word, human society, are held together. The People are the only court to decide matters of life and death; also even cases where the penalty is a fine, if the assessment be a heavy one, and especially where the accused have held high magistracies. . . . Men who are on trial for their lives at Rome, while the sentence is in process of being voted — if even only *one* of the tribes whose votes are needed to ratify the sentence has not voted, have the privilege at Rome of openly departing and condemning themselves to a voluntary exile. Such men are safe at Naples, or Præneste, or Tibur, and other towns with whom this arrangement has been duly ratified on oath.

Again the People bestow public offices on the deserving, which are the most honorable rewards of virtue. It [the Popular Assembly] has the absolute power of passing or repealing laws; and, most important of all, it is the People who deliberate on the question of peace or war. And when provisional terms are made for alliance, suspension of hostilities or treaties, it is the People who ratify or reject them.

These considerations would lead one to say that the chief power in the state was the People's, — that the constitution was a democracy.

The Relations of Each Part to the Other

I must now show how each of these several parts can, when they choose, oppose or support one another.

The Consul, then, when he has started on an expedition, seems to be absolute, still he needs both the People and the

Senate to help him, otherwise he will have no success. Plainly he must have supplies sent his legions occasionally ; but without a decree of the Senate they can get neither corn, clothes, nor pay ; so that all the plans of a general are futile, if the Senate is resolved either to shrink from danger, or to hamper his plans. And again, whether a Consul shall bring any undertaking to a conclusion or not, depends entirely on the Senate ; for it has absolute authority at the end of the year to send another Consul to supersede him, or to continue the existing one in his command as [proconsul]. [Again the Senate controls the matter of the much-prized triumphs] for the generals cannot celebrate them with the proper pomp, nor sometimes celebrate them at all, unless the Senate concurs and grants the necessary money. As for the People, that body ratifies or rejects treaties, terms of peace and the like ; and especially when the Consuls lay down their office they have to give an account of their adminis- tration, before it. [Consequently the Consuls are obliged to court popular favor.]

As for the Senate, it is obliged to take the multitude into account and respect the wishes of the People. It cannot execute [death sentences] unless the People first ratify its decrees. Also in matters directly affecting Senators — e.g. laws diminishing the Senate's traditional authority, or de- priving Senators of certain dignities and office, or even actually cutting down their property, — even in such cases the People have the sole power of passing or rejecting the law. But most important of all is the fact that, if the [Popular] Tribunes interpose their veto, the Senate not merely cannot pass a decree, but cannot even hold a meeting at all, — formal or informal. Now the Tribunes are always bound to execute the will of the People, and above all things to have regard to the public wishes ; therefore for all these reasons the Senate stands in awe of the multitude, and cannot neglect the feelings of the People.

In like manner the People are far from being independent
of the Senate.   For contracts innumerable are given out by
the Censors to all parts of Italy for the repair or construction of public buildings; there is also the collection of
revenues from many rivers, harbors, forests, mines, and
land, — everything in a word that comes under the control
of the Roman government; and in all these the People at
large are engaged; so that there is scarcely a man, so to
speak, who is not interested either as a contractor or as
being employed in the works.   For some purchase the contracts from the censors themselves; others go partners with
them, while others again go security for these contractors,
and actually pledge their property to the treasury for them.
Now over all these transactions the Senate has absolute
control; it can grant an extension of time, [in emergency it
can lighten or release the contract, or enforce it on the
contractors with such severity as to ruin all involved.]
But most important of all is the fact that the judges are
taken from the Senate for most lawsuits, whether criminal
or civil, in which the charges are heavy.   Consequently all
citizens are at the Senate's mercy; they do not know when
they may need its aid, and are cautious about resisting or
actively opposing its will.   For a similar reason men do
not rashly resist the Consuls, because every one may become
subject to their absolute [military] authority on a campaign.

The Excellence of the Roman Constitution

The result of this power of the several estates for mutual
help or harm is a union sufficiently firm for all emergencies,
and a constitution which it is impossible to find a better.
Whenever any foreign danger compels them to unite and
work together, the strength which is developed by the
State is so extraordinary that everything required is un-
failingly carried out by the eager rivalry of all classes,

while each individual works, privately and publicly alike, for the accomplishment of the business in hand.

18. The Honesty of Roman Officials at the Best Period of the Republic

Polybius, "History," book VI, chap. 56. Shuckburgh's Translation

Before the decline of the old Roman spirit the honesty and general integrity of the Roman officials was something that excited the admiration and wonderment of the vastly more venal Greeks. Polybius also considers them far superior to the Carthaginians. Beyond a doubt this high standard of honor was as much of help to the Romans in their wars as many additional swordsmen.

The Roman customs and principles regarding money transactions are better than those of the Carthaginians. In the view of the latter nothing is disgraceful that makes for gain; with the former nothing is more disgraceful than to receive bribes and to make profit by improper means. For they regard wealth obtained by unlawful dealings as much a subject of reproach as a fair profit from the most unquestioned source is of commendation. A proof of the fact is this. The Carthaginians obtain office by open bribery, but among the Romans the penalty for it is death. With such a radical difference, therefore, between the rewards offered virtue among the two peoples, it is natural that the ways for obtaining them should be different also. . . .

[Again as contrasted with the Greeks, the Romans have the advantage, especially through their more sincere religious faith.] To my mind the Ancients were not acting at random when they brought in among the vulgar those opinions about the gods and the belief in the punishments in Hades; much rather do I think that men nowadays are acting rashly and foolishly in rejecting them. This is the reason, why apart from anything else, Greek statesmen, if intrusted with a single talent, though protected by ten checking clerks, as many seals, and twice as many witnesses, yet cannot be induced to keep faith; whereas the Romans, in their magistracies and embassies, have the handling of great sums of money, but from pure respect of their oath keep their faith intact. And again in other nations, it is a rare thing to find a man who keeps his hands out of the public purse, and is entirely pure in such matters; but among the Romans it is a rare thing to detect a man committing such a crime.

Some Specific Instances of Roman Honesty

[In another passage Polybius concedes that recently in his own day the Romans had declined from this high standard of virtue; still he holds them in the main highly honest.] [Book XVIII, chap. 35.]

As evidence that I am making no impossible assertion, I would quote two names, which will command general assent,—I name first Lucius Æmilius, who conquered Perseus and won the kingdom of Macedonia. In that kingdom, besides all the other splendor and wealth, was found in the treasury more than 6000 talents of gold and silver [over $6,000,000], yet he was so far from coveting any of this that he even refused to see it, and administered it by the hands of others. And this though he was not at all very rich; on the contrary, very poorly off. At least I know that on his death, which occurred shortly after the war, when his own sons Publius Scipio and Quintus Maximus wished to pay his wife her dowry, amounting to twenty-five talents [say $25,000], they were reduced to such straits they would have been unable to do so if they had not sold the household furniture and slaves, and some landed property besides. [This fact] seemingly incredible [can be readily ascertained on a few inquiries at Rome.]

Again Publius Scipio, son by blood of this Æmilius, and

[grandson by adoption of Scipio the Great], when he got possession of Carthage, reckoned the wealthiest city in the world, took absolutely nothing of it for his own private use, either by purchase or by any other means of acquisition whatever, although he again was by no means a rich man, but of very moderate estate for a Roman. But he not only abstained from all the wealth of Carthage, but refused to allow anything from Africa at all to be mixed up with his private property.

[Book XXXII, chap. 8, Polybius, speaking again of the disinterestedness and incorruptibility of many Romans, warns his Greek hearers against disbelief even if to them such probity seems incredible.]

Let my readers fully consider that the Romans more than any other people will take my books in their hands, — because the most splendid and numerous achievements recorded therein belong to them; and with them the truth about the facts could not possibly be unknown. No one then would voluntarily expose himself to certain disbelief and contempt. And let this be kept in mind when I seem to make a startling assertion about the Romans.

19. ROMAN STATE FUNERALS AND THEIR INFLUENCE

Polybius, "History," book VI, chaps. 52 and 53. Shuckburgh's Translation

How under the old Republican system, some even of the essentially private acts of society were made to minister to a worthy public end is set forth by Polybius. The great state funerals at Rome must have awakened almost as much interest as the games in the circus.

One example will be sufficient to show the pains taken by the Roman state to turn out men ready to endure anything to win a reputation in their country for valor. [It is this:] Whenever one of their famous men dies, in the course of his funeral, the body with all its paraphernalia is carried into the Forum to the Rostra, as a raised platform there is called, and sometimes is propped upright upon it so as to be conspicuous, or more rarely is laid upon it. Then with all the people standing around, the son of the deceased, if he has left one of full age and he is there, or failing him, one of his relations, mounts the Rostra and delivers a speech concerning the virtues of the departed, and the successful exploits performed by him in his lifetime.

By these means the people are reminded of what has been done, and made to see it with their own eyes: not only such as were engaged in the actual transactions, but those also who were not; and their sympathies are so deeply moved, that the loss appears not to be confined to the actual mourners, but to be a public one affecting the whole people. After the burial and the usual ceremonies have been performed, they place the likeness of the deceased in the most conspicuous spot in his house, surmounted by a wooden canopy or shrine. This likeness consists of a mask made to represent the deceased with extraordinary fidelity both in shape and color. These likenesses they display at public sacrifices adorned with much care.

When any illustrious member of the family dies, they carry these masks to the funeral, putting them on men whom they think as like the originals as possible, in height and other personal peculiarities. And these substitutes assume clothes, according to the rank of the person represented; if he was a consul or prætor, a toga with purple stripes; if a censor, a toga wholly of purple;[1] if he had celebrated a triumph or performed any like exploit, a toga embroidered with gold. These representatives also themselves ride in chariots, while the fasces and axes, and all the other customary insignia of the peculiar offices, lead

[1] There is some reason to doubt whether Polybius is correct here about the censor's robes.

the way, according to the dignity of the rank in the state enjoyed by the deceased in his lifetime. Upon reaching the Rostra they all take their seats on ivory [curule] chairs in their order.

The Public Gain from Such Display

There could not easily be imagined a more inspiring spectacle than this for a young man of noble ambitions and virtuous aspirations. For can we conceive any one to be unmoved at the sight of all the likenesses collected together of the men who have earned glory, all as it were living and breathing? Or what could be a more glorious spectacle?

[After the eulogy of the person just died, other eulogies are delivered recounting the great deeds of each ancestor represented.] By this means the glorious memory of brave men is continually renewed; the fame of those who have wrought any noble deed is never allowed to die; and the renown of those who have done good service to their fatherland becomes a matter of common knowledge to the multitude and part of the heritage of posterity. But the chief gain comes from inspiring young men to shrink from no exertion for the general welfare, in hope of obtaining the glory that awaits the brave; and many Romans have indeed volunteered to decide a whole battle by single combat, and not a few have accepted certain death. [There are many cases of heroic self-sacrifice for the sake of the fatherland.]

CHAPTER III

THE DEATH STRUGGLE WITH CARTHAGE

Almost no wars in history rise to the importance of the "Punic Wars" between Rome and Carthage. If Rome had been ruined soon after she united Italy under her sway; if the task of civilizing Spain, Gaul, Britain had been intrusted to the merchant princes and the priests of Baal of the great Semitic city of Africa, here again — as of the Persian Wars — one may say history would have been so altered, that it is waste of time to conjecture what might have emerged. Not merely did Rome destroy Carthage, but in the tremendous military effort involved she developed an army system which made her subsequent conquest of the discordant Hellenistic kingdoms mere child's play. The victory of Zama carried with it by implication the victories of Cynoscephalæ, Magnesia, Pydna, Corinth, and the great battles won over Mithridates.

In the Punic Wars we see the Roman national genius at its best. Brilliant individual leaders are few or none. Even Scipio the Elder barely rises to the rank of a genuine rival to Hannibal. But the spirit of the Roman people is superb. The courage and wisdom of the Senate in the great crises marks the Roman nobility on the whole as the ablest aristocracy the world has ever seen. We know that Rome conquered because she deserved to conquer, and no admiration naturally evoked for the dauntless achievements of Hannibal can destroy our greater admiration for the race of hard-headed, hard-handed Italian farmers, who never quailed at any disaster, who never "despaired of the Republic," who never counted treasure or effort or life too dear for the "Patria."

To one fact our study of merely military details must not make us blind. Rome was victorious, but at an exceedingly heavy price. Tens of thousands of her youth had perished. Industry, agriculture, and commerce had been nigh ruined throughout the peninsula. An undue accent had been laid upon the war virtues, so that it must have been exceedingly hard for very many Italians to settle down again to the quiet arts of peace. If the wars, however, had almost ruined the hardy country yeomanry, they had brought easily won riches to many of the aristocracy, who would be anxious for new wars, commands, and pillagings. The direct result of the Punic Wars was the conquests in the East and the extension of the Roman provincial system around the Mediterranean; but the period of civil war and of painful reconstruction which followed these conquests was likewise almost as truly the result of the great struggle with Carthage.

Nearly all the excerpts in this chapter relate of course to the Second Punic War, to which the first war was a mere prelude, the third an epilogue. We cannot complain that Roman annals for this period lack vividness or human interest; the only difficulty has been to select among the numerous first-class incidents, and to make the extracts as short as possible.

20. Horace's Ode on Regulus's Departure for Carthage

Horace, "Odes," book III, ode 5. De Vere's Translations

In 255 B.C. Regulus the consul with most of his army was taken prisoner by the Carthaginians. In 250 B.C. they sent an embassy to Rome to solicit peace, accompanied by Regulus, on the promise that he would return to Carthage if their proposals were not accepted. Coming before the Senate, Regulus urged the Romans to reject the terms of peace and, resisting the entreaties of his friends, returned to Carthage, where he was put to a cruel death. This incident became famous as an example of true Roman patriotism, and is thus glorified by Horace.

> With warning voice of stern rebuke
> Thus Regulus the Senate shook:
> He saw — prophetic — in far days to come
> The heart corrupt and future doom of Rome.

"These eyes," he cried, "these eyes have seen
Unbloodied swords from warriors torn,
And Roman standards nailed in scorn
On Punic shrines obscene;
Have seen the hands of free-born men
Wrenched back and bound; th' unguarded gate;
And fields our war laid desolate
By Romans tilled again.

"What! will the gold-enfranchised slave
Return more loyal or more brave?
    Ye heap but loss on crime?
The wool that Cretan dyes disdain
Can ne'er its virgin hue regain:
And valor fallen and disgraced
Revives not in a coward breast
    Its energy sublime.

"The stag released from hunters' toils
From the dread sight of man recoils,
Is he more brave than when of old
He ranged the forest free? Behold
In him your soldier! He has knelt
To faithless foes; he too has felt
The knotted cord; and crouched beneath
    Fear, not of shame, but death.

"He sued for peace tho' vowed to war;
Will such men, girt in arms once more,
Dash headlong on the Punic shore?
No! they will buy their craven lives
With Punic scorn and Punic gyves.
O mighty Carthage, rearing high
Thy fame upon our infamy,
A city, aye, an empire built
On Roman ruins, Roman guilt!"

From the chaste kiss and wild embrace
Of wife and babes he turned his face,
   A man self-doomed to die :
Then bent his manly brow, in scorn,
Resolved, relentless, sad, but stern,
   To earth, all silently ;
Till counsel never heard before
Had nerved each wavering Senator ;
Till flushed each cheek with patriot shame,
And surging rose the loud acclaim : —
Then from his weeping friends, in haste,
To exile and to death he passed.

He knew the tortures that Barbaric hate
Had stored for him.   Exulting in his fate
   With kindly hand he waved away
   The crowds that strove his course to stay.
He passed them all, as when in days of yore,
   His judgment given, thro' client throngs he pressed
   In glad Venafrian fields to seek his rest,
Or Greek Tarentum on the Southern shore.

21. The Youth and Character of Hannibal

Livy, " History," book XXI, chaps. 1, 3, 4

Very few military leaders can be compared to Hannibal; his
only real peers are Alexander, Cæsar, and Napoleon, and there is
some reason to think that he surpasses them all.   Considering the
very important part he plays in history, we know surprisingly
little about his personality.   This is partly due to the fact that
all Carthaginian accounts of his wars have been lost, and it was
very hard for Roman writers, *e.g.* Livy, as here quoted, to do
justice to their great enemy.   All that the latter say in his praise
may be accepted, and their derogatory remarks may well be questioned.   If Hannibal had been heartily sustained by the home government at Carthage, he might have conquered ; as it was, the

greatest military genius who ever lived attacked the *most military
people* which ever existed — and the genius was defeated, after a
sixteen years' war.

I [Livy] may be permitted to begin this part of my book
with saying what most historians have announced at the
beginning of their whole narrative, namely — that I am
about to relate *the most memorable of all the wars which were
ever waged:* the war which the Carthaginians, led by Hannibal, maintained with the Roman people. For never did any
other states or nations with mightier recourses join in combat, nor did these nations in question possess, at any other
time, such vast power and energy as then. They brought
into action, too, no arts of war unknown to each other, but
only those which had been previously tested in the First
Punic War; and again so fluctuating was the conflict, so
hesitant the award of victory, that the side which finally
conquered was for long the side most exposed to danger.
The hatred of the fighters was almost greater than their
power. The Romans were wrathful that those conquered
[in the last war] should take the offensive against their
conquerors: the Carthaginians [equally enraged] because
they felt that during their humiliation they had been lorded
over with haughtiness and rapacity.

The loss of Sicily and Sardinia[1] had grieved the high
spirit of Hamilcar [the father of Hannibal]; for he deemed
that Sicily had been surrendered out of premature despair,
and that Sardinia had been taken treacherously by the
Romans during the uproars [of insurrection against Car-
thage] in Africa; while in addition a heavy tribute had been
exacted.

[First Hamilcar, and then, after his death, his son-in-law,
Hasdrubal, carried the Carthaginian arms and influence into Spain

[1] These islands were of course the fruit of the final Roman victory in
the First Punic War.

until the peninsula was almost entirely in the power of the great African city. Presently Hasdrubal was murdered in a private quarrel, and the demand was made by the Spanish army that young Hannibal should take the command.]

No one doubted that in appointing a successor to Hasdrubal, the wishes of the commonalty [of Carthage] would agree with the desires of the soldiers. The latter indeed had at once carried Hannibal to the government house, and hailed him as "General" amid loud cheers and marked approval. Hasdrubal had earlier sent for him by letter while he was just arrived to manhood, and his case then had been discussed in the [Carthaginian] Senate, when the Barcine faction [to which Hannibal belonged] used all its influence to secure that he might be trained for military service, with a view to succeed to his father's command. Hanno, leader of the opposing party, then said, "Hasdrubal seems to ask what is reasonable, still I think his request ought to be refused." [He then went on to argue that rearing Hannibal in the expectation of a great command like that in Spain, would fit him only to play the tyrant over the Carthaginians. He concluded by saying:] "To my mind this young fellow should be kept at home, under the restraint of the laws and the power of the magistrates, and taught to live on an equal footing with the rest of the citizens, lest at some future time this small fire of his should kindle a vast conflagration."

A few [Senators] and those of the greatest worth, agreed with Hanno; but as usually happens the more numerous faction prevailed over their betters. Hannibal was sent to Spain, and from his first arrival caught the eye of the whole army. The veterans saw again, as it were, Hamilcar in his youth restored to them; they beheld the old accustomed vigor in his looks; and speedily Hannibal took care that the memory of his father should be the least of the reasons why they esteemed him.

Never was there a genius more fitted for those two most opposite duties — obeying and commanding. Not readily could one decide whether he was more the favorite of his general or of the army. To none did Hasdrubal prefer intrusting the command, rather than to him, when a deed needing activity and courage was called for. Under no other leader did the soldiers feel more confidence and boldness. Before perils Hannibal showed the uttermost fearlessness, and amid them the uttermost prudence. His body was not to be exhausted, nor his mind benumbed, however severe the toil. Heat or cold he endured alike.

The mere wants of nature, not appetite, dictated the amount of his food and drink. He could sleep or keep awake at any and all hours. What time he could spare he indeed devoted to slumber, but for that he asked neither a soft bed nor a quiet spot. Men have seen him, wrapped in his military cloak, lying on the bare ground, amid the watches and outposts of his soldiers. He did not dress more bravely than his social equals, but he was distinguished by fine horses and weapons. [In battle] he was preëminently the first alike of the horse and of the foot, — the foremost indeed in the charge, but also the last on the retreat.

Grievous shortcomings, however, counterbalanced these noble virtues of a true hero. He displayed excessive cruelty, and more than "Punic" perfidy.[1] He did not revere the ordinances of religion, and feared not gods, oaths, nor religious sentiments. With a character thus made up of a combination of virtues and vices, he served for three years under the command of Hasdrubal, without neglecting anything which ought to have been done or seen by a man who was to become a great general.

---

[1] As suggested in the introduction, Livy is hardly fair to Hannibal. There is no reason for believing that he was less humane and oath-keeping than the average military chieftain of his day.

22. Hannibal's Hostility to Rome

Cornelius Nepos, "Life of Hannibal," chap. 2.   Bohn Translation

Never was hatred keener than Hannibal's for Rome.   It should be remembered that he was an Oriental, a Semite, with all the powers of deep and inveterate passion peculiar to his race.   How in his boyhood he was taught to be the peculiar enemy of Rome is told in this narrative attributed to himself.

[When Hannibal was an exile at the court of Philip V of Macedonia, he said to that king:] "My father Hamilcar, when I was a very little boy, only some nine years old, offered sacrifices at Carthage, when he was going to take command in Spain, to 'Jupiter Best and Greatest,'[1] and while these rites were going on, he asked me 'Whether I should like to go with him to camp?' As I expressed extreme willingness to go, and begged him not to delay taking me, he replied, 'I will do so, if you will give me the promise which I ask.' Thereupon he led me to the altar at which he had begun to sacrifice, and, sending the rest of the company away, required me, taking hold of the altar, to swear '*That I would never hold friendship with the Romans.*' This oath, thus taken before my father, I have most strictly kept even to this day."

23. How the Second Punic War was Declared

Livy, "History," book XXI, chap. 18

In 219 B.C. Hannibal having completed his preparations in Spain, attacked Saguntum, a city on the coast of the peninsula allied to Rome ; thus precipitating the mighty Second Punic War. Probably neither side had the least realization of the tremendous

[1] This does not mean that the Carthaginians worshiped the same gods that the Romans did, but merely shows the Roman tendency to give their own names to foreign gods.   Probably Baal-Moloch was the deity to whom Hamilcar sacrificed.

and history-making struggle which they were commencing, and which was to end in the ruin of Carthage after almost ruining Rome.

In order that everything might be done that was proper, before they commenced the war, the Romans sent Quintus Fabius [and four others], men of advanced years as ambassadors, to go to Africa and ask the Carthaginians "whether Hannibal had laid siege to Saguntum by their public authority."[1] And if, as seemed likely, the Carthaginians did so confess, the envoys were then to declare war upon them.

When the Romans reached Carthage they were given an audience by the Council. Here Quintus Fabius simply pressed the question which had been laid upon him, whereat one of the Carthaginians answered : —

"Your former embassy [sent some time ago], good Romans, was precipitate enough, when you demanded that Hannibal be surrendered to you, because he had attacked Saguntum on his own authority. But for this last embassy, although your words are milder, your demands are really more severe. For then *Hannibal* was simply accused, and his surrender required. Now you require of us a [public] confession of wrong, and as though we had confessed to the fact, restitution is then promptly demanded. [But the treaty as to your rights in Spain — which is under discussion — was made by Hasdrubal, apparently without our proper authority. So we decline to argue about that case of Saguntum.] If your treaties do not bind you unless they are made by your proper authority, so neither can one bind us which Hasdrubal made without our knowledge. Cease then [to talk thereof], and tell us plainly what you have so long been really meditating."[2]

Then the Roman folded up his toga, and said, "Here we

---

[1] Hannibal's attack on Saguntum, a Spanish town allied to Rome, was the immediate cause of the war.

[2] Virtually defying the Romans to do their worst. Evidently the Carthaginian war party was predominant in the Council.

bring you peace and war.   Take whichever you please."
To that they cried out no less grimly, "You can give whichever you choose!"   Whereupon he shook out the toga.
"I GIVE WAR," he spoke; and they all cried back, "We take
it, and will wage it just as fiercely as we have received it."

24. HANNIBAL'S CROSSING OF THE ALPS

Livy, "History," book XXI, chaps. 32-38

Hannibal's famous crossing of the Alps was a sufficient prelude
to his momentous struggle in Italy.   He was unable to take the
road along the coast lest he fall in with the Roman army under
Publius Scipio [father of the famous Scipio Africanus] when, in
case of a defeat, his whole campaign would have been blasted ere
it had fairly begun.   It is usually considered that the pass by
which Hannibal reached Italy is that now known as the "Little
St. Bernard."   The greatness of Hannibal's feat is enhanced by
the fact that his army was not made up of patriots, sacrificing their all to avenge their country.   His troops were mostly mercenaries of every kind — Numidians, Spaniards, Gauls — held
together almost entirely by the spell of his genius.

From Druentia [in Gaul], by a road which ran mostly
across the plains, Hannibal reached the Alps without
molestation from the inhabitants of the region.   Now at
length, despite the very highly colored reports which had
come to them, the height of the mountains from near view,
with the snow almost mingling with the sky, the shapeless
huts clinging to the cliffs; the cattle and sumpter beasts
all withered by the cold, with everything, living or inani-
mate, stiffened with frost, and so many other like terrors;
all these, in short, smote the soldiers with alarm.

As they marched up the first slopes, overhead on the
heights they beheld the mountaineers [ready for sudden
attack.]   Hannibal ordered a halt and sent forward some
Gauls to view the ground.   And when he found no passage

in the direction* he had been following, he pitched camp in
the wildest possible valley, in country infinitely rugged.
At length he learned from the Gauls, who had mingled with
the mountaineers, and from whom indeed they differed little in language and habits, that the pass was only beset
during the day, for at nightfall the defenders withdrew,
each man to his own dwelling. He accordingly made a
feigned attempt during the daytime in another direction,
[but in the night] he put himself at the head of a body of
picked light troops, and rapidly cleared the pass; taking his
post on the very heights once held by the enemy.

Fighting the Mountaineers

At dawn the troops broke camp, and the rest of the army
moved forward. On a signal, the mountaineers swarmed
from their forts to their wonted stations, but they suddenly
beheld a part of their enemies clear above them, holding
their old positions, while the rest of the army was passing
up the road. For a little while they stood bewildered at all
they saw; but when speedily they perceived how the troops
were confused while going up the pass, and that the marching forces were disordered by the very tumult they were
making, — for the horses were especially terrified, — then the
mountaineers thought they could create enough additional
terror quite to annihilate the army. They therefore
scrambled along the dangerous rocks, accustomed as they
were to all this rough going; and now were the Carthaginians
indeed beset, opposed at once by the foe, and by the sheer
difficulties of the ground. Each man of them strove to escape the first, and there was actually more struggling among
themselves than against the enemy. Especially the horses
made danger in the lines, driven frantic as they were by the
discordant clamors which were echoed back from the forests
and valleys. They fell into dire confusion; and if any were

hit or wounded, they were so uncontrollable that they caused great loss both to men and baggage of every kind. As the pass was broken and steep on both sides, many were flung down to an awful depth, including some even of the soldiery; while the sumpter beasts, with their loads, rolled down like the fall of some vast fabric.

Distressing as was the sight of these losses, Hannibal for a while kept his place, lest he increase the danger, but later when he saw his line broken [he hastened down with his detatchment] from the higher ground [which they held]. At the first onset he routed the enemy ; and after the paths had been cleared of the mountaineers, the tumult [along the lines] soon ceased. He then took a fortified village, the chief town of the district, and fed his army for three days with the captured corn and cattle.

Hannibal then came to another canton, very populous for a mountainous country. Here he was almost overcome, not in open war, but in his own game of treachery and ambush. Some old men, commanders of the forts, came to the Carthaginians as envoys, and offered provisions, guides, and hostages. He answered them in a friendly manner, [fearing alike to reject or wholly trust them, and continued his advance most warily]. The elephants and cavalry formed the van of the advancing host, and he in person, watching everything that befell, followed with the picked infantry. When they came to a narrow pass, the barbarians rose at once on all sides from their ambush and assailed the Carthaginians, front and rear both at close quarters and at long range, while huge stones were rolled down upon the army. The greater number of the foe attacked the rear [where they were beaten off with great difficulty, and even as it was] one night was spent by Hannibal while separated from his cavalry and his baggage.

At the Summit of the Alps

[The next day the advance continued amid great loss, especially of the sumpter beasts.] Though the elephants were driven only with many delays over the steep and narrow paths, yet wherever they went they protected the army, because the enemy, to whom they were utterly strange, feared approaching them too closely.   On the ninth day they came to the summit of the Alps over regions trackless. For two days they remained encamped on the summit, and rest was given the soldiers, spent as they were by toil and battle.   A fall of snow, however, put the men in great panic, worn out as they were by so many hardships.[1]

[When the troops resumed the advance they went forward very wearily, until Hannibal ordered a halt] on a certain eminence whence there was a view reaching far and wide. Here he pointed out to them Italy, and the plains of the Po, extending themselves beneath the Alpine mountains. "Now," spoke he, "you are not merely surmounting the ramparts of Italy, but those of Rome.   The rest of the journey will be smooth and downward.   After one, or at most the second battle, you will have the citadel and capital of Italy in your power and possession!"

The army now began its advance, the enemy making no attempts against them except petty thefts, as chance offered. But the journey downward proved much more difficult than the ascent, as the slope of the Alps is shorter on the Italian side, and, as a consequence, steeper.

The Struggle through the Snow

At length they came to a rock so narrow and perpendicular that a light-armed soldier attempting it most carefully and clinging to the bushes and roots around could barely lower

---

[1] Remember, a large part of Hannibal's army was made up of Africans, to whom snow was a fearful wonder.

himself down. The ground, naturally very steep, had been broken by a recent avalanche into a precipice of nearly a thousand feet. Here the cavalry halted as at the end of their journey, and it was announced to Hannibal [in the rear] that the rock was impassable. He surveyed it personally, and imagined he must lead the army around it no matter how great the circuit, through regions pathless and untrodden. But this route proved impracticable [for it was entirely out of the question to force the army through the soft and yielding snowdrifts.]

At length after men and beasts had been uselessly fatigued, the camp was pitched on the summit; the ground being cleared for that purpose with great difficulty, so much snow was there to dig and to carry away. The soldiers were then set to work to make a way down the cliff, by which alone a passage could be won. It was needful to cut through the rocks themselves, and the men lopped down many large trees which grew around, and made a huge pile of timber. As soon as a strong wind came to stir the fire, they kindled the mass, and pouring vinegar upon the heated stones [beneath] rendered them soft and crumbling. They then could use their iron instruments upon the rock thus heated, and smoothed its slopes so that not merely the sumpter beasts but even the elephants could be led across and downward.

Four days had the army spent on this rock, the animals nearly perishing with hunger, for the mountain summits were mostly bare, and any pasturage was under the snows; but the lower parts [which they now reached] contained valleys and some sunny hills, with streams flowing through woods — scenes in short worthy for human abode. There the sumpter beasts were set out at pasture, and the men, so wearied with the passage, were given three days of rest; then they descended to the plains, where the country and the people were alike less rugged.

In this manner they came to Italy in the fifth month
after leaving New Carthage [in Spain], having crossed the
Alps in fifteen days.

25. How the Romans greeted Varro on his Return from Cannæ

Livy, "History," book XXII, chap. 61

In 216 b.c., largely owing to the blunders of the Consul Varro,
the Roman army was practically annihilated by Hannibal at
Cannæ ; yet because after the defeat Varro had done everything
possible to check the spread of disaster, and had clearly striven according to his best ability, the Roman government and people
refused to rebuke him.   The treatment accorded him was a moral
victory that did far to offset many Cannæs.

How much greater this disaster [at Cannæ] was than any
before it, is proved by the fact that certain allies [of Rome]
that had hitherto stood firm now began to waver, and the
only cause of this was that they despaired of the [Romans']
empire.   The peoples who went over to the Carthaginians
were these — the Atellani, the Calatini, the Hirpini, some
of the Apulians, the Samnites (except the Penetrians), all
the Bruttians and the Lucanians.   Besides these there were
included the Surrentinians and almost the whole coast possessed by the Greeks, the peoples of Tarentum, Metapon-
tum, Croton, the Locrians and all of Cisalpine Gaul.

Yet not even these losses and the falling away of their
allies so shook the Romans that any word touching " Peace "
was uttered amongst them ; either before the arrival of
[Varro] the consul at Rome, or after he came and renewed
the memory of the great calamity.   At this very juncture,
such was the height of public spirit, that when the consul
returned from such a fearful defeat, whereof he personally
was the main cause, he was met [before Rome] by multitudes of all classes of citizens, and thanks were given him

"*Because he had not despaired of the Republic.*" Although
had he been a Carthaginian general in like case, he would
have escaped no species of punishment.[1]

26. "HANNIBAL AT THE GATES"

Livy, "History," book XXVI, chaps. 7, 9, 10, 11

Hannibal's attempt to save Capua [211 B.C.] by a sudden
march on Rome, was a stirring passage in the Second Punic War.
In reality the danger to Rome was not great : Hannibal had no
time or men to waste on storming the gallantly defended capital :
but the event gave an admirable opportunity for Senate, people,
and army to exhibit their self-possession, and dogged purpose.

Hannibal, at length, when he saw that the Romans could
not be induced to join battle again, and that he was unable
to force his way through their lines into Capua, resolved to
remove his own camp thence, and give up the attempt, lest
the new consuls be able to cut off his provision supplies.
Whilst he deliberated anxiously what to do next, the impulse came to him to attack Rome itself, the very heart of
the war.   He believed there was some hope that he might
seize some part of the city, as result of the panic and confusion attending his unexpected approach ; also that if
Rome were imperiled either both, or at least one, of the
Roman generals, would retire from before Capua.   [And
if they divided their forces, he would surely gain some
advantage.]

He feared, however, lest his departure cause the Cam-
panians [in Capua] to surrender immediately [in despair.]
He bribed, therefore, a Numidian — a most daring fellow —
to convey a letter.   The man entered the Roman camp as a
deserter, then slipped across and got into Capua.   The letter
was full of encouragement.   "Hannibal's departure," it

---

[1] An entirely just observation. A defeated Athenian general would
probably have been condemned to drink poisonous hemlock, a Carthaginian to be trodden to death by an elephant.

ran, "would be highly beneficial [to the besieged.] It
would result in drawing off the Roman armies to the defense of Rome itself. They must not let their spirits sink.
After a few days more of patience the siege would be quite
over." He then ordered the boats on the Volturnus River
to be seized, and rowed up to the fort formerly erected
there for his protection. [Next laying in rations for ten
days he led his forces to the river by night, and crossed
before daylight.]

[When deserters brought news of this movement to the
Roman Senate, it was resolved most heroically not to withdraw the whole blockading army from Capua, but only a
fraction of the army to cover Rome. The rest was to maintain the siege.]

[Hannibal marched northward, devastating the country,
along the Latin Way, as far as the Liris, where he found
the bridges broken to hinder his advance; but at the same
time Fulvius, the proconsul, with a part of the army from
Capua was marching another road, parallel with Hannibal,
going at full speed to defend the city. As messengers came
in with tidings of Hannibal's advance] the whole city was
in a state of alarm. The confusion was increased by the
constant running to and fro of people bearing wild rumors.
Not merely in the houses were the lamentations of the
women to be heard, but matrons ran out upon the streets
from every direction and surged up and down around the
shrines of the gods, imploring them to "Save the city of
Rome from the clutches of the foe, and to keep the Roman
mothers and children from all harm!" The Senate sat at
the Forum near the magistrates in case the latter should
wish to consult with it. Some Senators [who held office]
were receiving orders and departing to their own spheres of
duty; others were offering themselves in whatever capacity
they might be of aid, while troops were stationed [at various
points in and around the city.]

During this confusion the news came. Fulvius, the proconsul, and his army had started from Capua, whereupon
the Senate ordered that his power should be the same as
that of the Consuls, lest when he entered the city his authority should cease.[1] Hannibal [ravaging direfully, pressed
on towards Rome until, marching his] troops into the confines
of the Pupinian tribe, he pitched his camp eight miles from
the city. The nearer the enemy came, the greater was the
number of the fugitives slain by the Numidians of his van,
and the greater the number of prisoners they made, of
every sort and condition.

Amid the confusion, Fulvius entered the city with his
troops [by another way] and camped between the Esquiline
and Colline gates. The Plebeian ædiles brought hither a
supply of provisions. The consuls and Senate came to the
camp and a council of war was held on the general state of
the Commonwealth. It was resolved the consuls should
camp near these gates, that Calpurnius, the city prætor,
should command at the Capitol, and that a full Senate should
be in continuous session at the Forum, in case of any sudden need for consulting it. Meantime Hannibal advanced
his camp to the Anio, *three miles from the city,* and when he
had established himself, he rode with two thousand horse
along from the Colline Gate as far as the temple of Hercules; and, galloping up, took as near a view as he could of
the walls and the site of the city. Fulvius, however, was
furious that he should do this so much at his ease, and sent
out a cavalry force with orders [to chase his escort back.
Meantime in Rome there was grievous panic, while the
rumor spread that the Aventine Hill had been taken.]

The cavalry battle, however, was in favor of the Romans,
and the enemy was driven [away to their camp.] Tumults,
however, were breaking out in different parts of the city,

---

[1] A proconsul's power ordinarily ceased when he entered the city of
Rome; but the regular consuls retained their power inside the city limits.

and it was resolved that all ex-dictators, ex-consuls, and ex-censors should exercise magisterial authority until the foe were driven from before the walls.   For the rest of the day and the night following tumults kept arising, unfounded though they were, and had to be repressed.

The next day Hannibal crossed the Anio and drew up, offering battle.   Flaccus and the consuls did not decline the issue, but when the troops on both sides were arrayed to join in a battle with Rôme for the prize of the victors, a violent rainstorm, with hail to boot, threw the lines in disorder, so that the [demoralized] troops must needs retire to their camp.[1]   [A second tempest prevented battle the next day.]   The Carthaginians considered this occurrence as " an act of the gods," and it is reported Hannibal remarked " At one time he wanted the resolution to take Rome, but at another time the opportunity." [2]

Two other things also brought down his hopes.   The more important one was that even while he lay with his forces near the city wall, he was informed that troops had marched from Rome with colors flying, as a reënforcement to go to Spain.[3]   The lesser matter was that a prisoner told him that the actual ground whereon his camp stood was sold [in Rome] at that very time, and at no lessened price.   [Stirred by this contempt and insult] Hannibal immediately called a crier, and ordered that the silversmiths' [and bankers'] shops which then stood around the Roman Forum should be put up for auction.

Thus baffled, he retired six miles from the city to the grove of Feronia, where was a temple famed for its riches.

[1] A lost battle then and there would not necessarily have ruined Rome. Hannibal would still have been forced to storm the city, desperately defended as it would surely have been.

[2] Referring to his failure to make the most of his alleged opportunity to seize Rome after the battle of Cannæ.

[3] A marvelous testimony to the confidence of the Romans in their ultimate victory.

[Having plundered this temple, Hannibal retreated sullenly into Campania. His effort to save Capua had failed, and that great city was presently starved out and forced to surrender on very severe terms.]

27. MARCELLUS AND ARCHIMEDES AT SYRACUSE

Plutarch, "Life of Marcellus," chaps. XIV–XIX

Marcellus was, on the whole, the most successful opponent of Hannibal, until the rise of Scipio Africanus; but his chief public service was the reduction of Syracuse [212 B.C.], which upon the death of King Hiero II had forsaken the Roman alliance for Carthage. What Nicias and Demosthenes had failed to do the grim and unrelenting Roman accomplished, and Syracuse sank to the level of a mere provincial subject town. How Archimedes, the famous mathematician-physicist, enabled the Syracusans to prolong the siege by his inventions, and the manner of his death during the capture, form together a time-honored story.

Marcellus proceeded to attack the city both by land and by sea. The land forces were conducted by Appius: Marcellus, with sixty galleys, each with five rows of oars, furnished with all sorts of arms and missiles, and a huge bridge of planks laid upon eight ships chained together, upon which was carried the engine to cast stones and darts, assaulted the walls, relying upon the abundance and magnificence of his preparations, and on his own previous glory; all which, however, were, it would seem, but trifles for Archimedes and his machines.

These machines he had designed and contrived, not as matters of any importance, but as mere amusements in geometry; in compliance with King Hiero's desire and request, some little time before, that he should reduce to practice some part of his admirable speculations in science and, by accommodating the theoretic truth to sensation and ordinary use, bring it more within the appreciation of people in general.

Archimedes, in writing to King Hiero, whose friend and near relation he was, had stated, that, given the force, any given weight might be moved, and even boasted, we are told, relying on the strength of demonstration, that if there were another earth, by going into it he could remove this. Hiero being struck with amazement at this, and entreating him to make good this problem by actual experiment, and show some great weight moved by a small engine, he fixed accordingly upon a ship of burden out of the king's arsenal, which could not be drawn out of the dock without great labor and many men; and, loading her with many passengers and a full freight, sitting himself the while far off, with no great endeavor, but only holding the head of the pulley in his hand and drawing the cord by degrees, he drew the ship in a straight line, as smoothly and evenly as if she had been in the sea. The king, astonished at this, and convinced of the power of the art, prevailed upon Archimedes to make him engines accommodated to all the purposes, offensive and defensive, of a siege. These the king himself never made use of, because he spent almost all his life in a profound quiet, and the highest affluence. But the apparatus was, in a most opportune time, ready at hand for the Syracusans, and with it also the engineer himself.

How Archimedes made Engines to resist Marcellus

When, therefore, the Romans assaulted the walls in two places at once, fear and consternation stupefied the Syracusans, believing that nothing was able to resist that violence and those forces. But when Archimedes began to ply his engines, he at once shot against the land forces all sorts of missile weapons, and immense masses of stone that came down with incredible noise and violence, against which no man could stand; for they knocked down those upon whom they fell, in heaps, breaking all their ranks and files.

In the meantime huge poles thrust out from the walls over the ships sunk some by the great weights which they let down from on high upon them; others they lifted up into the air by an iron hand or beak like a crane's beak, and, when they had drawn them up by the prow, and set them on end upon the poop, they plunged them to the bottom of the sea; or else the ships, drawn by engines within, and whirled about, were dashed against steep rocks that stood jutting out under the walls, with great destruction of the soldiers that were aboard them.

A ship was frequently lifted up to a great height in the air (a dreadful thing to behold), and was rolled to and fro, and kept swinging until the mariners were all thrown out, when at length it was dashed against the rocks or let fall. At the engine that Marcellus brought upon the bridge of ships, which was called *Sambuca* from some resemblance it had to an instrument of music, while it was as yet approaching the wall, there was discharged a piece of rock of ten talents' weight, then a second and a third, which, striking upon it with immense force and with a noise like thunder, broke all its foundation pieces, shook out all its fastenings, and completely dislodged it from the bridge. So Marcellus, doubtful what counsel to pursue, drew off his ships to a safer distance, and sounded a retreat to his forces on land.

The Scientific Spirit of Archimedes

[By these means Marcellus was compelled to reduce his attack to a mere blockade.] Yet Archimedes possessed so high a spirit, so profound a soul, and such treasures of scientific knowledge, that though these inventions had now obtained him the renown of more than human sagacity, he yet would not deign to leave behind him any commentary or writing on such subjects; but, repudiating as sordid and ignoble the whole trade of engineering, and every sort of art that lends itself to mere use and profit, he placed his whole affection and ambition in those purer speculations where there can be no reference to the vulgar needs of life.

The charm of his familiar and domestic Siren made him forget his food and neglect his person, to that degree that when he was occasionally carried by absolute violence to bathe, or have his body anointed, he used to trace geometrical figures in the ashes of the fire, and diagrams in the oil on his body, being in a state of entire preoccupation, and, in the truest sense, divine possession with his love and delight in science.

Taking of Syracuse and Fate of Archimedes

[At length after a tedious siege Marcellus was able to gain possession of Syracuse, while the inhabitants were celebrating a feast of Artemis and were off their guard.]

When looking down from the higher places upon the beautiful and spacious city below, he is said to have wept much, commiserating the calamity that hung over it, when his thoughts represented to him, how dismal and foul the face of the city would in a few hours be, when plundered and sacked by the soldiers. For among the officers of the army there was not one man that durst deny the plunder of the city to the soldiers' demands; nay, many were insistent that it should be set on fire and laid level to the ground: but this Marcellus would not listen to. Yet he granted, but with great unwillingness and reluctance, that the money and slaves should be made spoil; giving orders, at the same time, that none should violate any free person, nor kill, misuse, or make a slave of any of the Syracusans.

Though he had used this moderation, he still esteemed the condition of that city to be pitiable, and, even amidst the congratulations and joy, showed his strong feelings of

sympathy and commiseration at seeing all the riches accumulated during a long felicity, now dissipated in an hour.
For it is related, that no less spoil and plunder was taken
here, than afterward in Carthage. For not long after, they
obtained also the plunder of the other parts of the city,
which were taken by treachery; leaving nothing untouched
but the king's money, which was brought into the public
treasury.

Nothing, however, afflicted Marcellus so much as the death
of Archimedes; who was then, as fate would have it, intent
upon working out some problem by a diagram, and having
fixed his mind alike and his eyes upon the subject of his
speculation, he never noticed the incursion of the Romans,
nor that the city was taken. In this transport of study and
contemplation, a soldier, unexpectedly coming up to him,
commanded him to follow to Marcellus; which he declining
to do before he had worked out his problem to a demonstration, the soldier, enraged, drew his sword and ran him
through. Others write, that a Roman soldier, running upon
him with a drawn sword, offered to kill him; and that
Archimedes, looking back, earnestly besought him to hold
his hand a little while, that he might not leave what he
was then at work upon inconclusive and imperfect; but the
soldier, nothing moved by his entreaty, instantly killed him.
Others again relate, that as Archimedes was carrying to
Marcellus mathematical instruments, dials, spheres, and
angles, by which the magnitude of the sun might be
measured to the sight, some soldiers seeing him, and
thinking that he carried gold in a vessel, slew him. Certain it is that his death was very afflicting to Marcellus;
and that Marcellus ever after regarded the man that
killed him as a murderer; and that he sought Archimedes's
kindred and honored them with signal favors.

28. The Battle of Zama

Livy, "History," book XXX, chaps. 32–35

The battle of Zama (202 b.c.) ended the Second Punic War. It was fought after a vain attempt of the respective generals — Scipio and Hannibal — to arrange terms of peace at a personal interview. In the contest the Romans showed how much they had profited in the hard school of experience, by their former battles with Hannibal. The great Carthaginian did his best, but. he had a very heterogeneous army. Scipio, on the other hand, had a homogeneous, patriotic, well-disciplined force, and he handled it without a blunder.

When the two generals arrived back at their respective camps they both issued orders to their men to " make ready their arms, and prepare for the final battle; which, if they should win, would give them victory not for a day, but through all time." For the Romans on their part had no place of refuge in the strange and foreign land [of Africa]: and sheer destruction confronted Carthage if the troops who were her last hope were overcome.

[The generals on either side harangued their men, and urged them to strive to the uttermost: and then Scipio arrayed his lines, posting his " hastati " [1] in front, his "prin-cipes" behind them, and closing his rear line with the " triarii." He did not draw up his divisions in close order, instead he set each before its separate standard, and placed the companies at some little distance apart to leave a space through which the enemy's elephants might rush without breaking the Roman ranks.   Lælius [his favorite lieutenant] he put with the Italian cavalry on the left wing, Masinissa [2] and the Numidians were on the right. The open spaces between the [regular] companies of the van, he filled with

[1] These were the least seasoned troops in the legion; the " principes " were of better quality; the " triarii " were tested veterans.

[2] A claimant for the throne of Numidia, who had joined the Romans. He was a dashing and effective cavalry leader.

"velites" [Roman light-armed troops] with orders that when the elephants charged they were to retire behind the files, and leave a passage.

As for Hannibal, in order to terrify his foes, he set his elephants in front, for he had eighty of the beasts, more than in any of his former battles. Behind these lay his Ligurian and Gallic auxiliaries, and some Balearians and Moors, all intermixed. In the second line he set the Carthaginians, Africans, and a brigade of Macedonians; finally at a moderate interval he stationed a reserve of Italians, mainly from Bruttium.[1] As for his cavalry, he posted that upon the wings, the Carthaginians upon the right, the Numidians upon the left.

[Hannibal at the same time used every kind of argument to arouse enthusiasm and some kind of patriotism in this very diversely recruited army, especially appealing to the Carthaginians as having the most at stake.]

How the Battle Began

While Hannibal was thus employed, and his captains like-wise — most of them having to use interpreters among troops intermixed from such different nations — the trumpets and horns of the Romans sounded. Such a din did they make that the elephants, especially those by the left wing, turned around on their own party: [and practically drove Hannibal's cavalry on that side from the field.] A few of the elephants indeed were launched against the Romans, and made sore havoc among the "velites," though not without many wounds themselves. For the velites, giving ground [as ordered], pelted them with darts, until at last they were driven from the Roman lines by the showers of missiles from every side; and these elephants even put to flight the Carthaginian cav-

---

[1] This reserve comprised the remnant of his old army of veterans who had mostly left their bones in Italy fighting his battles, and now the survivors had followed him to Africa to die in the last struggle.

alry on the right wing also, whereupon Lælius, seeing the
disorder of the foe, dashed new terror into them whilst in
their confusion.

Stripped thus of their cavalry on either side, the Carthaginian foot now locked with the Romans, but they were no
match either in confidence or prowess.   Again, one circumstance, in itself a trifle, had no scant results.   With the
Romans the war cry was uniform, and therefore louder and
more terrific; but with the enemy, composed as they were
of so many peoples of varying tongues, the cry was disso-
nant.[1]   The Romans used the stationary kind of fighting,
pressing upon the enemy with their own weight and that
of their arms; but on the other side there was more of
skirmishing and rapid movement than real force.   Therefore the Romans, at the first charge, drove back the hostile
line; then pushing with their elbows and the bosses of their
shields, and thrusting forward into the spaces whence they
had pushed the foe, they advanced quite a space, as though
no one were resisting them; while the men in the rear
urged on their comrades in front as they felt the hostile
line yielding.

The Final Defeat of the Carthaginians

[The front ranks of the Carthaginians were thus forced
back upon Hannibal's veteran Italians, who angrily drove
them from the field as useless, and who themselves prepared
to face the Romans; while, however, they were reforming
for the final shock] Scipio promptly signaled to his spearmen to retreat, and had the wounded taken to the rear.
Then he brought up his "principes" and "triarii" from the
wings in order to strengthen the spearmen of the center.

---

[1] It is certain that mere *noise* had a great part in ancient battles, especially with its moral effects upon untried soldiers.   The Greeks and Romans
lacked modern cannon, but the din of one of their battles was doubtless
hideous.

Thus a fresh battle commenced, inasmuch as now the Romans had reached their genuine antagonists, men a match for them in their weapons, in their experience in war, and in their overwhelming hopes and fears. But both in numbers and in courage the Romans had advantage.[1] They had routed cavalry, elephants, and front line, and were now closing with the second line [and the last.]

Lælius and Masinissa, who had pursued the routed cavalry, now most opportunely returned, and charged the enemy's rear. Before this cavalry attack the Carthaginians at last succumbed. Many were surrounded and perished on the field; many, fleeing over the open plain, were slain by the [pursuing] cavalry. Of the Carthaginians and their allies about 20,000 that day perished, and about as many more were captured, as well as one hundred and thirty-three standards and eleven elephants.

Hannibal escaped with a few horsemen, not fleeing the field until he had tried every expedient both in the battle and before it began. [After having done everything possible for his country] he returned to Carthage in the six-and-thirtieth year after he had quitted it when a boy. There, in the Council House, he confessed he had lost not only the battle, but the war, and that the only hope of salvation was to make peace.

29. Why Rome was superior to Carthage

Polybius, "History," book VI, chap. 51.   Shuckburgh's Translation

The reasons why Rome was able in the end to master Carthage — despite the apparent great strength of the latter — are clearly stated by a Greek historian who had ample opportunity for collecting and judging all the facts.

[1] Probably a good many in this veteran reserve, the "Old Guard" of Hannibal, had joined in the slaughter of the Romans at Trasemene and Cannæ. Now finally their fates were reversed, but their last stand, when they were hopelessly outnumbered, did not belie their old glory.

As there is in every body politic a natural growth, then a zenith, then decay, and whereas everything in them is at its best when at the zenith, we may then judge of the difference between these two constitutions [Roman and Carthaginian] as they existed then [on the eve of the Second Punic War.] For exactly so far as the strength and prosperity of Carthage began earlier than that of Rome, by exactly so much was Carthage past its prime, while Rome was just at its zenith, so far as its political constitution was concerned. In Carthage, therefore, the influence of the Popular Assembly had risen already to be supreme, while at Rome the Senate was at the height of its power; and so, as in the one measures were deliberated upon by the multitude, and in the other by the best men, consequently the Romans in all public undertakings proved the stronger; on which account, though they met with capital disasters, by force of prudent councils they presently conquered the Carthaginians.

If we look, however, at separate details, *e.g.* at the provisions for carrying on a war, we shall find that whereas for a naval expedition the Carthaginians are the better trained and prepared — as is only natural with a people with whom it has been hereditary for many generations to practice this craft, and follow the seamen's trade above all nations in the world — yet, touching military service on land, the Romans train themselves to a much higher pitch than the Carthaginians. The former bestow their whole attention upon this department; whereas the Carthaginians, although they do take some slight interest in their cavalry, wholly neglect their infantry, the reason for this being that they employ foreign mercenaries, the Romans native and citizen levies.

It is in this point that the Roman polity is preferable to the Carthaginian. *They* have their hopes of freedom ever resting on the courage of mere mercenaries; the Romans on the valor

of their own citizens and the aid of their allies. The result
is that even if the Romans are beaten at first, they renew the
war with undiminished forces, which the Carthaginians cannot do. For as the Romans are fighting for native land and
children, it is impossible for them to relax the fury of their
struggle; but they persist with obstinate resolution until
they have triumphed over their enemies. What happened
in regard to their navy is an instance in point. In [nautical]
skill the Romans are much behind the Carthaginians, as I have
said, yet the upshot of the whole naval war was a decided
triumph for Rome, through the [personal] valor of her
men. For although nautical science contributes largely to
success in sea fights, still it is the courage of the marines
that turns the scale most decisively in favor of victory. The
fact is that Italians, as a nation, are by nature superior to
Phœnicians and Libyans both in physical strength and
courage. Likewise their habits also do much to inspire
their youth with enthusiasm for such exploits.

30. How Cato the Elder inveighed against Carthage

Plutarch, " Life of Marcus Cato the Elder," chaps. XXVI–XXVII

Marcus Cato the Elder was the very incarnation of the old
" Republican traditions " of Rome. He was born in 234 B.C.,
shortly after the end of the First Punic War, and he distinguished
himself in the Second Punic War. Considering the havoc Hannibal
had wrought in Italy, and the fierce hatreds and passions he had
engendered, it is in no wise surprising that to Cato any peace with
Carthage seemed only a truce; at any moment a new Hannibal
might arise and all the bloody drama be played over again. Besides this factor, also, Cato as a shrewd man of business shared,
no doubt, the jealousy with which the merchants and bankers of
Rome watched the commercial prosperity of their rival.

Some will have the overthrow of Carthage to have been
one of Cato's last acts of state; when, indeed, Scipio the

younger, did by his valor give it the last blow, but the war,
chiefly by the council and advice of Cato, was undertaken
on the following occasion.   Cato was sent to the Carthaginians and Masinissa, king of Numidia, who were at war
with one another, to know the cause of their difference.   He,
it seems, had been a friend of the Romans from the beginning; and they, too, since they were conquered by Scipio,
were of the Roman confederacy, having been shorn of their
power by loss of territory, and a heavy tax.   Finding Carthage, not (as the Romans thought) low and in an ill condition,
but well manned, full of riches and all sorts of arms and
ammunition, and perceiving the Carthaginians carry it high,
he conceived that it was not a time for the Romans to adjust
affairs between them and Masinissa ; but rather that they
themselves would fall into danger, unless they should find
means to check this rapid new growth of Rome's ancient
irreconcilable enemy.

Therefore, returning quickly to Rome, he acquainted the
Senate, that the former defeats and blows given to the Carthaginians, had not so much diminished their strength, as it had
abated their imprudence and folly ; that they were not become weaker, but more experienced in war, and did only
skirmish with the Numidians, to exercise themselves the
better to cope with the Romans : that the peace and league
they had made was but a kind of suspension of war which
awaited a fairer opportunity to break out again.

Moreover, they say that, shaking his gown, he took occasion to let drop some African figs before the Senate.   And
on their admiring the size and beauty of them, he presently
added, that the place that bore them was but three days'
sail from Rome.   Nay, he never after this gave his opinion,
but at the end he would be sure to come out with this sentence, " ALSO, CARTHAGE, METHINKS, OUGHT UTTERLY TO BE
DESTROYED."   But Publius Scipio Nasica would always
declare his opinion to the contrary, in these words, " It

seems requisite to me that Carthage should still stand."
For seeing his countrymen to be grown wanton and insolent,
and the people made, by their prosperity, obstinate and diso-
bedient to the Senate, and drawing the whole city, whither
they would, after them, he would have had the fear of
Carthage to serve as a bit to hold in the contumacy of the
multitude; and he looked upon the Carthaginians as too
weak to overcome the Romans, and too great to be despised
by them.

On the other side, it seemed a perilous thing to Cato, that
a city which had been always great, and was now grown
sober and wise, by reason of its former calamities, should
still lie, as it were, in wait for the follies and dangerous
excesses of the overpowerful Roman people; so that he
thought it the wisest course to have all outward dangers removed, when they had so many inward ones among themselves.

Thus Cato, they say, stirred up the third and last war
against the Carthaginians: but no sooner was the said war
begun, than he died [in 149 B.C., three years before Carthage
was taken].

CHAPTER IV

THE DECLINE OF THE ROMAN REPUBLIC

In the very victory over Carthage was the germ of the down-fall of the magnificent Republic that had destroyed Hannibal, and then, a half century later, his city. Few periods of ancient history are more interesting than the story of Rome from the rise of the Gracchi to the advent of Julius Cæsar, and no other period of ancient history is so charged with serious examples and warnings for thoughtful Americans. How Rome was undone by her very successes ; how her upper classes grew ever richer, while her lower classes were ground down by plutocratic oppression and slave competition ; how one after another reform and counter-reform were tried until the weary and war-racked commonwealth was glad to merge its public life in a monarchy, — these facts form some of the most instructive precedents in human annals.

In this culminating age of the Republic there is no lack of interesting personalities. Our literary evidence is abundant. The Gracchi, Marius, Sulla, Lucullus, Crassus, and their associates we can study almost intimately. Little as we may find that is admirable in the characters of many of these men, almost all we discover to be individuals of marvelous energy, usually of corresponding ability, and gifted in many cases with an aggressive egoism which was perhaps more developed in the Romans of this period than in any other race or century. From the ample material at our disposal no attempt is made to illustrate all the noteworthy events which follow one another in stirring succession from the tribunate of Tiberius Gracchus to the rise to prominence of Julius Cæsar. It has been possible to single out only certain typical incidents, also to add a few glimpses into the economic and social life of the upper and lower classes during this most interesting era.

The student should notice again that although this period is marked by grave domestic turmoils, the Roman armies did not cease to go forth conquering and to conquer. This is the age when Mithridates was overthrown, and the Eastern end of the Mediterranean brought fairly under the Roman yoke. As a result, the Italian conquerors were led into vital relations with Oriental luxury, morality, and religion — influences which were to affect the Western world mightily during the next three centuries.

31. How Polybius and Scipio the Younger became Friends

Polybius, "History," book XXXII, chaps. 9-15. Shuckburgh's Translation

About 163 B.C. the incident here narrated occurred. A large number of prominent Greeks from Achæa had been transported as prisoners to Italy, whereof one was Polybius, the future historian. How he became friends with Scipio Æmilianus, the future destroyer of Carthage, and what a high-minded, generous-hearted personage that great nobleman was in his youth, is admirably told. Incidentally many glimpses are given into society and manners at Rome in the second century B.C.

[When the Achæan exiles, of whom Polybius was one, were distributed among the various cities of Italy, Polybius, being already on terms of friendship with Fabius and Scipio, the sons of Lucius Æmilius Paulus, was assigned for residence at their house, and they became still more intimate.]

One day when all three were coming out of the house of Fabius, the latter left them to go to the Forum, and Polybius went in another direction with Scipio. As they were walking along, in a quiet, subdued voice and with the blood mounting to his cheeks, Scipio said, " Why is it, Polybius, that though my brother and I eat at the same table, you address all your conversation and all your questions to him and pass me over altogether ? Of course you have the same opinion of me as I hear the rest of the city has. For I am considered by everybody, I hear, to be a mild, effete person, and far removed from the true Roman character and ways, because I don't care for pleading in the law courts. And they say the family I come of requires a different kind of a representative, and not the sort that I am. It is that which annoys me the most."

Polybius was taken aback by the opening words of the young man, — for he was only just eighteen, — and replied that [he spoke mainly to Fabius because he was the elder; but that he would be delighted to help Scipio in any way possible to learn to come up to the family reputation].

While Polybius was still speaking the young man seized his right hand with both of his, and pressing it warmly said, "Oh, that I might see the day on which you would devote your first attention to me, and join your life with mine. From that moment I shall think myself worthy both of my family and my ancestors." Polybius was partly delighted at the sight of the young man's enthusiasm and affection, and partly embarrassed at the thought of the high position of his family and the wealth of its members. However, from the hour of this mutual confidence the young man never left the side of Polybius, but regarded his society as his first and dearest object.

From this time onward they continually gave each other practical proof of an affection which recalled the relationship of father and son, or of kinsmen of the same blood. The first impulse and ambition of a noble kind with which he was inspired was a desire to maintain a reputation for chastity, and to be superior to the standard observed in that respect among his contemporaries. [It was a time of great dissoluteness in Rome: young men wasted money and energies on mistresses, wine, and coarse banquets, for it was believed by the Romans that] owing to the destruction of the Macedonian monarchy, universal dominion was secured to them beyond dispute. Also a vast difference had been made both in public and private wealth and splendor, by the importation of the riches of Macedonia into Rome.

Scipio, however, set his heart on a different path of life; and by a steady resistance to his appetites, and by conforming his whole conduct to a consistent and undeviating standard, in about five years after this secured a general recognition of his character for goodness and purity.

His next object was to cultivate lofty sentiments in regard to money, and to maintain a higher standard of disinterestedness than other people. In this respect he had an excellent start in his association with his natural father [Æmilius]; but he also had good natural impulses to do right, and circumstances helped his success.

When the mother of his adoptive father, Æmilia, wife of Scipio the Great, died, she left him a great property. She had been accustomed to attend the women's religious processions in great state as sharing the life and high fortune of Scipio. For besides the magnificence of her dress and carriage, the basket, cups, and other sacrificial implements which were carried in her train were all of silver or gold on grand occasions; and the number of her maidservants and other slaves that made up her train had been proportioned to this splendor. All this establishment, immediately after Æmilia's funeral, Scipio presented to his own mother, who had long before been divorced by his father, Lucius, and who was badly off, considering her illustrious birth. She had previously refrained from taking part in grand public processions; but now, as there chanced to be a notable state sacrifice, she appeared surrounded with all the splendor and wealth which had once been Æmilia's, using among other things the same muleteers, pair of mules, and carriage. The ladies, therefore, who saw it were much impressed by the kindness and liberality of Scipio, and all raised their hands to heaven and prayed for blessings upon him.

[Scipio was remarkably liberal in the matter of the marriage portions of his adoptive aunts, the daughters of Scipio the Great, paying the fifty talents due three years in advance. When the husbands of these ladies applied for part of the money at Scipio's bankers, and were told they could have the whole on the spot, they at first thought there was some mistake] for at Rome so far from paying fifty talents [$50,000] three years in advance, no one will pay a talent before the appointed day; [1] so excessively particular are they about money, and so profitable do they consider time. . . .

Also Scipio by his strict chastity not merely saved his purse, but by refraining from many irregular pleasures he gained sound bodily health and a vigorous constitution for the whole of his life.

Courage, however, is an important element for public life in every country, but particularly in Rome; and he therefore was bound to give all his most serious attention to it. In this he was well seconded by Fortune, also. For as the Macedonian kings were especially keen after hunting, and [had great game preserves,] which were untouched during four years, owing to the public disturbances, the consequence was that they were full of every kind of animal. But when the [Macedonian] war was decided, Lucius Æmilius, thinking that hunting was the best training for body and courage his young soldiers could have, put the royal huntsmen under the charge of Scipio.

[As a result he became a highly proficient sportsman], and when he returned to Rome, instead, like the other young men, of hanging around the law courts, and paying calls, or haunting the Forum and trying to win popular favor, Scipio devoted his time to hunting, and by continually displaying brilliant and memorable acts of prowess won a greater reputation than others, whose only chance of gaining credit was by inflicting some damage on one of their fellow citizens, for that was the usual result of their law proceedings. Scipio, on the other hand, without inflicting

---

[1] A comment on the eminently "practical" spirit of the Romans.

annoyance on any one gained a popular reputation for manly courage, rivaling eloquence by action. The result was that in a short time he obtained a more decided superiority of position over contemporaries, than any Roman is remembered to have done; although he struck out a path for his ambition which, with a view to Roman customs and ideas, was quite different from that of others.

32. THE CONDUCT AND TREATMENT OF SLAVES

Plautus, (Comedy) " Pseudolus," Act I, Sc. 2. Bohn Translation

A Roman comedian, writing about the time of the end of the Second Punic War (201 B.C.), gives this picture of an inconsiderate master, and the kind of treatment his slaves were likely to get. Very probably conditions grew worse rather than better for the average slave household, for at least two centuries. As the Romans grew in wealth and the show of culture they did not grow in humanity.

[Ballio, a captious slave owner, is giving orders to his servants.]

Ballio. Get out, come, out with you, you rascals; kept at a loss, and bought at a loss. Not one of you dreams minding your business, or being a bit of use to me, unless I carry on thus! [*He strikes his whip around on all of them.*] Never did I see men more like asses [than you!] Why, your ribs are hardened with the stripes. If one flogs you, he hurts himself the most. [*Aside.*] Regular whipping posts are they all, and all they do is to pilfer, purloin, prig, plunder, drink, eat, and abscond! Oh! they *look* decent enough; but they're cheats in their conduct.

[*Addresses the slaves again.*] Now unless you're all attention, unless you get that sloth and drowsiness out of your breasts and eyes, I'll have your sides so thoroughly marked with thongs, that you'll outvie those Campanian coverlets in color, or a regular Alexandrian tapestry, purple-broidered all over with beasts. Yesterday I gave each of you his special job, but you're so worthless, neglectful, stubborn, that I must remind you with a good basting. So you think, I guess, you'll get the better of this whip and of me — by your stout hides! Zounds! But your hides won't prove harder than my good cowhide. [*He flourishes it.*] Look at this, please! Give heed to this! [*He flogs one slave.*] Well? Does it hurt? . . . Now stand all of you here, you race born to be thrashed! Turn your ears this way! Give heed to what I say. You fellow that's got the pitcher, fetch the water. Take care the kettle's full instanter. You who's got the ax, look after chopping the wood.

Slave. But this ax's edge is blunted.

Ballio. Well; be it so! And so are you blunted with stripes, but is that any reason why you shouldn't work for me? I order that you clean up the house. You know your business; hurry indoors. [*Exit first slave.*]

Now you [*to another slave*] smooth the couches, [for the dinner party]. Clean the plate and put in proper order. Take care that when I'm back from the Forum I find things *done,* — all swept, sprinkled, scoured, smoothed, cleaned, and set in order. To-day's my birthday. You should all set to and celebrate it. Take care — do you hear — to lay the salted bacon, the brawn, the collared neck, and the udder in water. I want to entertain some fine gentlemen in real style, to give the idea that I'm rich. Get in doors, and get these things ready, so there's no delay when the cook [1] comes. I'm going to market to buy what fish is to be had. Boy, you go ahead [*to a special valet*], I've got to take care that no one cuts off my purse.

33. Cato the Elder on how to manage Farm Slaves

Cato, Treatise on "Agriculture," chaps. 56-59

Cato the Elder passed as the incarnation of all worldly wisdom among Romans of the second century B.C. The precepts here

[1] Hired in from outside to help with the special banquet.

given were undoubtedly put in effect on his own farms.   During
the early Republic, when the estates were small, there seems to
have been a fair amount of kindly treatment awarded the slaves ;
as the farms grew larger the whole policy of the masters, by
becoming more impersonal, became more brutal.   Cato does not
advocate deliberate cruelty — he would simply treat the slaves
according to cold regulations, like so many expensive cattle.

Country slaves ought to receive in the winter, when they
are at work, four modii [1] of grain; and four modii and a half
during the summer.   The superintendent, the housekeeper,
the watchman, and the shepherd get three modii; slaves in
chains four pounds of bread in winter and five pounds from
the time when the work of training the vines ought to begin
until the figs have ripened.

Wine for the slaves.   After the vintage let them drink
from the sour wine for three months.   The fourth month
let them have a *hemina* (about half a pint) per day or two
congii and a half (over seven quarts) per month.   During the
fifth, sixth, seventh, and eighth months let them have a
sextarius (about a pint) per day or five congii per month.
Finally, in the ninth, tenth, and the eleventh, let them have
three *heminæ* (three fourths of a quart) per day, or an
amphora (about six gallons) per month.   On the Saturnalia
and on " Compitalia " each man should have a *congius* (something under three quarts).

To feed the slaves.   Let the olives that drop of themselves be kept so far as possible.   Keep too those har-
vested olives that do not yield much oil, and husband them,
for they last a long time.   When the olives have been consumed, give out the brine and vinegar.   You should dis-
tribute to every one a sextarius (about a pint) of oil per
month.   A modius (quarter bushel) of salt apiece is enough
for a year.

As for clothes, [give out] a tunic of three feet and a half,

[1] Modius = about a quarter bushel.

and a cloak (*sagum*) once in two years.   When you give a
tunic or cloak take back the old ones, to make cassocks (?)
out of.   Once in two years, good shoes should be given.

Winter wine for the slaves.   Put in a wooden cask ten
parts of must (non-fermented wine) and two parts of very
pungent vinegar, and add two parts of boiled wine and fifty
of sweet water.   With a paddle mix all these thrice per day
for five days in succession.   Add one forty-eighth of sea-
water drawn some time earlier.   Place the lid on the cask
and let it ferment for ten days.   This wine will last until
the solstice.   If any remains after that time, it will make
very sharp excellent vinegar.

34. How a Faithful Slave should Act

Plautus, (Comedy) "Menæchmi," Act V, Sc. 4.   Bohn Translation

What a slave of about 200 A.D. had to do in order to save himself from constant cuffs and stripes, is here set forth somewhat
humorously, but with a serious undercurrent of grim truth.   There
was no high motive for a slave to behave himself — simply a fear
of cruel punishment if he did not.   There might be a hope of ultimate freedom, but that depended entirely on the caprice of the
master.

Messenio, a slave, soliloquizes.

Well, this is the proof of a good servant : he must take care
of his master's business, look after it, arrange it, think about
it, when his master is away, take care of it diligently ; just as
much as if his master were present, or be even more careful.
He must take more care of his back than his appetite, his
legs than his stomach [1] — if he's got a good heart.   Just
let him think what those good-for-nothings get from *their*
masters, — lazy, worthless fellows that they are.   Stripes,
fetters, the mill, weariness, hunger, bitter cold — fine pay for

[1] *I.e.* take pains to avoid whippings and leg irons, even if sometimes
he is forced to go hungry.

idleness. That's what I'm mightily afraid of. Surely then it's much better to be good than to be bad. I don't mind tongue lashings, but I do hate real floggings. I'd rather eat meal somebody else grinds, than eat what I grind myself.[1] So I just obey what my master bids me; and I execute orders carefully and diligently. My obedience, I think, is such as is most for the profit of my back. And it surely *does* pay ! Let others do just as they think it worth while. I'll be just where I ought to be. If I stick to that, I'll avoid blunders; and I needn't be much afraid if I'm ready for my master, come what may. The time's pretty close when for this [faithful] service of mine, my master will give his reward.

35. SPARTACUS AND THE SLAVE REVOLT

Plutarch, "Life of Crassus," chaps. VIII–XI

In 73 B.C. the "Speaking Tools"—as the Romans called their slaves, especially those upon the great estates of Southern Italy—burst loose in a terrible insurrection, to quell which taxed the whole power of the government. Despite the sympathy one must have for these slaves and their gallant leader, their success would have been a calamity to civilization. An army of such brutalized wretches could only destroy ; they could never have erected a firm and tolerable government. There had already been two dangerous slave revolts in Sicily. After these outbreaks and the havoc and terror spread by them, the Romans out of sheer fear seem to have treated their slaves more harshly than ever.

The insurrection of the gladiators and the devastation of Italy, commonly called the war of Spartacus, began upon this occasion. One Lentulus Batiates trained up a great many gladiators in Capua, most of them Gauls and Thracians, who, not for any fault by them committed, but

[1] Refractory slaves were often sent to the hard labor of grinding grain in the hand mill.

simply through the cruelty of their master, were kept in confinement for the object of fighting one with another. Two hundred of these formed a plan to escape, but their plot being discovered, those of them who became aware of it in time to anticipate their master, being seventy-eight, got out of a cook's shop chopping knives and spits, and made their way through the city, and lighting by the way on several wagons that were carrying gladiators' arms to another city, they seized upon them and armed themselves. And seizing upon a defensible place, they chose three captains, of whom Spartacus was chief, a Thracian of one of the nomad tribes, and a man not only of high spirit and valiant, but in understanding, also, and in gentleness, superior to his condition, and more of a Grecian than the people of his country usually are.

First, then, routing those that came out of Capua against them, and thus procuring a quantity of proper soldiers' arms, they gladly threw away their own as barbarous and dishonorable. [Two prætors who were sent against them with small armies were defeated, while a third general's army was routed and himself slain.] After many successful skirmishes with Varinus, the prætor, himself, in one of which Spartacus took his lictors and his own horse, he began to be great and terrible; but wisely considering that he was not to expect to match the force of the empire, he marched his army towards the Alps, intending, when he had passed them, that every man should go to his own home, some to Thrace, some to Gaul. But they, grown confident in their numbers, and puffed up with their success, would give no obedience to him, but went about and ravaged Italy ; so that now the Senate was not only moved at the indignity and baseness, both of the enemy and of the insurrection, but, looking upon it as a matter of alarm and of dangerous consequence, sent out both the consuls to it, as to a great and difficult enterprise. The consul Gellius, falling suddenly upon a party of Germans, who through contempt and confidence had straggled from Spartacus, cut them all to pieces. But when Lentulus with a large army besieged Spartacus, he sallied out upon him, and, joining battle, defeated his chief officers, and captured all his baggage. As he made towards the Alps, Cassius, who was prætor of that part of Gaul that lies about the Po, met him with ten thousand men, but being overcome in battle, he had much ado to escape himself, with the loss of a great many of his men.

[The Senate in disgust now sent Crassus against the rebels. Spartacus, however, defeated Mummius, Crassus's lieutenant, and the general had to restore discipline among the demoralized Romans by executing fifty who had begun the flight; later he advanced again] . . . but Spartacus retreated through Lucania toward the sea, and in the straits, meeting with some Cilician pirate ships, he had thoughts of attempting Sicily, where, by landing two thousand men, he hoped to kindle anew the war of the slaves, which was but lately extinguished, and seemed to need but a little fuel to set it burning again. But after the pirates had struck a bargain with him, and received his earnest, they deceived him and sailed away. He thereupon retired again from the sea, and established his army in the peninsula of Rhegium. [Here Crassus tried to blockade him. Spartacus escaped with part of his army to Lucania, but some of Spartacus's followers mutinied, and left him. This division of malcontents was soon destroyed by Crassus.]

Spartacus, after this discomfiture, retired to the mountains of Petelia, but Quintius, one of Crassus's officers, and Scrofa, the quæstor, pursued and overtook him. But when Spartacus rallied and faced them, they were utterly routed and fled, and had much ado to carry off their quæstor, who was wounded. This success, however, ruined Spartacus, because it encouraged the slaves, who now disdained any longer to avoid fighting, or to obey their officers, but as they were upon their march, they came to them with their swords in their hand, and compelled them to lead them back again through Lucania, against the Romans, the very thing which Crassus was eager for. For news was already brought that Pompey [Crassus's rival for military glory] was at hand; and people began to talk openly that the honor of this war was reserved for him, who would come and at once oblige the enemy to fight and put an end to the war. Crassus, therefore, eager to fight a decisive battle, encamped very near the enemy, and began to make lines of circumvallation; but the slaves made a sally, and attacked the pioneers. As fresh supplies came in on either side, Spartacus, seeing there was no avoiding it, set all his army in array, and when his horse was brought him, he drew out his sword and killed him, saying, if he got the day, he should have a great many better horses of the enemies, and if he lost it, he should have no need of this. And so making directly towards Crassus himself, through the midst of arms and wounds, he missed him, but slew two centurions that fell upon him together. At last, being deserted by those that were about him, he himself stood his ground, and, surrounded by the enemy, bravely defending himself, was cut in pieces.

36. THE AUSTERITY OF CATO THE ELDER

Plutarch, "Life of Marcus Cato the Elder," chaps. IV–V

Cato the Elder (234 to 149 B.C.) during the eighty-five years of his life stood for almost all that was characteristically good and correspondingly bad in the Roman character. In his person was summed up the genius of the cold-blooded, hard-headed, practical, abstemious, money-grasping, yet strictly law-abiding and temperate race of Latin farmers who conquered the world. Few great peoples have more strictly excluded the spiritual and ideal from their lives than did the Romans.

Cato grew more and more powerful by his eloquence, so that he was commonly called the Roman Demosthenes, but his manner of life was yet more famous and talked of. For oratorical skill was, as an accomplishment, commonly studied and sought after by all young men; but he was very rare who would cultivate the old habits of bodily labor, or prefer a light supper, and a breakfast which never saw the fire; or be in love with poor clothes and a homely lodging, or could set his ambition rather on doing without luxuries than on possessing them. For now the state, unable to keep its purity by reason of its greatness, and having so many affairs, and people from all parts under its government, was fain to admit many mixed customs, and new examples of living.

With reason, therefore, everybody admired Cato, when they saw others sink under labors, and grow effeminate by pleasures; and yet beheld him unconquered by either, and that not only when he was young and desirous of honor, but also when old and grayheaded, after a consulship and triumph; like some famous victor in the games, persevering in his exercise and maintaining his character to the very last. He himself says, that he never wore a suit of clothes which cost more than a hundred drachmas; and that, when he was general and consul, he drank the same wine which his workmen did; and that the meat or fish which was bought in the market for his dinner did not cost above thirty *asses*. All of which was for the sake of the commonwealth, that so his body might be the hardier for the war.

Having a piece of embroidered Babylonian tapestry left him, he sold it; because none of his farmhouses were so much as plastered. Nor did he ever buy a slave for above fifteen hundred drachmas; as he did not seek for effeminate and handsome ones, but able, sturdy workmen, horse keepers and cowherds: and these he thought ought to be sold again, when they grew old, and no useless servants fed in a house.

In short, he reckoned nothing a good bargain, which was superfluous; but whatever it was, though sold for a farthing, he would think it a great price, if you had no need of it; and was for the purchase of lands for sowing and feeding, rather than grounds for sweeping and watering.

Some imputed these things to petty avarice, but others approved of him, as if he had only the more strictly denied himself for the rectifying and amending of others. Yet certainly, in my judgment, it marks an overrigid temper, for a man to take the work out of his servants as out of brute beasts, turning them off and selling them in their old age, and thinking there ought to be no further commerce between man and man, than whilst there arises some profit by it. We see that kindness or humanity has a larger field than bare justice to exercise itself in; law and justice we cannot, in the nature of things, employ on others than men; but we may extend our goodness and charity even to irrational creatures; and such acts flow from a gentle nature, as water from an abundant spring. It is doubtless the part of a kind-natured man to keep even worn-out horses and dogs, and not only take care of them when they are foals and whelps, but also when they are grown old.

37. How Cato the Elder governed as Censor

Livy, "History," book XXXIX, chaps. 40-44

In 184 b.c. Cato the Elder was elected censor. Under his administration the scourge was vigorously applied to the iniquities and follies of the younger generation of the Roman nobles, who, after the Second Punic War and the victories in Greece and Asia, were becoming lax and luxurious. No man ever stood for "the good old ways" more steadfastly than did Cato; and his censorship became a proverb for its severity.

[Among the numerous candidates for the censorship that year] Marcus Porcius Cato far surpassed them all. So great were his mental and intellectual powers that no matter how humbly he was born, he seemed capable of reaching the highest rank. No qualification for business, public or private, was wanting in him. Urban or rustic affairs he was alike skilled in. Some have won the highest honors, thanks to legal knowledge : some by their eloquence, some by military fame — but this man's genius was so versatile that whichever way it was engaged it might be said that nature formed him for that end alone.

In war he was most courageous, winning renown in many notable battles; and when he reached the generalship, he [won fame too] as a distinguished commander. In peace, if consulted on points of law, he was the wisest councilor; in litigation, he was the most eloquent advocate. Nor was his oratory only of temporary interest and force, during his own life, leaving no monument behind it. On the contrary, his eloquence still lives, and will long live, consecrated to memory by all kinds of writings. His orations were many, some in his own behalf, some for others, or against others; for he harassed his enemies [by continual litigation]. Enmities in abundance gave him plenty of employment, and he never suffered them to sleep, nor was it easy to tell whether the nobility labored harder to keep him down or he to oppress the nobility.

Cato's severity of Temper

No doubt his temper was sharp, his language bitter and absolutely reckless, but his mind was never conquered by his passions, his integrity was inflexible, and he looked with contempt on popular favor and riches. In spare diet, in enduring toil and danger, his body and mind were like iron; so that old age which brings all things to dissolution could not break his vigor. In his eighty-sixth year he stood a trial, pleaded his own cause, and published his speech; and in his ninetieth year he brought Servius Galba to trial before the People.

On the occasion when he was candidate for the censorship, as in all his previous career, the nobility tried to crush him. All the candidates, too, except Lucius Valerius Flaccus, who had been his colleague in the consulship, combined to defeat him [as being a personal enemy, and fearing a most severe censorship under him. Cato resisted them boldly and asked for Flaccus as colleague as being] "the only colleague, working with whom he could correct 'modern profligacy' and reëstablish the ancient morals." People were so inflamed by such harangues that in spite of the opposition of the nobility, they not only made Cato censor, but gave him Flaccus for his colleague.

How Cato dealt with Lucius Quintus

While anxious curiosity blended with fear [in all quarters], these censors made their survey of the Senate. Seven they expelled therefrom, one an ex-consul, highly distinguished by birth and honorable offices, — Lucius Quintius Flaminius. It is mentioned, as a usage instituted in memory of our forefathers, that the censors should annex marks of censure to the names of such as they degraded from the Senate. There are severe speeches of Cato, against those whom he either expelled from the Senate, or degraded from Equestrian rank, but by far the most so is that against Lucius Quintius. Had Cato given his speech as a mere prosecutor, not as a censor, not even Titus, Quintius's own brother could have suffered him to stay in the Senate.

Among other charges he declared that he had [taken one Philip, a Carthaginian and a favorite serving boy, to his province of Gaul] and this youth used frequently in wanton squabbling to upbraid him for quitting Rome just before the gladiator show. It chanced that during a feast, while they were hot with wine, a message was brought into the banqueting place, that a Boian nobleman had come as a deserter with his children, and wished to see the consul, that he might in person receive his pledge of protection. He was accordingly introduced into the tent, and began to talk through an interpreter, but even as he spoke Quintius said to his minion, "Since you left the show of gladiators, don't you want to see this Gaul dying?" When the other assented, but scarcely in earnest, the consul, drawing a sword that hung over his head, first struck the Gaul as he was speaking, and then when he was running out, begging for the "protection of the Roman People, and everybody present," ran him through the body.

[Other outrageous stories were told of the lust and cruelty of this Quintius.] In the latter part of Cato's speech he proposed to Quintius that if he denied this fact, and the other accusations, he should give security to stand a regular trial; but if he confessed them, could he suppose, he demanded, that any one would be sorry for his disgrace, — the disgrace of him who, in the midst of a feast, intoxicated as he was by wine and lust, had sported with the blood of a human being.

Other Censorial Measures

In the review of the equites, Lucius Scipio Asiaticus was degraded. In fixing the rates of taxation, also, the censor's conduct was harsh and severe on all ranks of men. People were ordered to give an account upon their oaths of women's dresses, and ornaments, and carriages exceeding in value 15,000 asses [about $250]. Also it was ordered that slaves, younger than twenty years, which since the last [censorial] survey had been sold for 10,000 asses [about $166] or more should be estimated at ten times their value [for taxation purposes, and that on all these articles a tax should be laid of three denarii for each thousand asses].[1]

[1] Ten asses at this time seem to have made one denarius. This then was a three per cent tax.

The censors took away water which belonged to the public, that was running or was carried into any private building or field; and they demolished within thirty days all buildings or sheds in possession of private parties that projected upon public ground. They then engaged contractors for executing government works, with the money decreed for this purpose, — for paving cisterns with stone, for cleansing the sewers when it was needful, for forming new ones on the Aventine, and in other quarters, where hitherto there had been none.

Dividing next their tasks, Flaccus built a mole to Neptunia on the coast, and made a road through the Formian hills. Cato bought for the public use two halls, the Marnian and the Titian in the Latumiæ, and four shops, and built there a court of justice which was called [from him] the Porcian. They farmed out the several branches of the revenue at the highest prices, and bargained with the contractors for the performance of the public services on the lowest terms. When the Senate, overcome by the prayers and lamentations of the tax contractors,[1] ordered these bargains revoked, the censors, by an edict, excluded from the bidding everybody who had evaded the former contracts, and relet the same branches [of public service] at very nearly the old rates.

This was a remarkable censorship, and the origin of many deadly feuds. It rendered Marcus Cato, to whom all the harshness was attributed, an uneasy man for the rest of his life. [He died thirty-five years later.]

38. THE AGRARIAN SITUATION IN ITALY IN 133 B.C.

Appian, "Civil Wars," book I, 7–9. White's Translation

The following extract makes fairly clear the condition of the farmers of Italy just before the rise of Tiberius Gracchus, and

[1] Who had found their contracts unprofitable.

shows what a terrible grievance the peasantry had against the owners and exploiters of the *latefundia* — the great estates worked usually by cheap slave labor.

The Romans, while they subdued one after another of the peoples of Italy, used to confiscate part of their lands, and build towns thereon, or established their own colonies in those already in existence, and used them in place of garrisons. Of the land acquired by war they granted the cultivated part promptly to settlers, or leased it, or sold it [outright]. Since they had no leisure, as yet, to allot the part which then lay desolated by war, usually the major part, they would proclaim that in the interval those who wished to till it might do so for a share of the yearly crops, — a tenth of the grain and a fifth of the fruit. Herdsmen had to give a share of their animals, both oxen and small cattle. This policy was followed to multiply the Italian race, which they reckoned the most laborious of peoples, in order to have plenty of allies at home.

The very opposite thing, however, happened; for the wealthy, getting hold of the greater part of the undistributed lands, growing bold by lapse of time and thinking they would never be ousted, added to their [original] holdings the small farms of their poor neighbors. This they did partly by purchase, yet partly by force; and so they cultivated vast tracts [of land] in lieu of mere private estates. To work them they used slaves as farm hands and herdsmen, lest free laborers should be forced to quit farm work for the army. The ownership of slaves brought huge profit from the multitude of the children [of the slaves], who increased because they were exempt from army service. Thus the magnates became marvelously rich, and the race of slaves multiplied through the land, while the [free] folk of Italy dwindled alike in numbers and power, ground down as they were by poverty, taxation, and [constant] service in the army. If any relaxation from these evils came, they passed their time in sheer idleness, for the land was in the clutches of the rich, who employed slaves as farm hands, not freemen.

These were the reasons why the people became [at last] troubled lest they should no longer have enough allies of the Italian stock, and lest the very government should be in danger by such a horde of slaves. They did not see any [real] remedy, for it was not easy, nay, it was hardly just, to deprive men of such large holdings which they had kept so long, and which included [the holder's own] trees, buildings, and fixtures. Once, indeed, a law had been passed on the motion of the tribunes, forbidding any one to hold more than 500 jugera (about 330 acres) of this [public] land, or pasture upon it more than 100 cattle or 500 sheep. To insure the observance of this law there must be a certain number of freemen kept upon the farms, whose business was to watch and report proceedings thereon. Persons holding [public] lands under the law were bound to swear to obey it, and penalties were laid for violation thereof. It was presumed that the rest of the [public] land would soon be divided in small lots among the poor. But not the least heed was paid to the law or the oaths. The few who seemed to respect them somewhat, conveyed their [surplus] lands to their relatives fraudulently; the majority disregarded them altogether. [At last Tiberius Gracchus arose in protest.]

39. The Murder of Tiberius Gracchus and the First Sedition in Rome

Plutarch, " Life of Tiberius Gracchus," chaps. XVI-XX

In 133 B.C. Tiberius Gracchus, having as tribune forced through legislation highly displeasing to the ruling nobility, sought reëlection to office from the people. To prevent this continuance of their enemy in power the aristocrats did not hesitate to resort

to violence. For practically the first time in Roman history a
political dispute was settled not peacefully, but with clubs and
swords. What made the murder of Tiberius Gracchus worse, was
the fact that he was still an "inviolate" tribune. The senatorial
oligarchy — be it noted — were the first to resort to violence and
precipitate civil war: and they gained their reward in the
triumph of Cæsarism.

Tiberius then went down into the market place amongst
the people, and made his addresses to them humbly and
with tears in his eyes; and told them he had just reason to
suspect that his adversaries would attempt in the night
time to break open his house, and murder him. This worked
so strongly with the multitude, that several of them pitched
tents round about his house, and kept guard all night for
the security of his person. By break of day [the soothsayer
tried to take the omens, but the chickens refused to eat,
— a very bad sign].

However, Tiberius went towards the Capitol, as soon as
he understood that the people were assembled there; but
before he got out of the house, he stumbled upon the
threshold with such violence, that he broke the nail of his
great toe, insomuch that blood gushed out of his shoe. He
was not gone very far before he saw two ravens fighting on
the top of a house which stood on his left hand as he passed
along; and though he was surrounded with a number of
people, a stone, struck from its place by one of the ravens,
fell just at his foot. This even the boldest men about him
felt as a check. But Blossius of Cuma, who was present,
told him, that it would be a shame, and an ignominious
thing, for Tiberius, who was the son of Gracchus, the grandson of Scipio Africanus, and the protector of the Roman
people, to refuse, for fear of a silly bird, to answer, when
his countrymen called to him; and that his adversaries
would represent it not as a mere matter for their ridicule,
but would declaim about it to the people as the mark of a

tyrannical temper, which felt a pride in taking liberties
with the people.   At the same time several messengers came
also from his friends, to desire his presence at the Capitol,
saying that all things went there according to expectation.
And indeed Tiberius's first entrance there was in every way
successful; [the people received him with loud cheers, but
in the crowd and confusion it was impossible to proceed
with the vote in an orderly way].

Whilst things were in this confusion, Fulvius Flaccus,
a senator, standing in a place where he could be seen, but
at such a distance from Tiberius that he could not make
him hear, signified to him by motions of his hand, that he
wished to impart something of consequence to him in
private.   Tiberius ordered the multitude to make way for
him, by which means, though not without some difficulty,
Fulvius got to him, and informed him, that the rich men, in
a sitting of the Senate, seeing they could not prevail upon
the consul to espouse their quarrel, had come to a final
determination amongst themselves, that he should be assassinated, and to that purpose had a great number of their
friends and servants ready armed to accomplish it.

Tiberius no sooner communicated this intelligence to
those about him, but they immediately tucked up their
gowns, broke into pieces the halberts which the officers used
to keep the crowd off, and distributed them among themselves, resolving to resist the attack with these.   Those
who stood at a distance wondered, and asked what was the
occasion; Tiberius, knowing that they could not hear him
at that distance, lifted his hand to his head, wishing to intimate the great danger which he apprehended himself to be
in.   His adversaries, taking notice of that action, ran off at
once to the senate house, and declared, that Tiberius desired
the people to bestow a crown upon him, as if this were the
meaning of his touching his head.

[The consul refused to order arms against Tiberius, but

Nasica urged stern measures.] "Since the consul," said he "regards not the safety of the commonwealth, let every one who will defend the laws follow me." He, then, casting the skirt of his gown over his head, hastened to the Capitol; those who bore him company wrapped their gowns also about their arms and forced their way after him. And as they were persons of the greatest authority in the city the common people did not venture to obstruct their passing, but were so eager to clear the way for them that they tumbled over one another in haste. The attendants they brought with them had furnished themselves with clubs and staves from their houses, and they themselves picked up the feet and other fragments of stools and chairs, which were broken by the hasty flight of the common people.

Thus armed, they made towards Tiberius, knocking down those whom they found in front of him, and those were soon wholly dispersed, and many of them slain. Tiberius tried to save himself by flight. As he was running, he was stopped by one who caught hold of him by the gown; but he threw it off, and fled in his undergarments only. And stumbling over those who before had been knocked down, as he was endeavoring to get up again, Publius Satureius, a tribune, one of his colleagues, was observed to give him the first fatal stroke, by hitting him upon the head with the foot of a stool. The second blow was claimed, as though it had been a deed to be proud of, by Lucius Rufus. And of the rest there fell above three hundred, killed by clubs and staves only, none by an iron weapon.

This, we are told, was the first sedition amongst the Romans, since the abrogation of kingly government, that ended in the effusion of blood. All former quarrels which were neither small nor about trivial matters, were always amicably composed, by mutual concessions on either side, the Senate yielding for fear of the commons, and the commons out of respect to the Senate. And it is probable indeed that Tibe-

rius himself might then have been easily induced, by mere
persuasion, to give way, and certainly, if attacked at all,
must have yielded without any recourse to violence and
bloodshed, as he had not at that time above three thousand
men to support him.   But it is evident that this conspiracy
was fomented against him, more out of the hatred and
malice which the rich men had to his person, than for the
reasons which they commonly pretended against him.   In
testimony of which, we may adduce the cruelty and unnatural
insults which they used to his dead body.   For they would
not suffer his own brother, though he earnestly begged the
favor, to bury him in the night, but threw him, together
with the other corpses, into the river.

40.   How Jugurtha corrupted the Degenerate Senate

Sallust, " Jugurthine War," chaps. 13, 16, 32, 33, 35.   Bohn Translation

Jugurtha, king of Numidia (118 to 106 B.C.), a sly and slippery African, was the occasion of revealing in plain day the
corruption that had penetrated the Roman Senate.   He was quite
familiar with the condition of affairs in Rome, and but for the fact
that the "popular" anti-senatorial party was again raising its
head against his noble friends, he would probably have bought his
way to perfect immunity.

Jugurtha [having murdered his kinsman Hiempsal, the
ally of Rome] began to feel a dread of the Roman people,
against whose wrath he had no hopes of safety save in the
avarice of the nobility and his own riches.   Therefore he
speedily sent envoys to Rome with a profusion of gold and
silver.   He ordered them in the first place to make abundant presents to his old friends and to get him new ones —
in short not to stickle at accomplishing everything possible
by bribery.

When these deputies reached Rome and had sent large

presents as directed, to his special friends and other men then very influential, so remarkable a change ensued that Jugurtha, from being an object of the greatest odium, grew into great regard and favor with the nobility, who, partly allured with hope, and partly with actual bribes, tried — by soliciting the members of the Senate individually — to prevent any severe measures from being adopted against him. When the envoys, therefore, felt sure of success the Senate, on an appointed day, gave an audience to both parties.[1]

[Despite the obvious justice of the complaints of the partisans of Hiempsal, and the denunciations of Jugurtha by several prominent Senators, the decision was in favor of Jugurtha; and commissioners were appointed to divide Numidia between him and Adherbal, the surving heir of the late king.]

Although Jugurtha had already counted Scaurus [one of these commissioners] among his friends at Rome, yet he received him with the most studied ceremony, and by presents and promises wrought on him so effectually that he preferred the prince's interest to his own character, honor, and all other considerations. The rest of the commissions he assailed in a similar way and gained over most of them; by a few only was integrity given more weight than lucre.

[Jugurtha accordingly had the kingdom divided altogether to his liking; nevertheless, he ultimately found himself at war with Rome, yet he soon found means to purchase a treaty of peace.]

Some [Roman officers] seduced by gold had restored to Jugurtha his war elephants; others had sold back to him his deserters; others had ravaged the lands of the population friendly to us [Romans], so strong was the spirit of rapacity, which like a contagious pestilence had pervaded the breasts of all.

---

[1] His cousin Adherbal, the cousin of Jugurtha, with whom he had been at war, had also sent an embassy to the Senate to make complaints against Jugurtha.

Jugurtha accordingly returned to Rome, but without any mark of royalty, and in the costume — so far as possible — of a suppliant; and though he felt great confidence on his own part, and was supported by everybody through whose influence or villainy he had executed his schemes, nevertheless he bought — with a huge bribe — the help of Gaius Bæbius, a plebeian tribune, by whose brazen help he trusted to be protected against the law or any other harm.

[He overreached himself, however, and popular clamor arising against him] he departed upon being ordered by the Senate to quit Italy. But, as he was leaving Rome, he, it is said, after frequently looking back on it silently, at last cried out, " *O venal çity! And soon to perish, — if but a purchaser be found!*"

[To conquer him and his Numidians cost the Romans a long and troublesome war.]

41. How Marius overthrew the Teutones

Plutarch, " Life of Marius," chaps. XVII–XXI

In the latter part of the second century B.C. the Germanic tribes of the north began their restless wanderings westward and southward — movements that never ceased until they had destroyed the Roman Empire. But their conquest was postponed for centuries by the victory of Marius (102 B.C.) at Aquæ Sextiæ in southern Gaul over the Teutones, a most formidable tribe threatening to overwhelm Italy. The deliverance was completed the next year by his victory over their allies, the Cimbri. This coming on the scene of the *Germans* is an event in world history, and worthy to be recorded.

Now the Teutones, whilst Marius lay quiet, ventured to attack his camp; from whence, however, being encountered with showers of darts, and losing several of their men, they determined to march forward, hoping to reach the other side of the Alps without opposition, and, packing up their baggage, passed securely by the Roman camp, where the greatness of their number was especially made evident by the long time they took in their march, for they were said to be six days in passing Marius's fortifications; they marched pretty near, and revilingly asked the Romans if they would send any commands by them to their wives, for they would shortly be with them. As soon as they were passed and had gone on a little distance ahead, Marius began to move, and follow them at his leisure, always encamping at some small distance from them; choosing also strong positions, and carefully fortifying them, that he might quarter with safety. Thus they marched till they came to the place called Sextilius's Waters,[1] from whence it was but a short way before being amidst the Alps, and here Marius put himself in readiness for the encounter.

He chose a place for his camp of considerable strength, but where there was a scarcity of water; designing, it is said, by this means, also, to put an edge on his soldiers' courage; and when several were not a little distressed, and complained of thirst, pointing to a river that ran near the enemy's camp: "There," said he, "you may have drink, if you will buy it with your blood." "Why, then," replied they, "do you not lead us to them, before our blood is dried up in us?" He answered, in a softer tone, "Let us first fortify our camp," and the soldiers, though not without repining, proceeded to obey. [A fight was precipitated, however, by the horse boys and camp servants of the Romans, who went down to the river for water and fell in with a small band of the enemy. After a sharp skirmish, the whole body of the Ambrones, a warlike tribe in alliance with the Teutones, came charging across the river against the Romans.]

[1] Aquæ Sextiliæ, more correctly Aquæ Sextiæ, the modern Aix of Provence, a little north of Marseilles.

How the Battle was Precipitated

The river disordered the Ambrones; before they could draw up all their army on the other side of it, the Ligurians [allies of the Romans] presently fell upon the van, and began to charge them hand to hand. The Romans, too, coming to their assistance, and from the higher ground pouring upon the enemy, forcibly repelled them, and the most of them (one thrusting another into the river) were there slain, and filled it with their blood and dead bodies. Those that got safe over, not daring to make head, were slain by the Romans, as they fled to their camp and wagons; where the women, meeting them with swords and hatchets, and making a hideous outcry, set upon those that fled as well as those that pursued, the one as traitors, the other as enemies; and, mixing themselves with the combatants, with their bare arms pulling away the Romans' shields, and laying hold on their swords, endured the wounds and slashing of their bodies to the very last, with undaunted resolution. Thus the battle seems to have happened at that river rather by accident than by the design of the general.

The Night after the First Day of Fighting

After the Romans were retired from the great slaughter of the Ambrones, night came on; but the army was not indulged, as was the usual custom, with songs of victory, drinking in their tents, and mutual entertainments, and (what is most welcome to soldiers after successful fighting) quiet sleep, but they passed that night, above all others, in fears and alarm. For their camp was without either rampart or palisade, and there remained thousands upon thousands of their enemies yet unconquered; to whom were joined as many of the Ambrones as escaped. There were heard, from these, all through the night, wild bewailings, nothing like the sighs and groans of men, but a sort of wild beastlike howling and roaring, joined with threats and lamentations rising from the vast multitude, and echoed among the neighboring hills and hollow banks of the river. The whole plain was filled with hideous noise, insomuch that the Romans were not a little afraid, and Marius himself was apprehensive of a confused tumultuous night engagement. But the enemy did not stir either this night or the next day, but were employed in disposing and drawing themselves up to the greatest advantage.

The Decisive Battle on the Second Day

Of this occasion Marius made good use; for there were beyond the enemies some wooded ascents and deep valleys thickly set with trees, whither he sent Claudius Marcellus, secretly, with three thousand regular soldiers, giving him orders to post them in ambush there, and show themselves at the rear of the enemies, when the fight was begun. The others, refreshed with victuals and sleep, as soon as it was day he drew up before the camp, and commanded the horse to sally out into the plain, at the sight of which the Teutones could not contain themselves till the Romans should come down and fight them on equal terms, but hastily arming themselves, charged in their fury up the hillside. Marius, sending officers to all parts, commanded his men to stand still and keep their ground; when they came within reach, to throw their javelins, then use their swords, and, joining their shields, force them back; pointing out to them that the steepness of the ground would render the enemy's blows inefficient, nor could their shields be kept close together, the inequality of the ground hindering the stability of their footing.

This counsel he gave them, and was the first that followed it; for he was inferior to none in the use of his body, and far excelled all in resolution. The Romans accordingly stood for their approach, and, checking them in their advance upwards, forced them little by little to give way and yield down the hill, and here, on the level ground, no sooner had the Ambrones begun to restore their van into a posture of resistance, but they found their rear disordered. For Marcellus had not let slip the opportunity; but as soon as the shout was raised among the Romans on the hills, he, setting his men in motion, fell in upon the enemy behind, at full speed, and with loud cries, and routed those nearest him, and they, breaking the ranks of those that were before them, filled the whole army with confusion. They made no long resistance after they were thus broke in upon, but having lost all order, fled.

The Romans, pursuing them, slew and took prisoners above one hundred thousand, and possessing themselves of their spoils, tents, and carriages, voted all that was not plundered to Marius's share, which, though so magnificent a present, yet was generally thought less than his conduct deserved in so great a danger.

42. THE REIGN OF TERROR UNDER SULLA

Plutarch's "Life of Sulla," chaps. XXXI–XXXII

In 82 B.C. Sulla, having become master of the state and being resolved upon a thorough reorganization of the government in favor of the aristocrats, undertook to eliminate every person who might prove an enemy to his scheme. He went about this policy with a cold-blooded and typically Roman thoroughness. What followed his edict is graphically told by Plutarch.

Few events in Roman history illustrate the lack of sentiment and the inherent lack of humanity among the Latins better than this. It is worth noticing that Sulla's cruelties did not succeed. Practically all his innovations in the constitution were overthrown in 70 B.C.

Sulla being thus wholly bent upon slaughter, and filling the city with executions without number or limit, many wholly uninterested persons falling a sacrifice to private enmity, through his permission and indulgence to his friends, Caius Metellus, one of the younger men, made bold in the Senate to ask him what end there was of these evils, and at what point he might be expected to stop? "We do not ask you," said he, "to pardon any whom you have resolved to destroy, but to free from doubt those whom you are pleased to save," Sulla answering, that he knew not as yet whom to spare. "Why then," said he, "tell us whom you will punish." This Sulla said he would do. These last words, some authors say, were spoken not by Metellus, but by Afidius,[1] one of Sulla's fawning companions. Immediately upon this, without communicating with any of the magistrates, Sulla proscribed eighty persons, and notwithstanding the general indignation, after one day's respite, he posted two hundred and twenty more, and on the third again, as many.

In an address to the people on this occasion, he told them he had put up as many names as he could think of; those which had escaped his memory he would publish at a future time. He issued an edict likewise, making death the punishment of humanity, proscribing any who should dare to receive and cherish a proscribed person, without exception to brother, son, or parents. And to him who should slay any proscribed person he ordained two talents reward, even were it a slave who had killed his master, or a son his father. And what was thought most unjust of all, he caused the attainder to pass to their sons, and son's sons, and made open sale of all their property.

Nor did the proscription prevail only at Rome, but throughout all the cities of Italy the effusion of blood was

1 *Afidius* is probably a mistake (of Plutarch or of a transcriber) for **Fufidius**.

such, that neither sanctuary of the gods, nor hearth of hospitality, nor ancestral home escaped. Men were butchered in the embraces of their wives, children in the arms of their mothers. Those who perished through public animosity or private enmity were nothing in comparison to the numbers of those who suffered for their riches. Even the murderers began to say, that "his fine house killed this man, a garden that, a third, his hot baths." Quintus Aurelius, a quiet, peaceable man, and one who thought all his part in the common calamity consisted in condoling with the misfortunes of others, coming into the Forum to read the list, and finding himself among the proscribed, cried out, "Woe is me, my Alban farm has informed against me." He had not gone far, before he was dispatched by a ruffian, sent on that errand.

Meantime, Marius [the Younger], when about to be taken, killed himself; and Sulla, coming to Præneste, at first proceeded judicially against each particular person, till at last, finding it a work of too much time, he cooped them up together in one place, to the number of twelve thousand men, and gave order for the execution of them all, his own host alone excepted. But he, brave man, telling him he could not accept the obligation of life from the hands of one who had been the ruin of his country, went in among the rest, and submitted willingly to the stroke.

What Lucius Catilina did was thought to exceed all other acts. For having, before matters came to an issue, made away with his brother, he besought Sulla to place him in the list of proscription, as though he had been alive, which was done; and Catiline, to return the kind office, assassinated a certain Marcus Marius, one of the adverse party, and brought the head to Sulla, as he was sitting in the Forum, and then going to the holy water of Apollo, which was nigh, washed his hands.

43. THE VAST POWER OF MITHRIDATES

Appian, "Mithridatic Wars," 118-119. White's Translation

In Mithridates, king of Pontus (reigned 120 to 63 B.C.), the Romans found their most formidable enemy, save only Hannibal. That he was a foeman worthy to contend with Sulla, Lucullus, and Pompey is testified to in the following from Appian. In conquering Mithridates the Romans, almost against their wish, were forced to conquer most of the nearer Orient, — especially all of Asia Minor and Syria, — and to come face to face with Parthia.

[When at last Mithridates had been overthrown the Romans called the victory over him "The Great Victory" and Pompey, his conqueror, "The Great" — on account of the magnitude and intensity of his resistance.]

Many times Mithridates had over 400 ships of his own, 50,000 cavalry, and 250,000 infantry, with engines and arms in proportion. For allies he had the king of Armenia and the princes of the Scythian tribes around the Euxine and the Sea of Azov and beyond, as far as the Thracian Bosphorus. He held communication with the leaders of the Roman civil wars, which were then fiercely raging, and with those who were inciting insurrections in Spain. He established friendly relations with the Gauls for the purpose of invading Italy.

From Cilicia to the Pillars of Hercules he also filled the sea with pirates, who stopped all commerce and navigation between cities, and caused severe famine for a long time. In short, he left nothing within the power of man undone or untried to start the greatest possible movement, extending from the Orient to the Occident, to vex, so to speak, the whole world, which was warred upon, tangled in alliances, harassed by pirates, or vexed by the neighborhood of the warfare. Such and so diversified was this one war [against Mithridates], but in the end it brought the greatest gain to the Romans; for it pushed the boundaries of their dominion from the setting of the sun to the river Euphrates.

44. LUCULLUS'S TRIUMPH OVER MITHRIDATES AND HIS LUXURIOUS MODE OF LIFE

Plutarch, " Life of Lucullus," chaps. XXXVII, XXXI–XLII

Lucullus (died about 56 B.C.) would have conquered Mithridates, had not Pompey been sent out (66 B.C.) to supersede him. As it was, he brought back from the East enough wealth for a magnificent triumph. Afterwards, disgusted at the political situation, he retired into private life and spent his days in a splendid luxury and gilded indolence that made his name proverbial. We still speak of "Lucullan banquets."

Lucullus, upon his return to Rome, found his brother Marcus accused by Caius Memmius for his acts as quæstor, done by Sulla's orders; and on his acquittal, Memmius changed the scene, and animated the people against Lucullus himself, urging them to deny him a triumph for appropriating the spoils and prolonging the war. In this great struggle, the nobility and chief men went down and, mingling in person among the tribes, with much entreaty and labor, scarce at length prevailed upon them to consent to his triumph. The pomp of which proved not so wonderful or so wearisome with the length of the procession and the number of things carried in it, but consisted chiefly in vast quantities of arms and machines of the king's, with which he adorned the Flaminian circus, a spectacle by no means despicable.

In his progress there passed by a few horsemen in heavy armor, ten chariots armed with scythes, sixty friends and officers of the king's, and a hundred and ten brazen-beaked ships of war, which were conveyed along with them, a golden image of Mithridates six feet high, a shield set with precious stones, twenty loads of silver vessels, and thirty-two of golden cups, armor, and money, all carried by men. Besides which, eight mules were laden with golden couches, fifty-six with bullion, and a hundred and seven with coined silver, little less than two millions seven hundred thousand pieces. There were tablets, also, with inscriptions, stating what moneys he gave Pompey for prosecuting the piratic war, what he delivered into the treasury, and what he gave to every soldier, which was nine hundred and fifty drachmas [about $150] each. After all which, he nobly feasted the city and adjoining villages.

Lucullus's Villas

And, indeed, Lucullus's life, like the Old Comedy, presents us at the commencement with acts of policy and of war, at the end offering nothing but good eating and drinking, feastings and revelings, and mere play. For I give no higher name to his sumptuous buildings, porticoes, and baths, still less to his paintings and sculptures, and all his industry about these curiosities, which he collected with vast expense, lavishly bestowing all the wealth and treasure which he got in the war upon them, insomuch that even now, with all the advance of luxury, the Lucullan gardens are counted the noblest the emperor has.

Tubero the stoic, when he saw his buildings at Naples, where he suspended the hills upon vast tunnels, brought in the sea for moats and fish ponds round his house, and built pleasure houses in the waters, called him 'Xerxes in a gown.' He had also fine seats in Tusculum, belvederes, and large open balconies for men's apartments, and porticoes to walk in, where Pompey coming to see him, blamed him for making a house which would be pleasant in summer, but uninhabitable in winter; whom he answered with a smile, "You think me, then, less provident than cranes and storks, not to change my home with the season."

When a prætor, with great expense and pains, was preparing a spectacle for the people, and asked him to lend him some purple robes for the performers in a chorus, he told him he would go home and see, and if he had got any, would let him have them; and the next day asking how many he wanted, and being told that a hundred would suffice, bade him to take twice as many; on which the poet Horace observes, that a house is but a poor one, where the valuables unseen and unthought of do not exceed all those that meet the eye.

Lucullus's daily entertainments were ostentatiously extravagant, not only with purple coverlets, and plate adorned with precious stones, and dancings, and interludes, but with the greatest diversity of dishes and the most elaborate cookery, for the vulgar to admire and envy. It was a happy thought of Pompey in his sickness, when his physician prescribed a thrush for his dinner, and his servants told him that in summer time thrushes were not to be found anywhere but in Lucullus's fattening coops, that he would not suffer them to fetch one thence, but observing to his physician, " So if Lucullus had not been an epicure, Pompey had not lived," ordered something else that could easily be got to be prepared for him. Cato was his friend and connection, but, nevertheless, so hated his life and habits, that when a young man in the Senate made a long and tedious speech, in praise of frugality and temperance, Cato got up and said, " How long do you mean to go on making money like Crassus, living like Lucullus, and talking like Cato? " There are some, however, who say the words were said, but not by Cato.

It is plain from the anecdotes on record of him, that Lucullus was not only pleased with, but even gloried in, his way of living. For he is said to have feasted several Greeks upon their coming to Rome day after day, who, out of a true Grecian principle, being ashamed, and declining the invitation, where so great an expense was every day incurred for them, he with a smile told them, " Some of this, indeed, my Grecian friends, is for your sakes, but more for that of Lucullus."

How Lucullus entertained Cicero and Pompey

Once when he supped alone, there being only one course, and that but moderately furnished, he called his steward and reproved him, who, professing to have supposed that there would be no need of any great entertainment, when nobody was invited, was answered, " What, did not you know, then, that to-day Lucullus dines with Lucullus ? " Which being much spoken of about the city, Cicero and Pompey one day met him loitering in the Forum, the former his intimate friend and familiar, and, though there had been some ill will between Pompey and him about the command in the war, still they used to see each other and converse on easy terms together. Cicero accordingly saluted him, and asked him whether to-day were a good time for asking a favor of him, and on his answering, " Very much so," and begging to hear what it was, " Then," said Cicero, " we should like to dine with you to-day, just on the dinner that is prepared for yourself." Lucullus being surprised, and requesting a day's time, they refused to grant it, neither suffered him to talk to his servants, for fear he should give order for more than was appointed before. But thus much they consented to, that before their faces he might tell his servant, that to-day he would sup in the Apollo (for so one of his best dining rooms was called), and by this evasion he outwitted his guests. For every room, as it seems, had its own assessment of expenditure, dinner at such a price, and all else in accordance ; so that the servants, on knowing where he would dine, knew also how much was to be expended, and in what style and form dinner was to be served. The expense for the Apollo was fifty thousand drachmas [$8000], and thus much being that day laid out, the greatness of the cost did not so much amaze Pompey and Cicero, as the rapidity of the outlay. One might believe Lucullus thought his money really captive and barbarian, so wantonly and contumeliously did he treat it.

Lucullus's Library

His furnishing a library, however, deserves praise and record, for he collected very many and choice manuscripts; and the use they were put to was even more magnificent than the purchase, the library being always open, and the walks and reading rooms about it free to all Greeks, whose delight it was to leave their other occupations and hasten thither as to the habitation of the Muses, there walking about, and diverting one another. He himself often passed his hours there, disputing with the learned in the walks, and giving his advice to statesmen who required it, insomuch that his house was altogether a home, and in a manner a Greek prytaneum for those that visited Rome. He was fond of all sorts of philosophy, and was well read and expert in them all. But he always from the first specially favored and valued the Academy; not the New one, which at that time under Philo flourished with the precepts of Carneades, but the Old one, then sustained and represented by Antiochus of Ascalon, a learned and eloquent man. Lucullus with great labor made him his friend and companion, and set him up against Philo's auditors, among whom Cicero was one, who wrote an admirable treatise in defense of his sect, in which he puts the argument in favor of *comprehension* [1] in the mouth of Lucullus, and the opposite argument in his own.

45. POMPEY'S CONQUEST OF THE EAST

Appian, "Mithridatic Wars," 114–119. White's Translation

Pompey is usually overshadowed in most histories by his greater rival, Cæsar, but he won marked successes along certain lines. The greatest thing that he did was to consolidate and organize the Roman power in Asia Minor, Syria, and Palestine. How impor-

---

[1] Or rather the book might be defined as "Apprehension" as opposed to mere sensation or impression.

tant this work was, and how magnificent was the triumph that
Pompey celebrate in Rome (September 30th, 61 B.C.) is told by
Appian. Incidentally a good idea is given of a typical Roman
triumph.

Pompey having cleaned out the robber dens, and pros-
trated the greatest king living [Mithridates] in one and
the same war; and having fought successful battles, besides
those of the Pontic war, with Colchians, Albanians, Iberians, Armenians, Medes, Arabs, Jews, and other Eastern
nations, extended the Roman sway as far as Egypt. He
let some of the subjugated nations go free, and made them
allies. Others he placed at once under Roman rule; still
others he distributed to [various vassal-] kings.

He founded cities also: in Lesser Armenia Nicopolis,
named for his victory, in Pontus Eupatoria, which Mithridates Eupator had built and named after himself, but destroyed because it had received the Romans. Pompey
rebuilt it, and named it Magnopolis. In Cappadocia he
rebuilt Mazaca, which had been completely ruined by the
war. He restored other towns in many places, that had
been destroyed or damaged, in Pontus, Palestine, Cœle-
Syria, and Cilicia, in which he settled the greater part of
the pirates [he had conquered], and where the city formerly called Soli is now known as Pompeiopolis. The city
of Talauri [in Pontus] Mithridates had used as a store-
house of furniture. Here were found 2000 drinking cups,
made of onyx welded with gold, and many cups, wine
coolers, and drinking horns, bridles for horses, etc. . . . all
ornamented in like manner with gold and precious stones.
The quantity of this store was so great that the inventory
of it occupied thirty days. These things had been inherited
from Darius [the Great of Persia and other mighty rulers].

At the end of the winter [63–62 B.C.] Pompey distributed
rewards to the army, 1500 Attic drachmas [about $270]
to each soldier, and in like proportion to the officers, the

whole, it was said, amounting to 16,000 talents [considerably over $16,000,000].   Then he marched to Ephesus, embarked for Italy, and hastened to Rome, having dismissed his soldiers at Brundisium to their homes, by which act his popularity was greatly increased among the Romans.

His Great Triumph at Rome

As he approached the city he was met by successive processions, first of youths, farthest from the city; then bands of men of different ages came out as far as they severally could walk; last of all came the Senate, which was lost in wonder at his exploits, for no one had ever before vanquished so powerful an enemy and at the same time brought so many great nations under subjection and extended the Roman rule to the Euphrates.

He was awarded a triumph exceeding in brilliancy any that had gone before.   It occupied two successive days; and many nations were represented in the procession from Pontus, Armenia, Cappadocia, Cilicia, all the peoples of Syria, besides Albanians, Heniochi, Achæans, Scythians, and Eastern Iberians; 700 complete ships were brought into the harbor;[1] in the triumphal procession were two-horse carriages and litters laden with gold or with other ornaments of various kinds, also the couch of Darius, the son of Hystaspes, the throne and scepter of Mithridates Eupator himself, and his image, eight cubits high, made of solid gold, and 75,000,000 drachmæ of silver coin [about $13,500,000.]   The number of wagons carrying arms was infinite and the number of prows of ships.   After these came the multitude of captives and pirates, none of them bound, but all arrayed in their native costume.

Before Pompey himself were led the satraps, sons and generals of the kings against whom he had fought, who were

[1] Probably of Ostia.

present — some having been captured, some given as hostages to the number of 324. Among them were [five sons of Mithridates, and two daughters; also Aristobulus, king of the Jews; the tyrants of the Cilicians, and other potentates].

There were carried in the procession images of those who were not present, of Tigranes [king of Armenia] and of Mithridates, representing them as fighting, as vanquished, and as fleeing. Even the besieging of Mithridates and his silent flight by night were represented. Finally, it was shown how he died, and the daughters who perished with him were pictured also, and there were figures of the sons and daughters who died before him, and images of the barbarian gods decked out in the fashion of their countries. A tablet was borne, also, inscribed thus : —

SHIPS WITH BRAZEN BEAKS CAPTURED DCCC:
CITIES FOUNDED IN CAPPADOCIA VIII:
IN CILICIA AND CŒLE-SYRIA XX:
IN PALESTINE THE ONE NOW CALLED SELEUCIS.

KINGS CONQUERED:

TIGRANES THE ARMENIAN: ARTOCES THE
IBERIAN: ORŒZES THE ALBANIAN:
ARETAS THE NABATÆAN: DARIUS
THE MEDE: ANTIOCHUS OF COMMAGENE.

Pompey himself was borne in a chariot studded with gems, wearing, it is said, the cloak of Alexander the Great, if any one can believe that. This was supposed to have been found among the possessions of Mithridates. . . . His chariot was followed by the officers who had shared the campaigns with him, some on horseback, and others on foot. When he reached the Capitol, he did not put any prisoners to death, as

had been customary at other triumphs, but sent them all home
at the public expense, except the kings.[1] Of these Aristobulus alone was shortly put to death, and Tigranes [son of
the king of Armenia] some time later.

Such was Pompey's triumph!

46. The Wealth and Habits of Crassus the Millionaire

Plutarch, "Life of Crassus," chaps. II–III

Marcus Licinius Crassus, the third member of the "First
Triumvirate," — along with Pompey and Cæsar, — was a soldier
of moderate capacity, and a somewhat abler politician. But his
chief power and distinction came through his wealth. He had
probably the largest private fortune made in Rome under the
Republic ; though under the Empire it seems in several instances
to have been surpassed. Some of the means whereby he grew rich
are here stated.

People were wont to say that the many virtues of Crassus
were darkened by the one vice of avarice, and indeed he
seemed to have no other but that; for it, being the most
predominant, obscured others to which he was inclined.
The arguments in proof of his avarice were the vastness of
his estate, and the manner of raising it ; for whereas at first
he was not worth above three hundred talents [$300,000],
yet, though in the course of his political life he dedicated
the tenth of all he had to Hercules, and feasted the people,
and gave to every citizen corn enough to serve him three
months, upon casting up his accounts, before he went upon
his Parthian expedition, he found his possessions to amount
to seven thousand one hundred talents [$7,100,000] ; most
of which, if we may scandal him with a truth, he got by fire
and rapine, making his advantage of the public calamities.
For when Sulla seized the city, and exposed to sale the

[1] Most unusual though highly politic clemency.

goods of those that he had caused to be slain, accounting them booty and spoils, and, indeed, calling them so too, and was desirous of making as many, and as eminent men as he could, partakers in the crime, Crassus never was the man that refused to accept, or give money for them.

Moreover, observing how extremely subject the city was to fire, and to the falling down of houses, by reason of their height and their standing so near together, he bought slaves that were builders and architects, and when he had collected these to the number of more than five hundred, he made it his practice to buy houses that were on fire, and those in the neighborhood which, in the immediate danger and uncertainty, the proprietors were willing to part with for little or nothing; so that the greatest part of Rome, at one time or other, came into his hands.

Yet for all he had so many workmen, he never built anything but his own house, and used to say that those that were addicted to building would undo themselves soon enough without the help of other enemies. And though he had many silver mines, and much valuable land, and laborers to work in it, yet all this was nothing in comparison to his slaves, such a number and variety did he possess of excellent readers, amanuenses, silversmiths, stewards, and table waiters, whose instruction he always attended to himself, superintending in person while they learned, and teaching them himself, as counting it the main duty of a master to look over the servants, that are, indeed, the living tools of housekeeping. But it was surely a mistaken judgment, when he said "no man was to be accounted rich that could not maintain an army at his own cost and charges, for war" . . . .

Crassus, however, was very eager to be hospitable to strangers; he kept open house, and to his friends he would lend money without interest, but called it in precisely at the time; so that his kindness was often thought worse

than the paying the interest would have been.   His entertainments were, for the most part, plain and citizenlike,
the company general and popular; good taste and kindness
made them pleasanter than sumptuosity would have done.

As for learning, he chiefly cared for rhetoric, and what
would be serviceable with large numbers; he became one of
the best speakers at Rome, and by his pains and industry
outdid the best natural orators.   For there was no trial
how mean and contemptible soever that he came to un-
prepared; nay, several times he undertook and concluded a
cause, when Pompey and Cæsar and Cicero refused to stand
up, upon which account particularly he got the love of the
people, who looked upon him as a diligent and careful
man, ready to help succor his fellow citizens.   Besides,
the people were pleased with his courteous and unpretend-
ing salutations and greetings; for he never met any citizen
however humble and low, but he returned him his salute by
name.   He was also looked upon as a man well read in
history, and pretty well versed in Aristotle's philosophy.

47. Quintus Cicero's Advice to his Brother when Candidate for the Consulship

Cicero, "Letters," Vol. I (Appendix, pp. 367 ff.).   Shuckburgh's Translation

In 63 b.c. Marcus Cicero, the great orator, was consul, having
been elected after a very lively canvass.   What a candidate had
to do while he paraded the Forum seeking for votes during the
days before the electoral comitia, is told in a lively manner in
this tract, which is ascribed to Quintus Cicero,[1] the brother of the
famous advocate.   It is impossible to quote more than a part.
The second selection is a letter from Marcus Cicero to his brother,
which tells its own story as to the illicit use of money in a Roman
election.

[1] Some doubts have been cast upon the authorship of this essay, but it
is undoubtedly true to conditions at Rome.

Almost every day as you go down to the Forum you must say to yourself, "I am a *novus homo*" [*i.e.* without noble ancestry]. "I am a candidate for the consulship." "This is Rome." For the "newness" of your name you will best compensate by the brilliance of your oratory. This has ever carried with it great political distinction. A man who is held worthy of defending ex-consuls, cannot be deemed unworthy of the consulship itself. Wherefore approach each individual case with the persuasion that on it depends as a whole your entire reputation. See that all those aids to natural ability, which I know are your special gifts are ready for use . . . and finally take care that both the number and rank of your friends are unmistakable. For you have, as few *novi homines*[1] have had, — all the tax-syndicate promoters, nearly the whole equestrian order, and many municipal towns, especially devoted to you, many people who have been defended by you, many trade guilds, and beside these a large number of the rising generation, who have become attached to you in their enthusiasm for public speaking, and who visit you daily in swarms, and with such constant regularity !

See that you retain these advantages by reminding these persons, by appealing to them, and by using every means to make them understand that this, and this only, is the time for those who are in your debt now, to show their gratitude,[2] and for those who wish for your services in the future, to place you under an obligation. It also seems possible that a "new man" may be much aided by the fact that he has the good wishes of men of high rank, and especially of ex-consuls. It is a point in your favor that you should be thought worthy of this position and

[1] Men, like Cicero, who had no ancestors who had held the upper ("curule") offices.

[2] Theoretically Roman advocates did not receive regular fees, but enjoyed the often substantial "gratitude" of their clients.

rank by the very men to whose position you are wishing to attain.

All these men must be canvassed with care, agents must be sent to them, and they must be convinced that we have always been at one with the Optimates (Aristocratic Party), that we have never been dangerous demagogues in the very least; that if we seem ever to have said anything in the spirit of the other party, we did it with a view of attracting Pompey, that we might have that man of the greatest influence either actively on our side of the canvass, or at least neutral.[1] Also take pains to get on your side the young men of high rank, and keep the friendship of those whom you already have. They will contribute much to your political position. You have many already : make them feel how much you think depends on them; if you rouse to zeal those who are now only lukewarm friends, that will be a vast gain.

[The writer then goes on to analyze the weak points in Cicero's leading rivals : their vile characters, their numerous personal crimes, their blunders as officials, etc., — all of which facts Cicero must take advantage.[2] He must also try to make " friends " of every kind of citizen.] " Whosoever gives any sign of inclination to you, or regularly visits your house, you must put down in the category of friends. But yet the most advantageous thing is to be beloved and pleasant in the eyes of those who are friends on the more regular grounds of relationship by blood or marriage, the membership in the same club, or some close tie or other. You must take great pains that [these men] should love you and desire your highest honor — as, for example, your tribesmen, neighbors, clients, and finally your

---

[1] Cicero's brother evidently fears he may be suspected of party irregularity — of having favored the rival *Populares* (Catiline's party).

[2] Politics in Cicero's day seem to have been on a fearfully scurrilous and personal basis.

freedmen, yes even your slaves: for nearly all the gossip that forms public opinion emanates from your own servants' quarters.

In a word, you must secure friends of every class, magistrates, consuls and their tribunes to win you the vote of the centuries [that elect the consuls]: men of wide popular influence. Those who either have gained or hope to gain the vote to a tribe or a century, or any other advantage, through *your* influence [for them], take all pains to collect and to secure.

[Cicero must not be squeamish about making friends; he can "without loss of dignity" affect familiarity with about any one and must by all means do so.] . . .

So you see that you will have the votes of all the centuries secured for you by the number and variety of your friends. The first and obvious thing is that you embrace the Roman senators and equites, and the active and popular men of all the other orders. There are many city men of good business habits, there are many freedmen engaged in the Forum who are popular and energetic: these men try with all your might, both personally and by common friends, to make eager in your behalf. Seek them out, send agents to them, show them that they are putting you under the greatest possible obligation. After that, review the entire city, all guilds, districts, neighborhoods. If you can attach to yourself the leading men in these, you will by their means easily keep a hold upon the multitude.

When you have done that, take care to have in your mind a chart of all Italy laid out according to the tribes in each town, and learn it by heart, so that you may not allow any chartered town, colony, præfecture, in a word, any spot in Italy to exist, in which you have not a firm foothold. Trace out also individuals in every region, inform yourself about them, seek them out, secure that in their own districts they shall canvass for you, and be, as it were, candi-

dates in your interest. Men in country towns think themselves in the position of friends if we of the city know
them by name; if, however, they think they are besides
getting some protection [by your legal talent] for themselves, they will not miss the chance of proving obliging.

[After having thus worked for the "rural vote"], the
centuries of the equites too seem capable of being won over
if you are careful. And you should be strenuous in seeing
as many people as possible every day of every possible
class and order, for from the mere numbers of these [who
greet you] you can make a guess of the amount of support
you will get on the balloting. Your visitors are of three
kinds: one consists of morning callers who come to your
house, a second of those who escort you to the Forum, the
third of those who attend you [constantly] on your canvass. In the case of the mere morning callers, who are less
select, and according to present-day fashion, are decidedly
numerous, you must contrive to think that you value even
this slight attention [of a call] very highly. It often happens that people when they visit a number of candidates,
and observe the one that pays special heed to their atten-
tions, leave off visiting the others, and little by little
become real supporters of this man.

Secondly, to those who escort you to the Forum: Since
this is a much greater attention than a mere morning
call, indicate clearly that they are still more gratifying to
you; and [with them], as far as it shall lie in your power,
go down to the Forum at fixed times, for the daily escort
[of a candidate] by its numbers produces a great impression
and confers great personal distinction.

The third class is that of people who continually attend
you upon your canvass. See that those who do so spontaneously understand that you regard yourself as forever obliged by their extreme kindness; from these on the
other hand, who *owe* you the attention [for services ren-

dered] frankly demand that so far as their age and business allow they should be constantly in attendance, and that those who are unable to accompany you in person, should find relatives to substitute in performing this duty. I am very anxious and think it most important that you should always be surrounded with numbers. Besides, it confers a great reputation, and great distinction to be accompanied by those whom you have defended and saved in the law courts. Put this demand fairly before them — that since by your means, and without any fee, — some have retained property, others their honor, or their civil rights, or their entire fortunes, — and since there will never be any other time when they can show their gratitude, they now should reward you by this service.

Letter of Cicero illustrating Bribery in Elections at Rome
54 B.C.

Epistles to Quintus, II, 14. Shuckburgh, I, p. 279.

" There is a fearful recrudescence of bribery. Never was there anything like it. On the 15th of July the rate of interest rose from four to eight per cent,[1] owing to the compact made by Memmius with the consul Domitius. I am not exaggerating. They offer as much as 10,000,000 sesterces [about $400,000] for the vote of the first century [in the consular elections]. The matter is a burning scandal. The candidates for the tribuneship have made a mutual compact; having deposited 500,000 sesterces [about $20,000] apiece with Cato, they agree to conduct their canvass according to his directions, with the understanding that any one offending against it will be condemned to forfeit by him.[2]

[1] All the available money on loan had been cornered to carry out a corrupt election bargain.

[2] Cato the Younger was famed for his personal probity. This mutual compact of the candidates for tribune was to insure a " clean canvass," with Cato acting as referee of the conduct of the candidates.

If this election [for tribunes] then turns out to be pure, Cato will have been of more avail than all the laws and jurors put together."

48. CONDITIONS IN ROME WHILE CATILINE WAS PLOTTING

Sallust, " Conspiracy of Catiline," chaps. 11–16.   Bohn Translation

Catiline's anarchistic conspiracy of 63 B.C. was, of course, only possible in a society in which there were a great number of depraved and desperate men, ready for any enterprise, however villainous. For such spirits Catiline was an ideal leader.   In this quotation from Sallust we see how it became possible for him to find a large following, and what manner of man he was personally.

After Sulla had recovered the government by force of arms, everybody became robbers and plunderers.   Some set their hearts on houses, some on lands.   His victorious troops knew no restraint, no moderation, but inflicted on the citizens disgraceful and inhumane outrages.   [The whole period was one of debauched tastes and lawlessness.]

When wealth was once counted an honor, and glory, authority, and power attended it, virtue lost her influence, poverty was thought a disgrace, and a life of innocence was regarded as a life of mere ill nature.   From the influence of riches, accordingly, luxury, avarice, pride came to prevail among the youth.   They grew at once rapacious and prodigal.   They undervalued what was their own; they set at nought modesty and continence; they lost all distinction between sacred and profane, and threw off all consideration and self-restraint.

The Spread of Evil Luxuries

It is a serious matter for reflection, after viewing our modern [town] mansions and villas, extended to the veritable size of cities, to contemplate the temples which our ancestors, a most devout race of men, erected to the gods.

But our forefathers adorned the fanes of the deities with devotion, and their homes with their own glory, and took nothing from what they conquered but the power of doing harm; their descendants on the contrary have even wrested from their allies, with rank injustice, whatever their brave and victorious ancestors had left to their vanquished enemies, — as if the only use of power was to inflict injury.

Why should I mention these displays of extraordinary luxury [which now set in], which can be believed only by those who have seen them; as, for example, how mountains have been leveled, and seas actually built over with edifices by many a private citizen, — men whom I deem to have made a sport of their wealth, since they were impatient to squander disreputably what they might have enjoyed with honor.

How Luxury promoted Bad Morals

But the love of irregular gratification, open debauchery, and all kinds of luxury had spread abroad with no less force. Men and women alike threw off all restraints of modesty. To gratify appetite they sought for every kind of production by land or sea. They slept before there was any [natural] inclination to sleep. They no longer waited to feel hunger, thirst, or fatigue, but anticipated them all by luxurious indulgence. Such propensities drove young men, when their patrimonies were run through, to criminal practices; for their minds, impregnated with evil habits, could not easily abstain from gratifying their passions, and were thus the more inordinately devoted in every way to rapacity and extravagance.

Character and Career of Catiline

In so populous and corrupt a city [as Rome] Catiline easily kept about him, as a bodyguard, crowds of the lawless and desperate. All the shameless libertines and profligate rascals were his associates and intimate friends, — the men who had squandered their paternal estates by gaming, luxury, sensuality, and all too who had plunged heavily into debt to buy immunity for crimes; all assassins or sacrilegious persons from every quarter, convicted, or dreading conviction for their misdeeds; all, likewise, for whom their tongue or hand won a livelihood by perjury or bloodshed; all, in short, whom wickedness, poverty, or a guilty conscience goaded [were friends to Catiline].

If any man of character as yet unblemished fell into his society, he presently rendered him by daily intercourse and temptation like to and equal to the rest. But it was the young whose acquaintance he chiefly courted [and easily ensnared]. For as the passions of each, according to his years, were aroused, he furnished mistresses to some, bought horses and dogs for others, and spared, in a word, neither his purse nor his character, if he could make them his devoted and trustworthy supporters.

[Catiline was alleged to have corrupted a Vestal Virgin, and wrought many vile crimes; at last, smitten with a passion for a certain Aurelia, he murdered his own grown-up son, because she objected to marrying him and having in the house a grown-up stepson.] And this crime seems to me to have been the chief cause of hurrying forward his conspiracy. For his guilty mind, at peace neither with gods nor men, found no comfort either waking or sleeping, so utterly did conscience desolate his tortured spirit. His complexion, in consequence, was pale, his eyes haggard, his walk sometimes quick and sometimes slow, and distraction was plainly evident in every feature and look.

The young men [his boon companions] . . . he enticed by various methods into evil practices. From among them he furnished false witnesses and forgers of signatures;[1] and he taught them all to regard with equal unconcern property

[1] To any rascal who needed such assistance.

and danger. At length when he had stripped them of all character and shame he led them to other and greater iniquities. When there was no ready motive for crime, he nevertheless stirred them up to murder quite inoffensive persons, just as if they had injured him, lest their hand or heart should grow torpid for want of employment.

Trusting to such confederates and comrades, and knowing that the load of debt was everywhere great, and that the veterans of Sulla, having spent their [bounty] money too freely, now were longing for a civil war, remembering their spoils and former victory, Catiline accordingly formed the design of overthrowing the government.

49. THE EARLY CAREER OF JULIUS CÆSAR

Suetonius, "Life of Julius Cæsar," I–XIX. Bohn Translation

Cæsar was born in 100 B.C. The story of his boyhood and young manhood is known to us mainly through the biography here quoted, and through a similar biography by Plutarch. On the whole, Suetonius seems to be the better informed. It is needless to comment on the value of every authentic incident illustrating the education and character of the man who was, on the whole, the greatest personage produced by the Græco-Roman world.

Julius Cæsar the " Divine "[1] lost his father when he was in the sixteenth year of his age, and the next year, when he was named as Flamen Dialis [high priest of Jupiter], he repudiated Cossutia, who was very wealthy — though her family was only of the equestrian order — and to whom he had been betrothed when he was a mere boy. He then wedded Cornelia, the daughter of Cinna, [the famous Cinna] who was four times Consul, and by her he shortly afterwards had a daughter named Julia. He resisted the efforts of the dictator Sulla to get him to divorce Cornelia, and suffered the penalty of being stripped of his priestly office, his wife's

[1] He was enrolled among the gods after his death.

dowry, and his own patrimonial estates.   Since he was iden-
tified with the adverse [anti-Sullan] faction, he was compelled to leave Rome.

At last he got a pardon through the good offices of the
Vestal Virgins and of Mamercus Æmilius and Aurelius
Cotta, his near kinsmen.   We are assured that when Sulla,
having withstood for a while the entreaties of his own
best friends, men of high rank, at last gave way to their
importunity [in Cæsar's behalf], he exclaimed, — whether
by divine impulse or shrewd conjecture, —

"Your suit is granted, and you can take him among you;
but know," he added, "that this man for whose safety you
are so very anxious, will some day or other, be the ruin of
the party of the nobility, in defense whereof you have
leagued with me! *for in this one Cæsar you will find many
Mariuses.*"   [For a while he served in Bithynia and Cilicia
on governmental and military service.   While on his way
to Rhodes to study rhetoric] he was taken prisoner by
pirates near the isle of Pharmacusa [near Miletus], and
detained by them — to his great wrath — for nearly forty
days, his only attendants being a physician and two body
servants.   For he had at once sent his other servants and
traveling companions to raise his ransom money.   Fifty
talents [$50,000] were paid, and he was landed on the
coast.   Whereupon he collected some ships and promptly
put to sea after the pirates, captured them, and inflicted on
them the punishment that he had so often threatened them
[as] in jest.[1]

His First Public Offices

During his quæstorship [at Rome] he pronounced funeral
orations from the rostra, according to custom, — in praise of
his aunt Julia and his wife, Cornelia.   In the panegyric
upon his aunt he gives the following account of her own

[1] Crucifixion.

and his father's genealogy on both sides: "My aunt Julia
derived her descent by her mother from a race of kings;
and by her father from the Immortal Gods. For the Marcii
Reges, her mother's family, deduce their pedigree from
Ancus Marcius, and the Julii, her father's, from Venus; of
which stock we are a branch. We therefore unite in our
descent the sacred majesty of kings, the chiefest among
men, and the divine majesty of gods, to whom kings themselves are subject."

[While he was serving in Spain as proquæstor] at Gades,
on seeing a statue of Alexander the Great in the temple of
Hercules he sighed deeply, as if weary of his sluggish life
— as having wrought nothing memorable at an age at which
Alexander had already conquered the world.[1] . . .

While he was Ædile at Rome he not only embellished the
comitium and the rest of the Forum and the adjoining basilicas, but adorned the Capitol also with temporary piazzas —
built in order to display for the popular amusement, a part of
his vast collections.[2] He entertained the people both by himself and along with his colleagues — with wild beast hunts,
and with games. On this account he obtained the whole
credit of the expense to which they had jointly contributed,
insomuch that his colleague, Marcus Bibulus, could not
forbear remarking that he was treated in the manner of Pol-
lux. For as the temple erected in the Forum to the "Two
Brothers" went by the name of Castor alone, so his and
Cæsar's joint munificence was imputed to the latter only.

How he acted as Prætor

[He next was elected prætor, and he now boldly attacked
the noble party and was nearly murdered for his alleged
sympathies with Catiline. He was fairly embarked among

---

[1] Alexander died at only thirty-three.
[2] Probably of Greek paintings, statues, etc.

the anti-aristocrats and while in this office] he proved him-self a most resolute supporter of Cæcilius Metellus, tribune of the Plebs, who, despite all opposition from his col-leagues, had proposed some laws of "violent tendency,"[1] until they both [Metellus and Cæsar] were dismissed from office by a vote of the Senate.[2] Cæsar ventured, however, to retain his post and continue in the administration of justice [as prætor]: but finding that preparations were being made to obstruct him by force of arms, he dismissed the lictors, threw off his [magistrate's] robe, and betook himself pri-vately to his own house, with the resolution to be quiet in a time so unfavorable to his interests. He likewise pacified the mob which two days afterward flocked about him, and in a riotous manner made a voluntary tender of their assist-ance in the vindication of his honor. This all happening contrary to expectation, the Senate, meeting in haste on ac-count of the tumult, gave him its thanks through some leading members of the house, and sending for him, after highly commending his conduct, canceled its former vote, and restored him to his office.

How he was refused a Triumph

At the expiration of his prætorship he obtained by lot the province of Farther Spain, and pacified his creditors, who were detaining him, by finding sureties for his debts.[3] Contrary to both law and custom, he took his departure be-fore the usual equipage and outfit [for a governor] were provided. It is uncertain whether this haste rose from the fear of an impeachment, with which he was threatened at

[1] Among others to recall Pompey from his command in Asia.

[2] Probably a very illegal act for the Senate.

[3] According to Plutarch, the great millionaire Crassus went surety for him. His debts were so great that he is alleged to have declared he was "needing 25,000,000 ses. [$1,000,000] to be worth nothing at all." (Ap-pian's Civil War, book II, chap. 2.) Practically all Roman politicians of the day were terribly in debt.

the expiration of his former office, or his anxiety to lose no time in relieving the [Roman] allies, who implored him to come to their aid. He had no sooner established tranquillity in the province than, without waiting for the arrival of a successor, he returned to Rome, with equal haste, to sue for a triumph[1] and the consulship. The day of election, however, being already fixed by proclamation, he could not be legally admitted as a candidate, unless he entered the city as a private person.[2] In this emergency he asked a suspension in his favor of the law [governing the case] : but such an indulgence was strongly opposed — and he found himself forced to abandon all thoughts of a triumph, lest he be disappointed in the consulship.

[He therefore made the alliance with Pompey and Crassus, known as the " First Triumvirate," as consul passed many laws displeasing to the aristocracy, and got himself appointed proconsul of Gaul, with a powerful army.]

[1] He had won some considerable victories over the tribes in western Spain.

[2] And so gave up his generalship and claim to a triumph.

CHAPTER V

THE FOUNDING OF THE ROMAN EMPIRE

The Empire was inevitable unless Republican Rome was capable of reforming herself, or the Roman power should cease to live. It was, however, beyond the ability of any statesman to make the Republic able to grapple with the responsibilities of a great imperial system; and Julius Cæsar neither could nor would perpetuate the old conditions of chaos and misrule. If he had been allowed to round out a normal span of life and execute his complete policy, there is little doubt that we would have found the world under a highly articulated centralized monarchy. His assassination taught his cautious successor, Octavian (or, to use his later title, Augustus), that while monarchy was unavoidable, it must be monarchy so disguised and hedged in by ostentatious safeguards as not to trample very wantonly on Roman public opinion. The result was the device of the "Principate" — the leadership of the state by a "First Citizen"; and the bestowal of abundant honor and apparent responsibility upon the Senate, which was to share the administration with the *Princeps, i.e.* the establishment of that dual sway of the Empire, which modern scholars call the *Dyarchy*.

It took three centuries for the system of Augustus to break down, when it was at length replaced by the unveiled despotism of Diocletian; although within less than a century after Augustus's death, with the reign of Domitian (died 96 A.D.), the pretenses of the Principate had almost ceased to impose upon any thinking man. Taken in their entirety, considering the multitude of human beings their actions affected, considering how many of their institutions remained even after Diocletian, and how many of the things which began with the Empire actually affect the life and thought of to-day, it is fair to assert that Julius Cæsar and Augustus were among the most influential personages in all secular history. Nor can their part in the founding of Christianity be ignored. Without a Roman Empire, with its removal of national boundaries, and with its law, peace, relative good government, Græco-Latin civilization and speech, and similar unifying influences, it is hard to see how Christianity could ever have developed into a world religion. Imagine St. Paul compelled to carry abroad his "Gospel to the Gentiles," when every mountain valley or island had been held by a jealous king or oligarchy, excluding all strangers and foreign ideas; and zealously suppressing as treason any trifling divergence from the cultus of the local gods! The persecution the Christians presently endured from the Roman government was a mere drop in the bucket compared with such a disadvantage.

To Julius Cæsar it was given to be an unflinching destroyer of institutions which had long been worthy of destruction; to Augustus to be one of the most significantly constructive statesmen in universal history. Fortunately our literary records for both of them are fairly complete. Julius Cæsar was often his own literary advocate; Augustus has left us an autobiographal statement in a stately inscription; while Suetonius, Plutarch, Appian, and others each contribute part of the story. Once more the difficulty is to select that which is best told by the ancient writers themselves, and to omit what is as well told by the pens of moderns.

50. CÆSAR'S ACCOUNT OF HOW HE WAS FORCED TO TAKE UP ARMS

Cæsar, "Civil War," book I, chaps. 1–6. Bohn Translation

Whether Cæsar or his enemies were to blame when (in January, 49 B.C.) he "crossed the Rubicon," is still debated. In the main, opinion is on Cæsar's side, holding: (1) that his enemies tried to force him to quit his province before the time permitted by law; (2) that if he had come back to Rome as an unarmed man, as they intended, his life would have been in imminent danger. Trusting foolishly for their military support to Pompey, — who now had deserted his one-time ally, Cæsar, — the great nobles precipitated the civil war which Cæsar seems to have tried hard to prevent. His own story of the matter will have perennial interest.

When Cæsar's letter [with conciliatory proposals] was delivered to the consuls, it was with great difficulty, and a hard struggle by the tribunes [on Cæsar's side], that they were prevailed upon to suffer it to be read in the Senate; the tribunes, however, could not prevail that any question should be put to the Senate on the subject of the letter. The consuls put the question on "The Regulation of the State." Lucius Lentulus [one of them] promised that "he would not fail the Senate and the Republic if they declared their sentiments resolutely and boldly, but if they turned their regard to Cæsar and courted his favor, as formerly, he would strike out on his own plan, and not truckle to the authority of the Senate; and [added] that he had a way of again getting Cæsar's favor and friendship." Scipio talked in the same strain, that "it was Pompey's intention not to abandon the Republic if the Senate would support him; but if they should hesitate and act without energy, they would in vain implore his aid, if ever they should need it later."

How the Moderates in the Senate were Silenced

This speech of Scipio's — as the Senate was convened inside the city, and Pompey was near at hand — seemed to fall from Pompey's own lips.[1] Some spoke with a certain moderation, as Marcellus first, who said at the outset that "the question ought not thus to be put before the Senate until levies had been made through Italy, and armies raised under whose protection the Senate might freely and safely vote what resolutions seemed proper"; [and two other Senators spoke in like vein]. They were all harshly rebuked by Lentulus, who peremptorily refused to put their motions. Marcellus, overawed by his reproofs, retracted his opinion. Thus most of the Senate, intimidated by the expressions of the consul, by the fears of an army close at hand, and the

---

[1] This Metellus Scipio was the father-in-law of Pompey.

threats of Pompey's friends, unwillingly and reluctantly adopted Scipio's opinion, that Cæsar should disband his army by a certain day, and should he not do so, he should be considered as a public enemy. Marcus Antonius and Quintus Cassius, tribunes of the people, here announced their vetoes. At once the question was raised as to the validity of their vetoes. Violent opinions were uttered. Whoever spoke with the greatest bitterness and cruelty was most loudly applauded by Cæsar's enemies.

The Senate having broken up in the evening, all who belonged to that body were summoned by Pompey. He commended the bold talkers and secured their votes for the next day; the more moderate he reproved and excited against Cæsar. Many veterans from all parts, who had served in Pompey's armies, were invited to his standard by the hopes of rewards and promotions. Several officers of the two legions that had been delivered up by Cæsar [to Pompey] were sent for. The city and assembly place were crowded with tribunes, centurions, and veterans. All the consul's friends, all Pompey's connections, all those who bore any old grudge against Cæsar, were forced into the Senate House. By their concourse and asseverations the timid were awed, the irresolute confirmed, and the actual majority deprived of the power to speak their minds freely.

The Violent Party Prevails

Lucius Piso, the censor, offered to go to Cæsar, and so did Lucius Roscius, the prætor, to tell him of how matters stood, and they asked only six days to dispatch their business. Also some opinions were expressed that commissioners should be sent to Cæsar to acquaint him with the Senate's pleasure; [but] all these proposals were rejected, and all were opposed in the harangues of the consul [Lentulus], Scipio, and Cato.

An old enmity against Cæsar and chagrin at a [former] defeat goaded on Cato. Lentulus was spurred by the magnitude of his debts, and the hopes of having the government of an army and provinces, and by the presents which he expected from such princes as should get the title of "Friends of the Roman People." He boasted among his friends that, " He would be a second Sulla, and to him the supreme power would return." Like hopes of a province and armies which he expected to share with Pompey on account of his [marriage] connection prompted Scipio. Besides that, he had the fear of being called to trial; and he was moved too by the adulation and an ostentatious display of himself and his friends in power, who at that time had great influence in the administration and the law courts.

As for Pompey, he was stirred up by Cæsar's enemies, and was also unwilling that any man should be his equal in public dignity ; consequently, he was now utterly cut off from Cæsar's friendship. He had reconciled himself with their common enemies, though most of these enemies he had himself brought upon Cæsar, while the latter was his ally. Then, too, he was chagrined at the disgrace he had incurred by converting two legions from their expedition through Asia and Syria to increase his own power. He was, therefore, anxious for war.

The Votes are passed against Cæsar

Under these circumstances everything was done in a hasty and disorderly manner, and no time was given to Cæsar's kinsmen to inform him of what was happening, nor liberty to the tribunes of the plebs to set forth the peril they were exposed to, or even to retain the last privilege which Sulla had left them, of using their vetoes. On the seventh day [of the new year] they were obliged to think of their personal safety, something that the most violent plebeian tribunes had not been accustomed to be troubled about, or to fear being brought to book for their actions before the eighth month. Recourse was had to that extreme and final decree of the Senate, — though never had it been resorted to by daring innovators save when the city was in peril of incendiarism, or public safety was despaired of, — " That the Consuls, Prætors, and Plebeian Tribunes, and Proconsuls in the City should see to it that the state suffers no hurt."[1] These decrees were dated the 8th of January, therefore, in the first five days on which the Senate could meet, from the day on which Lentulus entered into his consulate, the two [intervening] days of election excepted, the severest and most virulent decrees were passed against Cæsar's government, and against those most illustrious dignitaries — the Plebeian Tribunes. The latter at once made their escape from the city and withdrew to Cæsar, who was then at Ravenna awaiting an answer to his moderate demands, [hoping that] matters could be brought to a peaceful termination by any act of justice on the part of his enemies.

During the next days the Senate was convened outside the city. Pompey repeated the same things which he had declared through Scipio. He applauded the courage and firmness of the Senate, acquainted them with his force, and told them that he had ten legions ready ; besides he was informed and assured that Cæsar's soldiers were disaffected, and he could not persuade them to defend or even to follow him. [The Senate then voted all kinds of military levies and money for Pompey. The provinces were distributed among Cæsar's enemies in a most headlong and disorderly manner.] Levies were made throughout Italy, arms demanded and money exacted from the municipal towns, and violently taken from the temples. . . .

[When the news came to Cæsar he appealed to his army,

---

[1] This " final decree " practically established martial law.

especially dwelling on the unprecedented wrongs done the tribunes, and the troops cried out they would follow him.]

51. The Crossing of the Rubicon

Suetonius, "Life of Julius Cæsar," chaps. 31–33.   Bohn Translation

The famous story of the "crossing of the Rubicon" by Cæsar in January, 49 B.C., has been attacked by modern historians. They argue that it is unlikely that a man like Cæsar would not have known his own mind when things came to a grave issue. Yet the story is one the student is fain to believe; and there seems nothing improbable in assuming that even Cæsar was glad to weigh the issues for the last time before forcing a civil war.

When the news came [to Ravenna, where Cæsar was staying] that the interposition of the tribunes in his favor had been utterly rejected, and that they themselves had fled Rome, he immediately sent forward some cohorts, yet secretly, to prevent any suspicion of his plan; and to keep up appearances, he attended the public games and examined the model of a fencing school which he proposed building, then — as usual — sat down to table with a large company of friends.

However, after sunset some mules from a near-by mill were put in his carriage, and he set forward on his journey as privately as possible, and with an exceedingly scanty retinue. The lights went out. He lost his way and wandered about a long time — till at last, by help of a guide, whom he discovered towards daybreak, he proceeded on foot through some narrow paths, and again reached the road. Coming up with his troops on the banks of the Rubicon, which was the frontier of his province,[1] he halted for a while, and revolving in his mind the importance of the step he meditated, he turned to those about him, saying:

[1] A very ancient law forbade any general to cross the Rubicon into Italy proper with his troops under arms.

"Still we can retreat! But once let us pass yon little bridge, — and nought is left but to fight it out with arms!"

Even as he hesitated this incident occurred. A man of strikingly noble mien and graceful aspect appeared close at hand, and played upon a pipe. To hear him not merely some shepherds, but soldiers too came flocking from their posts, and amongst them some trumpeters. He snatched a trumpet from one of them and ran to the river with it; then sounding the "Advance!" with a piercing blast he crossed to the other side. At this Cæsar cried out, "Let us go where the omens of the Gods and the crimes of our enemies summon us! THE DIE IS NOW CAST!"

Accordingly he marched his army over the river; [then] he showed them the tribunes of the Plebs, who on being driven from Rome had come to meet him, and in the presence of that assembly, called on the troops to pledge him their fidelity; tears springing to his eyes [as he spoke] and his garments rent from his bosom.

[The soldiery showed remarkable enthusiasm in his cause; the Pompeian resistance collapsed; and in a surprisingly short time Cæsar was master of Italy.]

52. CÆSAR'S REFORMS WHILE DICTATOR

Suetonius, " Life of Julius Cæsar," chaps. 40-44. Bohn Translation

Less than four years passed between the great victory of Cæsar at Pharsalia (48 B.C.) to his murder (44 B.C.). During most of this time he was busy with wars in Egypt, Asia Minor, Africa, and Spain, but in the interval left him for peaceful business he displayed a marvelous activity in executing every kind of reform. It is hardly too much to imagine that if he had lived twenty years longer, he would have changed the whole face of ancient society.

Turning his attention to the regulation of the Republic, he corrected the calendar[1] which had for some time been

[1] In this task Cæsar was aided by the learned Græco-Egyptian Sosigenes.

direfully confused through the unwarrantable liberty which the pontiffs had taken in the matter of intercalation.[1] To such a height had this abuse proceeded that neither the festivals designed for the harvest fell in the summer, nor those for the vintage fell in autumn. He accommodated the year to the course of the sun, ordaining that in the future it should consist of 365 days without any intercalary month; and that every fourth year an extra day should be inserted.

He filled up the vacancies in the Senate by advancing divers plebeians to the rank of patricians, and also he increased the number of prætors, ædiles, quæstors, and lesser magistrates. The method he used in those cases was to recommend such persons as he had pitched upon, by notices distributed among the several [Roman] tribes, thus, "Cæsar Dictator to such a tribe [name given], I recommend to you — [the persons are named], that by the favor of your votes, they may obtain the honors which they are seeking." He likewise admitted to office the sons of those who had been proscribed.

The trial of lawsuits he restricted to the two orders of judges, — the equestrian and the senatorial, — excluding the "tribunes of the treasury"[2] who had formerly made up a third class. The revised census of the people he ordered to be taken neither in the usual manner or place, but street by street, by the leading inhabitants of the several quarters of the city; and he reduced the number of those who received corn at the public cost[3] from 320,000 to 120,000. To prevent any tumults on account of the census, he ordered that the prætor should every year fill up by lot the vacancies occasioned by death, from those who were not enrolled for the corn doles.

[1] The old calendar was so unscientific it was necessary to insert arbitrarily extra months to make the years of something like equal length.

[2] The exact nature of these "tribunes of the treasury" is very uncertain.

[3] A prolific source of pauperism and general abuse.

After having distributed 80,000 citizens among foreign colonies,[1] he enacted, — to halt the drain on the population, — that no freeman of the city, above the age of twenty or under forty, who was not in the army, should absent himself from Italy for more than three years running; also no Senator's son was to go abroad, save in the retinue of some high officer. As to those who tended flocks and herds [he required] that no less than one third of their free-born shepherds should be youths.[2] He bestowed on all physicians and professors of liberal arts the "freedom of the city" in order to fix them [at Rome] and induce others to settle there.

With respect to debts he disappointed the expectation that was generally entertained, that they would be totally canceled. He ordered that debtors should satisfy their creditors according to the value of their estates, at the rate at which they were purchased before the Civil War began. However, from the debt was to be deducted everything that had been paid as interest, either in money or in bonds; as a result of this about one fourth of the [average] debt was lost. He dissolved all the guilds save such as were of ancient foundation.[3] Crimes [under him] were punished with extreme severity; and since the rich were more prone to commit them, because they were [hitherto] liable to banishment without loss of property, he stripped murderers — as Cicero remarks — of their whole estates, and other offenders of a half.

He was extremely constant and strict in the administration of justice. He expelled from the Senate such members as had been convicted of bribery. He dissolved the marriage of a man of prætorian rank who had married a lady

---

[1] Mostly at Corinth and Carthage, which cities he rebuilt.

[2] The object was to "keep the young men on the farm," to prevent them from flocking to Rome.

[3] The guilds were probably dangerous centers of political agitation.

two days after her divorce from a former husband, although there was no suspicion of any illicit [previous] connection. He imposed custom duties on foreign goods.[1] The use of litters for traveling, of purple robes, and of jewels he allowed only to persons of a certain age and rank, and on particular days. He enforced rigid execution of the sumptuary laws, placing officers about the markets to seize upon all meats offered for sale contrary to the rules, and to bring them to him. Sometimes he actually sent his lictors and soldiers to carry away such viands as had escaped the notice of his officers, even when they were upon the table.

His thoughts were now fully employed from day to day in a great variety of projects, for the beautifying and improvement of Rome, as well as for guarding and extending the bounds of the Empire. [He planned a magnificent temple of Mars, and also a splendid theater near to the Tarpeian Rock.] He proposed to reduce the civil law to a reasonable compass, and out of that immense and undigested mass of statutes to abridge the best and most necessary parts into a few books; also to make as large a collection of books as possible in the Greek and Latin languages, for the public use — the province of providing and putting them in proper order being assigned to [the noted savant] Marcus Varro.

Then too he intended to drain the Pontine marshes, to cut a channel for the discharge of the waters of the Fucine lake, to form a road from the Upper Sea [Adriatic] through the ridge of the Apennines, to make a canal through the Isthmus of Corinth, to drive the Dacians — who had overrun Pontus and Thrace, within their proper limits, and then to make war upon the Parthians, [marching] through Lesser Armenia, but not risking a general engagement [with the Parthians] until he had made some trial of their prowess in

[1] Probably to discourage outlandish luxuries, rather than to afford "protection" to home wares.

war. But in the midst of all his undertakings and projects
he was carried off by death.

53. The Funeral of Cæsar

Appian, "Civil Wars," book II, 143–148. White's Translation

How after the murder of Julius Cæsar (15th of March, 44 B.C.)
Marcus Antonius ("Mark Antony"), his friend, and in virtue of
the consulship, chief magistrate, roused the Roman multitude
against the assassins by his famous funeral oration is known
mainly through the incomparable version given by Shakespeare.
The account by Appian which Shakespeare adapted differs in
some particulars from its great imitation. For this reason, as
well as for its inherent historic value, the narrative of Appian
possesses high interest. It is, of course, far less dramatic, but it is
more nearly history.

Cæsar's will was now produced and the people ordered
that it be read at once. In it Octavian, his sister's grandson, was adopted by Cæsar. His gardens were given to the
people as a place of recreation, and to every Roman living
in the city, he gave 75 Attic drachmas [about $13]. The
people too were stirred to anger when they saw the will of
this lover of his country, whom they had before heard
accused of tyranny. Most of all did it seem pitiful to them
that Decimus Brutus, one of the murderers, should have
been named by him for adoption in the second degree; for
it was usual for the Romans to name alternate heirs in case
of the failure of the first.

When Piso brought Cæsar's body into the Forum a countless multitude ran together with arms to guard it, and with
acclamations and magnificent display placed it on the
rostra. Wailing and lamentation were renewed for a long
time; the armed men clashed their shields. Antony, seeing
how things were going, did not abandon his purpose, but
having been chosen to deliver the funeral oration, as a con-

sul for a consul, as a friend for a friend, a relative for a
relative (he was akin to Cæsar on the mother's side),
resumed his artful design, and spoke thus:[1]

Antony's Oration

"It is not fitting, fellow citizens, that the funeral oration
of so great a man should be pronounced by me alone, but
rather by his whole country. The decrees which all of us,
in equal admiration for his merit, voted to him while he
was alive — Senate and People acting together — I will read,
so that I may voice your sentiments rather than merely
mine."

Then he began to read with a severe and gloomy countenance; pronouncing each sentence distinctly, and dwelling
especially on those decrees which declared Cæsar to be
"superhuman, sacred and inviolable," and which named
him "The Father of his Country," or "The Benefactor," or
"The Chieftain without a Peer." With each decree, Antony
turned his face and his hand towards Cæsar's corpse, illustrating his discourse by his action, and at each appellation
he added some brief remark full of grief and indignation;
as, for example, where the decree spoke of Cæsar as "The
Father of his Country," he added that this was a testimonial
of his clemency; and again, where he was made "Sacred
and Inviolable," and that "everybody was to be held sacred
and inviolate who should find refuge in him."

"Nobody," said Antony, "who found refuge in him was
harmed, but *he*, whom you declared sacred and inviolate was
killed, although he did not extort these honors from you as
a tyrant, and did not even ask them. Most servile are we
if we give such honors to the unworthy who do not ask
for them. But you, faithful citizens, vindicate us from

---

[1] The Romans had fairly good shorthand reporters ; and even if these
were not present, we may imagine Appian followed notes giving substantially what Antonius said.

this charge of servility by paying such honors as you now pay to the dead."

Antony resumed his reading, and recited the oaths by which all were pledged to guard Cæsar and Cæsar's body with all their strength, and all were devoted to perdition who should not avenge him in any conspiracy. Here lifting up his voice, and extending his hand toward the Capitol, he exclaimed, "Jupiter, Guardian of this City, and ye other gods, I stand here ready to avenge him as I have sworn and vowed, but since those that are of equal rank with me have considered the decree of amnesty[1] beneficial, I pray that it may prove so."

A commotion arose among the Senators in consequence of this exclamation which seemed to have special reference to them. So Antony quieted them again and recanted, saying, "To me, fellow citizens, this deed seems to be not the work of human beings, but of some evil spirit. It becomes us to consider the present rather than the past. Let us then conduct this sacred one to the abode of the blest, chanting our wonted hymn of lamentation for him."

Having thus spoken, he gathered up his garments like a man inspired, girded himself so that he might have free use of his hands, took his position in front of the bier, as in a play, bending down to it, and rising again, and sang first as to a celestial deity. . . . [He declaimed on Cæsar's "god-like origin," victories, and spoils he had brought to Rome] exclaiming, "Thou alone hast come forth unvanquished from all the battles thou hast fought! Thou alone hast avenged thy country of the outrages put upon it 300 years ago [by the Gauls], bringing to their knees the savage

[1] The Senate shortly after the murder had declared a general amnesty on the motion of Cicero. The Senators had considered declaring Cæsar a tyrant, but as this would have annulled all his appointments they preferred this compromise because some of the chief conspirators had been assigned by Cæsar to provinces and were loath to give up the prospect of command.

tribes, the only ones that ever broke into and burned Rome."

Carried away by extreme passion, he uncovered the body of Cæsar, lifted his robe on the top of a spear, and shook it aloft, pierced with the dagger thrusts, and red with the Dictator's blood. Whereupon the people, like a [theatric] chorus, mourned with him in a most doleful manner, and [then] from sorrow became again filled with anger.

The People break out in Fury

[After more lamentations] the people could stand it no longer. It seemed to them monstrous that all the murderers, who, save Decimus Brutus, had been made prisoners while siding with Pompey, and who, instead of being punished, had been advanced by Cæsar to the magistracies of Rome, and to the command of provinces and armies, should have conspired against him, and that Decimus should have been deemed by him worthy of adoption as a son.

While they were in this temper, and were already nigh to violence, some one raised above the bier an image of Cæsar himself, wrought of wax. As for the actual body, since it lay on its back upon the couch, it could not be seen. The image was turned around and around by a mechanical device, showing the twenty-three wounds on all parts of the body and the face, — which gave him a shocking appearance. The people could no longer bear the pitiful sight presented to them. They groaned, and girding themselves, they burned the Senate chamber, where Cæsar had been slain, and ran hither and thither searching for the murderers, who had fled some time previously.

They were so mad with rage and grief, that, like wild beasts, they tore in pieces the tribune Cinna on account of the similarity of his name to the prætor Cinna, who had made a speech against Cæsar, not waiting to hear any explanation about the similarity of name, — so that no part of him was ever found for burial. They carried fire to the houses of the other murderers, but the servants bravely fought them off, and the neighbors begged them to desist. So the people abstained from using fire, but threatened to come back with arms on the following day.

Cæsar's Funeral Pyre

The murderers fled from the city secretly. The people returned to Cæsar's bier, and bore it as something consecrated to the Capitol in order to bury it in the temple and place it among the gods. Being prevented from so doing by the priests, they placed it again in the Forum, where of old had stood the palace of the kings of Rome. There they collected together sticks of wood and benches, of which there were many in the Forum, and anything else that they could find of this sort, for a funeral pile, throwing on it the adornments of the procession, some of which were very costly. Some of them cast their own crowns upon it and many military gifts.[1] Then they set fire to it, and the entire people remained by the funeral pile throughout the night.

There an altar was at first erected, but now stands [on the spot] the Temple of Cæsar himself, for he was deemed worthy of divine honors; since Octavius, his adoptive son, who took the name of Cæsar, and following in his footsteps in political policy, greatly strengthened the government founded by Cæsar, [which government] remains to this day, — and decreed divine honors to his "fathers." From this example the Romans now pay like honors to each emperor at his death, if he has not reigned in a tyrannical manner or made himself odious, although at first they could not bear to call them kings while living.[2]

[1] The rewards of their valor.
[2] Thus Augustus, Vespasian, and Trajan were "deified," but not Tiberius or Nero.

54. The Personal Traits of Julius Cæsar

Suetonius, " Life of Julius Cæsar," chaps. 45-57, 62, 72-73. Bohn Translation

Thanks to Suetonius we gain a fairly complete view of the personal traits of the greatest man produced by Antiquity. Considered as a public man, Cæsar impresses us by his marvelous versatility — orator, politician, constructive statesman, and general; as a private individual he seems to have been a charming and genial gentleman, by no means impeccable, even according to the lax standards of his age, but a man who could command warm and abiding friendship.

He was tall, of a fair complexion, round limbed, rather full faced, with eyes black and piercing; he enjoyed excellent health except toward the close of his life when he was subject to sudden fainting fits and disturbances in his sleep. He was likewise twice seized with the " falling sickness," while engaged in active service. He was extremely nice in the care of his person, and kept the hair of his head closely cut and had his face smoothly shaved. His baldness gave him much uneasiness, having often found himself on that score exposed to the jibes of his enemies. He used therefore to brush forward the hair from the crown of his head, and of all the honors conferred on him by the Senate and People, there was none which he either accepted or used with greater pleasure than the right of wearing constantly a laurel crown. It is said that he was particular in his dress, for he wore the *latus clavus*[1] with fringes about the wrists, and always had it girded about him, but rather loosely.

He first inhabited a small house in the Suburra,[2] but after his advancement to the office of Pontiff, he occupied a palace belonging to the government on the Via Sacra. He liked

---

[1] Toga with a broad strip of purple, such as only senators were allowed to wear.

[2] One of the noisiest and least select quarters in Rome.

his residence to be elegant and his entertainments sump, tuous. He pulled down entirely a villa near the grove of Aricia, which he built from the foundation, and finished at heavy cost, because it did not meet his taste, although at that time he had only limited means, and was in debt Also he used to carry about on his expeditions tesselated and marble slabs for the floor of his tent.

It is said he actually invaded Britain in hopes of finding pearls there. He was accustomed to compare the size of these and ascertain their weight merely by poising them in his hand. At any cost he would purchase gems, carved work, statues, and pictures, executed by eminent masters of antiquity. For young and handy slaves he would pay a price so extravagant that he forbade its being entered in his daily expense book.

We are also told that in the provinces he constantly maintained two tables, one for the army officers and the local country gentleman, the other for Romans of the highest rank and distinguished provincials. He was so very exact in the management of his domestic affairs that he once threw a baker into prison for serving him a finer sort of his bread than his guests.

[He was a notable lady's man, and indulged in many intrigues; he was especially intimate with Servilia, the mother of Marcus Brutus,]for whom he purchased in his first consulship . . . a pearl which cost him 6,000,000 sesterces [$240,000], and in the Civil War, besides other presents assigned to her — for a trifling consideration — some valuable farms that had been set up at public auction.

It was confessed even by his enemies that in regard to wine he was abstemious. A remark is ascribed to Marcus Cato, that "Cæsar was the only sober man amongst all those engaged in the design to subvert the government."

In eloquence and warlike achievements he equaled, if he did not surpass, the greatest of men. After his prosecution of Dolabella he was indisputably reckoned one of the most distinguished advocates. Cicero in recounting to Brutus the famous orators declares " he does not see that Cæsar was inferior to any of them, and says " that he had an elegant, noble, and magnificent vein of eloquence." In his delivery Cæsar is said to have had a shrill voice, and his action was animated, but not ungraceful.

He was perfect in the use of arms, an accomplished rider, and able to endure fatigue beyond all belief. On a march he used to go at the head of his troops, sometimes on horseback, but oftener on foot, with his head bare in all kinds of weather. He would travel post in a light carriage without baggage, at the rate of one hundred miles per day ; and if he was stopped by floods in the rivers, he swam across, or floated on skins inflated in the wind, so that he often anticipated the tidings of his movements. Often he rallied his troops by his own personal exertions, stopping those who fled, keeping others in their ranks, and seizing men by the throat, turned them again towards the enemy, although numbers [of his men] were [sometimes] so terrified that an eagle bearer[1] thus stopped made a thrust at him with the spearhead [on the eagle], and another on a like occasion left the standard in his hand.

He always treated his friends with such kindness and good nature, that when Gaius Oppius, in traveling with him through a forest, was suddenly taken ill, he resigned to him the only place there was to shelter them at night, and lay on the ground in the open air. The resentment he entertained towards any one was never so implacable but that he did not very willingly renounce it when opportunity offered [and various instances are cited of how he forgave enemies and detractors, and worked for their interests after reconciliation].

[1] The eagle was the great standard of a legion.

55. How Cleopatra bewitched Antony

Plutarch, " Life of Mark Antony," chaps. XXV–XXIX

The romance of Antony (more properly Antonius) and Cleopatra was an event affecting the history of the world. Recently an attempt has been made to show that the element of
genuine passion was largely absent — that it was a union founded
mainly on mere political advantage. This seems very improbable.
Antony was exactly the kind of a man to sacrifice his interests to
a fierce and skillfully enkindled passion. If he had possessed the
strength to resist the seductions of the Egyptian queen, very likely
he could have undermined the power of Octavian, and become master of the world — changing the whole story of the Roman Empire.

When making preparation for the Parthian war, Antony
sent to command her to make her personal appearance in
Cilicia, to answer an accusation, that she had given great
assistance, in the late wars, to Cassius. Dellius, who was
sent on this message, had no sooner seen her face, and remarked her adroitness and subtlety in speech, but he felt
convinced that Antony would not so much as think of giving
any molestation to a woman like this; on the contrary, she
would be the first in favor with him. So he set himself at
once to pay his court to the Egyptian, and gave her his advice, " to go," in the Homeric style, to Cilicia, " in her best
attire," and bade her fear nothing from Antony, the gentlest
and kindest of soldiers.

She had some faith in the words of Dellius, but more in
her own attractions, which, having formerly recommended
her to Cæsar and the young Cnæus Pompey, she did not
doubt might prove yet more successful with Antony. Their
acquaintance was with her when a girl, young, and ignorant
of the world, but she was to meet Antony in the time of life
when women's beauty is most splendid, and their intellects
are in full maturity.[1] She made great preparations for her

---

[1] She was then about twenty-eight years old.

journey, of money, gifts, and ornaments of value, such as so wealthy a kingdom might afford, but she brought with her her surest hopes in her own magic arts and charms.

She received several letters, both from Antony and from his friends, to summon her, but she took no account of these orders; and at last, as if in mockery of them, she came sailing up the river Cydnus, in a barge with gilded stern and out-spread sails of purple, while oars of silver beat time to the music of flutes and fifes and harps. She herself lay all along, under a canopy of cloth of gold, dressed as Venus in a pic-ture, and beautiful young boys, like painted Cupids, stood on each side to fan her. Her maids were dressed like Sea Nymphs and Graces, some steering at the rudder, some working at the ropes. The perfumes diffused themselves from the vessel to the shore, which was covered with multitudes, part following the galley up the river on either bank, part running out of the city to see the sight. The market place was quite emptied, and Antony at last was left alone sitting upon the tribunal; while the word went through all the multitude, that Venus was come to feast with Bacchus for the common good of Asia.

On her arrival, Antony sent to invite her to supper. She thought it fitter he should come to her; so, willing to show his good humor and courtesy, he complied, and went. He found the preparations to receive him magnificent beyond expression, but nothing so admirable as the great number of lights; for on a sudden there was let down altogether so great a number of branches with lights in them so ingeniously disposed, some in squares, and some in circles, that the whole thing was a spectacle that has seldom been equaled for beauty.

The next day, Antony invited her to supper, and was very desirous to outdo her as well in magnificence as contrivance; but he found he was altogether beaten in both, and was so well convinced of it, that he was himself the first to jest and mock at his poverty of wit, and his rustic awkwardness. She, perceiving that his raillery was broad and gross, and savored more of the soldier than the courtier, rejoined in the same taste, and fell into it at once, without any sort of reluctance or reserve.

For her actual beauty, it is said, was not in itself so remarkable that none could be compared with her, or that no one could see her without being struck by it, but the contact of her presence, if you lived with her, was irresistible; the attraction of her person, joining with the charm of her conversation, and the character that attended all she said or did, was something bewitching. It was a pleasure merely to hear the sound of her voice, with which, like an instrument of many strings, she could pass from one language to another; so that there were few of the barbarian nations that she answered by an interpreter; to most of them she spoke herself, as to the Æthiopians, Troglodytes, Hebrews, Arabians, Syrians, Medes, Parthians, and many others, whose language she had learnt; which was all the more surprising, because most of the kings, her predecessors, scarcely gave themselves the trouble to acquire the Egyptian tongue, and several of them quite abandoned the Macedonian.

Antony was so captivated by her, that while Fulvia his wife maintained his quarrels in Rome against Cæsar by actual force of arms, and the Parthian troops, commanded by Labienus (the king's generals having made him commander-in-chief), were assembled in Mesopotamia, and ready to enter Syria, he could yet suffer himself to be carried away by her to Alexandria, there to keep holiday, like a boy, in play and diversion, squandering and fooling away in enjoyment that most costly, as Antiphon says, of all valuables, time. They had a sort of company, to which they gave a particular name, calling it that of the "Inimitable Livers." The members entertained one another daily in turn, with an extravagance of expenditure beyond measure or belief.

Philotas, a physician of Amphissa, who was at that time a student of medicine in Alexandria, used to tell my [Plutarch's] grandfather Lamprias, that, having some acquaintance with one of the royal cooks, he was invited by him, being a young man, to come and see the sumptuous preparations for supper. So he was taken into the kitchen, where he admired the prodigious variety of all things; but particularly, seeing eight wild boars roasting whole, says he, " Surely you have a great number of guests."   The cook laughed at his simplicity, and told him there were not above twelve to sup, but that every dish was to be served up just roasted to a turn, and if any thing was but one minute ill timed, it was spoiled; "And," said he, " maybe Antony will sup just now, maybe not this hour, maybe he will call for wine, or begin to talk, and will put it off. So that," he continued, " it is not one, but many suppers must be had in readiness, as it is impossible to guess at his hour."

To return to Cleopatra; Plato admits four sorts of flattery, but she had a thousand. Were Antony serious or disposed to mirth, she had at any moment some new delight or charm to meet his wishes; at every turn she was upon him, and let him escape her neither by day nor by night. She played at dice with him, drank with him, hunted with him; and when he exercised in arms, she was there to see. At night she would go rambling with him to disturb and torment people at their doors and windows, dressed like a servant woman, for Antony also went in servant's disguise, and from these expeditions he often came home very scurvily answered, and sometimes even beaten severely, though most people guessed who it was. However, the Alexandrians in general liked it all well enough, and joined good humoredly and kindly in his frolic and play, saying they were much obliged to Antony for acting his tragic parts at Rome, and keeping his comedy for them.

It would be trifling without end to be particular in his

follies, but his fishing must not be forgotten. He went out one day to angle with Cleopatra, and, being so unfortunate as to catch nothing in the presence of his mistress, he gave secret orders to the fishermen to dive under water, and put fishes that had been already taken upon his hooks; and these he drew so fast that the Egyptian perceived it. But, feigning great admiration, she told everybody how dexterous Antony was, and invited them next day to come and see him again. So, when a number of them had come on board the fishing boats, as soon as he had let down his hook, one of her servants was beforehand with his divers, and fixed upon his hook a salted fish from Pontus. Antony, feeling his line give, drew up the prey, and when, as may be imagined, great laughter ensued, " Leave," said Cleopatra, "the fishing-rod, general, to us poor sovereigns of Pharos and Canopus; your game is cities, provinces, and kingdoms."

56. THE DEEDS OF AUGUSTUS

Extracts from the "Monumentum Ancyranum." Adapted from University of Pennsylvania, "Historical Reprints," vol. 5, No. 1

This is, perhaps, the most famous inscription left us by Antiquity. It is inscribed on marble in a building which was a temple of Augustus in Ancyra, Asia Minor. The original of this document seems to have been set up in bronze before the great Emperor's mausoleum in Rome, and this is one of the copies distributed through the provinces. Only a fraction of the long inscription can be cited, and it is hard to abridge what is throughout of high historical value. It gives us what Augustus *wished* to have regarded as the leading glories of his reign, distorting and suppressing some facts, but adding much to our knowledge of others.

Below is a copy of the deeds of the divine Augustus, by which he subjected the whole world to the dominion of the Roman People, and of the sums of money he spent upon the Republic and the Roman People, even as they are graven on the two brazen columns which are set up in Rome.

In my twentieth year [44 B.C.], acting on my own initiative and at my own charges, I raised an army wherewith I brought again liberty to the Republic oppressed by the dominance of a faction. Therefore did the Senate admit me to its own order by honorary decrees, in the consulship of Gaius Pansa and Aulus Hirtius. At the same time they gave unto me rank among the consulars in the expressing of my opinion [in the Senate]; [1] and they gave unto me the *imperium*.[2] It also voted that I, as proprætor, together with the consuls, should "see to it that the state suffered no harm." In the same year, too, when both consuls had fallen in battle, the people made me consul and triumvir for the reëstablishing of the Republic.

The men who killed my father [Julius Cæsar] I drove into exile by strictly judicial process,[3] and then, when they took up arms against the Republic, twice I overcame them in battle.[4]

I undertook civil and foreign wars both by land and by sea; as victor therein I showed mercy to all surviving [Roman] citizens. Foreign nations, that I could safely pardon, I preferred to spare rather than to destroy. About 500,000 Roman citizens took the military oath of allegiance to me. Rather over 300,000 of these have I settled in colonies, or sent back to their home towns (municipia) when their term of service ran out; and to all of these I have given lands bought by me, or the money for farms — and this out of my private means. I have taken 600 [war] ships, besides those smaller than triremes.

---

[1] He could speak in the Senate when the presiding officer summoned the ex-consuls to speak, *i.e.* among the first.

[2] In Augustus's case this amounted to confirming him in his exceptional command over an army raised by him without public authority.

[3] Augustus wants to pose as a close adherent to legal processes — not martial power.

[4] Not actually true; in the first battle at Philippi Augustus was worsted, though Antonius's half of the army succeeded.

Offices and Honors given to Augustus

Twice have I had the lesser triumph [ovation]; thrice the [full] curule triumph; twenty-one times have I been saluted as "Imperator." After that, when the Senate voted me many triumphs, I declined them. Also I often deposited the laurels in the Capitol, fulfilling the vows which I had made in battle. On account of the enterprises brought to a happy issue on land and sea by me, or by my legates, under my auspices, fifty-five times has the Senate decreed a thanksgiving unto the Immortal Gods. The number of days, too, on which thanksgiving was professed, fulfilling the Senate's decrees, was 890. Nine kings, or children of kings, have been led before my car in my triumphs. And when I wrote these words, thirteen times had I been consul, and for the thirty-seventh year was holding the tribunician power.

The dictatorship which was offered me by the People and by the Senate, both when I was present and when I was absent, I did not accept. The annual and perpetual consulship I did not accept.

Ten years in succession I was one of the "triumvirs for the reëstablishing of the Republic." Up to the day that I wrote these words I have been *princeps* of the Senate forty years. I have been *pontifex maximus,* augur, member of the "College of XV for the Sacred Rites" [and of the other religious brotherhoods].

Augustus's Acts as Censor

In my fifth consulship, by order of the People and the Senate, I increased the number of patricians. Three times I revised the Senate list. In my sixth consulship, with my colleague, Marcus Agrippa, I made a census of the People. [By it] the number of Roman citizens was 4,063,000. Again in the consulship of Gaius Censorinus and Gaius Asinus

[8 B.C.] I [took the census, when] the number of Roman citizens was 4,230,000. A third time . . . in the consulship of Sextus Pompeius and Sextus Appuleius [14 A.D.], with Tiberius Cæsar as colleague, I [took the census when] the number of Roman citizens was 4,937,000. By new legislation I have restored many customs of our ancestors which had begun to fall into disuse, and I have myself also set many examples worthy of imitation by those to follow me.

By decree of the Senate my name has been included in the hymn of the Salii,[1] and it has been enacted by law that as long as I live I shall be invested with the tribunician power. I refused to be *pontifex maximus* in place of a colleague still living, when the people proffered me [that] priesthood which my father had held.

Benefactions and Public Works conducted by Augustus

[The temple of] Janus Quirinus, which it was the purpose of our fathers to close when there was a victorious peace throughout the whole Roman Empire, — by land and sea, — and which — before my birth — had been alleged to have been closed only twice at all, since Rome was founded : thrice did the Senate order it closed while I was princeps.[2]

To each of the Roman plebs I paid 300 sesterces [$12] in accord with the last will of my father [Cæsar]. In my own name in my fifth consulship [29 B.C.] I gave 400 sesterces [$16] from the spoils of war. Again in my tenth consulship [24 B.C.] I gave from my own estate to every man [among the Romans] 400 sesterces as a donative. In my eleventh, twelve times I made distributions of food, buying grain at my own charges. [And I made like gifts on several other occasions.] The sum which I spent for Italian farms [for the veterans] was about 600,000,000 sesterces [$24,000,000] and for lands in the provinces about 260,-

---

[1] As if Augustus were a god.
[2] 29 B.C., 25 B.C., and probably again in 8 B.C.

000,000 [$10,400,000]. . . . Four times have I aided the public treasury from my own means, to such extent that I furnished to those managing the treasury department 150,000,000 sesterces [$6,000,000].

I built the Curia [Senate House], and the Chalcidicum adjacent thereunto, the temple of Apollo on the Palatine with its porticoes, the temple of the deified Julius [Cæsar], the Lupercal, the portico to the Circus of Flaminius [and a vast number of other public buildings and temples].

Aqueducts which have crumbled through age I have restored, and I have doubled the water [in the aqueduct] called the Marcian by turning a new stream into its course. The Forum Julium and the basilica which was between the temple of Castor and the temple of Saturn, works begun and almost completed by my father, I finished.

Three times in my own name and five times in that of my [adoptive] sons or my grandsons I have given gladiator exhibitions; in these exhibitions about 10,000 men have fought. [Besides other games] twenty-six times in my own name, or in that of my sons and grandsons I have given hunts of African wild beasts in the circus, the Forum, the amphitheaters — and about 3500 wild beasts have been slain.

I gave the people the spectacle of a naval battle beyond the Tiber where is now the grove of the Cæsars. For this purpose an excavation was made 1800 feet long and 1200 wide. In this contest thirty warships — triremes or biremes — took part, and many others smaller. About 3000 men fought on these craft beside the rowers.

Conquests wrought by Augustus

I have cleared the sea from pirates. In that war with the slaves [1] I delivered to their masters for punishment

---

[1] The reference is to Sextus Pompeius's forces overthrown in 36 B.C., which were largely recruited from runaway slaves.

30,000 slaves who had fled their masters and taken up arms against the Republic. The provinces of Gaul, Spain, Africa, Sicily, and Sardinia swore the same allegiance to me. I have extended the boundaries of all the provinces of the Roman People which were bordered by nations not yet subjected to our sway. My fleet has navigated the ocean from the mouth of the Rhine as far as the boundaries of the Cimbri where aforetime no Roman had ever penetrated by land or by sea. The German peoples there sent their legates, seeking my friendship, and that of the Roman people. At almost the same time, by my command and under my auspices two armies have been led into Ethiopia and into Arabia, which is called "The Happy," and very many of the enemy of both peoples have fallen in battle, and many towns have been captured.

I added Egypt to the Empire of the Roman People. When the king of Greater Armenia was killed I could have made that country a province, but I preferred after the manner of our fathers to deliver the kingdom to Tigranes [a vassal prince]. . . . I have compelled the Parthians to give up to me the spoils and standards of three Roman armies, and as suppliants to seek the friendship of the Roman people. Those [recovered] standards, moreover, I have deposited in the sanctuary located in the temple of Mars the Avenger.

In my sixth and seventh consulships [28 and 27 B.C.] when I had put an end to the civil wars, after having obtained complete control of the government, by universal consent I transferred the Republic from my own dominion back to the authority of the Senate and Roman People. In return for this favor by me, I received by decree of the Senate the title AUGUSTUS, the door-posts of my house were publicly decked with laurels, a civic crown[1] was fixed above

---

[1] A "civic crown" was given for saving a citizen. Augustus had saved the state.

my door, and in the Julian Curia [Senate-house] was set a
golden shield, which by its inscription bore witness that it
was bestowed on me, by the Senate and Roman People, on
account of my valor, clemency, justice, and piety. After
that time I excelled all others in dignity, but of power I
held no more than those who were my colleagues in any
magistracy.

[A kind of supplement to the inscription adds]: The sum
of money which he gave into the treasury or to the Roman
People or discharged soldiers was 600,000,000 *denarii*
($96,000,000) [and names many other public works].

57. Egypt and its Condition and Government under Rome

Strabo's " Geography," book XVIII, chap. I, ¶¶ 12–13. Bohn Translation

Everywhere under the Early Empire the Roman rule meant
peace, law and order, justice and prosperity. A notable example
of this was the great and rich province of Egypt, which had been
woefully ruled by the last kings of the Ptolemy line, ending with
the famous Cleopatra. Augustus organized the country as the
Emperor's own special domain land. The Emperor was considered the successor of the ancient Pharaohs ; his deputy — the
præfect — ruled the country with an authority permitted to few
other governors. Under Roman rule Egypt experienced a marked
increase in prosperity.

At present [in Augustus's time] Egypt is a Roman
province, and pays considerable tribute, and is well
governed by prudent persons sent there in succession.
The governor thus sent out has the rank of king. Sub-
ordinate to him is the administrator of justice, who is the
supreme judge in many cases. There is another officer
called the Idologus whose business is to inquire into
property for which there is no claimant, and which of right
falls to Cæsar. These are accompanied by Cæsar's freed-

men and stewards, who are intrusted with affairs of more
or less importance.

Three legions are stationed in Egypt, one in the city [of
Alexandria], the rest in the country. Besides these, there
are also nine Roman cohorts quartered in the city, three on
the borders of Ethiopia in Syene, as a guard to that tract,
and three in other parts of the country. There are also
three bodies of cavalry distributed at convenient posts.

Of the native magistrates in the cities, the first is the
" Expounder of the Law " — who is dressed in scarlet. He
receives the customary honors of the land, and has the care
of providing what is necessary for the city. The second is
the " Writer of the Records "; the third is the " Chief
Judge "; the fourth is the " Commander of the Night
Guard." These officials existed in the time of the [Ptole-
maic] kings, but in consequence of the bad administration
of the public affairs by the latter, the prosperity of the city
[of Alexandria] was ruined by licentiousness. Polybius
expresses his indignation at the state of things when he
was there. He describes the inhabitants of Alexandria as
being composed of three classes, — first the Egyptians
and natives, acute in mind, but very poor citizens, and
[wrongfully] meddlesome in civic affairs. Second were the
mercenaries, — a numerous and undisciplined body, — for it
was an old custom to keep foreign soldiers — who from the
worthlessness of their sovrans knew better how to lord it
than to obey. The third were the [so-called] " Alexan-
drines," who, for the same reason, were not orderly citizens ;
however they were better than the mercenaries, for although they were a mixed race, yet being of Greek origin
they still retained the usual Hellenic customs.

Such, then, if not worse, were the [social] conditions [of
Alexandria] under the last kings. The Romans, as far as
they were able, corrected — as I have said — many abuses,
and established an orderly government — by setting up

vice-governors, "nomarchs," and "ethnarchs," whose business it was to attend to the details of administration.

58. HORACE'S SECULAR HYMN

Horace. De Vere's Translation

In 17 B.C. Augustus celebrated the "Secular Games," a peculiarly solemn event, supposedly permitted only once in a century.
The occasion was one of general jubilation over the notable peace
and prosperity of the age. The "Secular Hymn" by the court
poet Horace is perhaps the most successful poem of occasion ever
written. It fits admirably into the spirit of the occasion with its
references to the old divinities and the contemporary rulers and
their triumphs. It was probably sung on the third day of the
festival at the temple of Apollo on the Palatine by a choir of
twenty-seven noble boys and maidens.

Phœbus! and Dian, thou whose sway,
 Mountains and woods obey!
Twin glories of the skies, forever worshiped, hear!
 Accept our prayer this sacred year
 When, as the Sibyl's voice ordained
  For ages yet to come,
 Pure maids and youths unstained
Invoke the Gods who love the sevenfold hills of Rome.

  All bounteous Sun!
 Forever changing, and forever one!
Who in thy lustrous car bear'st forth light,
And hid'st it, setting, in the arms of Night,
Look down on worlds outspread, yet nothing see
Greater than Rome, and Rome's high sovereignty.
 Thou Ilithyia, too, whatever name,
  Goddess, thou dost approve,
 Lucina, Genitalis, still the same
 Aid destined mothers with a mother's love;

Prosper the Senate's wise decree,[1]
Fertile of marriage faith and countless progeny!
As centuries progressive wing their flight
For thee the grateful hymn shall ever sound;
  Thrice by day, and thrice by night
For thee the choral dance shall beat the ground.

  Fates! whose unfailing word
Spoken from lips Sibylline shall abide,
  Ordained, preserved and sanctified
By Destiny's eternal law, accord
    To Rome new blessings that shall last
    In chain unbroken from the Past.
Mother of fruits and flocks, prolific Earth!
Bind wreaths of spiked corn round Ceres's hair:
And may soft showers and Jove's benignant air
  Nurture each infant birth!

  Lay down thine arrows, God of day!
  Smile on thy youths elect who singing pray.
Thou, Crescent Queen, bow down thy star-crowned head
And on thy youthful choir a kindly influence shed.
If Rome be all your work — if Troy's sad band
Safe sped by you attained the Etruscan strand,
  A chosen remnant, vowed
To seek new Lares, and a changed abode —
Remnant for whom thro' Ilion's blazing gate
Æneas, orphan of a ruined State,
  Opened a pathway wide and free
  To happier homes and liberty : —
Ye Gods! If Rome be yours, to placid Age
  Give timely rest: to docile Youth
    Grant the rich heritage

---

[1] Augustus's law to promote fruitful marriages.

Of morals, modesty, and truth.
On Rome herself bestow a teaming race
Wealth, Empire, Faith, and all befitting Grace.

Vouchsafe to Venus' and Anchises' heir,
    Who offers at your shrine
    Due sacrifice of milk-white kine,
Justly to rule, to pity and to dare,
To crush insulting hosts, the prostrate foeman spare
  The haughty Mede has learned to fear
  The Alban axe, the Latian spear,
  And Scythians, suppliant now, await
  The conqueror's doom, their coming fate.
  Honor and Peace, and Pristine Shame,
  And Virtue's oft dishonored name,
  Have dared, long exiled, to return,
  And with them Plenty lifts her golden horn.

Augur Apollo! Bearer of the bow!
  Warrior and prophet! Loved one of the Nine!
Healer in sickness! Comforter in woe!
  If still the templed crags of Palatine
And Latium's fruitful plains to thee are dear,
  Perpetuate for cycles yet to come,
    Mightier in each advancing year,
  The ever growing might and majesty of Rome.
Thou, too, Diana, from thine Aventine,
  And Algidus's deep woods, look down and hear
The voice of those who guard the books Divine,
  And to thy youthful choir incline a loving ear.

    Return we home! We know that Jove
    And all the Gods our song approve
    To Phœbus and Diana given;
    The virgin hymn is heard in Heaven.

59. STORY ILLUSTRATING THE MAGNANIMITY OF AUGUS-TUS IN HIS LATER YEARS

Seneca, " Essay on Benefits," book III, chap. 27.   Bohn Translation

While struggling for power Augustus had been ruthless and unscrupulous in clearing away any enemy who crossed his path. When he felt his throne secure, he deliberately reversed this policy, and made his leniency proverbial.   He refused to hear charges of conspiracy, promoted men who had opposed him, and went to great lengths to refute any charge that he was a despot founding his power on cruelty and blood.   Of this mild policy the following story gives striking illustration.

In the reign of Augustus, men's own words were not yet able to ruin them [as under later and worse Emperors] yet they sometimes brought them into trouble.   A Senator named Rufus, while at dinner, expressed a hope that Cæsar [Augustus] would not return safe from a journey for which he was preparing, and added that all the bulls and calves wished the same thing.[1]   Some of those present carefully noted these words.   At daybreak the slave who had stood at his feet during the dinner, told him of what he had said in his cups, and urged him to be the first to go to Cæsar and denounce himself.   Rufus followed this advice, met Cæsar as he was going down to the Forum, and swearing that he was out of his mind the day before, prayed that " what he had said might fall upon his own head and that of his children."   He then begged Cæsar to pardon him and to take him back into favor.   When Cæsar said he would do so, Rufus added, " No one will believe that you have taken me back into favor unless you make me a present of something," and he asked for and obtained a sum of money so large that it would have been a gift not to be

[1] They feared lest they be slaughtered in the thanksgiving sacrifices on his return.

slighted, even if bestowed by an unoffended prince. Cæsar added, "In the future I will take care never to quarrel with you, — for my own sake."

60. Vergil's Glorification of the Julian Line

Æneid, book VI, ll. 789-800, 847-853.   H. H. Ballard's Translation

Vergil's Æneid — rightly understood — is one long pæan, glorifying Rome, its founders, and its greatness in the Augustan age. How skillfully the courtly poet paid his tribute to the reigning Julii and especially to Augustus is shown in the following lines from the great Latin epic. In calling Augustus's age "Golden," Vergil is merely voicing the public gratitude for the good government and general prosperity that marked the Early Empire; few rulers were more popular than Augustus.

[Anchises, in the realms of the dead, is reciting to his son Æneas the future glories of the Roman race.]

Lo! Cæsar and all the Julian
Line, predestined to rise to the infinite spaces of heaven.
This, yea, this is the man, so often foretold thee in promise,
Cæsar Augustus, descended from God, who again shall a
    golden
Age in Latium found, in fields once governed by Saturn
Further than India's hordes, or the Garymantian peoples
He shall extend his reign; there's a land beyond all of our
    planets
'Yond the far track of the year and the sun, where sky-
    bearing Atlas
Turns on his shoulders the firmament studded with bright
    constellations;
Yea, even now, at his coming, foreshadowed by omens from
    heaven,
Shudder the Caspian realms, and the barbarous Scythian
    kingdoms,
While the disquieted harbors of Nile are affrighted!

[Anchises now points out the long line of worthies and conquerors who are to precede Augustus, and adds these lines.]

Others better may fashion the breathing bronze with more
    delicate fingers;
Doubtless they also will summon more lifelike features
    from marble:
They shall more cunningly plead at the bar; and the mazes
    of heaven
Draw to the scale and determine the march of the swift
    constellations.
Thine be the care, O Rome, to subdue the whole world for
    thine empire!
These be the arts for thee, — the order of peace to establish,
Them that are vanquished to spare, and them that are haughty
    to humble! [1]

61. THE GLORIES OF ROME

Strabo, " Geography," book V, chap. 3, ¶ 8.   Bohn Translation

Addressing a Greek audience, Strabo gives us this impression
of the physical aspect of the mighty city that had mastered all
Hellendom.   He wrote in the age of Augustus.   The city probably continued to increase in magnificence for the next two hundred years, and a number of the most famous buildings, *e.g.* the
Flavian Amphitheater, were not yet erected.

The Greek cities are thought to have flourished mainly
on account of the felicitous choice made by their founders,
in regard to the beauty and strength of their sites, their
proximity to some haven, and the fineness of the country.
But the Roman prudence was more particularly employed
on matters which have received but little attention from the
Greeks, — such as paving their roads, constructing aqueducts,
and sewers.   In fact they have paved the roads, cut through

[1] Perhaps the most famous lines in Latin poetry.

hills, and filled up valleys, so that the merchandise may be conveyed by carriage from the ports. The sewers, arched over with hewn stones, are large enough in parts for actual hay wagons to pass through, while so plentiful is the supply of water from the aqueducts, that rivers may be said to flow through the city and the sewers, and almost every house is furnished with water pipes and copious fountains.

We may remark that the ancients [of Republican times] bestowed little attention upon the beautifying of Rome. But their successors, and especially those of our own day, have at the same time embellished the city with numerous and splendid objects. Pompey, the Divine Cæsar [i.e. Julius Cæsar], and Augustus, with his children, friends, wife, and sister have surpassed all others in their zeal and munificence in these decorations. The greater number of these may be seen in the Campus Martius which to the beauties of nature adds those of art. The size of the plain is remarkable, allowing chariot races and the equestrian sports without hindrance, and multitudes [here] exercise themselves with ball games, in the Circus, and on the wrestling grounds. The structures that surround [the Campus], the greensward covered with herbage all the year around, the summit of the hills beyond the Tiber, extending from its banks with panoramic effect, present a spectacle which the eye abandons with regret.

Near to this plain is another surrounded with columns, sacred groves, three theaters, an amphitheater, and superb temples, each close to the other, and so splendid that it would seem idle to describe the rest of the city after it. For this cause the Romans esteeming it the most sacred place, have erected funeral monuments there to the illustrious persons of either sex. The most remarkable of these is that called the "Mausoleum" [the tomb of Augustus] which consists of a mound of earth raised upon a high foundation of white marble, situated near the river, and covered on the top with evergreen shrubs. Upon the summit is a bronze statue of Augustus Cæsar, and beneath the mound are the funeral urns of himself, his relatives, and his friends. Behind is a large grove containing charming promenades. In the center of the plain [the Campus Martius] is the spot where [the body of] this prince was reduced to ashes. It is surrounded by a double inclosure, one of marble, the other of iron, and planted within with poplars. If thence you proceed to visit the ancient Forum, which is equally filled with basilicas, porticoes, and temples, you will there behold the Capitol, the Palatine, and the noble works that adorn them, and the piazza of Livia [Augustus's Empress], — each successive work causing you speedily to forget that which you have seen before. Such then is Rome!

CHAPTER VI

THE DEEDS OF THE EMPERORS

No political experiment was ever a greater immediate success than the Roman Empire. Down to the death of Antoninus Pius it must have appeared the final solution of all governmental problems. Even after the Roman World became convulsed with the civil wars and barbarian invasions of the third century, no one seems really to have doubted the permanence of the Empire as an institution divinely ordained and perpetuated.

It is sometimes complained that too much time has been wasted upon the study of the personal biographies, crimes, exploits, etc., of the individual Emperors, and not enough upon the general features of the government and society of their day ; and it is perfectly true that court gossip and the anecdotes, *e.g.* of the gluttony of a Vitellius, do not constitute the most valuable history. Yet on the other hand, a study of the personalia of the Emperors is by no means useless. Sooner or later representatives of almost all the more usual human types within the Empire found their way to the throne ; and in the long line of the Cæsars we can study in the concrete what was best and what was worst in the first three Christian centuries. There were many potential Neroes in the Empire of the first century, and it is also safe to assume that Marcus Aurelius had many humble yet high-minded comrades in his courageous philosophy, during the second century.

Naturally one's eyes are focused upon the crimes of a Nero, a Domitian, or an Elagabalus. It should never be forgotten, however, that these evil Emperors were only in power a small fraction of the time ; and even under their sway, the average provincials probably were not misgoverned. The typical Roman Emperor was very far removed from an irascible and arbitrary Oriental sultan. He was often a tried soldier, taught in the camps to obey before he

could command; he had frequently held important administrative
offices; and so was an experienced civil governor, and in most
cases he took a highly serious view of the dignity and respon
sibility of his great office, and was keenly conscious that the
prosperity of his subjects rested largely in his keeping.   In
discharging his duties of course no tender scruples nor squeamish
sympathies were likely to prevent him from doing what he
conceived to be for the good of the " Roman World"; and it
is useless to look for the Christian virtues of charity and mercy
to enemies and evildoers.   The Roman Empire did not fall, however, through the personal inefficiency of its rulers.   The evils
which undermined it were probably beyond remedy at the hands
of any single Cæsar.

In this chapter a number of typical cases are presented of
great events which affected the woe or weal of the Empire ; and
of incidents which illustrate the characters of certain famous
Emperors.   The citations, of course, could be vastly multiplied.
Excerpts dealing with the life and thought of the Empire are reserved for the next chapter (VII).

62. The Defeat of Varus

Velleius Paterculus, " History of Rome," book ii, chaps. 117-119.
Bohn Translation

In the years 12 to 9 B.C. the vast region known as Germany
had been brought under Roman control by Drusus, the stepson
of Augustus.   Up to 9 A.D. it seemed likely that the whole
country and its inhabitants would be peacefully Romanized.
How this scheme came to nought, thanks to the folly of Varus
the Roman governor, and the patriotism of the chieftain Arminius
(or Hermann), is told by the contemporary historian Velleius
Paterculus.   The event was an important one: — for the first
time in history the Roman eagles were forced back.

Quintilius Varus [the new governor of Germany] was
born of a noble rather than an illustrious family ; he was
of a mild disposition, and of a sedate manner, and being

rather indolent both in mind and body was more accustomed to ease in a camp than action in the field. How far he was from despising money, Syria — where he had been governor — gave the proof; for when he went there the province was rich and he was poor; when he departed it was poor and he was rich! On appointment to the command in Germany, he imagined that the inhabitants had nothing human but their voice and limbs, and that creatures who could be tamed by the sword might be civilized by [the intricacies of] law. With this notion, once in the heart of Germany, as if among a most peace-loving folk, he spent the summer deciding litigation, and ordering the pleadings before a tribunal. [The Germans, though exasperated by such strange proceedings, pretended to be grateful for them] and they at length lulled Varus into such a perfect security that he fancied himself a city prætor [at Rome] handing out justice in the Forum, instead of commanding an army in the middle of Germany.

It was at this time, that a young man of high birth, Arminius, son of the German prince, Segimer, — brave in action, quick in understanding and with an activity of mind far beyond his barbarian condition, a youth who had regularly accompanied our army in the former war, and had been made a Roman citizen and even an eques, — took advantage of the general's indolence to perpetrate an act of atrocity; cleverly judging that a man is most easily destroyed when he is most secure, and that security very often is the commencement of calamity. He communicated his thoughts at first to a few, then to more friends, assuring them that the Romans might readily be surprised. Then he proceeded to add action to resolution, and fixed a time for executing the plot. Notice of his intent was given to Varus by Segestes, a German of high credit and rank; but fate was not to be opposed by warnings, and had already darkened the Roman general's vision. . . .

Varus refused to credit the information, asserting that "he felt a trust in the good will of the [subject] people, proportioned to his kindness to them." And after this first warning there was no time for a second.

[The Roman army was therefore surprised in the forest by the Germans of Arminius.] An army unrivaled in bravery, the flower of the Roman troops in discipline, vigor and military experience, was thus brought through supine leadership, the perfidy of the foe, and a cruel Fortune into an utterly desperate situation. The troops did not even have the opportunity of fighting as they wished . . . and hemmed in by woods, lakes and the bands of ambushed enemies, were entirely cut off by those foes, whom they had used to slaughter like cattle. Their leader, Varus, showed some spirit in dying, though none in fighting — for, imitating the example of his father and grandfather, he ran himself through with his sword. Of the two præfects of the camp Lucius Eggius gave an honorable example, but Ceionius one of baseness, for after the bulk of the army had perished, Ceionius advised a surrender, preferring to die by the executioner than in battle. Numonius Vala, Varus's lieutenant, a man hitherto of good reputation, this time proved guilty of foul treachery, for leaving the infantry unguarded he fled with the allied cavalry, trying to reach the Rhine. But Fortune avenged his crime; he perished in this act of deserting his countrymen. The savage enemy mangled the half-burned body of Varus.[1] His head was cut off and sent to Marobodus [a barbarian king] and by him sent to the Emperor; and so at length received honorable burial in the sepulcher of his family.

[1] The Romans in their last stand seem to have tried to burn his body on a funeral pyre.

63. A Discourse of Claudius in the Senate

Inscription.   Published in Zell's "Opuscula," and now translated

Claudius, the third successor of Augustus (41 to 54 A.D.), was a fearfully pedantic and long-winded individual. He was not without abilities as a ruler, however, and did much to equalize the condition of the Italians and the Provincials. The following speech of his in the Senate (luckily preserved on an inscription) illustrates at once the nature of an imperial harangue before the Conscript Fathers, the interruptions that seem to have been allowed even in the speech of an Emperor, the broad personalities in which Claudius indulged, and his liberal policy withal, especially to the Gauls.

"It is surely an innovation of the divine Augustus, my great-uncle, and of Tiberius Cæsar, my uncle, to desire that particularly the flower of the colonies and of the municipal towns, that is to say, all those that contain men of breeding and wealth, should be admitted to this assembly."

[*Interruption, seemingly by a senator*]: "How now? Is not an Italian senator to be preferred to a provincial senator!"

"I will soon explain this point to you, when I submit that part of my acts which I performed as censor, but I do not conceive it needful to repel even the provincials who can do honor to the Senate House. Here is this splendid and powerful colony of Vienna;[1] is it so long since it sent to us senators? From that colony comes Lucius Vestinus, one of the glories of the equestrian order, my personal friend, whom I keep close to myself for the management of my private affairs. Let his sons be suffered — I pray you — to become priests of the lowest rank, while waiting till, with the lapse of years, they can follow the advancement of their dignity. As for that robber, [Valerius Asiaticus from Vienna] I will pass over his hateful name. For I detest

[1] Not the great Vienna on the Danube, but the modern town of Vienne in southern France.

that hero of the gymnasium, who brought the consulship
into his family before even his colony had obtained the full
rights of Roman citizenship. I could say as much of his
brother, stamped as unworthy by this unlucky relationship,
and incapable henceforth of being a useful member of
your body."

[*Interrupting shout*]: "Here now, Tiberius Cæsar Ger-
manicus! It's time to let the Conscript Fathers understand what your talk is driving at — already you've
reached the very limits of Narbonnese Gaul!"

[*Claudius resumes*]: "All these young men of rank, on
whom I cast my glance, you surely do not regret to see
among the number of the senators; any more than Persicus,
that most high-born gentleman and my friend, is ashamed
when he meets upon the images of his ancestors the name
Allobrogius.[1] And if such is your thought, what would
you desire more? Do I have to point it out to you?
Even the territory which is located beyond the province
of [Gallia] Narbonnensis, has it not already sent you
senators? For surely we have no regrets in going clear
up to Lugdunum [2] for the members of our order. Assuredly,
Conscript Fathers, it is not without some hesitation that
I cross the limits of the provinces which are well known
and familiar to you, — but the moment is come when I
must plead openly the cause of Further Gaul. It will
be objected that Gaul sustained a war against the divine
Julius for ten years. But let there be opposed to this
the memory of a hundred years of steadfast fidelity, and
a loyalty put to the proof in many trying circumstances.
My father, Drusus, was able to force Germany to submit,
because behind him reigned a profound peace assured
by the tranquillity of the Gauls. And note well, that at

---

[1] In memory of a victory by a certain ancestor of Persicus, who defeated the Allobroges in 121 B.C.

[2] Modern Lyons.

the moment he was summoned to that war, he was busy
instituting the census [in Gaul], a new institution among
them, and contrary to their customs. And how difficult
and perilous to us is this business of the census,[1] although
all we require is that our public resources should be known,
we have learned by all too much experience."

64. A Typical Neronian Crime: the Murder of Britannicus

Tacitus, "Annals," book XIII, chaps. 15-17.   Church and Broadrib Translation

Nero's crimes have become proverbial, and the repetition of
them a dreary catalogue. The following story of the death of
his stepbrother Britannicus (the true son of Claudius, the late
Emperor) is typical of most of the others. It was the first of
Nero's great iniquities, being perpetrated in 55 A.D., when the
young sovereign was only eighteen years old.

[Agrippina, Nero's mother, was disappointed in her hopes
of controlling the government through her son. She complained of the efforts of his ministers Seneca and Burrhus
against her, and threw out hints that Britannicus, Claudius's
real heir, and stepbrother to Nero, was coming of age and
must have his rights.]

Nero was confounded at this, and as the day was near on
which Britannicus was to complete his fourteenth year,[2] he
reflected on the domineering temper of his mother, and now
again on the character of the young prince, which a trifling
circumstance had lately tested, — trifling, yet sufficient to
gain him wide popularity. During the Saturnalia amid
other pastimes of his playmates, at a game of lot drawing
for "king" [of the revels], the lot fell upon Nero, upon

---

[1] Perilous, of course, because it was detested by the Provincials as the
basis for Roman taxation.

[2] When by Roman usage youths took the manly toga and came of age.

which he gave all his other companions various orders but of such a character as would not put them to the blush; but when he told Britannicus to step forward and begin a song, hoping for a laugh at the expense of a boy who knew nothing of sober, much less of riotous, society, the lad had with perfect coolness commenced some verses which hinted at his expulsion from his father's house, and from supreme power. This procured him pity, which was all the more conspicuous, as night with its merriment had stripped off all disguise [of men's feelings].

Nero saw the reproach and doubled his hate. Pressed by Agrippina's menaces, having no charge against his "brother," and not daring openly to order his murder, he meditated a secret device, and directed poison to be prepared through the agency of Jullius Pollio, a tribune of the prætorians, who had in his custody a woman under sentence for poisoning, — one Locusta, — a person with a vast reputation for crime. That all the people waiting upon Britannicus should care nothing for right or honor had been long since provided for. He actually received his first dose of poison from his tutors [but it did not prove deadly, and he suffered no great hurt]. But Nero, impatient at such slow progress in crime, threatened the tribune and ordered the prisoner to execution, for prolonging his anxiety while they were thinking of the popular gossip and preparing their own defense. Then they promised that that death should be as sudden as if it were the hurried work of the dagger, and a rapid poison of ingredients previously tested was prepared close to the Emperor's chamber.

It was customary for the [young] imperial princes to sit during their meals with other nobles of the same age, in the sight of their kinsfolk, but at a table of their own, furnished somewhat frugally. There Britannicus was dining, and as whatever he ate and drank was always tested by the taste of a select attendant, the following device was contrived, that the usage might not be dropped, or the crime betrayed by the death of both prince and attendant. — A cup as yet harmless, but extremely hot and already tested was handed to Britannicus; — then, on his refusing it because of its warmth, poison was poured in with some cold water, and this so penetrated his entire frame that he lost alike voice and breath.

There was a stir among the company; some, taken by surprise, ran hither and thither, while those whose discernment was keener remained motionless, with their eyes fixed on Nero, — who, as he reclined in seeming unconcern, said that, — "this was a common occurrence, from a periodic epilepsy, which had afflicted Britannicus from infancy, and his sight and senses would presently return." As for Agrippina, her terror and confusion, though her countenance struggled to hide it, so visibly appeared, that she was clearly ignorant, as was Octavia, Britannicus's own sister [and Nero's wife]. She saw in fact that she was robbed of her only remaining refuge, and that here was a precedent for parricide. Even Octavia, — notwithstanding her useful inexperience, — had learned to hide her grief, her affection, and indeed every emotion.

And so after a brief pause the company resumed its mirth. One and the same night witnessed Britannicus's death and funeral, preparations having already been made for his obsequies, which were on a humble scale. [A violent storm, testified, in popular opinion, to the wrath of heaven at the whole proceeding.] The emperor apologized for the hasty funeral by reminding people that it was the practice of our ancestors to withdraw from view any grievously untimely death, and not to dwell on it with panegyrics or display. "For himself," said he, "as he had now lost a brother's help, his remaining hopes centered in the State, and all the more tenderness ought to be shown by the Senate and People towards a prince who was the only survivor of a family born to the highest greatness."

65. The Great Fire at Rome in the Days of Nero

Cassius Dio, "Roman History," book 62, chaps. 16-18

Most historians charge Nero with having caused the great fire that nearly destroyed Rome in 64 A.D. Modern criticism makes it very doubtful whether the Emperor really *caused* the fire; although his life was so iniquitous that people readily believed that he was guilty. The city of Rome was, for the most part, composed of very ill-built and inflammable *insulæ* (tenement houses), and a blaze once under headway was almost impossible to check. In any case, the burning of Rome was one of the famous events of the age; and it is likely enough that thugs and bandits pretended they had the Emperor's orders, when they spread the flames in the hope of getting new chances for plunder.

Nero had the wish — or rather it had always been a fixed purpose of his — to make an end of the whole city in his lifetime. Priam he deemed wonderfully happy in that he had seen Troy perish at the same moment his authority over her ended. Accordingly, Nero sent out by different ways men feigning to be drunk, or engaged in some kind of mischief, and at first had a few fires kindled quietly and in different quarters; people, naturally, were thrown into extreme confusion, not being able to find either the cause of the trouble nor to end it; and meantime met with many strange sights and sounds. They ran about as if distracted, and some rushed one way, some another. In the midst of helping their neighbors, men would learn that their own homes were blazing. Others learned, for the first time, that their property was on fire, by being told it was burned down. People would run from their houses into the lanes,[1] with a hope of helping from the outside, or again would rush into the houses from the streets seeming to imagine they could do something from the inside. The shouting and screaming of children, women, men, and gray beards

[1] These were fearfully narrow and tortuous in Rome.

mingled together unceasingly; and betwixt the combined smoke and shouting no one could make out anything.

All this time many who were carrying away their own goods, and many more who were stealing what belonged to others kept encountering one another and falling over the merchandise. It was impossible to get anywhere; equally impossible to stand still. Men thrust, and were thrust back, upset others, and were upset themselves, many were suffocated or crushed; in short, no possible calamity at such a disaster failed to befall.

This state of things lasted not one day, but several days and nights running. Many houses were destroyed through lack of defenders; and many were actually fired in more places by professed rescuers. For the soldiers (including the night watch) with a keen eye for plunder, instead of quenching the conflagration, kindled it the more. While similar scenes were taking place at various points, a sudden wind caught the fire and swept it over what [of the city] remained. As a result nobody troubled longer about goods or homes, but all the survivors, from a place of safety, gazed on what appeared to be many islands and cities in flames. No longer was there any grief for private loss, public lamentation swallowed up this — as men reminded each other how once before the bulk of the city had been even thus laid desolate by the Gauls.

While the whole people was in this state of excitement, and many driven mad by calamity were leaping into the blaze, Nero mounted upon the roof of the palace, where almost the whole conflagration was commanded by a sweeping glance, put on the professional harpist's garb, and sang "The Taking of Troy"[1] (so he asserted), although to common minds, it seemed to be "The Taking of Rome."

The disaster which the city then underwent, had no parallel save in the Gallic invasion. The whole Palatine

[1] A poem probably composed by himself.

hill, the theater of Taurus, and nearly two thirds of the rest of the city were burned. Countless persons perished. The populace invoked curses upon Nero without intermission, not uttering his name, but simply cursing "those who set the fire";[1] and this all the more because they were disturbed by the recollection of the oracle recited in Tiberius's time, to this effect,

> "After three times three hundred rolling years
> In civil strife Rome's Empire disappears."

And when Nero to encourage them declared these verses were nowhere to be discovered, they changed and began to repeat another oracle — alleged to be a genuine one of the Sibyl,

> "When the matricide reigneth in Rome,
> Then endeth the race of Æneas."

And thus it actually turned out, whether this was really revealed in advance by some divination, or whether the populace now for the first time gave it the form of a sacred utterance merely adapted to the circumstances. For Nero was indeed the last sovran of the Julian line, descended from Æneas.

Nero now began to collect vast sums both from individuals and nations, sometimes using downright compulsion, with the conflagration as his excuse, and sometimes obtaining funds by "voluntary" offers. As for the mass of the Romans they had the fund for their food supply withdrawn.[2]

---

[1] This was not merely through fear of the Emperor. It probably took some time for the rumor to spread that Nero had caused the fire.

[2] It ought in fairness to be said Nero did everything possible to relieve the suffering after the fire, giving freely from the treasury as well as levying on the provinces.

66. How the Emperor Domitian tried to amuse the Roman Populace

Suetonius, " Life of Domitian," chap. IV.   Bohn Translation

Despite their control of the army and the subservience of the Senate, the average Emperor quailed before the hootings and ill will of the Roman mob.   Thus Domitian (81–96 A.D.), a bad and tyrannical Cæsar, tried to win popularity by providing the idle masses of the capital with their favorite games and arena massacres.

He frequently entertained the people with the most magnificent and costly shows, not only in the amphitheater, but in the circus; where, besides the usual chariot races, with two or four horses abreast, he exhibited the imitation of a battle betwixt cavalry and infantry; and in the amphitheater a sea fight.   The people too were entertained with wild-beast hunts, and gladiator fights even in the night-time, by torchlight.   He constantly attended the games given by the quæstors, which had been disused for some time, but were revived by him; and upon those occasions, he always gave the people the liberty of demanding two pair of gladiators out of his own [private] " school," who appeared last in court uniforms.

He presented the people with naval fights, performed by fleets almost as numerous as those usually employed in real engagements; making a vast lake near the Tiber, and building seats around it.   And he witnessed these fights himself during a very heavy rain.

He likewise instituted in honor of Jupiter Capitolinus, a solemn contest in music to be performed every five years; besides horse-racing and gymnastic exercises.   There was too a public performance in elocution both Greek and Latin, and beside the musicians who sung to the harp, there were others who played concerted pieces or solos without vocal accompaniment.

Thrice he bestowed upon the people[1] a bounty of 300 sesterces [$12] per man, and at a public show of gladiators a very plentiful feast. At the "Festival of the Seven Hills" [held in December], he distributed large hampers of provisions to the Senatorial and Equestrian orders, and small baskets to the commonalty, and encouraged them to eat by setting the example. The day after, he scattered among the people a variety of cakes and other delicacies to be scrambled after; and on the greater part of them falling amidst the seats of the lower classes, he ordered 500 tickets[2] to be thrown into each range of benches belonging to the Senatorial and Equestrian orders.

67. The Poet Statius banquets with his Lord God the Emperor

Statius, "Silvæ," book IV, 2. Slater's Translation

How servile Roman society had become before the end of the first century A.D., and how ready literary men were to heap adulation upon even a very morose and despotic Emperor, is shown by this extract from a poem by Statius (a writer of some ability) on the occasion of an invitation to dine with Domitian. When a poet could prostitute his genius in this manner, it is evident that literature was bound to decline.

The royal feast of Sidonian Dido is sung by him who brought the great Æneas to the Laurentine fields : the banquet of Alcinöus is celebrated in deathless verse by him who sang the return over the broad seas of Ulysses outworn; but I — to whom •Cæsar has even now for the first time granted to enjoy the bliss of that holy banquet, and to rise up from an Emperor's table — how shall I sound my vows upon the lyre; how avail to pay my thanks ?

[1] Presumably the male adult citizens in Rome are meant.

[2] These were probably lottery tickets: the lucky numbers drew articles of value, — vases, slaves, money, possibly a small villa.

Barren are the years of my past. This is the beginning of my days, this the threshold of life !

Ruler of the world, great father of the conquered globe : hope of mankind, darling of the gods, can it be that I behold thee as I recline [at the feast] ? Is it thou ? And dost thou suffer me to see thy face, *thy* face hard by at the board over the wine, and must I not rise up to do thee homage ? . . .

Not on the feast : not upon the slabs of Moorish citronwood set on pillars of ivory, not upon the long array of henchmen — on *him*, on him alone I gaze. Calm was his countenance ; with a quiet majesty he tempered the brightness and gently abated the blazoned pomp of his grandeur ; yet the radiance he sought to hide shone out upon his brow.[1]

68. DEEDS AND ANECDOTES OF THE EMPEROR HADRIAN

Ælius Spartianus, " Life of Hadrian," in the " Augustan History "

Under Hadrian (Emperor 117–138 A.D.) the Roman Empire reached its acme of prosperity. The Emperor, himself a man of remarkable and varied genius, although not always of just and even temperament, seemed anxious to conceal the real despotism of his government, by the enlightened use of his power. No new conquests were made, but many internal reforms were executed. Hadrian also was a great traveler, and spent much of his reign going up and down his vast empire, heaping benefits upon the communities with which he sojourned.

In many places where he visited the frontiers, which were not separated from the Barbarians by rivers, Hadrian raised a kind of wall, by driving into the ground great piles. He set up a king over the Germans ; he quenched the seditious movements of the Moors — for which deed the Senate

---

[1] The flattery seems more pronounced, when it is recalled that Domitian was an extremely gloomy and forbidding monarch.

ordered thanksgivings to the Gods. A single interview was sufficient for Hadrian to stop a war with the Parthians that seemed to threaten. Then he sailed by way of Asia and the Islands to Achaia; and after the example of Hercules and Philip he was admitted to the Eleusinian mysteries. He bestowed many benefits upon the Athenians and presided at their games. It was noticed in Achaia, that though many persons with swords assisted at the religious ceremonies, nevertheless none of the suite of Hadrian came armed. He passed next into Sicily, where he ascended Mt. Ætna to see the sun rise, which seems there to form a bow of variegated colors. Next he went to Rome, and thence to Africa, where he heaped benefactions upon the province. Never did a Prince traverse over the Empire with such celerity!

After that, returning from Africa to Rome, he went quickly again to the East, and passing by way of Athens, he dedicated the public works which he had [formerly] commenced there; such as a temple to Jupiter the Olympian, and an altar upon which he bestowed his own name.

In Cappadocia he took some slaves which he intended for camp service. He proffered his friendship to the princes and kings of the region, and he did the same to Chosroës, king of Parthia, to whom he returned the latter's daughter, who had been made captive by Trajan.

While traversing the provinces he punished according to their crimes the [various] governors and procurators; and did so with such severity that he seemed actually to stimulate their accusers. After having crossed Arabia, the Emperor came to Pelusium, where he erected a splendid monument to Pompey. While sailing on the Nile he lost his beloved favorite Antinoüs, whom he mourned as over a woman. There are various stories about this young man. Some say he sacrificed himself [to save] Hadrian's life;

[others give widely differing accounts as to the Emperor's liking for him]. The Greeks, with their sovran's consent accorded [the memory of Antinoüs] divine honors.

This ruler loved poetry, and cultivated carefully all branches of literature. He understood likewise arithmetic, geometry, and painting. He danced and sang extremely well, his bent for [sensuous] pleasure being extreme. He made many verses for his favorites, and wrote love poems. He handled weapons with much skill, and was a master of the military art. He also devoted some little time to the exercises of gladiators. Now severe, now merry, now voluptuous, now self-contained, now cruel, now merciful, this Emperor seemed never the same. [He enriched his friends liberally, but finally growing suspicious of some put them to death or ruined them.]

[He enjoyed literary and philosophical discussions, but it was not safe to defeat him in them.] Favorinus [a famous philosopher and orator], when his friends blamed him for surrendering to Hadrian's criticism as to his use of a word — when he had good authority on his side — laughed and replied, " You can never persuade me, good friends, that the commander of thirty legions is not the best-qualified [critic] in the world ! "

When he sat as judge he was aided not merely by his friends and his courtiers, but by [many famous] *Juris consulti*, all approved by the Senate. He enacted among other things that no one should destroy houses in one city to transport the materials[1] to another city. He awarded to children of proscribed persons, a twelfth part of their father's estate. He did not admit accusations for the crime of *lese-majesté*. He refused the bequests of persons whom he had not known, and did not accept those of personal acquaintances, if they had children. He enacted that whoever found a treasure on his own land should keep

[1] *I.e.* Choice marbles, frescoes, paintings, columns, statues, etc.

it.[1] If one found treasure on the property of some one else, he could keep half — the rest went to the proprietor.

He took away the right of masters to kill their slaves, requiring that if the slaves deserved it, they should be condemned [to death] by the regular judges. He abolished the special dungeons for slaves and freedmen. Also hereafter not all the slaves of a master who was murdered in his home [by a slave] were to suffer death [as formerly], but only those within reach of his outcries.

Hadrian had also a most agreeable style of conversation, even towards persons of decidedly humble rank. He hated those who seemed to envy him this natural pleasure, under pretext of causing "the Majesty of the Throne" to be respected. At the University of Alexandria [the Museum] he proposed many questions to the professors there, and satisfied himself [as to the facts]. He had a remarkable memory, and great talents (for oratory), preparing his own orations and responses [without aid of a secretary]. He had a great faculty for remembering names without prompting; it was enough to have met persons once, he could then even aid the nomenclators if they made a mistake. He remembered all the old veterans whom he had pensioned off. He wrote, dictated, heard others, and conversed with his friends; and all at the same time!

69. The Character of Antoninus Pius

Marcus Aurelius, "Meditations," book I, 16. Casaubon's Translation

Antoninus Pius (reigned 138–161 A.D.) had a singularly untroubled reign, although there is reason to believe that the forces which later ruined the Roman world were allowed by him to work unchecked. No one, however, has questioned the purity of his life and the simplicity and nobility of his character. His personality is

[1] That it should not be confiscate to the state, as had been the custom with treasure-trove.

described by his adopted son — the famous Marcus Aurelius.   It is a high tribute to the ancient civilization and the Stoic philosophy that they could produce two such characters and bestow on them successively the government of the world.

"In my father [Antoninus Pius] I observed his meekness; his constancy without wavering in those things which after due examination . . . he had determined.   How free from all vanity he carried himself in matters of honor and dignity (as they are esteemed); his laboriousness and assiduity, his readiness to hear any man that had aught to say tending to any common good! how generally and impartially he would give every man his due: his skill and knowledge when rigor or extremity, when indulgence or moderation were in season.   His moderate condescending to other men's occasions as an ordinary man, neither absolutely requiring his friends that they should wait on him at his ordinary meals, nor that they should of necessity accompany him in his journeys.   His sociability, his gracious and delightful conversation never reached satiety, his care of his body was within bounds and measures, not as one who did not wish to live long, or overstudious of neatness and elegancy; yet not as one that did not regard it, so that through his own [care of his health] he seldom needed any medicine.

"He was not easily moved and tossed up and down, but loved to be constant, both in the same places and businesses; and after his great fits of headache he would return fresh and vigorous to his wonted affairs.   He was very discreet and moderate in exhibiting public sights and shows for the pleasure and pastime of the people; in public buildings, congiaria [i.e. general distribution of money or corn doles], and the like.   He did not use the baths at unseasonable hours.   He was never curious or anxious about his food, or about the style or color of his clothes, or about any mere matter of external beauty.   In all his conversation, he was

far from all inhumanity, boldness, incivility, greediness, or
impetuosity; never doing anything with such earnestness
and intention that a man could say of him, that he flew
into a heat about it, but contrariwise, all things distinctly,   ·
as at leisure, without trouble, orderly, soundly, and agree-
ably.   A man [in short] might have applied to him what
is recorded of Socrates."

[Again Marcus Aurelius says (book VI, 27) :]

"Remember Antoninus Pius's constancy in things that
were done by him in accordance with reason, his equability
in all things; how he would never give over a matter until he
understood the whole state of it fully and plainly; and how
patiently and without any resentment he would bear with
them that did unjustly condemn him; how he would never
be overhasty in anything, nor give ear to slanders or false
accusations, but examine and observe with the best diligence
the several actions and dispositions of men.   He would
easily be content with a few things — [mere] lodgings, bed-
ding, the ordinary food and attendance.   He bore with those
who opposed his opinions and even rejoiced if any man
could better advise him, and finally he was exceedingly
religious without superstition."

70. The Reign of Marcus Aurelius

Eutropius, "Compendium of Roman History," book VIII, chaps. 12-14.
Bohn Translation

Marcus Aurelius was Emperor from 161 to 180 A.D.   No ruler
ever came to power with higher ideals and purposes, but the reign
was not a very prosperous one.   The philosopher in the purple
was afflicted by the widespread pestilences in the Empire, and by
the dangerous wars on the frontiers.   He struggled against the
difficulties manfully, and overcame most of them; but his reign
marks the beginning of the long slow decline of the Empire.

Marcus Aurelius was trained in philosophy by Apollonius of Chalcedon: in the Greek language by Sextus of Chæronea, the grandson of Plutarch, while the eminent orator Fronto instructed him in Latin literature.   He conducted himself towards all men at Rome, as if he had been their equal, being moved by no arrogance by his elevation to the Empire. He exercised prompt liberality, and managed the provinces with the utmost kindness and indulgence.

Under his rule affairs were successfully conducted against the Germans.   He himself carried on a war with the Marcomanni, which was greater than any in the memory of man [in the way of wars with the Germans] — so that it was compared to the Punic Wars, for it was exceedingly formidable, and in it whole armies were lost; especially as in this reign, after the victory over the Parthians [1] there occurred a great pestilence so that at Rome, and throughout Italy and the provinces a large fraction of the population, and actually the bulk of the regular troops perished from the plague.

With the greatest labor and patience he persevered for three whole years at Carnutum [a strategically located fortress town in Pannonia] — and brought the Marcomannic war to an end; a war in which the Quadi, Vandals, Sarmatians, Suevi and all the barbarians in that region, had joined the outbreak of the Marcomanni.   He slew several thousand men, and having delivered the Pannonians from bondage [to the invaders] held a triumph at Rome.   As the treasury was drained by the war, and he had no money to give his soldiers; and as he would not lay any [extra] tax on the provinces or Senate, he sold off all his imperial furniture and decorations by an auction held in the Forum of Trajan, consisting of gold and cups of crystal and precious stone, silk garments belonging to his wife and to himself, embroidered — as they were — with gold, and numbers of jeweled ornaments.   This sale was kept up through two

[1] Won for Marcus Aurelius by his generals.

successive months and a great deal of money was raised by it. After his [final] victory, however, he refunded the money to such purchasers as were willing to restore what they had bought, but was by no means troublesome to those who wished to keep their purchase.

After his victory he was so magnificent in his display of games [at Rome] he is said to have exhibited in the arena one hundred lions at once.[1] Having then at last rendered the state happy by his excellent management and gentleness of character, he died in the eighteenth year of his reign, in the sixty-first of his life. He was enrolled among the gods, all [the Senate] voting unanimously that he should have such honor.

71. How Didius Julianus bought the Roman Empire at Auction

Herodianus, "History of the Emperors," book II, chap. 6 ff.

In 193 A.D. the Prætorian Guards murdered the virtuous Emperor Pertinax, who had striven to reduce them to discipline. The sale of the purple which followed forms one of the most fearful and dramatic incidents in the history of the Empire, illustrating: (1) how completely the guardsmen had lost all sense of decency, discipline, and patriotism; (2) how the idea that all things were purchasable for money had possessed the men of ·the Empire. It ought to be said that the Prætorians were an especially pampered corps, and probably the rest of the army was less corrupted.

When the report of the murder of the Emperor [Pertinax] spread among the people, consternation and grief seized all minds, and men ran about beside themselves. An undirected effort possessed the people, — they strove to hunt out the doers of the deed, yet could neither find nor

---

[1] In giving such a show Marcus Aurelius simply complied with Roman public sentiment, despite his philosophic contempt for such displays.

punish them. But the Senators were the worst disturbed, for it seemed a public calamity that they had lost a kindly father and a righteous ruler. Also a reign of violence was dreaded, for one could guess that the soldiery would find that much to their liking.

When the first and the ensuing days had passed, the people dispersed, each man fearing for himself; men of rank, however, fled to their estates outside the city, in order not to risk themselves in the dangers of a change on the throne. But at last when the soldiers were aware that the people were quiet, and that no one would try to avenge the blood of the Emperor, they nevertheless remained inside their barracks and barred the gates; yet they set such of their comrades as had the loudest voices upon the walls, and had them declare that the Empire was for sale at auction, and promise to him who bid highest that they would give him the power, and set him with the armed hand in the imperial palace.

When this proclamation was known, the more honorable and weighty Senators, and all persons of noble origin and property, would not approach the barracks to offer money in so vile a manner for a besmirched sovranty. However, a certain Julianus — who had held the consulship, and was counted rich — was holding a drinking bout late that evening, at the time the news came of what the soldiers proposed. He was a man notorious for his evil living; and now it was that his wife and daughter and fellow feasters urged him to rise from his banqueting couch and hasten to the barracks, in order to find out what was going on. But on the way they pressed it on him that he might get the sovranty for himself, and that he ought not to spare the money to outbid any competitors with great gifts [to the soldiers].

When he came to the wall [of the camp], he called out to the troops and promised to give them just as much as they desired, for he had ready money and a treasure room full of gold and silver. About the same time too came Sulpicianus, who had also been consul and was præfect of Rome and father-in-law of Pertinax, to try to buy the power also. But the soldiers did not receive him, because they feared lest his connection with Pertinax might lead him to avenge him by some treachery. So they lowered a ladder and brought Julianus into the fortified camp; for they would not open the gates, until they had made sure of the amount of the bounty they expected. When he was admitted he promised first to bring the memory of Commodus again into honor[1] and restore his images in the Senate house, where they had been cast down; and to give the soldiers the same lax discipline they had enjoyed under Commodus. Also he promised the troops as large a sum of money as they could ever expect to require or receive. The payment should be immediate, and he would at once have the cash brought over from his residence.

[According to the other contemporary historian, Cassius Dio, Julianus and Sulpicianus now bid against another "one from within the camp, and one without." By their increases they speedily reached the sum of 4000 denarii[2] per man; some of the guard kept reporting and saying to Julianus, "'Sulpicianus offers so much; now how much will you add to that?' And again to Sulpicianus, 'Julianus offers so much, how much will you raise it?'" Sulpicianus seemed about to win the day, when Julianus advanced to 6250 denarii[3] "which he offered with a great shout, indicating the amount likewise upon his fingers," whereupon the troops accepted his bid.]

Captivated by such speeches, and with such vast hopes awakened, the soldiers hailed Julianus as Emperor, and de-

---

[1] Commodus (Pertinax's predecessor) had been most popular with the pampered guards, though hated by the civilians.

[2] About $800.   [3] About $1000.

manded that along with his own name he should take that
of Commodus. Next they took their standards, adorned
them again with the likeness of Commodus and made ready
to go with Julianus in procession.

The latter offered the customary imperial sacrifices in
the camp; and then went out with a great escort of the
guards. For it was against the will and intention of the
populace, and with a shameful and unworthy stain upon
the public honor that he had bought the Empire, and not
without reason did he fear the people might overthrow
him. The guards therefore in full panoply surrounded him
for protection. They were formed in a phalanx around
him, ready to fight; they had "their Emperor" in their
midst; while they swung their shields and lances over his
head, so that no missile could hurt him during the march.
Thus they brought him to the palace, with no man of the
multitude daring to resist; but just as little was there any
cheer of welcome, as was usual at the induction of a new
Emperor. On the contrary the people stood at a distance
and hooted and reviled him as having bought the throne
with lucre at an auction.

[Didius Julianus held his ill-gotten power only from March 28th,
193 A.D., to June 1st of the same year, being deposed and slain
when Septimius Severus and the valiant Danube legions marched
on Rome to avenge Pertinax. The ringleaders of the Prætorians
were executed; the rest of the guardsmen dishonorably discharged
and banished from Italy.]

72. How the Goths devastated the Empire in the Reign of Gallienus

Jordanes, "History of the Goths," chap. 20.   Mierow's Translation

Under Gallienus (260 to 268 A.D.) the Empire was in desperate straits and seemed on the eve of dissolution. Since 250 A.D.
the Goths had been flinging their hordes over the Danube, and

committing devastations which required decades of peace to repair. It is a tribute to the strength of the Empire that it did not perish in the third century A.D.

While Gallienus was given over to luxurious living of every sort, Respa, Veduc, and Thuruar, leaders of the Goths, took ship and sailed across the strait of the Hellespont to Asia. There they laid waste many populous cities and set fire to the renowned temple of Diana at Ephesus, which, as we [Jordanes] said before, the Amazons built. Being driven from the neighborhood of Bithynia they destroyed Chalcedon, which Cornelius Avitus afterward restored to some extent. Yet even to-day, though it is happily situated near the royal city [Constantinople], it still shows some traces of its ruin as a witness to posterity.

After their success the Goths recrossed the strait of the Hellespont, laden with booty and spoil, and returned along the same route by which they had entered the lands of Asia, sacking Troy and Ilium on the way. These cities, which had scarce recovered a little from the famous war of Agamemnon, were thus devastated anew by the hostile sword. After the Goths had thus devastated Asia, Thrace next felt their ferocity.

[After continuing their havoc for a long time unchecked, they were at last expelled for more than a century, by the arms of Claudius II, Aurelian, and Probus.]

73. How AURELIAN CONQUERED ZENOBIA

From Vopiscus, "Life of Aurelian" (in the "Augustan History")

During the disasters of the middle of the third century A.D. the Asiatic provinces of the Empire were nearly torn away, first by the Persians, then by the rulers of Palmyra, a thriving and powerful city situated upon an oasis in the Syrian desert. From 266 to 273 A.D. the sovereign of this city and the "Queen of the East," was Zenobia, a woman of masculine courage and energy, who almost founded an Oriental empire to the detriment of Rome. From this dismemberment the Roman world was saved by the valor of the great Emperor Aurelian, who among his other conquests overcame Zenobia and destroyed Palmyra (273 A.D.), after no puny struggle.

After taking Tyana and winning a small battle near Daphne, Aurelian took possession of Antioch, having promised to grant pardon to all the inhabitants, and — acting on the counsel of the venerable Apollonius — he showed himself most humane and merciful. Next, close by Emessa, he gave battle to Zenobia and to her ally Zaba, — a great battle in which the very fate of the Empire hung in the issue. Already the cavalry of Aurelian were weary, wavering, and about to take flight, when, by divine assistance, a kind of celestial apparition renewed their courage, and the infantry coming to the aid of the cavalry, they rallied stoutly. Zenobia and Zaba were defeated, and the victory [of Aurelian] was complete. Aurelian, thus made master of the East, entered Emessa[1] as conqueror. First of all he presented himself in the temple of Elagabalus, as if to discharge himself of an ordinary vow, — but there he beheld the same divine figure which he had seen come to succour him during the battle. Therefore in that same place he consecrated some temples, with splendid presents; he also erected in Rome a temple to the Sun, and consecrated it with great pomp.

Afterward he marched on Palmyra, to end his labors by the taking of that city. The robber bands of Syria, however, made constant attacks while his army was on the march; and during the siege he was in great danger by being wounded by an arrow.

Finally wearied and discouraged by his losses, Aurelian undertook to write to Zenobia, pledging her — if she would surrender, to preserve her life, — in the following letter.

---

[1] A very sacred city, and a great seat of the worship of the Syrian sun-god Elagabalus.

"*Aurelian, Emperor of Rome and 'Restorer of the Orient'
to Zenobia and those waging war on her side.* You should
have done what I commanded you in my [former] letter. I
promise you life if you surrender. You, O Zenobia, can live
with your family in the place which I will assign you upon
the advice of the venerable Senate. You must deliver to the
treasury of Rome your jewels, your silver, your gold, your
robes of silk, your horses and your camels. The Palmyrenes,
however, shall preserve their local rights."[1]

Zenobia replied to this letter with a pride and boldness,
not at all in accord with her fortune. For she imagined
that she could intimidate him.

"*Zenobia, Queen of the East, to Aurelian Augustus.* No
one, saving you, has ever required of me what you have in
your letter. One ought in war to hearken only to the voice
of courage. You demand that I surrender myself, as if you
did not know that the Queen Cleopatra preferred to die
rather than to live in any other save her [royal] station.
The Persians do not abandon us, and we will wait their succours. The Saracens and the Armenians are on our side.
The brigands of Syria have defeated your army, O Aurelian;
— what will it be when we have received the reënforcements
which come to us from all sides. You will lower then that
tone with which you, — as if already full conqueror, — now
bid me to surrender."

On the reading of this letter the Emperor did not blush,
yet he was angered, and at once assembling his army with
his generals, and surrounding Palmyra on all sides, the
great Emperor devoted his attention to everything; for he
cut off the succours from the Persians, and corrupted the
hordes of Saracens and Armenians, winning them over sometimes by his severity, sometimes by his adroitness; in brief,
after many attacks, the valiant Queen was vanquished. Al-

---

[1] The genuineness of this letter and its answer has been questioned, but
they certainly illustrate the true spirit both of Aurelian and of Zenobia.

though she fled on camels by which she strove to reach the Persians, the cavalrymen sent in pursuit captured her, and brought her to Aurelian.

The tumult of the soldiers — requiring that Zenobia be given up for punishment — was very violent; but Aurelian conceived that it would be shameful to put to death a woman; so he contented himself with executing most of those [men] who had fomented, prepared, and conducted this war, reserving Zenobia to adorn his triumph and to feast the eyes of the Roman People. It is grievous that he must needs place in the number of those massacred the philosopher Longinus, who was, — it is said, — the master of Zenobia in the Greek tongue. It is alleged that Aurelian consented to his death because there was attributed to him that [aforenamed] letter so full of offensive pride.

It is seldom and even difficult that Syrians remain faithful. The Palmyrenes, who had been defeated and conquered, seeing that Aurelian [had gone away and] was busy with the affairs of Europe, wished to give the power to one Achilleus, a kinsman of Zenobia, and stirred up a great revolt. They slew six hundred archers and Sandrion, whom Aurelian had left [as governor] in their region; but the Emperor, ever in arms, hastened back from Europe, and destroyed Palmyra, even as it deserved.

[In his magnificent triumph, celebrated in Rome after Aurelian had conquered Tetricius, the usurping "Emperor of Gaul," and other enemies,] Zenobia was led in procession, exposed to public view, adorned with jewels, and loaded with chains of gold [so heavy that] some of her guards had to hold them up for her. [Later, however, she was treated with great humanity, granted a palace near Rome, and spent her last days in peace and luxury.]

CHAPTER VII

PUBLIC AND PRIVATE LIFE UNDER THE EMPIRE

This is naturally a wide topic. For no other period of antiquity have we so much illuminating material as for the two centuries following the battle of Actium. The result is that we can enter into the life, thoughts, habits, philosophy of the typical "man of the Empire" as is impossible when we come to periods much nearer chronologically to our own. In many of its phases, — its vast private fortunes, its teeming cities, its swarming commerce, and the refinements and artificiality of its general life, — the "Imperial Age" reminds us much of the twentieth century. There is no need to dwell here on the divergencies — caused usually by the presence of slavery and the absence of Christianity. Probably men never came nearer to being able to "fleet the time carelessly as they do in the golden world," than did the upper classes in Italy during the reigns of the better Emperors.

The picture is given a clearer setting when one remembers how, while the "Eternal Empire" seemed daily growing mightier, while wealth, intellect, and inherited nobility seemed never more secure of holding their preëminence, silent social forces were at work which were to undermine the whole glittering fabric, and small bands of "insane" worshipers of a crucified malefactor in Judea were preparing for the mightiest intellectual and religious revolution the world has ever seen.

Although this chapter is necessarily long, it needs little introduction. With the use of his general knowledge of the political history, the student should sift and understand the various extracts given. Thus focussed, the scattered pictures will at length come together into a comprehensive panorama, and an insight will be gained alike into the glory and the rottenness of "Imperial Rome."

74. A Debate in the Senate in Imperial Times

Pliny the Younger, " Letters," book II, letter 11.   Firth's Translation

The letter here presented from the correspondence of Pliny the Younger will give a fairly clear idea of a typical debate in the Senate during the reign of Trajan, and also of the extortions practiced by Roman governors upon the provincials.   It ought to be said that compared with Republican times such malfeasance in office was comparatively and honorably rare.   The Emperors, as a rule, punished oppressive subordinates with a heavy hand, if for no other reason than that it paid to keep the provincials contented. Africa, which Priscus here named had ruled, was under the direct control of the Senate, not of the Emperor, and so more exposed to lax administration.

Marius Priscus, on being accused by the people of Africa whom he had ruled as proconsul, declined to defend himself before the Senate, and asked to have judges appointed to hear the case.   Cornelius Tacitus [the great historian] and myself were instructed to appear [as advocates] for the provincials, and we came to the conclusion that we were bound in honesty to our clients to notify the Senate that the charges of inhumanity and cruelty against Priscus were too serious to be heard by ordinary judges, inasmuch as he was accused of taking bribes to condemn and even to put to death innocent men.

[After considerable debate the Senate ordered that the case should be taken up temporarily by the judges, but that the bribe givers should be summoned to Rome.]   So these witnesses came to Rome,— Vitellius Honoratus and Flavius Martianus.   Honoratus was charged with bribing Priscus to the tune of 300,000 sesterces to exile a Roman eques and put seven of his [non-noble] friends to death.   Martianus was accused of giving Priscus 700,000 sesterces to sentence one Roman eques to still more grievous punishment — for he was beaten with rods, condemned to the mines, and then stran-

gled in prison.   Honoratus — luckily for him — escaped the
investigation of the Senate by dying.   Martianus was
brought before the Senate when Priscus was not present
[and the case was postponed until the next meeting of the
Senate when it came up for disposal].

A very august assembly it was !   The Emperor [Trajan]
presided in his capacity as consul; besides, the month of
January brings crowds of people to Rome, especially Senators ;[1] besides the importance of the case and its notoriety
— increased by the very delays that had occurred — and the
ingrained curiosity of all men to know all details of something very important, had made everybody flock to Rome
from all quarters.   You can imagine how nervous and anxious we were in having to speak in such a gathering, and in
the presence of the Emperor on such an important case.

However, as soon as I had pulled myself together and
collected my thoughts, I began my address, and though
I was nervous, I was on the best of terms with my audience.   I spoke for nearly five hours,[2] for, besides the
twelve water clocks — the biggest I could get — which
had been assigned me, I obtained four others.   And as
things turned out, everything I had feared beforehand
would prove an obstacle to a good speech, really helped
me.

Claudius Marcellinus answered me in behalf of Martianus
[one of the co-defendants], then the Senate was dismissed
and met again on the next day ; for there was no time
to begin a fresh speech, as it would have been broken
off by the fall of night.   On the following day Salvius
Liberalis, a man of shrewd wit, careful in the arrangement
of his speeches, with a pointed style and a fund of learning,
spoke for Priscus, and in his speech he certainly brought

[1] Pliny would imply that in the summer months the Senate meetings
were often very thin.

[2] The Conscript Fathers were patient listeners !

out all that he knew. Cornelius Tacitus replied to him
in a wonderfully eloquent address, marked by that lofty
dignity which is the chief charm of his oratory.   Then
Fronto Catius made another speech on Priscus's behalf,
and he spent more time in appeals for mercy than in
rebutting evidence — as befited the part of the case he
had to deal with. Nightfall halted his speech, but did not
break it off altogether, and so the proceedings lasted over
into the third day. This was quite fine, and just as it
used to be, for the Senate to be interrupted by nightfall,
and for the members to be called upon to sit for three days
running.

Cornutus Tertullus, the consul-designate, a man of high
character, and a devoted champion of justice, gave as his
opinion that the seven hundred thousand sesterces that
Priscus had received should be confiscated to the Treasury ;
that Priscus should be banished from Rome and Italy, and
Martianus [the bribe giver] should be banished from Rome,
Italy, and Africa.[1] Toward the end of his speech, he added
that the Senate felt that, since Tacitus and I, who had been
summoned to plead for the provincials, had fulfilled our
duties with diligence and fearlessness, we had acted in a
manner worthy of the commission intrusted to us.   The
other consul-designate agreed, and all the consulars[2] did
likewise, until it was Pompeius Collega's turn to speak.

He moved that the money received by Priscus be confiscated for the Treasury ; that Martianus should be banished
for five years [only], and Priscus should suffer no other
penalty than that for extortion [i.e. the loss of his dignities]
which had been already passed on him. Opinion was much
divided, and perhaps there was a majority in favor of [this]
less severe proposal — for even some who had supported

[1] Martianus had evidently a business residence in Africa — so this was
a heavy penalty for him.
[2] Ex-consuls.

Cornutus changed sides, and seemed ready to vote for
Collega, who had spoken after them.   But when the House
divided, those who stood near the seats of the consuls [1] began to cross to the side of Cornutus.   Then those who were
allowing themselves to be counted as supporters of Collega
also crossed over.   He was with a mere handful of votes.
Later he complained bitterly of those who led him into his
proposal, especially of Regulus,[2] who failed to support the
measure he himself had suggested [should be made].   But
Regulus is a fickle fellow, rash to a degree, yet a great
coward to boot.

75. The Correspondence of a Provincial Governor and the Emperor Trajan

Pliny the Younger, " Letters," book X, letters 25 ff.   Firth's Translation

About 112 A.D. Trajan appointed Pliny the Younger, a distinguished Senator and literary man, as governor of Bithynia —
a province suffering from previous maladministration.   The nature
of the governor's problems and the obligation he was under of referring very petty matters to the Emperor appears clearly in the
following letters.   This correspondence of Trajan and Pliny (given
here only in small part) is among the most valuable bits of
historical data we have for the whole Imperial Age.

Pliny to Trajan:

The people of Prusa, Sire, have a public bath in a neglected
and dilapidated state.   They wish — with your kind permission — to restore it; but I think a new one ought to be
built, and I reckon you can safely comply with their wishes.

[Then the governor names various ways to find the money,
especially cutting down the free distribution of oil.]

---

[1] *I.e.* the Senators most in honor.
[2] A wealthy, but very unscrupulous, lawyer and advocate, whom Pliny
regarded with especial aversion.

Trajan to Pliny:

If the building of a new bath will not cripple the finances of Prusa, we can indulge their wishes; only it must be understood that no new taxes are to be raised to meet the cost, and that their contributions for necessary expenses shall not show any falling off.

Pliny to Trajan:

A desolating fire broke out in Nicomedia, and destroyed a number of private houses, and two public buildings — the almshouse and the temple of Isis — although a road ran between them. The fire was allowed to spread farther than it need, first owing to the violent wind; second, to the laziness of the citizens, it being generally agreed they stood idly by without moving, and simply watched the conflagration. Besides there was not a single public fire engine or bucket in the place, and not one solitary appliance for mastering a fire. However, these will be provided upon orders I have already given. But, Sire, I would have you consider whether you think a fire company of about 150 men ought not to be formed? I will take care that no one not a genuine fireman shall be admitted, and that the guild should not misapply the charter granted it. Again there would be no trouble in keeping an eye on so small a body.

Trajan to Pliny:

You have formed the idea of a possible fire company at Nicomedia on the model of various others already existing; but remember that the province of Bithynia, and especially city states like Nicomedia, are the prey of factions. Give them the name we may, and however good be the reasons for organization, such associations will soon degenerate into [dangerous] secret societies. It is better policy to provide fire apparatus, and to encourage property holders to make use of them, and if need comes, press the crowd which collects into the same service.

Pliny to Trajan:

Sire, the people of Nicomedia spent 3,229,000 sesterces [about $130,000] upon an aqueduct, which was left in an unfinished state, and I may say in ruin, and they also levied taxes to the extent of 2,000,000 ses. [$80,000] for a second one. This, too, has been abandoned, and to get a water supply those who have wasted these vast sums must go to a new expense. I have visited a splendid clear spring, from which it seems to me the supply ought to be brought to the town [and have formed a scheme that seems practicable].

Trajan to Pliny:

Steps must certainly be taken to provide Nicomedia with a water supply ; and I have full confidence you will undertake the duty with all due care. But I profess it is also part of your diligent duty to find out who is to blame for the waste of such sums of money by the people of Nicomedia on their aqueducts, and whether or no there has been any serving of private interests in this beginning and then abandoning of [public] works. See that you bring to my knowledge whatever you find out.

Pliny to Trajan:

The theater at Nicæa, Sire, the greater part of which has already been constructed — though it is still unfinished — has already cost over 10,000,000 sesterces [$400,000]; — at least so I am told, for the accounts have not been made out; and I am fearful lest the money has been thrown away. For the building has sunk and there are great gaping crevices to be seen, either because the ground is damp, or owing to the [bad quality] of the stone. [It is doubtful if the affair is worth completing.] Just before I came the Nicæans also began to restore the public gymnasium, which had been destroyed by fire, on a larger scale than the old building, and they have already disbursed a considerable sum thereon, and I fear to little purpose [for it is very ill constructed]. Moreover the architect — the rival, to be sure, of the man who began the work — asserts that the walls, although twenty-two feet thick cannot bear the weight placed upon them, because they have not been put together with cement in the middle and have not been strengthened with brickwork. [At Claudiopolis too the public money, it seems, is being wasted on some vast public baths. What is Pliny to do in both cases?]

Trajan to Pliny:

You are the best judge of what to do at Nicæa. It will be enough for me to be informed of the plan you adopt. All Greek peoples have a passion for gymnasia, so perhaps the people of Nicæa have set about building one on a rather lavish scale, but they must be content to cut their coat according to their cloth. You again must decide what advice to give the people of Claudiopolis.

Pliny to Trajan:

When I asked for a statement of the expenditures of the city of Byzantium — which are abnormally high — it was pointed out to me, Sire, that a delegate was sent every year with a complimentary decree to pay his respects to you, and that he received 12,000 sesterces [$480] for so doing. Remembering your instructions [I ordered him to stay at home and to forward the decree by me] in order to lighten the expenses. [I beg you to tell whether I have done right.]

Trajan to Pliny:

You have done quite right, my dear Pliny, in canceling the expenditure of the Byzantines ... for that delegate. ... They will in the future do their duty well enough, even though the decree alone is sent me through you.

Pliny to Trajan :

Sire, a person named Julius Largus of Pontus, whom 1 have never seen or heard of before, has intrusted me with the management of his property with which he seeks to prove his loyalty to you. For he has asked me in his will to undertake as heir the division of his property, and after keeping 50,000 sesterces [$2000], hand over all the remainder to the free cities of Heraclea and Teos. He leaves it to my discretion whether I think it better to erect public works and dedicate them to your glory, or to start an athletic festival, to be held every five years, and to be called the "Trajan Games." I have decided to lay the facts before you [and ask your decision].

Trajan to Pliny :

Julius Largus, in picking you out for your trustworthiness, has acted as though he knew you intimately. So do you consider the circumstances of each place, and the best means of perpetuating his memory, and follow the course you think best.

Pliny's Dealings with the Christians

Pliny to Trajan : [1]

It is my custom, Sire, to refer to you in all cases where I am in doubt, for who can better clear up difficulties and inform me ? I have never been present at any legal examination of the Christians, and I do not know, therefore, what are the usual penalties passed upon them, or the limits of those penalties, or how searching an inquiry should be made. I have hesitated a great deal in considering whether any distinctions should be drawn according to the ages of

---

[1] This letter about the Christians is of unique value. It proves clearly that in Pliny's time the Christians in Asia Minor were decidedly numerous, and it sets forth some of the difficulties the government confronted in dealing with them.

the accused; whether the weak should be punished as severely as the more robust, or whether the man who has once been a Christian gained anything by recanting? [Again] whether the *name* [of being a Christian], even though otherwise innocent of crime, should be punished, or only the crimes that gather around it?

In the meantime, this is the plan which I have adopted in the case of those Christians who have been brought before me. I ask them whether they are Christians, if they say "Yes," then I repeat the question the second time, and also a third — warning them of the penalties involved; and if they persist, I order them away to prison. For I do not doubt that — be their admitted crime what it may — their pertinacity and inflexible obstinacy surely ought to be punished.

There were others who showed similar mad folly, whom I reserved to be sent to Rome, as they were Roman citizens. Later, as is commonly the case, the mere fact of my entertaining the question led to a multiplying of accusations and a variety of cases were brought before me. An anonymous pamphlet was issued,[1] containing a number of names [of alleged Christians]. Those who denied that they were or had been Christians and called upon the gods with the usual formula, reciting the words after me, and those who offered incense and wine before your image — which I had ordered to be brought forward for this purpose, along with the [regular] statues of the gods, — all such I considered acquitted, — especially as they cursed the name of Christ, which it is said *bona fide* Christians cannot be induced to do.

Still others there were, whose names were supplied by an informer. These first said they were Christians, then denied it, insisting they had been, "but were so no longer"; some of them having "recanted many years ago," and more than

---

[1] Probably the work of the Pagan priests.

one "full twenty years back." These all worshiped your
image and the god's statues and cursed the name of Christ.

But they declared their guilt or error was simply this —
on a fixed day they used to meet before dawn and recite a
hymn among themselves to Christ, as though he were a god.
So far from binding themselves by oath to commit any
crime, they swore to keep from theft, robbery, adultery,
breach of faith, and not to deny any trust money deposited
with them when called upon to deliver it. This ceremony
over, they used to depart and meet again to take food — but
it was of no special character, and entirely harmless.[1] They
[also] had ceased from this practice after the edict [I
issued] — by which, in accord with your orders, I forbade
all secret societies.

I then thought it the more needful to get at the facts behind their statements. Therefore I placed two women,
called "deaconesses," under torture, but I found only a de-
based superstition carried to great lengths,[2] so I postponed
my examination, and immediately consulted you. This
seems a matter worthy of your [prompt] consideration,
especially as so many people are endangered. Many of all
ages and both sexes are put in peril of their lives by their
accusers; and the process will go on, for the contagion of
this superstition has spread not merely through the free
towns, but into the villages and farms. Still I think it can
be halted and things set right. Beyond any doubt, the
temples — which were nigh deserted — are beginning again
to be thronged with worshipers; the sacred rites, which
long have lapsed, are now being renewed, and the food for
the sacrificial victims is again finding a sale — though up to
recently it had almost no market. So one can safely infer

[1] Christians were accused of fearful orgies and cannibalism.
[2] Note the irony of this statement. We know that Pliny was a high-
minded, honorable, and kindly man, who would surely have found a vast
deal to commend in Christianity — if he had truly understood it.

how vast numbers could be reclaimed, if only there were a chance given for repentance.

Trajan to Pliny:

You have adopted the right course, my dear Pliny, in examining the cases of those cited before you as Christians; for no hard and fast rule can be laid down covering such a wide question. The Christians are not to be hunted out. If brought before you, and the offense is proved, they are to be punished, but with this reservation — if any one denies he is a Christian, and makes it clear he is not, by offering prayer to our gods, then he is to be pardoned on his recantation, no matter how suspicious his past. As for anonymous pamphlets, they are to be discarded absolutely, whatever crime they may charge, for they are not only a precedent of a very bad type, but they do not accord with the spirit of our age.

76. A Business Panic in Rome

Tacitus, "Annals," book VI, chaps. **16–17**.   Church and Broadrib's Translation

In 33 A.D. occurred a direful business panic in Rome, which probably caused far more stir than the report — very likely that year — of a petty outbreak in Judæa against the procurator Pontius Pilate.   A careful study of the story will reveal a good deal as to business conditions at Rome, the state of the currency, the laws as to the taking of interest, etc.

[At this time, 33 A.D.] a powerful host of accusers fell with sudden fury on the class which systematically increased its wealth by usury in defiance of the law of Cæsar the Dictator, defining the terms of lending money, and of holding estates in Italy, a law long obsolete because the public good is sacrificed to private interest. The curse of usury was indeed of old standing in Rome, and a most frequent cause of sedition and discord, and it was therefore

repressed even in the early days of a less corrupt morality.
[Various laws were enacted to check it.]   On this occasion,
however, Gracchus the prætor, to whose jurisdiction the
inquiry had fallen, felt himself compelled by the number
of persons endangered to refer the matter to the Senate.
In their dismay, the Senators, not one of whom was free
from similar guilt, threw themselves on the Emperor's
indulgence.   He yielded, and a year and six months was
granted — within which every one was to settle his private
accounts conformably to the requirements of the law.

Hence followed a scarcity of money, a great shock being
given to all credit, the current coin too, — in consequence of
the conviction of so many persons, and the sale of their
property, — being locked up in the imperial Treasury or the
public exchequer.   To meet this, the Senate had directed
that every creditor should have two thirds of his capital
secured on estates in Italy.   Creditors, however, were suing
for payment in full, and it was not respectable for persons
when sued to break faith.   So, at first, there were clamorous
meetings and importunate entreaties; then noisy applica-
tions to the prætor's court.   And the very device intended
as a remedy, the sale and purchase of estates, proved the
contrary, as the usurers had hoarded up all their money for
the buying of land.

The facilities for selling were followed by a fall in prices,
and the deeper a man was in debt, the more reluctantly did
he part with his property, and many were utterly ruined.
The destruction of private wealth precipitated the fall of
rank and reputation; till at last the Emperor interposed
his aid by distributing throughout the banks 100,000,000
sesterces [$4,000,000], and allowing freedom to borrow
without interest for three years, provided the borrower gave
security to the state in land to double the amount.   Credit
was thus restored, and gradually private lenders were
found.   The purchase, too, of estates was not carried out,

according to the letter of the Senate's decree, rigor at the outset, as usual with such matters, becoming negligent in the end.

77. SUMMARY OF SOME BENEFACTIONS TO ROMAN CITIES BY PRIVATE INDIVIDUALS

Summarized from Duruy, "History of Rome"

The Imperial Age was one of great benevolence if we are willing to give that name to acts of generosity which were often too showy and ostentatious to merit the highest praise. The cases here cited are nearly all (except that of Pliny) based upon the evidence of inscriptions.

Ummidia Quadratilla built at Casinum an amphitheater and a temple.

Secundus at Bordeaux built an aqueduct costing 2,000,000 ses [$80,000].

Perigrinus [a character in Lucian] is represented as giving during his lifetime his whole property, 30 talents, to his native city.

Crinas of Marseilles expended 10,000,000 sesterces [$400,000] in rebuilding the walls of that city.

The two brothers Stertinus [1] gave a still larger sum than the last for erecting public buildings in their native Naples.

Hiero gave 2000 talents [over $2,000,000] to Laodicea, his native town.

The younger Pliny spent on his native town of Como, 11,000,000 ses. [$440,000], though by no means a very rich man. He founded a library, a school, and a charity institute for poor children; also a temple to Ceres, with spacious porticoes to shelter tradespeople who came to the fair held in honor of that goddess. His grandfather had already built

[1] One of these men was a famous physician who boasted that he gained 600,000 ses. ($24,000) by yearly fees.

for the town a costly portico, and provided the money for decorating the city gates.

[Like instances of civic spirit and benevolence could be multiplied ad infinitum.]

78. MARTIAL ON PHASES OF LIFE IN ROME

Martial, " Epigrams," book IX, 3. Bohn Translation

In the reign of Domitian the capital was utterly overrun by a discordant, heterogeneous multitude of foreigners, making the city resemble New York or Chicago of to-day, and almost swamping the old Italian element.   The courtly poet seizes the fact to pay a compliment to the Emperor.

What race is so distant from us, what race is so barbarous, O Cæsar, that from it no spectator is present in thy city!   The cultivator of Rhodope[1] is here from Hæmus[1] [sacred to] Orpheus.   The Scythian who drinks the blood of his horses is here; he, too, who quaffs the waters of the Nile nearest their springing; and he also whose shore is laved by the most distant ocean.   The Arabian has hastened hither; the Sabæans have hastened; and here the Cilicians have anointed themselves with their own native perfume. Here come the Sicambrians with their hair all twisted into a knot, and here the frizzled Ethiopians.   Yet though their speech is all so different, they all speak together hailing thee [O Emperor] as the true father of thy country.

[Rome had her great shopping district (mainly on streets leading into the Forum), and seemingly her " department stores "; also her class of inveterate shoppers, as Martial here testifies. (*Epigrams*, IX, 49.)]

Mamurra, after having walked long and anxiously in the bazaars where golden Rome proudly displayed her riches, examined the handsome young slaves, yes devoured them

[1] High mountains in Thrace.

with his eyes — not those slaves exposed in the open shops,
but those kept for [sale to] select people in private rooms,
and are not exhibited to common folk, such as I.   Tired of
this inspection he uncovers various tables, square ones and
round; next asks to see some rich ivory ornaments displayed on the upper shelves.   Then, after four times
measuring a dinner couch for six guests, all adorned as it
was with tortoise shell, he regretted sorrowfully "that it
was not big enough for his citron wood table."   He consulted
his nose to find out if the bronzes had the true Corinthian
aroma, and criticized some statues by Polycletus!   Next,
complaining that some crystal vases had been spoiled by
mixing in glass, he marked and had set aside ten myrrhine
cups.   He weighed ancient bowls, and inquired for goblets
that had been ennobled by the hand of Mentor.   He counted
emeralds set in chased gold, and examined the largest pearl
ear-pendants.   He sought on every counter for real sar-
donyxes, and cheapened some large jaspers.   At last, when
forced by fatigue to retire, at the eleventh hour he bought
two small cups for one small coin and bore them home
himself.[1]

[What a modest dinner party ought to be like is thus expounded.
(*Epigrams*, X, 48.)]

The priesthood of Isis proclaim the eighth hour,[2] and the
guard with their javelins march back to quarters.   Now
the warm baths have reached the right temperature; an
hour before they exhaled a dreadful excess of steam; at
noon the baths of Nero had been insufferably hot.   Stella,
Nepos, Canius, Cerialis, Flaccus, are you coming to dine with
me?   The dinner couch holds seven, we are only six: —

[1] Anybody of real gentility would at least have had a slave to carry
his purchases.
[2] Two o'clock. The hours seem to have been called off at the Temple
of Isis.

so add Lupus. My bailiff's wife has brought me mallows
to aid digestion, and other treasures of the garden, lettuce,
sliced leeks, and mint; slices of egg shall crown anchovies
dressed with rue; and there shall be sows' teats swimming
in tunny sauce. These will serve as whets to our appetite.
My little dinner will be put on the table at once. There
will be a kid snatched from the jaws of a hungry wolf;
that will be nice tidbits that do not need to be carved;
there will be haricot beans, and young cabbages. To these
a chicken will be added; and a ham that has already graced
the table thrice. For dessert I will give ripe fruits, wine
from a Nomentan flagon [of a choice old vintage]. All
shall be seasoned with mirth free from bitterness; there
shall be no license of speech that brings repentance on the
morrow, and nothing shall be said that we would wish
unsaid.[1] But my guests may talk of the rival factions of
the circus, and my cups shall make no man guilty [of in-
discretions].

79. How Horace got an Education

Horace, "Satires," book I, 6, ll. 70-90. Adapted from the Bohn Translation

During the later Republic and Early Empire the craving for a
good education was probably more prevalent than in any other age,
barring the present. Even the lower classes were not usually
illiterate (witness the numerous wall scribblings at Pompeii), although there was no system of free public schools. What one
father did to give his son all possible advantages is told in this
noble and touching tribute by Horace.

If I dare venture to speak in my own praise, and say that
I live undefiled, innocent, and dear to my friends, let me
confess that I owe all this to my father. A poor man he
was, and on a lean farm, yet he was not content to send me

---

[1] *I.e.* vain talk on political matters which might be seized upon by
professional " accusers " [*delatores*] for ruinous prosecutions.

to a local school [at Venusia, his home town] under the
pedant Flavius, though boys of pretensions, sons of prominent centurions, went there with their school bags and writing tablets slung over their left arms, and carrying their
teacher the fee in their hands on the Ides of eight months
in the year.[1] On the contrary, he had the spirit to bring
me even as a child to Rome, to be taught those liberal arts
which a senator or eques requires for his children. If any
one had seen my dress and the slaves that attended me in
the big city, he would have guessed that I was maintained
by some hereditary estate. My father — most faithful of
guardians — was ever present at all my studies.[2] Why
need I say more? He preserved my modesty (the first
point of virtue) not merely untainted, but free from the
very rumor of taint. He was not afraid lest any one should
reproach him [for giving an education to a son] who turned
out to be an auctioneer, or as my father was, a taxgatherer.
I should not then have complained. But all the more is
praise due to him, and from me the greater gratitude. As
long as I keep my senses I will never be ashamed of such a
father, nor apologize for my [humble] birth as do so many,
asserting "it is no fault of theirs."

80. How Pliny Endowed a School

Pliny the Younger, "Letters," book IV, letter 13.   Firth's Translation

The following letter by Pliny to the famous historian Tacitus is
witness to the interest taken in education under the Empire.   The
school here mentioned was, of course, not a mere primary school, —
that existed surely already at Comum, — but one of the higher
learning.   Pliny's munificence was by no means unique.   Prob-

---

[1] Roman schoolmasters were paid usually once per month for the eight
months per year that school was kept.

[2] He did not let his son fall into the care of an irresponsible slave pedagogue.

ably in no other age was so much money donated by wealthy men for education, — especially in their home towns, — until recently in America.

[This letter contains a request] let me tell you why I ask it. When I was last in my native district [Comum, North Italy] a son of a fellow townsman of mine, a youth under age, came to pay his respects to me. I said to him, "Do you keep up your studies?" "Yes," he answered. "Where?" I asked. "At Milan," was the reply. "But why not here?" I pressed. Then the lad's father, who was with him, . . . said, "Because we have no teachers here." "How is that?" I asked. "It is a matter of urgent importance to you who are fathers," and it so chanced that luckily quite a number of fathers were listening to me,[1] "that your children should get their education here at home."

"For where can they pass their time so pleasantly as in their native town, where can they be brought up so virtuously as under their parent's eyes; or so inexpensively as at home? If you put your money together, you could hire teachers at a trifling cost, and you could add to their stipends the sum you now spend on your son's lodgings and travel money — no small sum. I have no children of my own, still, in the interests of the community — which I may consider as my child or my parent — I am ready to contribute a third part of what you may decide to club together upon. I would even promise the whole sum if I did not fear that if I did so, my generosity might be corrupted to serve private interests, as I see is the case in many places where teachers are employed at the public charge. There is only one way of preventing the evil, and that is by leaving the right of employing the teachers to the parents alone, who will be careful to make a right choice if they are obliged to find [part of] the

[1] We may imagine the conversation taking place in a crowded atrium, where many provincial gentlemen had come to pay respects to their very distinguished townsman. Pliny was consul in 100 A.D.

money.[1] You cannot make your children a better present
than this, nor can you do your place a better turn."

And now [my friend Tacitus] since this is a serious matter,
I beg you to look out for some teachers among the throng
of learned men who gather around you, whom we can sound
on the matter, but not in such a way as to pledge ourselves
to employ any of them. For I wish to give the parents a
perfectly free hand. They must judge and choose for
themselves : I have only a sympathetic interest and a share
in the cost. So if you find any one who thinks himself
capable, let him go to Comum, but on the express understanding that he builds upon no certainty beyond his confidence in himself. Farewell.

81. Flogging Schoolmasters at Rome

Martial, " Epigrams," book X, 62. Adapted from Bohn Translation

That the Roman schoolmasters, no less than their Greek predecessors, relied on the scourge to quicken slow wits is shown in
the following from this writer of the end of the first century A.D.

Sir Schoolmaster — show pity upon your simple scholars,
at least if you wish to have many a long-haired boy attendant upon your lectures, and the class seated around your
critical table love you. Then would no teacher of arithmetic or swift writing [2] have a greater ring of pupils around
him. Hot and bright are the days now under the flaming
constellation of the lion ; and fervid July is ripening the
bursting harvest. So let your Scythian scourge with its
dreadful thongs, such as flogged Marsyas of Celænæ,[3] and
your formidable cane — the schoolmaster's scepter — be laid
aside, and sleep until the Ides of October. Surely in summer time, if the boys keep their health, they do enough.

---

[1] Pliny is evidently thinking of Roman towns where the schools had
"gone into politics " with the usual unhappy results.

[2] A kind of shorthand.

[3] Who rashly challenged Apollo to a flute contest.

82. CONTEMPORARY TESTIMONY TO THE GREATNESS AND BENEFICENCE OF THE ROMAN EMPIRE

Collected in Duruy, "History of Rome," vol. VI

There is a wealth of evidence that from the days of Augustus down, say, to the death of Alexander Severus (235 A.D.) the Roman Empire was regarded as an almost unqualified success. This is true not merely of the ruling classes, but especially true with the provincials; indeed for long the latter, who were the direct beneficiaries of the law, order, and good government brought by the Cæsars, were far more enthusiastic about the Imperial régime than the lordly senatorial families which had been omnipotent in the days of the Republic.

Plutarch speaks of Rome, though a firm admirer himself of conquered Greece, as "a sacred and beautiful goddess," and again, as "the firm anchor which stops and holds securely all things human in the midst of the whirlwind by which they are driven."

Aristeides the Orator, writing in the reign of Antoninus Pius, thus apostrophizes the Roman power, "Men have laid off their iron armor to put on festal garments, and your provinces are covered with rich cities, jewels of your Empire, which glitter like the costly necklace of a rich matron. Your land is but one immense garden."

Tertullian (a strict Christian, and no friendly critic of Pagan power) thus speaks of the empire, writing about 200 A.D. (De Anima, 30): "The world is every day better known, better cultivated and more wealthy. The roads are open to commerce. The deserts are changed into fruitful domains; agriculture is pursued where once rose forests; sowing, where once could be seen only barren rocks. Drained are the marshes. No more do the flocks fear the wild beast. No longer is there any island to fill men with horror; no rocks to strike them with fear. Everywhere there are houses, people, cities. Everywhere there is life!"

Appian, the second-century historian, says less rhetori-
cally on the same subject (Præf., 6): "For two hundred
years this imperial system has lasted. In that period the
city [of Rome] has been adorned in a marvelous manner,
the revenues of the Empire have been increased, and by the
blessing of continual peace the [provincial] peoples have
attained to the height of happiness."

A maxim of the Emperor Tiberius well illustrates the
attitude of the imperial government, touching the taxation
of the provincials, " A good shepherd shears his sheep, but
does not flay them."

83. THE GREAT BUILDINGS IN ROME ABOUT 75 A.D.

**Pliny the Elder, " Natural History," book XXXVI, chap. 24. Bohn
Translation**

We have this description, written about 75 A.D., of some of
the remarkable buildings and other public works at Rome, which
made the city unrivaled in Antiquity, and venerable and wonderful to-day.

[In great buildings] as well as in other things the rest
of the world has been outdone by us Romans. If, indeed,
all the buildings in our City are considered in the aggregate,
and supposing them — so to say — all thrown together in
one vast mass, the united grandeur of them would lead
one to imagine that we were describing another world,
accumulated in a single spot.

Not to mention among our great works the Circus Maximus, that was built by the Dictator Cæsar — one stadium
broad and three in length — and occupying with the adjacent buildings no less than four jugera [about 2½ acres]
with room for no less than 160,000 spectators seated, — am
I not, however, to include in the number of our magnificent
structures the Basilica of Paulus with its admirable Phry-
gian columns [built also in Julius Cæsar's day], the

Forum of the late Emperor Augustus, the Temple of Peace
erected by the Emperor Vespasian Augustus — some of
the finest work the world has ever seen? [and many
others].

We behold with admiration pyramids that were built
by kings, while the very ground alone that was purchased
by the Dictator Cæsar, for the construction of his Forum,
cost 100,000,000 sesterces [$4,000,000]. If, too, an enor-
mous expenditure has its attractions for any one whose
mind is influenced by money matters, be it known that
the house in which Clodius [Cicero's enemy] dwelt . . .
was purchased by him at a price of 14,800,000 sesterces
[$592,000] — a thing which I for my part look upon as
no less astonishing than the monstrous follies that have
been displayed by kings.

[Frequently praise is given to the great sewer system
of Rome.] There are seven "rivers" made to flow, by
artificial channels, beneath the city. Rushing onward like
so many impetuous torrents, they are compelled to carry
off and sweep away all the sewerage; and swollen as they
are by the vast accession of the rain water, they reverberate
against the sides and bottoms of their channels. Occasionally too the Tiber, overflowing, is thrown backward in its
course, and discharges itself by these outlets. Obstinate
is the struggle that ensues between the meeting tides, but
so firm and solid is the masonry that it is able to offer an
effectual resistance. Enormous as are the accumulations
that are carried along above, the work of the channels
never gives way. Houses falling spontaneously to ruins,
or leveled with the ground by conflagrations are continually battering against them; now and then the ground is
shaken by earthquakes, and yet — built as they were in
the days of Tarquinius Priscus, seven hundred years ago —
these constructions have survived, all but unharmed.

[Passing to the dwellings of the city] in the consulship

of Lepidus and Catulus [78 B.C.] we learn on good authority there was not in all Rome a finer house than that belonging to Lepidus himself, but yet — by Hercules! — within
twenty-five years the very same house did not hold the hun-
dredth rank simply in the City![1] Let anybody calculate —
if he please — considering this fact, the vast masses of marble, the productions of painters, the regal treasures that must
have been expended in bringing these hundred mansions to
vie with one that in its day had been the most sumptuous
and celebrated in all the City; and then let him reflect that,
since then and down to the present, these houses had all
of them been surpassed by others without number. There
can be no doubt that the great fires [in Rome] are a punishment inflicted upon us for our luxury; but such are our
habits, that in spite of such warnings, we cannot be made to
understand that there are things in existence more perish-
able than even man himself.

But let us now turn our attention to some marvels that,
if justly appreciated, may be pronounced to remain unsur-
passed. Quintus Marcius Rex [prætor in 144 B.C.] upon
being commanded by the Senate to repair the Appian Aqueduct and that of the Anio, constructed during his prætorship
a new aqueduct that bore his name, and was brought
hither by a channel pierced through the very sides of mountains. Agrippa [prime minister of Augustus] during his
ædileship, united the Marcian and the "Virgin" Aqueducts
and repaired and strengthened the channels of others. He
also formed 700 wells, in addition to 500 fountains, and 130
reservoirs, many of them magnificently adorned. Upon
these works too he erected 300 statues of marble or bronze,
and 400 marble columns, and all this in the space of a
single year! In the work which he has written in com-
memoration of his ædileship, he also informs us that public
games were celebrated for the space of fifty-seven days and

[1] Not to mention, of course, the notable country villas.

170 gratuitous bathing places were opened [to the public].
The number of these [public baths] at Rome has vastly
increased since his time.

The preceding aqueducts, however, have all been surpassed
by the costly work which has more recently been completed
by the Emperors Gaius [Caligula] and Claudius. Under
these princes the Curtian and the Cærulean Waters with
the "New Anio" were brought a distance of forty miles,
and at so high a level that all the hills — whereon Rome
is built — were supplied with water. The sum expended
on these works was 350,000,000 sesterces [$14,000,000].
If we take into account the abundant supply of water to
the public, for baths, ponds, canals, household purposes,
gardens, places in the suburbs and country houses, and then
reflect upon the distances that are traversed [from the
sources on the hills], the arches that have been constructed,
the mountains pierced, the valleys leveled, — we must perforce admit that there is nothing more worthy of our admiration throughout the whole universe.

84. The Extent of the City of Rome

Pliny the Elder, "Natural History," book III, chap. 9.   Bohn Translation

The following short sketch of Rome, its streets, buildings, etc.,
is given us by a careful author, writing in the reign of Vespasian
(69–79 A.D.).   While the area of Rome was far inferior to various
great modern capitals, probably the masses of the population were
so compactly housed that the inhabitants in Pliny's time numbered
well up to 1,500,000, although any estimates must be very uncertain.

Romulus left the city of Rome, if we are to believe those
who state the very greatest number, with only three gates,
and no more. When the Vespasians[1] were Emperors and
Censors in the year of the building of the city, 826 [73 A.D.],

---

[1] Titus was colleague with his father, Vespasian.

the circumference of the walls which surrounded it was thirteen and two-fifths miles. Surrounding as it does the Seven Hills, the city is divided into fourteen districts, with 265 crossroads under the guardianship of the Lares.[1] If a straight line is drawn from the mile column placed at the entrance of the Forum to each of the gates, which are at present thirty-seven in number — taking care to count only once the twelve double gates, and to omit the seven old ones, which no longer exist — the total result will be a straight line of twenty miles and 765 paces. But if we draw a straight line from the same mile column to the very last of the houses, including therein the Prætorian camp [in the suburb] and follow throughout the line ot the streets, the result will be something over seventy miles. Add to these calculations the [great] height of the houses, and then a person may form a fair idea of this city, and surely he must confess that no other place in the world can vie with it in size.

On the eastern side it is bounded by the mound (*agger*) of Tarquinius Superbus — a work of surpassing grandeur; for he raised it so high as to be on a level with the walls on the side on which the city lay most exposed to attack from the neighboring plains. On all the other sides it has been fortified — either with lofty walls, or steep and precipitous hills; yet it has come to pass, that the buildings of Rome — increasing and extending beyond all bounds — have now united many [outlying] towns to it.[2]

85. The Collapse of Houses and the Fires in Rome

Strabo, "Geography," book V, chap. 3.   Bohn Translation

Only the upper classes at Rome dwelt in marble palaces. The majority of people lodged in *insulæ*, huge tenement houses, high,

[1] A little chapel to the Lares would stand at each crossing.

[2] Thus the houses were practically continuous all the way to Tibur, Arcia, and other suburban towns.

ill ventilated, unsanitary.   Often these must have been vile rook-
eries, but fortunately in Italy one can live most of the time in the
open air.   Houses of this type were exposed to constant danger
by collapse or conflagration, as is told by Strabo.

[In Rome there is continual need] of wood and stone for
ceaseless building caused by the frequent falling down of
houses, and on account of conflagrations and of sales which
seem never to cease.   These sales are a kind of voluntary
falling down of houses, each owner knocking down and re-
building according to his individual taste.   For these purposes the numerous quarries, forests, and rivers [in the
region] which convey the materials, offer wonderful facilities.

Augustus Cæsar endeavored to avert from the city the
dangers alluded to, and instituted a company of freedmen,
who should be ready to lend their assistance in the case of
conflagration, while as a preventive against falling houses
he decreed that all new buildings should not be carried to
the same height as formerly, and those erected along the
public ways should not exceed seventy feet in height.[1]   But
these improvements must have ceased except for the facilities
afforded [to Rome] by the quarries, the forests, and the ease
of transport.

86. THE MANIA FOR LITERARY FAME IN IMPERIAL TIMES

Friedlaender, " Roman Life and Manners," English Translation, vol. III, p. 45

A well-known German writer has collected these instances of the
intense yearning of the men of the Empire for literary celebrity.
Vast quantities of Greek and Latin prose and poetry were ground
out, and inflicted on the age.   It is a pathetic sign of the decline
of true literary taste and ability that so little of what once passed
as the work of genius has survived ; while probably most of what
was lost deserved its fate !

[1] Rome was evidently cursed with many flimsily constructed "sky
scrapers."   Trajan about a hundred years after Augustus reduced the
maximum building height to only sixty feet.

The grave of a Roman boy, apparently the son of a freedman, named Quintus Sulpicius Maximus, who died early in
his twelfth year, has been discovered at Rome.   According
to the inscription on his tomb, he competed for the prize in
the Capitoline *agon* [1] in the year 94, with fifty-two Greek
poets; "owing to the talent he displayed, the favor which
his tender years aroused became admiration; he came out of
the contest with honor."   The 43 Greek hexameters impro-
vised by him on the theme "What Zeus said when he
reproached Helios for lending his chariot to Phaethon"(probably a common subject for the rhetoric schools) were engraved
upon the monument, "that it might not be thought the
parents were influenced in their judgment by their affection."
They give evidence of a diligent study of the Greek epic.
Of two Greek epigrams in praise of the deceased, one asserts
that sickness and exhaustion carried him off, since he devoted himself day and night to the Muses.

In 110 the thirteen-year-old Lucius Valerius Prudens of
Histonium [an Italian town] was unanimously awarded the
prize.

Besides the Capitoline contest, Domitian held another
competition yearly on March 19, the festival of Minerva, the
object of his special worship at his country seat near Alba.
One of the members of a college founded by the Emperor,
elected by lot to preside, superintended the arrangements;
in addition to theatrical representations and magnificent
combats of wild beasts, there were oratorial and poetical
competitions.   As late as the fourth century poets as well
as athletes and musicians took part in the Pythian *agon*
(contest) at Carthage, as is shown by Saint Augustine's
mention of his own coronation as a poet by the proconsul
[of Africa].

[1] A contest especially between composers of Greek and Latin poetry.

87. ORATORY IN THE ROMAN COURTS

Pliny the Younger, "Letters," book II, letter 14. Firth's Translation

As political freedom gradually ceased under the Empire, oratory was more and more confined to the courts but in the argument of cases an interest was maintained that was often entirely disproportionate to the importance of the suit. Forensic oratory was practically the only public way a young man of good family could distinguish himself unless he joined the army. In the opinion of true lovers of the art, however, by 100 A.D. the advocate's profession was in a very bad state, and in great danger of falling into contempt. Its evils and abuses are here explained by Pliny.

Yes [you Maximus, my correspondent] are quite right: my time is fully taken up by cases in the Centumviral Court, but they give me more worry than pleasure, for most of them are of a minor and unimportant nature. [Most of the advocates are young men without standing, and] make their first beginnings on the hardest subjects. Yet, by Heaven, before my time — to use an old man's phrase — not even the highest-born youths had any standing here, unless they were introduced by a man of consular rank.

Now all modesty and respect are thrown to the winds, and one man is as good as another. So far from being introduced they burst in. The audiences follow them as if they were actors, bought and paid to do so; the agent [of the orator] is there to meet them in the middle of the court-house (basilica), where the doles of money are handed over as openly as doles of food at a banquet; and they are ready to pass from one court to another for a bribe. [They are made fun of for their readiness to cry "bravo"] yet this disgraceful practice gets worse every day. Yesterday two of my own nomenclators — young men I admit, about the age of those who have just assumed the toga — were enticed off to join the claque for three denarii [about 50 cents]

apiece.　Such is the outlay you must make to get a reputa‐
tion for eloquence !

At that price you can fill the benches, however many
there are; you can obtain a great throng and get thunders
of applause as soon as the conductor gives the signal.　For
a signal is absolutely necessary for people who do not
understand, and do not even *listen* to the speeches; and
many of these fellows do not listen at all, though they
applaud as heartily as any.　If you chance to be crossing
the courthouse, and wish to know how any one is speaking,
there is no need to stop to listen.　It is quite safe to guess
on the principle that he who is speaking worst gets the most
applause.

The singsong style [of this claque] only wants the clap‐
ping of hands, or rather cymbals and drums, to make them
like the priests of Cybele, for as for howlings, — that is the
only word to express the unseemly applause, — they have
enough and to spare.

88. The Life of a Refined Roman Gentleman

Pliny the Younger, "Letters," book III, letter 1.　Firth's Translation

If at its worst a Roman magnate's life was one of stupid sensu‐
ality, at its best it represented an almost ideal refinement and
cultivated leisure.　Pliny's friend here described must have been a
most charming companion　Very pleasant, indeed, might life be
during the early Empire — if one belonged to the favored classes.

I do not think I have ever spent a more delightful time
than during my recent visit to Spurinna's house; indeed
I enjoyed myself so much that if it is my fortune to grow
old, there is no one whom I should prefer to take as my
model in old age, as there is nothing more methodical than
that time of life.　Personally I like to see men map out
their lives with the regularity of the fixed courses of the
stars, and especially old men.　For while one is young a

little disorder and rush — so to speak — is not unbecoming; but for old folks, whose days of exertion are past, and in whom personal ambition is disgraceful, a placid and well-ordered life is highly suitable. That is the principle upon which Spurinna acts most religiously; even trifles, or what would be trifles were they not of daily occurrence, he goes through in fixed order, and, as it were, orbit.

In the morning he keeps his couch; at the second hour he calls for his shoes and walks three miles, exercising mind as well as body. If he has friends with him, the time is passed in conversation on the noblest of themes, otherwise a book is read aloud, and sometimes this is done even when his friends are present, but never in such a way as to bore them. Then he sits down, and there is more talk for pref-erence; afterward he enters his carriage, taking with him either his wife — who is a pattern lady — or one of his friends, a distinction I recently enjoyed. How delightful, how charming that privacy is! What glimpses of old times one gets! What noble deeds and noble men he tells you of! What lessons you drink in! Yet at the same time it is his wont to so blend his learning with modesty, that he never seems to be playing the schoolmaster.

After riding seven miles he walks another mile, then resumes his seat, or betakes himself to his room and his pen; for he composes, both in Latin and Greek, the most scholarly lyrics. They have a wonderful grace, wonderful sweetness and wonderful humor, and the chastity of the writer enhances its charm. When he is told that the bath-ing hour has come — which is the ninth hour in winter and the eighth in summer — he takes a walk naked in the sun, if there is no wind. Then he plays at ball for a long spell, throwing himself heartily into the game, for it is by means of this kind of active exercise that he battles with old age.

After his bath he lies down and waits a little while ere taking food, listening in the meantime to the reading of

some light and pleasant book. All this time his friends
are at perfect liberty to imitate his example or do anything
else they prefer. Then dinner is served, the table being as
bright as it is modest, and the silver plain and old-fashioned:
he has also some Corinthian vases in use, for which he has
a taste but not a mania. The dinner is often relieved by
actors of comedy, so that the pleasures of the table may
have a seasoning of letters. Even in the summer the meal
lasts well into the night, but no one finds it long, for it has
kept up with such good humor and charm. The consequence
is that, though he has passed his seventy-seventh year, his
hearing and eyesight are as good as ever, his body is still
active and alert, and the only symptom of his age is his
wisdom.

This is the sort of life that I [Pliny] have vowed and
determined to forestall, and I shall enter upon it with zest,
as soon as my age justifies me in beating a retreat.

89. A WEALTHY ROMAN'S FORTUNE

**Pliny the Elder, "Natural History," book XXXIII, chap. 47. Bohn
Translation**

Great fortunes under the Empire fell into two general classes, —
those founded on commerce, and those founded on land. A good
instance of the latter is here cited from Pliny. Isidorus must
have been a great territorial lord, — almost a petty prince upon
his vast domains. It was estates like his — worked by cheap
slave labor — which ruined the honest peasant farmers of Italy.

Gaius Cæcilius Claudius Isidorus in the consulship of
Gaius Asinius Gallus and Gaius Marcius Censorinus [8 B.C.]
upon the sixth day before the calends of February declared
by his will, that though he had suffered great losses by the
civil wars, he was still able to leave behind him 4116 slaves,
3600 yoke of oxen, and 257,000 head of other kinds of

cattle,[1] besides in ready money 60,000,000 sesterces [about $2,400,000]. Upon his funeral he ordered 1,100,000 sesterces [about $44,000] to be expended.

90. A Roman Seaside Villa

Statius, " Silvæ," book II, 2 (abridged).   Slater's Translation

About 90 A. D. a Roman poet wrote this description of a friend's villa on the beautiful bay of Naples.   Despite somewhat strained and flowery language, we get a good idea of the charms of the location and the elegance and luxury of the building.   There is no reason, however, to believe that this villa surpassed many others of its kind.

Between the walls that bear the name of the Sirens and the rocks burdened with Tyrrhene Minerva's temple, stands a lofty mansion that looks out upon the Bay of Puteoli.   This is ground dear to Bromius.   On the high hills ripens a vintage that need not be jealous of Falernian vats.

The sheltered waters, the crescent bay break a passage through the arc of cliff on either hand.   The charm that first meets the sight is a steaming bathhouse with twin cupolas.   From the land a rivulet of fresh water flows to meet the brine.   From the shore, along the long counterscarps of cliff, the colonnade makes its way, worthy of a city.   The long platform dominates the rough rocks.   Where once was blinding dust and dazzling sunshine — a wild, unlovely track — it is now a joy to pass.

One hall [of the villa] looks out upon the sunrise and the fresh beams of Phœbus, another keeps him back at his setting and will not suffer the afterglow to pass.   Here are rooms that resound with the voices of the sea : here are others that refuse to know the thunderous surges, but rather the silence of the land.

[1] Note how cattle and slaves are lumped together as property of essentially the same kind.

What need to tell of statues fashioned long since in wax and bronze? [Masterpieces of Apelles and Myro and Phidias]; bronzes from the funeral fire of Corinth; busts of great captains, and bards, and wise men of old [fill the villa].

Why should I rehearse the countless roof tops and the ever changing view? Each has a charm of its own; every chamber window has its own [private] view of the sea.

There is one hall that quite outshines them all; one hall that straight across the sea presents to thee, [the view of] Parthenope.[1] Therein are marbles chosen from the heart of the quarries in Greece, [and the other marbles from Egypt, or from Phrygia]: green marbles from Laconia and yellow from Numidia. Here are the Carystian pillars that delight to face seaward. These all front and greet the towers of Naples. A blessing on the fancy that prefers the Greek, that makes a Grecian land thy home!

91. LETTERS ABOUT PRIVATE LIFE IN EGYPT UNDER THE EMPIRE

Oxyrhynchos, "Papyri." Quoted in Milne's "Egypt under Roman Rule," pp. 160-162

Most of the letters here given explain themselves. They are from papyri of the Imperial period, found at the Egyptian town of Oxyrhynchos, and serve to give a curious and valuable light upon the life of an obscure provincial community.

[Relating to gymnastic sports in 323 A.D.]

"Dioscorides, logistes,[2] of the Oxyrhyncite nome (subprovince). The assault at arms by the youths will occur to-morrow, the 24th. Tradition, no less than the distinguished character of the festival, requires that they do their uttermost in the gymnastic display. The spectators will be present at the two performances."

---

[1] Naples.　　　[2] A high local magistrate in Roman Egypt.

[Announcing privileges to a victor in the games; a letter by Senate of Oxyrhynchos in 292 A.D. to the district governor.]

" At a meeting of our body a dispatch was read from Theodorus, recently chosen in place of Areion, the scribe, to proceed to his highness, the Præfect [of Egypt] and attend his 'immaculate' court.   In this dispatch he explained that he is victor in the games and exempted from inquiries.   We have, therefore, nominated Aurelianus to serve [as deputy to the Governor at Alexandria] and we send you word accordingly that this fact may be brought to his knowledge, and no time be lost in his departure and attendance upon the court."[1]

[From a petty local magistrate of a small village in the Egyptian Fayum; about some public amusements.]

" To Aureleus Theon, keeper of the training school, from Aurelius Asclepiades, son of Philadelphus, president of the council of the village of Bacchias.   I desire to hire from you Tisais, the dancing girl, and another, to dance for us at the above village for (fifteen ?) days from the 13th Phaophi by the old [Egyptian] calendar.   You shall receive as pay 36 drachmæ a day, and for the whole period 3 artabai of wheat, and 15 couples of loaves; also three donkeys to fetch them and take them back."

[Invitations in " good society " at Oxyrhynchos.]

" Chæreman requests your company at dinner, at the table of the lord Serapis[2] at the Serapæum, to-morrow the 15th, at 9 o'clock."

" Herais requests your company at dinner, in celebration of the marriage of her children, in her house to-morrow, the 5th, at 9 o'clock."

[1] Evidently attendance upon the præfect's court was an unwelcome and probably expensive duty.

[2] Dinner parties seem to have been given in temples, as to-day in hotels.

"Greeting, my dear Serenia, from Petosiris. Be sure, dear, to come upon the 20th for the birthday festival of the god, and let me know whether you are coming by boat or by donkey, in order that we may send for you accordingly. Take care not to forget. I pray for your continued health."

[Declaration to a local magistrate by an egg seller, showing the close watch kept by city authorities over the trades.]

"To Flavius Thennyras, logistes of the Oxyrhynchite district, from Aurelius Nilus, son of Didymus, of the illustrious and most illustrious city of Oxyrhynchos, an egg seller by trade. I hereby agree on the august, divine oath by our lord the Emperor and the Cæsars to offer my eggs in the market place publicly for sale, and to supply to the said city, every day without intermission; and I acknowledge that it shall be unlawful for me in the future to sell secretly or in my house. If I am detected in so doing, I shall be liable to penalty." [1]

[Complaint by an outraged husband — Syrus, son of Petechon — of the "Great Oasis" to the Egyptian Præfect as to lawless conditions among the lower classes of Egypt.]

"I married a woman of my own tribe . . . a free-born woman, of free parents, and have children by her. Now Tabes, daughter of Ammonios and her husband Laloi, and Psenesis and Straton their sons, have committed an act that disgraces all the chiefs of the town, and shows their recklessness; they carried off my wife and children to their own house, calling them their slaves, although they were free, and my wife has brothers living who are free. When I remonstrated, they seized me and beat me shamefully."

[Another complaint by a woman, Tarmouthis, a seller of vegetables in the Arsinote district in Egypt, to the authorities.]

[1] There is evidently fear that a conspiracy to " enhance " the price of eggs is impending, hence the exaction of this oath.

"On the fourth of this month, Taorsenouphis, wife of Ammonios Phimon, an elder of the village of Bacchias although she had no occasion against me, came to my house, and made herself most unpleasant to me. Besides tearing my tunic and cloak, she carried off 16 drachmæ that I had put by, the price of vegetables I had sold. And on the fifth her husband, Ammonios Phimon, came to my house, pretending he was looking for my husband, and took my lamp and went up into the house. And he went off with a pair of silver armlets, weighing forty drachmæ, while my husband was away from home."

92. A DIATRIBE AGAINST THE WOMEN OF ROME

Juvenal, " Satires," VI, ll. 199-304, 475-503. Gifford's Translation

About 100 A.D. a keen and bitter satirist delivered himself as follows against the women of Rome. Some of his charges are clearly overwrought; but there is no doubt that the Roman ladies often abused the very large liberties allowed them, and that divorce, unfaithfulness, wanton extravagance, and many other like evils were direfully common. Also the women were invading the arts and recreations of men, — a proceeding the present age will view more leniently than did Juvenal.

[Now] tell me — if thou canst not love a wife,
Made thine by every tie, and thine for life,
Why wed at all?   Why waste the wine and cakes,
The queasy-stomach'd guest, at parting, takes?
And the rich present, which the bridal right
Claims for the favors of the happy night,
The platter where triumphantly inscroll'd
The Dacian hero shines in current gold?[1]
If thou canst love, and thy besotted mind
Is so uxoriously to one inclined,

[1] On the wedding night the husband presented the wife with some gold pieces.   The "Dacian Hero" is a sarcastic allusion to Domitian.

Then bow thy neck, and with submissive air,
Receive the yoke thou must forever wear.

To a fond spouse, a wife no mercy shows
But warmed with equal fires, enjoys his woes.
She tells thee where to love and where to hate,
Shuts out the ancient friend, whose beard thy gate
Knew from its downy to its hoary state:
And when rogues and parasites of all degrees
Have power to will their fortune as they please,
She dictates thine, and impudently dares
To name thy very rivals for thy heirs.

" Go crucify that slave."   " For what offence ?
Who's the accuser ?   Where's the evidence ?
Hear all ! no time, whatever time we take
To sift the charges, when man's life's at stake,
Can e'er be long: hear all, then, I advise ! " —
" Thou sniveler ! is a slave a *man ?* " she cries:
" He's innocent ? — be it so, — 'tis *my* command,
My will: let that, sir, for a reason stand."

Thus the virago triumphs, thus she reigns:
Anon she sickens of her first domains,
And seeks for new ; — husband on husband takes,
Till of her bridal veil one rent she makes.
Again she tires, again for change she burns,
And to the bed she lately left returns,
While the fresh garlands and unfaded boughs,
Yet deck the portal of her wondering spouse.
Thus swells the list — " *Eight husbands in five years ;* "
A rare inscription on their sepulchres !

While thy wife's mother lives, expect no peace.
She teaches her with savage joy to fleece
A bankrupt spouse ; kind creature ! she befriends

The lover's hopes, and when her daughter sends
An answer to his prayer, the style inspects,
Softens the cruel, and the wrong corrects. . .

Women support the bar, they love the law,
And raise litigious questions for a show,
They meet in private and prepare the Bill
Draw up instructions with a lawyer's skill,
Suggest to Celsus[1] where the merits lie,
And dictate points for statement or reply.

Nay more, they fence, who has not marked their oil,
Their purple rugs,[2] for this preposterous toil?
Equipped for fight, the lady seeks the list
And fiercely tilts at her antagonist,
A post! which with her buckles she provokes,
And bores and batters with repeated strokes,
Till all the fencer's art can do she shows,
And the glad master interrupts her blows. . . .

[Or when the lady is being dressed to receive a gentleman friend,
it is a sad time for her maid trying to please her mistress.]

The house appears
Like Phalaris's[3] court, all bustle, gloom and tears.
The wretched Psecas, for the whip prepared,
With locks disheveled, and with shoulders bared,
Attempts her hair; fire flashes from her eyes,
And "wretch! why this curl so high?" she cries.
Instant the lash, without remorse, is plied,
And the blood stains her bosom, back and side.
Another trembling on the left prepares
To open and arrange the straggling hairs

[1] A well-known Roman jurist.
[2] Wrapped around them after violent exercise.
[3] Phalaris was a frightfully cruel tyrant of Agrigentum.

To ringlets trim; meanwhile the council meet,
And first the nurse, a personage discreet,
Gives her opinion; then the rest in course
As age or practice lend their judgment force,
So warm they grow, and so much pains they take,
You'd think her honor or her life at stake,
So high they build her head, such tiers on tiers,
With wary hands, they pile, that she appears
Andromache before; — and what behind?
A dwarf, a creature of a different kind!

93. The Gormandizing of the Emperor Vitellius

Suetonius, "Life of Vitellius," chap. 13　　Bohn Translation

The Emperor Vitèllius, who had a very brief and insignificant reign (69 A. D.), was mainly distinguished for his gormandizing and gluttony. How he enjoyed himself during his short lease of power is told by Suetonius. Probably there were a good many in Rome who would have imitated him, if given a similar opportunity.

Vitellius always made three meals per day, sometimes four: breakfast, dinner and supper and a drunken revel after all. This load of victuals he could bear well enough, from a custom to which he had enured himself of frequently vomiting. For these several meals he would make different appointments at the houses of his friends on the same day. None ever entertained him at a less expense than 400,000 sesterces [about $16,000]. The most famous was a set entertainment given him by his brother, at which were served up no less than two thousand choice fishes, and seven thousand birds. Yet even this supper he himself outdid at a feast which he gave upon the first use of a dish which had been made for him, and which from its extraordinary size he called "The Shield of Minerva." In this dish were tossed together the livers of charfish, the brains of pheasants and peacocks, with the tongues of flamingoes and the entrails of lampreys, which had been brought in ships of war as far as from the Carpathian Sea [between Crete and Rhodes] and the Spanish Straits.

He was not only a man of insatiable appetite, but he would gratify it at unseasonable times, and with any garbage that came his way. Thus at a sacrifice he would snatch from the fire the flesh and cakes and eat them on the spot. When he traveled, he did the same at inns upon the road, whether the meat was fresh dressed and hot, or whether it had been left from the day before and was half eaten.

[After a reign of a little less than a year this glutton was slain by troops of his worthier rival Vespasian.]

94. LUXURY IN THE USE OF RINGS

Pliny the Elder, "Natural History," book XXXIII, chap. 6. Bohn Translation

To what absurd lengths Roman foppery and luxury could go is exemplified in the following. There was about equal affectation in fashionable circles, as to all kinds of raiment, furniture, etc.

It was the custom at first to wear rings on a single finger only, — the one next to the little finger, and this we see to be the case in the statues of Numa and Servius Tullius. Later it became usual to put rings on the finger next to the thumb, even with statues of the gods; and more recently still it has been the fashion to wear them upon the little finger too. Among the Gauls and Britons the middle finger — it is said — is used for the purpose. At the present day, however, with us, this is the only finger that is excepted, for all the others are loaded with rings, smaller rings even being separately adapted for the smaller joints of the fingers.

Some people thrust several rings upon the little finger alone; while others wear but one ring upon this finger, the ring that carries the seal upon the signet ring itself, this last being carefully shut up as an object of rarity, too precious to be worn in common use, and only to be taken from the coffer as from a sanctuary. And thus is the wearing of a single ring upon the little finger, no more than an ostentatious advertisement that the owner has property of a more precious nature under seal at home.

Some too make a parade of their rings, whilst to others it is a decided labor to wear more than one at a time; some, in their solicitude for the safety of their gems, make the hoop of gold tinsel, and fill it with lighter material than gold, thinking thereby to diminish the risks of a fall. Others again, are in the habit of concealing poisons beneath their ring stones, and so wear them as instruments of death; so *e.g.* did Demosthenes, mightiest of Greek orators. And besides, how many of the crimes that are stimulated by cupidity, are committed by the instrumentality of rings!

Happy the times; yes, truly innocent when no seal was ever put on anything! At the present day, indeed, our very food and drink even have to be kept from theft through the agency of the [seal] ring. This of course is thanks to those legions of slaves, those throngs of foreigners who are introduced into our houses, multitudes so great that we have to have a nomenclator [professional remembrancer] to tell us even the names of our own servants. Different surely it was in the times of our forefathers, when each person possessed a single slave only, one of his master's own lineage, called Marcipor [Marcus's boy] or Lucipor [Lucius's boy], from his master's name, as the case might be, and taking all his meals with him in common; when, too, there was no need to take precautions at home by keeping a watch upon the servants. But at present, we not only buy dainties that are sure to be pilfered but hands to pilfer them as well; and so far from its being enough to keep the very keys sealed, often the signet ring is taken from the owner's finger while he is overpowered with sleep, or actually lying on his death bed.[1]

[1] According to Suetonius the signet ring was removed from the finger of the Emperor Tiberius while he lay dying.

95. The Bill of Fare of a Great Roman Banquet

Macrobius, "Saturnalia Convivia," book III, chap. 13.   Abstract in
Mommsen, "History of Rome" (new edition), vol. V, p. 387, note

The sensual and unrefined society of the Roman age laid a vast
stress upon the joys of *eating*.   Probably never before or since
has greater effort been expended upon gratifying the palate.   The
art of cooking was placed almost on a level with that of sculpture
or of music.   It is worth noticing that the ancient epicures were,
however, handicapped by the absence of most forms of modern ices,
and of sugar.   The menu here presented was for a feast given by
Mucius Lentulus Niger, when, in 63 B.C., he became a pontiff.
There were present the other pontifices including Julius Cæsar,
the Vestal Virgins, and some other priests, also ladies related to
them.   While this banquet took place under the Republic, it was
probably surpassed by many in Imperial times.

Before the dinner proper came sea hedgehogs; fresh oys-
ters, as many as the guests wished; large mussels;
sphondyli; field fares with asparagus; fattened fowls;
oyster and mussel pasties; black and white sea acorns;
sphondyli again; glycimarides; sea nettles; becaficoes [1]; roe
ribs; boar's ribs; fowls dressed with flour; becaficoes; purple
shellfish of two sorts.   *The dinner itself* consisted of sows'
udder; boar's head; fish-pasties; boar-pasties; ducks; boiled
teals; hares; roasted fowls; starch pastry; Pontic pastry.

96. The Banquet of Trimalchio, the Rich Parvenu

Petronius, "Satyricon."   Ryan's Translation

The following is a mere excerpt from a comic romance probably
composed during the reign of Nero.   The picture of Trimalchio,
the coarse freedman parvenu, who has nothing to commend him
but his money, and who is surrounded by countless parasites and
creatures of his whims, is one of the most clever and unsparing
delineations in ancient literature.   Much of the *Satyricon* is too

---

[1] A kind of small thrush.

coarse for reproduction. The passage here given will, however, present some notion of Roman " luxury " at its extremes.

At last we went to recline at table where boys from Alexandria poured snow water on our hands, while others, turning their attention to our feet, picked our nails, and not in silence did they perform their task, but singing all the time. I wished to try if the whole retinue could sing, and so I called for a drink, and a boy, not less ready with his tune, brought it accompanying his action with a sharp-toned ditty; and no matter what you asked for it was all the same song.

The first course was served and it *was* good, for all were close up at the table, save Trimalchio, for whom, after a new fashion, the place of honor was reserved.[1] Among the first viands there was a little ass of Corinthian bronze with saddle bags on his back, in one of which were white olives and in the other black. Over the ass were two silver platters, engraved on the edges with Trimalchio's name, and the weight of silver. Dormice seasoned with honey and poppies lay on little bridgelike structures of iron; there were also sausages brought in piping hot on a silver gridiron, and under that Syrian plums and pomegranate grains.

We were in the midst of these delights when Trimalchio was brought in with a burst of music. They laid him down on some little cushions, very carefully; whereat some giddy ones broke into a laugh, though it was not much to be wondered at, to see his bald pate peeping out from a scarlet cloak, and his neck all wrapped up and a robe with a broad purple stripe hanging down before him, with tassels and fringes dingle-dangle about him.

Then going through his teeth with a silver pick, " my

[1] Trimalchio is made out such a boor that he does not yield the place of honor to a guest.

friends," quoth he, " I really didn't want to come to dinner
so soon, but I was afraid my absence would cause too great
a delay, so I denied myself the pleasure I was at — at any
rate I hope you'll let me finish my game." A slave followed,
carrying a checkerboard of turpentine wood, with crystal
dice; but one thing in particular I noticed as extra nice —
he had gold and silver coins instead of the ordinary black
and white pieces. While he was cursing like a trooper
over the game and we were starting on the lighter dishes, a
basket was brought in on a tray, with a wooden hen in it,
her wings spread round, as if she were hatching.

Then two slaves came with their eternal singing, and
began searching the straw, whence they rooted out some
peahen's eggs, and distributed them among the guests.
At this Trimalchio turned around — " Friends," he says,
" I had some peahen's eggs placed under a hen, and so help
me Hercules ! — I hope they're not hatched out; we'd better
try if they're still tasty." Thereupon we took up our
spoons — they were not less than half a pound weight [of
silver] — and broke the eggs that were made of rich pastry.
I had been almost on the point of throwing my share away,
for I thought I had a chick in it, until hearing an old hand
saying, "There must be something good in this," I delved
deeper — and found a very fat fig-pecker inside, surrounded
by peppered egg yolk.

At this point Trimalchio stopped his game, demanded the
same dishes, and raising his voice, declared that if any one
wanted more liquor he had only to say the word. At once
the orchestra struck up the music, as the slaves also struck
up theirs, and removed the first course. In the bustle a
dish chanced to fall, and when a boy stooped to pick it up,
Trimalchio gave him a few vigorous cuffs for his pains, and
bade him to " throw it down again " — and a slave coming
in swept out the silver platter along with the refuse.
After that two long-haired Ethiopians entered with little

bladders, similar to those used in sprinkling the arena in the amphitheater, but instead of water they poured *wine* on our hands. Then glass wine jars were brought in, carefully sealed and a ticket on the neck of each, reading thus:

"Opimian Falernia[1]
One hundred years old."

[Presently one of the guests remarks, first on how completely Trimalchio is under the thumb of his wife; next he comments on the gentleman's vast riches.]

"So help me Hercules, the tenth of his slaves don't know their own master. . . Some time ago the quality of his wool was not to his liking; so what does he do, but buys rams at Tarentum to improve the breed. In order to have Attic honey at home with him, he has bees brought from Attica to better his stock by crossing it with the Greek. A couple of days ago he had the notion to write to India for mushroom seed. And his freedmen, his one-time comrades [in slavery] they are no small cheese either; they are immensely well-off. Do you see that chap on the last couch over there? To-day he has his 800,000 sesterces [$32,000]. He came from nothing, and time was when he had to carry wood upon his back. . . . He has been manumitted only lately, but he knows his business. Not long ago he displayed this notice:

CAIUS · POMPEIUS · DIOGENES
HAVING · TAKEN · A · HOUSE · IS · DISPOSED
TO · LET · HIS · GARRET · FROM · THE
KALENDS · OF · JULY.

[After a very long discussion in like vein and a vulgar display of luxuries and riches, Trimalchio condescends to tell the company how he came by his vast wealth.]

---

[1] An extremely choice and famous vintage.

"When I came here first [as a slave] from Asia, I was only as high as yonder candlestick, and I'd be measuring my height on it every day, and greasing my lips with lamp oil to bring out a bit of hair on my snout.

"Well, at last, to make a long story short, as it pleased the gods, I became master in the house, and as you see, I'm chip of the same block. He [my master] made me coheir with Cæsar,[1] and I came into a royal fortune, but no one ever thinks he has enough. I was mad for trading, and to put it all in a nutshell, bought five ships, freighted them with wine — and wine was as good as coined money at that time — and sent them to Rome. You wouldn't believe it, — every one of those ships was wrecked. In one day Neptune swallowed up 30,000,000 sesterces [$1,200,000] on me. D'ye think I lost heart? Not much! I took no notice of it, by Hercules! I got more ships made, larger, better, and luckier; that no one might say I wasn't a plucky fellow. A big ship has big strength — that's plain! Well I freighted them with wine, bacon, beans, perfumes, and slaves. Here Fortuna (my consort) showed her devotion. She sold her jewelry and all her dresses, and gave me a hundred gold pieces — that's what my fortune grew from. What the gods ordain happens quickly. For on just one voyage I scooped in 10,000,000 sesterces [$400,000] and immediately started to redeem all the lands that used to be my master's. I built a house, bought some cattle to sell again — whatever I laid my hand to grew like a honeycomb. When I found myself richer than all the country round about was worth, in less than no time I gave up trading, and commenced lending money at interest to the freedmen. 'Pon my word, I was very near giving up business altogether,

---

[1] It was hardly safe for a rich man to fail to remember the Emperor in his will, lest the latter in his wrath at being slighted confiscate the whole estate.

only an astrologer, who happened to come into our colony, dissuaded me.

"And now I may as well tell you it all, — I have thirty years, four months and two days to live, moreover I'm to fall in for an estate, — that's [the astrologer's] prophecy anyway. If I'm so lucky as to be able to join my domains to Apulia, I'll say I've got on pretty well. Meanwhile under Mercury's[1] fostering, I've built this house. Just a hut once, you know — now a regular temple! It has four dining rooms, twenty bedrooms, two marble porticoes, a set of cells [for the slaves?] upstairs, my own bedroom, a sitting room for this viper [my wife!] here, a very fine porter's room, and it holds guests to any amount. There are a lot of other things too that I'll show you by and by. Take my word for it, if you have a penny you're worth a penny, you are valued for just what you have. Yesterday your friend was a frog, he's a king to-day — that's the way it goes."

[Trimalchio goes on to show off to his guests the costly shroud, perfumes, etc., he has been assembling for his own funeral; and at last] we, the guests were already disgusted with the whole affair when Trimalchio, who, by the way, was beastly drunk, ordered in the cornet players for our further pleasure, and propped up with cushions, stretched himself out at full length.

"Imagine I'm dead," says he, "and play something soothing!" Whereat the cornet players struck up a funeral march, and one of them especially — a slave of the undertaker fellow — the best in the crowd, played with such effect that he roused the whole neighborhood. So the watchmen, who had charge of the district, thinking Trimalchio's house on fire, burst in the door, and surged in — as was their right — with axes and water ready. Taking advantage of such an opportune moment . . . we bolted incontinently, as if there had been a real fire in the place.

[1] The patron god of traders and thieves.

97. SENECA ON THE GLADIATORIAL BUTCHERIES

Seneca, "Epistles," 7. Henderson's Translation

The following letter indicates how by the age of Nero cultured and elevated souls were beginning to revolt at the arena butcheries which still delighted the mob.

I turned in to the games one mid-day hoping for a little wit and humor there. I was bitterly disappointed. It was really mere butchery. The morning's show was merciful compared to it. *Then* men were thrown to lions and to bears: but at midday to the audience. There was no escape for them. The slayer was kept [fighting] till he could be slain. "Kill him! flog him! burn him alive" [was the cry:] "Why is he such a coward? Why won't he rush on the steel? Why does he fall so meekly? Why won't he die willingly?" Unhappy that I am, how have I deserved that I must look on such a scene as this? Do not, my Lucilius, attend the games, I pray you. Either you will be corrupted by the multitude, or, if you show disgust, be hated by them. So stay away."

98. SENECA'S OPINIONS UPON SLAVERY

Collected from Seneca's writings in B. W. Henderson's "Life and Principate of Nero," p. 92

With all his shortcomings Seneca was undoubtedly the most advanced pagan thinker of his day. The following extracts from his writings indicate clearly that by about 60 A.D. the old ideas of the inevitableness and desirability of slavery were beginning to crumble. The spread of the Stoic philosophy as well as the final triumph of Christianity did much to mitigate and finally almost to abolish the Roman slave system.

"It is a savage pride which quotes the proverb '*So many slaves, so many foes.*'[1] They are no foes to us until we make them so."

[1] A proverb probably very often in Roman mouths.

"Slaves, do I say? Rather 'men.' 'Slaves?' No, but comrades. 'Slaves?' Say rather 'humble friends.' Nay — 'slaves' if you like, but fellow slaves with you, who own one arbiter of destiny — Fate. See your modern master deeming it a disgrace if no throng of slaves surrounds his couch at dinner. Poor wretches! Flogged for a murmur, a cough, a sneeze, a sigh. In olden time slaves who might speak not only in the presence of, but even face to face with, their masters, were found ready to lay down their lives for their master's sakes. Is not a slave of the same stuff as you, his lord? Does he not enjoy the same sun, breathe the same air, die, even as do you? Let then your slave worship rather than dread you. Is it too little for a master, which is enough for God? *For love casts out fear.*" [1]

"Shall a slave be counted as one that can do benefits to his lord? Surely. Virtue recks not of the birth but of the purpose. She resides not in the person, nor nobility in the pedigree. She deals not with citizen or slave, but rests content with man as man. Scorn not any man. The Universe is the common parent of us all."

99. Wall Inscriptions from Pompeii

Collected in Kelsey's Translation of Mau's "Pompeii," chap. 57 passim

There are almost no literary remains from Antiquity possessing greater human interest than these inscriptions scratched on the walls of Pompeii (destroyed 79 A.D.). Their character is extremely varied, and they illustrate in a keen and vital way the life of a busy, luxurious, and, withal, tolerably typical, city of some 25,000 inhabitants in the days of the Flavian Cæsars. Most of these inscriptions carry their own message with little need of a commentary. Perhaps those of the greatest importance are the ones relating to local politics. It is very evident that the so-called "monarchy" of the Emperors had not involved the destruction of political life, at least in the provincial towns.

[1] Compare this to the teachings of the New Testament.

Notices of Gladiatorial Games, etc.

" Twenty pairs of gladiators provided by Quintus Monnius Rufus, are to fight at Nola May 1, 2 and 3, and there will be a hunt."

" Thirty pairs of gladiators provided by Gnæus Alleius Nigidius Maius quinquennial duumvir, together with their substitutes, will fight at Pompeii on November 24, 25, 26. There will be a hunt. Hurrah for Maius the Quinquennial! Bravo, Paris!"[1]

" The gladiatorial troop of the ædile Aulius Suettius Certus will fight at Pompeii May 31. There will be a hunt, and awnings will be provided."

" Twenty pairs of gladiators furnished by Decimus Lucretius Satrius Valens perpetual priest of Nero, son of the Emperor, and ten pairs of gladiators furnished by Decimus Lucretius Valens his son, will fight at Pompeii April 8, 9, 10, 11, and 12. There will be a big hunt and awnings. Æmilius Celer wrote this by the light of the moon."[2]

Election Notices and Appeals

" The dyers request the election of Postumius Proculus as ædile."

" Vesonius Primus urges the election of Gnæus Helvius as ædile, — a man worthy of public office."

" Vesonius Primus requests the election of Gaius Gavius Rufus as duumvir, a man who will serve the public interest — do elect him, I beg of you."

" Primus and his household are working for the election of Gnæus Helvius Sabinus as ædile."

[1] Maius was as ' quinquennial ' holding a position practically the same a the censors in Republican Rome. He seems to have been a wealthy and important man. Paris was probably a well-known gladiator.

[2] Celer seems to have been a regular notice painter at Pompeii.

"Make Lucius Cæserninus quinquennial duumvir of Nuceria,[1] I beg you: he is a good man."

"His neighbors request the election of Tiberius Claudius Verus as duumvir."

Various candidates are commended in different inscriptions as "worthy of public office," "an upright young man," "a youth of remarkable modesty," "a careful watcher of the treasury."

Guilds and tradespeople unite to support favorite candidates, thus: "The worshipers of Isis[2] as a body ask for the election of Gnæus Helvius Sabinus as ædile."

Again, "The inhabitants of the Campanian suburb ask for the election of Marcus Epidius Sabinus as ædile."[3]

"At the request of the neighbors Suedius Clemens, most upright judge, is working for the election of Marcus Epidius Sabinus, a worthy young man, as duumvir with judicial authority.   He begs you to elect him."

The ease with which notices could be scribbled on the walls of the streets of Pompeii, enabled enemies to deliver satirical attacks on candidates, as well as for friends to praise, thus: "The sneak thieves request the election of Vatia as ædile." "The whole company of late drinkers (favor Vatia)." "The whole company of late risers (favor Vatia)."

Inscriptions of General and Various Interest

Notice on the "Elephant Inn," — ornamented with the sign of an elephant in the coils of a snake, and defended by a pigmy, — "Inn to let.   Triclinium (dining room) with three couches."

---

[1] Nuceria was a town neighboring to Pompeii.
[2] A quasi-religious fraternity.
[3] Sabinus evidently represents some "local interest."

Written on the walls of a sleeping room in another inn, by some affectionate husband, " Here slept Vibius Restitutus all by himself his heart filled with longings for his Urbana."

Advertisement painted on a wall, " To rent from the first day of next July, shops with the floors over them, fine upper chambers, and a house, in the Arnius Pollio block, owned by Gnæus Alleius Nigidius Maius. Prospective lessees may apply to Primus, slave of Gnæus Alleius Nigidius Maius." [1]

Another advertisement, " To let, for the term of five years, from the thirteenth day of next August to the thirteenth day of the sixth August thereafter, the Venus bath, fitted up for the best people, shops, rooms over shops, and second-story appartments in the property owned by Julia Felix, daughter of Spurius."

Notice for a lost article, "A copper pot has been taken from this shop. Whoever brings it back will receive 65 sesterces [$2.60]. If any one shall hand over the thief [he will be rewarded (?)]."

Messages and expressions from lovers are many; examples: " He who has never been in love can be no gentleman." " Health to you, Victoria, and wherever you are may you sneeze sweetly." [2] " Restitutus has many times deceived many girls." (Written on a wall.) " Romula keep tryst here with Staphylus."

Some lovers expressed themselves in verse, thus: —

> " If any man seek
> My girl from me to turn,
> On far-off mountains bleak,
> May Love the scoundrel burn!"

---

[1] Primus was evidently a trusted house agent, even if still a slave.
[2] To sneeze implied having good luck.

Again, —

> " If you a man would be, —
> If you know what love can do, —
> Have pity and suffer me
> With welcome to come to you."

Notice by a gamester, " At Nuceria, I won $855\frac{1}{2}$ denarii [about \$138] by gaming, — fair play."

Notice about the advent of some young pigs or puppies, " On October 17 Puteolana had a litter of three males and two females."

Proverbs, " The smallest evil if neglected, will reach the greatest proportions." " If you want to waste your time, scatter millet and pick it up again."

[There are also a good many quotations from the Latin poets marked on the walls by school children, lovers, and others ; Ovid, Vergil, Lucretius, and divers other poets are represented. Thus we find the familiar " *Arma virumque cano* " scratched by some school boy.]

Copies of Wax Tablets relating to Business Transactions

[These are not scratched on the walls, but are business documents found carefully packed in a wooden box in the house of Lucius Cæcilius Jucundus, which was excavated in 1875. The wooden bases of the tablets had turned to charcoal, but it was possible to decipher much of the writing.]

Entry of account of Umbricia Januaria. Umbricia Januaria declares that she has received from Lucius Cæcilius Jucundus 11,039 sesterces [about \$440] which sum came into the hands of Lucius Cæcilius Jucundus by agreement as the proceeds of an auction sale for Umbricia Januaria, the commission due him having been deducted.

"Done at Pompeii, on the 12th of December, in the consulship of Lucius Duvius and Publius Clodius." (56 A.D.)
(Many witnesses follow.)

(A receipt.) "On the 18th of June in the duumvirate of
Lucius Veranius Hypsæus and Lucius Albucius Justus, I,
Privatus,[1] slave of the colony of Pompeii, declared in writing that I had received from Lucius Cæcilius Jucundus 1675
sesterces [about $67], and previous to this day, on June
6, I received 1000 sesterces [about $40] as rent for the
public pasture.

"Done at Pompeii in the consulship of Gnæus Fonteius
and Gaius Vipstanus" (59 A.D.). (Many witnesses follow.)

[1] The city of Pompeii, evidently, like other ancient towns, owned slaves
in its corporate capacity; and these men might be petty officials of some
importance, and intrusted with the letting of the public property.

CHAPTER VIII

PHILOSOPHICAL AND RELIGIOUS LIFE IN THE LAST PAGAN CENTURIES

The last three pagan centuries were a period of great religious and intellectual unrest. Probably never was there an age when a greater proportion of educated men were religious skeptics than the last era of the Roman Republic. For example, Julius Cæsar was as close to being an atheist as any great figure in history. Then came the revival of the formal state religion by Augustus for the real purpose, probably, of fostering mere public morality and good citizenship throughout the unthinking masses. But behind this *formal* revival of the old religion went an awakening craving among intelligent persons for something better. The selfish materialism of the Epicureans could not satisfy them, nor the cold formulas of the nobler forms of Greek philosophy. The dissatisfaction with the old religion and the desire for one nobler had assumed three distinct forms before the final triumph of Christianity. These were: (I) a bold and audacious criticism of the old Græco-Roman religion as presented in its original forms (cf. selection 100). (II) The development of the Stoic philosophy which represented what were ethically some of the noblest products of ancient intelligence, and which was the result of a sincere and painful seeking after God on the part of many souls who were alike disgusted with the old "Olympian" system, and with the later selfish atheism. (III) The spread of Oriental religions over the West, — religions which were avowedly mere additions to the Græco-Roman system, but which had in them a spiritual appeal, a promise of immortality, a pledge of reconciliation with God, such as never entered into the cults of Jupiter or Apollo.

It is perfectly safe to assert that even if Christianity had never arisen, the religion of the Roman Empire would have undergone a pronounced change.   From great incredulity the pendulum swung back to extreme credulity.   There was firm credence — even among thoughtful men — in magic formulas, alleged miracles, dreams, ghosts, and the like.   The last great pagan critic of Christianity, the Emperor Julian the Apostate (died 363), complained that the miracles of Jesus were mean, puny, and unworthy of a son of God : and that a true deity would have wrought far greater ones.

It is easy to cite passages illustrating the criticism of the older type of paganism, also examples from the Stoic philosophers, but the evidence for the later Oriental cults (Mithraism, Isis-worship, the cult of the " Great Mother," etc.) is not of a kind easy to present in a book like this, being mainly based on very scattered inscriptions.   (See, however, § 108.)   It should never be forgotten that Christianity triumphed because it met a need whereof the age was extremely conscious, a need whereof men were seeking a satisfaction most eagerly.

100. A Skeptic's Mockery of the Multiplicity of Pagan Gods

Lucian, " The Convention of the Gods."   Adapted from the Bohn Translation

How absurd the old pagan system seemed to educated men of the second century A.D. is illustrated by this keen satire by a clever and unbelieving Greek writer.   Lucian had little use for Christianity : it comes in for a share of his ridicule, but few did more than he to prepare for the triumph of Christianity, by pulling down the fabric of time-honored superstitions on which the outworn pagan religions rested.

[The gods are in solemn assembly, discussing the right of new candidates — especially from barbarous countries — to their company.   Olympus is at length getting overpopulated.   Momus — god of mockery — speaks to the following effect.]

Now Attis, and Korybus and Sabazius — from what part of the world have *they* been rolled in upon us, one after another ?   Or that Mithras the Median, with his Oriental mantle and tiara, who doesn't speak a word of Greek, so

that even if one drink his health he doesn't understand.
. . . And you with the dog-face [Anubis] the Egyptian,
wrapped all up in linen, who are you, fine Sir, or how do
you put in a claim to be divine with your barking? And
what is the meaning of this bull [Apis] from Memphis, that
spotted individual, being worshiped and delivering oracles,
and having prophets? I blush to speak of the ibises and
apes and goats [which have . . .] stuffed Heaven from
Egypt. . . . [Other evils nearer home in Greece are cited
and] if you desire to end these evils, Zeus, I will read off a
certain resolution, composed just now by me.

Zeus [president of the assembly]. Read — for all your
charges are not without some reason.

[The decree is read. It is couched in the regular style of an
Athenian decree and is to the following effect.]

In the name of God :
In a lawfully convoked popular assembly, on the seventh
day of the first decade of the month, under the presidency
of Zeus,[1] and the vice presidency of Poseidon, Apollo in the
chair, Momus the son of Nux, acting as registrar and Hyp-
nus brought forward the following motion. — Seeing that
many unauthorized strangers, both Greeks and barbarians,
have forced their way into the company of the gods, that the
supply of ambrosia and nectar has begun to fail, that the
great demand for them has sent the price up to a mina per
jar, that strange gods shamelessly push themselves forward
and turn the old gods out of their places : *be it decreed* that
a commission of seven first-class gods be appointed to sift
all claims of each of their colleagues, etc.

Zeus. Very just Momus. All in favor hold up their
hands! Or rather let it be declared carried at once; for I
know the majority are against it. The Assembly is dismissed. But be ready each of you with clear proofs of your

[1] An accurate parody upon the Greek legal formula.

titles, — the certificates of your father's and mother's names, whence and how he or she became a divinity, his tribe, and fellow demesmen. All without these cannot be considered by the Commission.

101. A Famous Religious Impostor of the Second Century

Lucian: abridged in Friedlaender, "Roman Life and Manners." (English edition, vol. III, p. 131)

While mere skepticism allied to the nobler Stoicism undermined the old religious faith of the educated classes, the multitude still kept its belief in the old gods, and was liable to be led off into all kinds of absurd superstition. Under these conditions religious impostors were bound to reap rich harvests.

Alexander [105–175 A.D.] was as a boy remarkable for his beauty. He was early instructed in magic arts, and wandered about the country, but at last resolved to found an oracle in his native town of Aboniteichos on account of the crass superstition of the people. Tablets of bronze were buried by him and conveniently dug up, announcing that Apollo and his son Asclepius were coming to Aboniteichos. The inhabitants in delight began building a temple to Asclepius. Presently Alexander entered the town; magnificently clad in a white and purple tunic and carrying a sickle in his hand, after the manner of the hero Perseus, whose son he claimed to be. The god Asclepius is said to have revealed himself in the form of a snake. Prompted by Alexander the townsmen soon found an empty goose egg, with a little snake within it, near the spot where they had begun the new temple. Soon afterward he exhibited a large tame snake — long in readiness — and the rapid growth of the divine snake seemed a matter of course.

Appearing with the snake round his neck in a dimly lighted room, he thrust out from his robe a snake's head made of painted linen, somewhat resembling a human face, the mouth of which could be opened and shut by a horse-hair attachment inside. Sometimes this snake uttered oracles; more often questions propounded at the shrine were handed back with written answers. Vast crowds came to consult the oracle. The fee was small, but the multitude so vast that Alexander's profits were great. Many prominent people, Roman governors and the like, were among the inquirers. The time was one of famine, earthquake, pestilence, and the like, and the oracle affected to give sure directions for avoiding calamity. An occasional error or false prophesy did not injure its prestige.

Alexander died at the age of seventy, full of honor, wealth, and influence. Even after his death it was believed that his statue in the market place of Parium in Mysia delivered oracles.

102. The Nature of Demons

Appuleius, "The God of Socrates." Works of Appuleius, chap. XX. Bohn Translation

The second century A.D. was marked by a very waning faith in the old gods among the educated classes, but it was not free from a recrudescence of curious theories as to the nature of the soul, nor from downright superstition. The writings of Appuleius, a very typical author, are sufficient evidence of this. It should be noticed that a pagan "demon," was by no means always a noxious creature like the later Christian "demon."

According to a certain signification the human soul, even when it is still situate in the body, is called a "Demon." . . . If then this is the case, a longing of the soul that is of good tendency is a good demon. Hence some think, that the blessed are called *Eudaimones*, the *demon* of whom is good, that is, whose mind is perfect in virtue. You may call this demon in our [Latin] language, according to my mode of interpretation by the name   .

of " Genius," because this God, who is in the mind of
every one, though immortal, is nevertheless after a certain
manner generated with man; so that those prayers in
which we implore the Genius, and which we employ when
we embrace the knees (*genua*) of those whom we supplicate,
seem to me to testify to this connection and union, since
they comprehend in two words the body and the mind,
through the communion and conjunction of which we exist.

There is also another species of demons, according to a
second signification, and that is the human soul *after* it has
performed its duties in the present life, and quitted the
body. I find that this is called in the ancient Latin language by the name of " Lemur." Now, of these Lemures,
the one who, undertaking the guardianship of his posterity,
dwells in a house with propitious and tranquil influence,
is called the " familar" Lar. But those who, having no
fixed habitation of their own, are punished with vague
wandering, as with a kind of exile, on account of the evil
deeds of their life, are usually called " Larvæ," thus becoming a vain terror to the good, but a source of punishment to the bad.

But when it is uncertain what is the allotted condition
of any of these, and whether it is Lar or Larvæ, it is called
a God Manes, the name of God being added for the sake
of honor. For only those are called Gods, who being in
the number of the Lemures, and having regulated the
course of their life justly and prudently, have later been
celebrated by men as divinities, and are generally worshiped with temples and religious rites. Such are, for
example, Amphiaraus in Bœotia, Mopsus in Africa, Osiris
in Egypt, and others in other nations, but especially
Esculapius[1] everywhere. All this distribution, however,
has been made of those demons who once existed in a
human body.

[1] The Greek Asclepius.

But there is another species of demons, more exalted and august, not fewer in number, but far superior in dignity, who [in no wise attached to the body . . .] preside over certain powers.   In the number of these are Sleep and Love, which possess powers of a different nature; Love, of exciting to wakefulness; Sleep, of lulling to rest.

From this more elevated order of demons Plato is of the opinion that a peculiar demon is allotted to every man, to be a witness and a guardian of his conduct in life, who, without being visible to any one, is always present, and is an overseer not only of his actions, but even of his thoughts. But when life is finished the soul has to return to its judges; then the demon who has presided over it immediately seizes and leads it as his charge to judgment, and is there present with it, while it pleads its cause; and censures it if it is guilty of any untruthfulness; corroborates what it says, if it asserts what is true, and conformably to its testimony, sentence is passed.

[This demon] is entirely our guardian, our individual keeper, our watcher at home, our special regulator, a searcher into our inmost fibers, a reprover of our evil deeds, an approver of our good ones.   He is our forewarner in uncertainty, our monitor in matters of doubt, our defender in danger, and our assistant in need.   He is able also by dreams and by tokens, and perhaps even openly, when necessity demands it, to avert from you evil, to increase your blessings, to lighten your darkness, to regulate your prosperity, and modify your adversity.

103. A Stoic on the Endurance of Hardship

Seneca, " Essay on Providence," chap. IV.   Bohn Translation

Seneca, the prime minister of Nero, affected an austere stoical philosophy, that did not always correspond with the fact that he was among the wealthiest and most powerful men in Rome.

Nevertheless, his *theories* are often very noble; and in them we discover the best substitute paganism could present for Christianity. Indeed, there are even letters supposed to have been exchanged between Seneca and St. Paul, although these are clearly spurious.

Prosperity comes to the mob and to the low-minded men as well as to the great, but it is the privilege of great men alone to send under the yoke[1] the disasters and terrors of mortal life; whereas to be always prosperous, and to pass through life without a twinge of mental distress is to remain ignorant of one half of nature. You are a great man [no doubt]; but how am I to know it, if Fortune sends you no chance to show your virtue? You have entered the arena of the Olympic games, but no one else has done so; you have the crown but not the victory. I do not congratulate you as I would a brave man, but as one who has obtained a consulship, or a prætorship. You have gained dignity. I may say the same of every good man, if troublous circumstances have never given him a chance to show forth the strength of his mind. I think you unhappy because you have never been unhappy; you have passed through your life without meeting an antagonist; no one will know your powers, not even yourself.

For a man cannot know himself without a trial; no one has ever learnt what he could do without putting himself to the test; for which reasons many have of their own free will exposed themselves to misfortunes which no longer came in their way, and have sought for an opportunity of making their virtue, which otherwise would have been lost in darkness, shine before the world. Great men, I say, often rejoice at crosses of fortune, just as brave soldiers do at wars. I recall hearing Triumphus, who was a gladiator in the reign of Tiberius Cæsar, complaining about the scarcity of prizes. "What a glorious time," said he, "is past." [For]

---

[1] A humiliation inflicted upon a conquered army, making them walk between two spears while a third was fastened across the top.

"valor is greedy of danger, and thinks only of whether it strives to go, not of what it will suffer, since even what it will suffer is part of its glory." . . . God, I say, favors those whom He wishes to enjoy the greatest honors, whenever He affords them the means of performing some exploit of spirit and courage, something not easily to be accomplished. You can judge a pilot in a storm, a soldier in a battle. How can I know with how great a spirit you could endure poverty, if you overflow with riches?

Do not, I beg you, dread those things which the immortal Gods apply like spurs to our minds; misfortune is virtue's opportunity. The recruit turns pale at the thought of a wound; the veteran who knows that he has often won the victory after losing blood, looks boldly at his own flowing gore. In a like manner God hardens, reviews, and exercises those whom He tests and loves;[1] those whom He seems to indulge He is keeping out of condition for their coming misfortune.

104. How a Stoic met Calamity in the Days of Nero

Epictetus, "Discourses," book I, chap. 1.   Carter's Translation

What meeting misfortune "like a Stoic" implied, is shown by this anecdote preserved from the evil days of Nero. Agrippinus was banished in 67 A.D. In such troublous days a part of the education of every man of the upper classes seems to have been the deliberate steeling himself to endure calamity.

[Paconius Agrippinus, a famous Stoic, was put on trial before the Senate for disaffection to the Emperor. He did not deign even to appear to defend himself before such a servile body.]

They brought Paconius the news, "You are this moment being tried before the Senate."

---

[1] Cf. "Whom the Lord loveth He chasteneth."

"The case goes well, I trust," replied he, "but see — it is
eleven, our time for exercise."

As he took exercise, in came another messenger.

"Condemned!" he cried.

"To exile," asked Paconius, "or to death?"

"Exile!"

"And is my property confiscate?"

"It is not taken."

"Well then, — let us go as far as Aricia, and dine there."[1]

105. How all Things are under the Divine Inspection

Epictetus, "Discourses," book I, chap. 14. Carter's Translation

Epictetus, the famous freedman, philosopher, and Stoic, had an
almost Christian concept of the power and goodness of God.
Indeed the spread of teachings like his went far to make the
world ready to accept Christianity.

When a person asked Epictetus how any one might be
convinced that each of his actions is under the inspection
of God; do you not think, says Epictetus, that all things
are mutually bound together and united?

I do.

Well, and do you not think that things on earth feel the
influence of the heavenly bodies?

Yes.

Else how do the trees come so readily, as if by God's
express command; bud, blossom, bring forth fruit and ripen
it; then let it drop, and shed their leaves . . . all when
He says the word? Whence again are there seen, on the
increase and decrease of the moon, and the approach and
departure of the sun, so great vicissitudes and changes to
the direct contrary in earthly things? Have then the very

[1] A town about 16 miles from Rome, and on the road to the region of
banishment.

leaves, and our own bodies, this connection and sympathy with the whole, and have not our souls much more ? But our souls are thus connected and intimately joined to God, as being indeed members and distinct portions of His essence; and must He not be sensible of every movement of them as belonging, and with like nature to himself ?

"But I cannot" — you say — "attend to all things at once." Why, does any one tell you that you have equal power with Zeus ? No! but nevertheless He has assigned to each man a director, his own good "genius," and committed him to his guardianship; a director whose vigilance no slumbers interrupt, and whom no false reasoning can deceive. For to what better and more careful guardian could He have committed us ? So that when you have shut your doors, and darkened your room, remember never to say that you are alone, for you are not; but God is within, and your genius is within, and what need have they of light to see what you are doing ?

Elsewhere Epictetus enjoins these rules to be followed by a true philosopher. (From his "Manual," § XXXIII)

Be for the most part silent, or speak merely what is necessary and in few words. We may, however, enter, though sparingly, into discourse sometimes, when occasion calls for it, but not on any of the common subjects, of gladiators, or horse races, or athletic champions, or feasts, the vulgar topics of conversation; but principally not of men, so as either to blame or praise, or make comparisons. If you are able, then, by your own conversation, bring over that of your company to proper subjects, but if you happen to be taken among strangers, be silent.

Let not your laughter be much, nor on many occasions, nor profuse.

Avoid swearing, if possible, altogether; if not, as far as **you** are able.

Avoid public and vulgar[1] entertainments, but if ever an occasion calls you to them, keep your attention upon the stretch that you may not slide imperceptibly into vulgar manners.   For be assured that if a person be ever so sound himself, yet if his companion be infected, he who converses with him will be infected likewise.

Provide things relating to the body no further than mere use; as meat, drink, clothing, house, family.

When you are going to confer with any one, and particularly those in a superior station, represent to yourself how Socrates or Zeno would behave in such a case, and you will not be at a loss to make proper use of whatever may occur.

In parties of conversation avoid a frequent and excessive mention of your own actions and doings.   For however agreeable it may be to *yourself* to mention the risks which you have run, it is not equally agreeable to others, to hear your adventures. . . .

When you do anything from a clear judgment that it ought to be done, never shun the fact that you are seen to do it, even though the world should make a wrong supposition about it, for if you do not act right, shun the action itself; but, if you do, why are you afraid of those who censure you wrongly?

106. Letters of Marcus Aurelius to his Master Fronto

Appendix to Meditations of Marcus Aurelius.   Translated in Everyman Library Edition

That Marcus Aurelius while "Cæsar" (*i.e.* Crown Prince) (about 150 A.D.) was not utterly engrossed in philosophy or the cares of state, is shown delightfully in these letters to Fronto, his beloved rhetoric teacher.   We see by them a very simple and beautiful family life in the imperial household — a charming contrast to the courts of some of the earlier Emperors.

[1] *I.e.* entertainments that catch the "vulgar," ignorant multitude.

My dearest Master, — I am well. To-day I studied from
the ninth hour of the night [3 P.M.] to the second hour
[8 A.M.] of the day, after taking food. I then put on my
slippers and from the second to the third hour had a most
enjoyable walk up and down my room. Then booted and
cloaked — for so we were commanded to appear — I went
to wait upon my lord the Emperor.[1] We went a-hunting, did
doughty deeds, heard a rumor that boars had been caught,
but there was nothing to see. However, we climbed a
pretty steep hill, and in the afternoon returned home. I
went straight to my books. Off with the boots, down with
the cloak! I spent a couple of hours in bed. I read Cato's
speech on the Property of Pulchra, and another in which he
impeaches a tribune. I think I have caught cold, whether
from walking in slippers, or writing [an essay] badly, I
don't know. To-day I seem to snivel more than usual.
Well, I will pour oil on my head, and go off to sleep. I
don't mean to put one drop in my lamp to-day, so weary
am I from riding and sneezing.

[Another letter from the country.] After attending to
my throat [a cold still remaining] I went to my father [An-
toninus Pius] and stood at his side as he sacrificed. Then
to luncheon. What do you think I had to eat? A bit of
bread fairly big — while I watched others gobbling boiled
beans, onions, and fish full of roe. Then we went to work
at gathering the grapes with plenty of sweat and shouting,
and as the quotation runs, "A few high-hanging clusters
did we leave survivors of the vintage." After the sixth
hour we returned home. I did a little [literary work] and
poor work at that. Then I had a long gossip with my dear
mother[2] sitting on the bed. [After a talk about Fronto's
wife and little daughter] the gong sounded, the signal that
my father had gone to bath. We supped — after bathing —

---

[1] Antoninus Pius.   [2] His adoptive mother, wife of Antoninus Pius.

in the wine cellar, and listened with enjoyment to the chatter of the rustics.

[Another letter, puts the supposedly grave philosopher Cæsar in a new light.] When my father returned home from the vineyards, I mounted my horse as usual and rode on ahead some little way. Well, there on the road was a herd of sheep, standing all crowded together as though the place were a desert with four dogs and two shepherds, but nothing else. Then one shepherd says to the other shepherd, on seeing a number of horsemen, "I say, look at those riders: they do a deal of robbery." When I hear this, I clap spurs to my horse and ride straight for the sheep. In consternation the sheep scatter; hither and thither they are fleeting and bleating. A shepherd throws his fork, and the fork falls on the horsemen who rode next to me. We make our prompt escape.

[Fronto, writing to Marcus Aurelius of the latter's little daughters, says after a visit to the two baby princesses :[1]]

I have seen your little ones, and no sight could have been more charming to me, for they are so like you in face that nothing could be more striking. I was well rewarded for my pains in journeying to Lorium, for the slippery road and the rough ascent. For I had two copies of yourself beside me. By the mercy of heaven they have healthy color and strong lungs! One clutched a piece of white bread, fit indeed for the child of a prince ; one a hard black crust fit for the child of a true philosopher. In the pleasant prattle of their little voices I seemed to recognize already the clear tones of your harmonious speech.

[And of his children, Marcus Aurelius once wrote :] Today the weather is bad, and I feel ill at ease, but when my

[1] See version given in Cape's *Age of the Antonines*, p. 86.

little girls are well, it seems that my own pains are of slight moment, and the weather is quite fair.

107. The Precepts of Marcus Aurelius

"Meditations of Marcus Aurelius," passim.   Adapted from Long's Translation

Never did a mighty ruler, actuated by noble theories, set for himself a higher standard of personal conduct than Marcus Aurelius (reigned 161 to 180 A.D.). His "Meditations" were composed in large part whilst he was in camp on the Danube waging war against the Germanic invaders of the Empire. Despite the lofty and courageous tone of these exhortations addressed to himself, despite the constant profession of trust in an all good Deity, they are imbued with a profound spirit of pessimism and soul weariness. Marcus Aurelius courageously resolved to do his duty, but there was little real joy displayed in so doing. He lacked the enkindling hope and enthusiasm which possessed the persecuted Christians.

[IX. 40.] Why dost thou not pray to the gods to give thee the faculty of not fearing the things which thou fearest, nor of desiring the things which thou desirest, nor of being pained at anything, rather than pray that any of these things should not happen? For certainly if the gods can coöperate with men, they can coöperate for these purposes.

[VI. 30.] Reverence the gods and help men. Short is life. There is only one fruit of this mundane life — a pious disposition and acts of social helpfulness.

[IX. 1.] He who acts unjustly acts impiously. For since the universal Nature has made rational animals for the sake of one another to help one another according to their deserts, but in no way to injure one another, he who trangresses her will is clearly guilty of impiety towards the highest divinity

[III. 5.] Be cheerful and seek not external help nor the tranquillity which others give. A man must stand erect, not be kept erect by others.

[XI. 1.] This again is a property of a rational soul — love of one's neighbor.

[III. 6.] [There is nothing better in life than] thy own mind's self-satisfaction in the things which it enables thee to do according to right reason.

[VII. 1.] There is nothing new: all things are both familiar and short lived.

[II. 5.] Every moment think steadfastly as a Roman and as a man to do what thou hast in hand with perfect and simple dignity, and feeling of affection, and freedom and justice, and to give thyself relief from all other thoughts; and thou wilt give thyself relief if thou dost every act in thy life as if it were the last.

[VIII. 24.] Such as bathing appears to thee, — oil, sweat, dirt, filthy water, all things disgusting, — so is every part of life and everything [else].

[IV. 49.] Think of any trouble not that "this is a misfortune," but that "to bear it nobly is good fortune."

[III. 12.] If thou workest at that which is before thee, following right reason seriously, vigorously, calmly, without allowing anything else to distract thee, but keeping thy divine part pure, as if thou were bound to give it back [to God] immediately; if thou holdest to this, expecting nothing, fearing nothing, but satisfied with thy present activity according to nature, and with heroic truth in every word and sound that thou utterest, thou wilt live happy. And there is no man who is able to prevent this.

[IV. 5.] Death is even as the act of being born is, — a mystery of nature.[1]

---

[1] Marcus Aurelius makes it plain that he has no expectation — possibly no desire — of a personal immortality (IV. 21).

108. Isis and Her Worship

Appuleius, "The Golden Ass," book XI, passim. Bohn Translation

In Appuleius's romance we are given a fairly clear idea of the cult of Isis, that Egyptian goddess who became almost naturalized in the Græco-Roman world.   Unfortunately the real dogmas of the devotees of Isis, like those of their rivals of Cybele, Mithras, etc., were genuine "mysteries" and their secrets have perished with the last initiates.   Very likely the outward display of the other Oriental cults would have resembled that of Isis herein described ; and for any one of the prominent deities might it be claimed, as is here claimed for Isis, — that she is the true manifestation of many other divinities.

[The goddess Isis appears in a vision to Lucius, the supposed narrator of the story, and declares herself.]

Behold me, I who am Nature, the parent of all things, the mistress of all elements, the primordial offspring of time, the supreme among the Divinities, the queen of departed spirits, *whose one sole divinity the whole earth venerates under a manifold form.*   The "Mother of the Gods" is what the Phrygians call me, Cecropian Athena I am styled at Athens, Paphian Aphrodite by the Cyprians in their sea-girt isle, Artemis Dictynna by the arrow-bearing Cretans, and the ancient goddess Demeter by the Eleusinians.   But those who are illuminated by the first rays of that holy divinity the Sun — the Ethiopians and the Egyptians so wise in the ancient lore, who worship me in the meetest fashion — they call me by my true name, Queen Isis.

[And after further expatiating upon her power, Isis says :]

Under my protection you will live happy, you will live glorious, and when having accomplished the span of this life you shall descend to the realms below, even there, dwelling as you shall in the Elysian fields, you shall frequently adore me.

[A little later in the story is given this picture of a procession in honor of Isis.]

The marchers were all finely arrayed in divers manners. One man was belted as a soldier, another came as a hunter with a short scarf, a hunting-knife and a javelin. There were those in the arms of gladiators, and one in the purple robes of a magistrate, another like a philosopher with his cloak, his staff, his wooden clogged shoes and his goatish beard. There was a she-bear wearing the dress of a woman, an ape with a plaited straw hat on its head, and an ass on which wings were glued [as representing Bellerophon].

After this merry masquerade the regular procession of the goddess advanced. There were women in white garments with vernal chaplets, scattering flowers along the way. Others sprinkled the streets with drops of balsam and other perfumes. Also there came a multitude of men and women with torches. After them musicians, then a host of both sexes who had been initiated into the sacred rites, resplendent in their white linen garments. The women had their anointed hair enveloped in a transparent veil, but the men had shaven and shining pates, and these "earthly stars" kept up an incessant tinkling upon brazen, silver and even golden sistra.[1]

[Then followed the priests themselves all in white linen and each carrying some holy vessel, or sacred symbol; *e.g.* a miniature palm tree of gold, or a golden corn-fan, and finally one came with a kind of ark] an effable symbol of sublime religion, the mysteries of which are forever to be kept in deep silence. It was of burnished gold, and consisted of a small urn, hollowed out most artistically, and covered with the wonderful Egyptian hieroglyphics. The spout of this urn was very long and not much elevated; a handle was

---

[1] A kind of elaborate rattles, much used in Oriental worships.

attached to the other side, and projected from the urn with a wide sweep. On this lay an asp, uplifting its scaly, wrinkled and swollen throat, and embracing it with its winding folds.[1]

[1] The interpretation of this urn, the hieroglyphics, the snake, etc., was of course a part of the "mysteries" for the initiates.

CHAPTER IX

THE LATER ROMAN EMPIRE AND THE CHRISTIANS

The fourth century was one of the most momentous epochs in history : in it the old paganism was dethroned, Christianity became the recognized religion of the civilized world, and the barbarians effected such a lodgment within the decrepit Empire that its dissolution in the West became merely a matter of years. The story of this period cannot be told by a series of contemporary extracts, however numerous. Still it is possible to illustrate a number of phases of the last era before the downfall of the ancient world. In this chapter will be found first a few excerpts relating to typical persecutions of the Christians, then others illustrating the triumph of Christianity and the new and elaborate institutions of despotism with which Diocletian and Constantine strove to prop up the tottering empire, also a few pictures, *e.g.* from Ammianus Marcellinus, of the splendor, luxury, and withal moral worthlessness which prevailed down to the greatest of historical catastrophes.

As for the triumph of Christianity, no student of civilization will ever underestimate its importance. Here, again, conjecture loses itself asking what would have become of arts, laws, and letters if the Germanic invaders had conquered a world knowing no better deities than Jupiter or Isis. The victory of Christianity over paganism was, as the great German scholar Ulhorn [1] has well said, "the purest ever won. For it was won by witnessing and enduring, by loving and suffering, by pouring out innocent blood." It was won by weak men and women, slaves often, opposed to the mightiest of governments and all the social and intellectual pride and prejudice of the civilized world. Nevertheless it is useless to expect to find a complete regeneration of the ancient world wrought

[1] See his *Conflict of Christianity with Heathenism*, p. 477.

by the mere fiat of a Constantine. Christianity had imbued the Roman Empire very feebly with its vital spirit before the Empire perished from western Europe. Only in the nations which rose on the ruins of that Empire has Christianity been working out slowly and painfully the realization of its precepts.

Turning to the secular side of this period, the importance of the governmental reforms of Diocletian and Constantine are not to be ignored — for it was *their* empire, with its absolute monarch and centralized corps of officials, which the medieval potentates had in mind when they looked back to Rome for law and example, not the Principate of Augustus with its Republican fictions. Nor again should the weakness of the Roman Empire and of its new despotic constitution be exaggerated. If the successors of Augustus ceased to rule in the west in 476 A.D., the successors of Constantine were to reign in Constantinople until 1453. A large part of the stability possessed by the Eastern Empire during its long history is to be attributed to the institutions given it by Diocletian and by the first Christian Emperors.

109. Nero's Persecution of the Christians

Tacitus, " Annals," book XV, chap. 44. Bohn Translation

After the great fire of 64 A.D. Nero — to find some scapegoat for the calamity — singled out the Christians. The passage here given from Tacitus is of enormous importance. It testifies (1) that a generation after the Crucifixion the Christians were an appreciably numerous element in the population of Rome; (2) that they drew their converts from the lowest classes; (3) that the educated classes, though regarding them as innocent of incendiarism, considered them worthy of little pity. Tacitus was a boy in Rome when the persecution took place.

[Not all the efforts of Nero to shift the onus for the fire at Rome from himself] availed to relieve him from the infamy of being believed to have ordered the conflagration [at Rome]. Therefore, to stop the rumor, he falsely charged with guilt, and punished with the most fearful tortures, the persons commonly called Christians, who were [generally] hated for their enormities. Christus, the founder of that "name,"[1] was put to death as a criminal by Pontius Pilate, procurator of Judea, in the reign of Tiberius, but the pernicious superstition — repressed for a time, broke out yet again, not only through Judea, — where the mischief originated, but through the city of Rome also, whither all things horrible and disgraceful flow from all quarters, as to a common receptacle, and where they are encouraged. Accordingly first those were arrested who confessed they were Christians; next on their information,[2] a vast multitude were convicted, not so much on the charge of burning the city, as of " hating the human race."

In their very deaths they were made the subjects of sport : for they were covered with the hides of wild beasts, and worried to death by dogs, or nailed to crosses, or set fire to, and when the day waned, burned to serve for the evening lights. Nero offered his own garden players for the spectacle, and exhibited a Circensian game, indiscriminately mingling with the common people in the dress of a charioteer, or else standing in his chariot. For this cause a feeling of compassion arose towards the sufferers, though guilty and deserving of exemplary capital punishment, because they seemed not to be cut off for the public good, but were victims of the ferocity of one man.

110. How a Female Martyr faced Her Persecutors

Extracts from the "Memoirs of St. Perpetua of Carthage." Translated in Workman, "Persecution in the Early Church," p. 319

St. Perpetua was put to death about 212 A.D. She wrote her own story of her experiences in prison, relating herself the narrative almost down to the time of her actual martyrdom, when other hands completed the story. Few documents give us the uncompro-

---

[1] *I.e.* religious following or sect. Note how Tacitus takes the fact of the historical existence of Jesus and of his crucifixion as a matter of course.

[2] Doubtless wrung from them by torture.

mising spirit of the early Christians better than this.   For the pagan side of a "persecution story" see the very important letter of Pliny the younger to Trajan on page 219.

When I was in the hands of the persecutors, my father in his tender solicitude[1] tried hard to pervert me from the faith.

"My father," I said, "you see this pitcher.   Can we call it by any other name than what it is?"

"No," he said.

"Nor can I," [I said], "call myself by any other name than that of Christian."

So he went away, but, on the rumor that we were to be tried, wasted away with anxiety.

"Daughter," he said, "have pity on my gray hairs; have pity on thy father.   Do not give me over to disgrace.   Behold thy brothers, thy mother, and thy aunt: behold thy child who cannot live without thee.   Do not destroy us all."

Thus spake my father, kissing my hands, and throwing himself at my feet.   And I wept because of my father, for he alone of all my family would not rejoice in my martyrdom.   So I comforted him, saying:

"In this trial what God determines will take place.   We are not in our own keeping, but in God's."   So he left me — weeping bitterly.

[Perpetua and another Christian woman, Felicitas, were tossed and gored by a bull; but despite cruel manglings yet survived.   Perpetua, says a sympathizing recorder] seemed in a trance.   "When are we to be tossed?" she asked, and could scarcely be induced to believe that she had suffered, in spite of the marks on her body.   [They were presently stabbed to death by gladiators] after having exhorted the others to "stand fast in the faith and love one another," she guided to her own throat the uncertain hand of the young gladiator.

---

[1] She was a young wife and mother of barely twenty-two years.

111. CERTIFICATE OF HAVING SACRIFICED TO THE PAGAN GODS

Issued in Egypt during the persecution of Decius from a Papyrus found in the Fayûm District in 1893. Quoted in Workman, "Persecutions in the Early Church," p. 340

About 250 A.D., during Decius's short but furious persecution persons suspected of Christianity were evidently obliged to clear themselves by sacrificing to the old gods, then taking out a certificate to protect themselves against further legal proceedings. This example comes from a small village in Egypt.

To the Commissioners of Sacrifice of the Village of Alexander's Island: from Aurelius Diogenes, the son of Satabus, of the Village of Alexander's Island, aged 72 years: — scar on his right eyebrow.

I have always sacrificed regularly to the gods, and now, in your presence, in accordance with the edict, I have done sacrifice, and poured the drink offering, and tasted of the sacrifices, and I request you to certify the same, Farewell.

Handed in by me, *Aurelius Diogenes.*

I certify that I saw him sacrificing . . .[1]

Done in the first year of the Emperor, Cæsar Gaius Messius Quintus Trajanus Decius, Pius, Felix, Augustus: the second of the month Epith.[2]

112. HOW THE ROMAN OFFICIALS TRIED TO SEIZE CHRISTIAN BOOKS IN 303 A.D.

Workman, "Persecutions in the Early Church" (p. 272), quoting "Deeds of Zenophilus," an early Christian writing

In the great persecution started by Diocletian an especial effort was made to seize all the copies of the Christian scriptures, in the

---

[1] The magistrate's signature is obliterated.
[2] June 26, 250 A.D.

hope of depriving the persecuted sect of the means of preserving and propagating its doctrines. The following tells how the search for the books was conducted in Cirta, an important city of Numidia.

When [the magistrates and a policeman, guided by the apostizing secretaries of the Bishop] came to the house of Felix the tailor, he brought out five books, and when they came to the house of Projectus he brought out five big and two little books. Victor the schoolmaster brought out two books, and four books of five volumes each. Felix the "Perpetual Flamen"[1] said to him,

"Bring your Scriptures out: you have more."

Victor the schoolmaster said, "If I had had more I should have brought them out."

When they came to the house of Eutychius who was a "Cæsarian" [i.e. in the government civil service], the flamen said, "Bring out your books that you may obey the law."

"I have none," he replied.

"Your answer," said Felix, "is taken down."[2]

At the house of Coddeo, Coddeo's wife brought out six books. Felix said, "Look and see if you have not got some more."

The woman said, "I have no more."

Felix said to Bos, the policeman, "Go in and see if she has any more."

The policeman reported, "I have looked and found none."

[Another account tells of a wily bishop, Mensurius of Carthage, who removed all the library of his church, but took care not to leave the shelves bare, but left a number of heretical works. These the pagans seized and were satisfied with, to the secret glee of the orthodox Christians.]

[1] A pagan priest helping with the search.
[2] In order that you may be prosecuted if your assertion is false.

113. How Constantine overthrew Maxentius and favored Christianity

Eusebius, " Life of Constantine," book I, chap. 24 ff.   Bagster's
Translation

In 312 A. D. Constantine the Great, — already master of Gaul
and Spain, — overthrew Maxentius, the evil ruler of Italy, at the
Mulvian Bridge near to Rome.   The victory was followed by dec-
larations by Constantine in favor of Christianity, although he did
not formally become a Christian himself until on his deathbed.
The story of his great change towards a hitherto despised and
persecuted sect, naturally became the subject of miraculous and
semimiraculous stories among the delighted Christians.   The
narrative given by Eusebius, represents at least what was repeated
in Constantine's own lifetime by his Christian subjects.

God the Supreme Governor of the world appointed Constantine to be prince and sovran . . . so that while others
have been raised to this eminence by the election of their
fellow men, he is the only one to whose elevation no mortal
may boast to have contributed.

As soon as he was established on the throne, he began to
care for the interests of his paternal inheritance [especially
Gaul and Britain], and visited with much considerate kindness all those provinces which had previously been under
his father's government.

[Having subdued various barbarian neighbors of his part
of the Empire, he beheld Rome the imperial city oppressed
by the tyranny of Maxentius, emperor of Italy and Africa,
and Constantine speedily resolved to deliver her.]   Being
convinced however that he needed some more powerful aid
than his military forces could afford him, on account of the
wicked and magical enchantments which were so diligently
practiced by the tyrant, he began to seek for Divine assistance,
[as more important even than] weapons, and a huge army.
[He considered how divers emperors had invoked the
heathen gods yet had come to destruction.]   On the other

hand he recollected that his father, who had pursued an entirely opposite course, who had condemned their error
and honored one supreme God during his whole life, had
found Him to be the Savior and Protector of his Empire,
and the Giver of every good thing.

Accordingly he called on Him with earnest prayer and
supplications that He would reveal to him who He was, and
stretch forth His right hand to help him in his present
difficulties. And while Constantine was thus praying with
fervent entreaty, a most marvelous sight appeared to him
in heaven, the account of which might have been difficult to
receive with credit had it been related by any other person.
But since the victorious emperor himself not long afterward
declared it to the writer of this history, when he was honored
with his acquaintance and society, and confirmed this statement with an oath,[1] who could refuse to accredit the relation,
since the testimony of after times has established its truth?
He said that about mid-day, when the sun was beginning to
decline, he saw with his own eyes the trophy of a cross of
light in the heavens, above the sun, and bearing the inscription "BY THIS CONQUER." [2]   At this sight he himself was
struck with amazement, and his whole army also, which
happened to be following him on some expedition and witnessed the miracle.

He said, also, that he doubted within himself what this
apparition could mean. [Presently he fell asleep] and in
his sleep the Christ of God appeared to him with the same
sign which he had seen in the heavens, and commanded
him to procure a standard made in the likeness of that sign,
and to use it as a safeguard in all engagements with his
enemies.

---

[1] Constantine clearly saw the value of Christian support and how by
circulating the story of this wonder he could give his cause a divine sanc-
tion which would encourage the Christians to adhere to him.

[2] "*In hoc signo vinces.*"

At dawn of day he arose and told his friends his secret, then he called together his goldsmiths and jewelers, and sat in their midst, and described to them the figure of the sign which he had seen, bidding them copy it in gold and precious stones.   It was made in the following manner.   A long spear overlaid with gold formed the figure of the cross by means of a piece transversely laid over it.   On the top of the whole was fixed a crown, formed by the intertexture of gold and precious stones ; and thereon were two letters indicating the name of Christ, . . . the [Greek] letter P [Latin *R*] being intersected by X [Latin CH] exactly in its center ; and these letters the Emperor was in the habit of wearing on his helmet at a later period.   From the traverse piece which crossed the spear [was a purple streamer, embroidered with jewels and gold ; and on the staff hung a square banner bearing] a golden portrait, half length, of the pious Emperor and of his children.

[Constantine now devoted himself to the study of Christianity and the Bible,] and he made the priests of God his councilors and deemed it incumbent upon him to honor the God who appeared to him with all devotion. After this, being fortified by well-grounded hopes in Him, he undertook to quench the fury of the fire of tyranny.

[Meantime Maxentius at Rome was giving himself utterly over to deeds of cruelty and lust, and on one occasion caused his guards to massacre a great multitude of the Roman populace.]

In short it is impossible to describe the manifold acts of oppression by which this tyrant of Rome oppressed all his subjects ; so that by this time they were reduced to the most extreme penury and want of necessary food, a scarcity such as our contemporaries do not remember ever to have existed before at Rome.

Constantine, however, filled with compassion on account of all these miseries, began to arm himself with all warlike preparations against the tyranny, and marched with his forces eager to reinstate the Romans in the freedom they had inherited from their ancestors. . . . The Emperor, accordingly, confiding in the help of God, advanced against the first, second, and third divisions of the tyrant's forces, defeated them all with ease at the first assault, and made his way into the very interior of Italy.

Already he was close to Rome, when to save him from the need of fighting with all the Romans for the tyrant's sake, God Himself drew the tyrant, as it were by secret cords, a long way outside the gates. For once, as in the days of Moses and the Hebrew nation, who were worshipers of God, He cast Pharaoh's chariots and his host into the waves of the Red Sea, so at this time did Maxentius, and the soldiers and guards with him, sink to the bottom as a stone, when in his flight before the divinely aided forces of Constantine, he essayed to cross the river [the Tiber] which lay in his way, over which he had made a strong bridge of boats, and had framed an engine of destruction — really against himself, but in hope of ensnaring thereby him who was beloved by God. [But God brought this engine to be Maxentius's undoing:] for the machine, erected on the bridge with the ambuscade concealed therein, giving way unexpectedly before the appointed time, the passage began to sink down, and the boats with the men in them went bodily to the bottom. And first the wretch himself, then his armed attendants and guards, even as the sacred oracles had before described "sank as lead in the mighty waters." [So Constantine and his men might well have rejoiced, even as did Moses and the Israelites over the fate of Pharaoh's host in the Red Sea.]

Then Constantine entered the imperial city in triumph. And here the whole body of the Senate, and others of rank and distinction in the city — freed as it were from the restraint of a prison, along with the whole Roman populace,

their faces expressing the gladness in their hearts, received
him with acclamations and excess of joy — men, women,
and children, with countless multitudes of servants, greeting him as "Deliverer, Preserver, and Benefactor" with
incessant plaudits.

114. How Constantine founded Constantinople

Sozomen, "Ecclesiastical History," book II, chap. 3.   Bohn Translation

Nothing that Constantine the Great did shows his ability more
clearly than his seizing upon the site of old Byzantium for the
location for his new capital.   The place was admirably suited for
an imperial residence, being over against Asia which the Persians
were threatening, and in easy touch with the Danube, where the
Northern Barbarians were always swarming.   Note that Constantinople was from the outset (330 A.D.) a *Christian* city; as
contrasted with old Rome, where paganism still kept a firm grip,
at least on much of the population, for nearly a century.

The Emperor [Constantine] always intent on the advancement of religion erected splendid [Christian] temples to
God in every place — especially in great cities such as
Nicomedia in Bithynia, Antioch on the Orontes, and
Byzantium.   He greatly improved this latter city, and
made it equal to Rome in power and influence; for when
he had settled his empire as he was minded, and had freed
himself from foreign foes, he resolved on founding a city
which should be called by his own name, and should equal
in fame even Rome.   With this intent he went to the plain
at the foot of Troy on the Hellespont . . . and here he
laid out the plan of a large and beautiful city, and built
gates on a high spot of ground, whence they are still visible
from the sea to sailors.   But when he had proceeded thus
far, God appeared to him by night and bade him seek
another site for his city.

Led by the divine hand, he came to Byzantium in Thrace,

beyond Chalcedon in Bithynia, and here he desired to build
his city, and render it worthy of the name of Constantine.
In obedience to the command of God, he therefore enlarged
the city formerly called Byzantium, and surrounded it with
high walls; likewise he built splendid dwelling houses; and
being aware that the former population was not enough for
so great a city, he peopled it with men of rank and their
families, whom he summoned from Rome and from other
countries. He imposed [special] taxes to cover the expenses of building and adorning the city, and of supplying
the inhabitants with food. He erected all the needed
edifices [for a great capital] — a hippodrome, fountains,
porticoes and other beautiful adornments. He named it
Constantinople and *New Rome*, — and established it as the
Roman capital for all the inhabitants of the North, the
South, the East, and the shores of the Mediterranean, from
the cities on the Danube and from Epidamnus and the
Ionian Gulf to Cyrene and Libya.

He created another Senate which he endowed with the
same honors and privileges as that of Rome, and he strove
to render the city of his name equal in every way to Rome
in Italy; nor were his wishes in vain, for by the favor of
God, it became the most populous and wealthy of cities.
As this city became the capital of the Empire during the
period of [Christian] religious prosperity, it was not
polluted by altars, Grecian temples, nor [pagan] sacrifices.
Constantine also honored this new city of Christ by adorning it with many and splendid houses of prayer, in which
the Deity vouchsafed to bless the efforts of the Emperor by
giving sensible manifestations of his presence.[1]

[1] Sozomen goes on to state a remarkable miracle of healing at one of
the churches in Constantinople.

115. A CHRISTIAN'S TESTIMONY TO THE DIVINE SANCTION FOR THE ROMAN EMPIRE

Aurelius Prudentius, Poem "Against Symmachus"

The following was written about 400 A.D. or a little later. It shows how the Christian writers joined with the pagan in ascribing universal and abiding sovereignty to Rome, — only they would see in this the favor of Christian Providence, not of Jupiter, Mars, and the other heathen deities. The theory that there must be one universal (Catholic) Church and one universal Empire possessed the Christians very speedily after the Roman government ceased to persecute them.

O Roman, wouldst thou have me tell what is the true cause of thy triumphs, the hidden seat of thy glory, the arms by which thou hast enchained the world? It is God. . . .

From the shores of the Western Ocean even unto the glittering sea where the day springs, war aforetime vexed humanity. Hands cruel and ever armed knew only to smite and how to wound. God desired to tame their rage. He taught the people to bow their head under one law; to become one and all *Romans,* even all those who dwelt hard by the Rhine and the Danube, from the Elbe to the vasty deep, from the Tagus to the fleece of gold,[1] and those whose cities the Po courses, or where goes the Nile with her tepid waters, fertilizing the fields, ere she loses herself through her seven mouths. An equal law has made all men equal. The same name has bound them together. The chain which assures their obedience has become the chain of fraternal concord. *No matter where we are in the world we live as fellow citizens,*[2] born close by one to another, inclosed within the circuit of the same city, and grown up at the same domestic hearth.

---

[1] Colchis in the Euxine region.

[2] There are few truer or stronger statements of the work of unification wrought by the Roman Empire than this.

This hath been wrought by so many successes and triumphs of Rome. Now, verily, the way is made straight for the coming of Christ; whilst peace and public concord prevail far and wide under a mild governance. Rome and Peace are the two bonds of the universe, and now are they blended in one. O Christ, thou didst not permit the dominion of Rome without Peace [as her consort]. For Peace is Thy delight, and that Peace is wrought by the excellence of Rome : — [of Rome] who knows as well how to govern as she knows how to vanquish.[1]

116. How St. Ambrose Humiliated Theodosius the Great

Theodoret, "Ecclesiastical History," book V, chaps. 17 and 18.
Bohn Translation

What vast power the Christian bishops and clergy were able to assume less than one hundred years after they ceased to be subject to dire persecution, is shown by the following story of the humiliation and penance St. Ambrose, the masterful bishop of Milan, inflicted upon Theodosius I, the last ruler of the undivided Empire.

Thessalonica is a large and populous city, in the province of Macedonia. [In consequence of a sedition there] the anger of the Emperor [Theodosius] rose to the highest pitch, and he gratified his vindictive desire for vengeance by unsheathing the sword most unjustly, and tyrannically against all, slaying the innocent and guilty alike. It is said 7000 perished without any forms of law, and without even having judicial sentence passed upon them; but that, like ears of corn in the time of harvest, they were alike cut down.

When Ambrose [Bishop of Milan] heard of this deplor-

---

[1] There is infinite irony in the fact that these proud lines were written very shortly before the great Empire began to dissolve.

able catastrophe, he went out to meet the Emperor, who —
on his return to Milan — desired as usual to enter the holy
church, but Ambrose prohibited his entrance, saying, "You
do not reflect, it seems, O Emperor, on the guilt you have
incurred by that great massacre; but now that your fury is
appeased, do you not perceive the enormity of your crime?
You must not be dazzled by the splendor of the purple you
wear, and be led to forget the weakness of the body which
it clothes. Your subjects, O Emperor, are of the same
nature as yourself, and not only so, but are likewise your
fellow servants; for there is one Lord and Ruler of all, and
He is the Maker of all creatures, whether princes or people.
How would you look upon the temple of the one Lord of
all? How could you lift up in prayer hands steeped in the
blood of so unjust a massacre? Depart then, and do not by
a second crime add to the guilt of the first."

The Emperor, who had been brought up in the knowledge
of Holy Writ, and who knew well the distinction between
the ecclesiastical and the temporal power, submitted to the
rebuke, and with many tears and groans returned to his
palace. More than eight months after, occurred the festival
of our Saviour's birth. The Emperor shut himself up in
his palace . . . and shed floods of tears.

[After vain attempts by intermediaries to appease the
bishop, Theodosius at last went to Ambrose privately and
besought mercy, saying], "I beseech you, in consideration
of the mercy of our common Lord, to unloose me from these
bonds, and not to shut the door which is opened by the
Lord to all that truly repent." [Ambrose stipulated that
the Emperor should prove his repentance by recalling his
unjust decrees, and especially by ordering] "that when sentence of death or of proscription has been signed against
any one, thirty days are to elapse before execution, and on
the expiration of that time the case is to be brought again
before you, for your resentment will then be calmed [and

you can justly decide the issue]." The Emperor listened to this advice, and deeming it excellent, he at once ordered the law to be drawn up, and himself signed the document. St. Ambrose then unloosed his bonds.

The Emperor, who was full of faith, now took courage to enter holy church, [where] he prayed neither in a standing, nor in a kneeling .posture, but throwing himself on the ground. He tore his hair, struck his forehead, and shed torrents of tears, as he implored forgiveness of God. [Ambrose restored him to favor, but forbade him to come inside the altar rail, ordering his deacon to say], "The priests alone, O Emperor, are permitted to enter within the barriers by the altar. Retire then, and remain with the rest of the laity. A purple robe makes Emperors, but not priests." . . .

[Theodosius uttered some excuses, and meekly obeyed, praising Ambrose for his spirit, and saying], "Ambrose alone deserves the title of 'bishop.'"

117. A Part of the Register of Dignitaries of the Roman Empire

Portion of the "Notitia Dignitatum." Translated in the University of Pennsylvania Historical Reprints, vol. VI, No. 4

Whether this document dates from about 402 A.D. or whether from before 378 A.D. is a little uncertain. Probably the former date is correct ; in any event it gives a good idea of the endless gradations and extreme elaboration of later Roman officialdom ; how every person, high or low, tended to settle into a "status" ; and how, as the spirit died out of the old society, accent upon the form and letter grew ever more extreme. Yet this governmental machine was not useless ; it kept up the administration under very bad and weak Emperors, and probably prolonged the life of the Empire not a little. It is impossible to cite more than a very small portion of this catalogue of high officers.

REGISTER OF DIGNITARIES

Register of the Dignitaries both Civil and Military in the Districts of the East[1]

The Prætorian Præfect of the East.

The Prætorian Præfect of Illyricum.

The Præfect of the City of Constantinople.

Two Masters of the horse and foot in the presence [of the Emperor — *i.e.* at Court ?].

The Master of the horse and foot in the East.

The Master of the horse and foot in Thrace.

The Master of the horse and foot in Illyricum.

The Provost of the " Sacred " Bedchamber.

The Master of the Offices.

The Quæstor.

The Count of the " Sacred " Largesses.

The Count of the Private Domains.

Two Counts of the Household Troops.

The Superintendent of the " Sacred " Bedchamber.

The Chief of the Notaries.

The Warden of the " Sacred " Palace.

The Masters of the Bureaus [of government].

  of memorials.

  of correspondence.

  of requests.

  of Greek [correspondence].

Two Proconsuls : of Asia and of Achaia.

The Count of the East.   [Diocese embracing Syria and Palestine.]

The Augustal Præfect.   [Governing Egypt.]

Four Vicars : for [the diocese] of Asia, of Pontus, of Thraces, of Macedonia.

Two military Counts : of Egypt, and of Isauria [district in Asia Minor].

[1] The officials for the West appear on a separate list here omitted.

Thirteen "Dukes."[1]   [Their districts are given.]
Fifteen "Consulars."   [Their districts are given.]
Forty "Presidents."   [Their districts are given.]
Two "Correctors."   [Their districts are given.]

The Prætorian Præfect of the East.   Under the control of the "Illustrious"[2] prætorian præfect of the East are the dioceses below mentioned, of the East, of Egypt, of Pontus, of Thrace : —

Provinces of [the diocese of the East] fifteen, — Palestine, Phœnicia, Cilicia, Cyprus, Arabia . . . Isauria, Palestina salutaris, Palestina secunda, Mesopotamia, etc.
Provinces of the diocese of Egypt five [list given].
Provinces of the diocese of Asia ten [list given].
Provinces of the diocese of Pontus ten [list given].
Provinces of the diocese of Thrace six [list given].
The staff of the illustrious prætorian præfect of the East: a chief of staff, a chief deputy, a chief assistant, a custodian, a keeper of records, a receiver of taxes, a curator of correspondence, a registrar [and many more].

[And similar lists are given for the other Prætorian Præfect.]

The Master of the Soldiery in the [Imperial] Presence. Under the command of the illustrious Master of the Soldiery in the Presence are : —

Five squadrons of "Palatine" horse : —
The "senior promoted" horse.
The companion cuirassiers.
The junior companion archers.
The companion Taifalians.
The Arcadian horse.

[1] The Dukes are military officers : the last three grades of officials named are provincial governors.

[2] "Illustrious" was the highest official title in the later Empire, next in honor was "Worshipful" (*Spectabilis*), and next "Right Honorable" (*Clarissimus*). About all high dignitaries had one of these titles.

Seven squadrons of the horse of the line : —
[Names of the divisions follow.]
Six " Palatine " [Infantry] Legions : —
  The senior lancers.
  The junior Jovians.
  The junior Herculeans.
  The Fortenses.
  The Nervii.
  The junior Martiarii.
Eighteen " Palatine " *Auxilia* : —
  [Names of divisions follow.]

The staff of the aforesaid Master in the Presence is [made up from officers] enrolled with the forces and assigned to staff duty.   It includes the officers named below : —

  A chief of staff.
  Two accountants.
  A custodian.
  Chief clerks who become accountants [and many others].

[Omitting the forces and subordinates of the " Master of the Soldiery in East," of the " Keeper of the Sacred Bedchamber," and of several high civil officials, a typical governmental department may be taken up.]

The Count of the Sacred Largesses.   Under the control of the illustrious Count of the Sacred Largesses [are the following] : —

The Counts of the Largesses in all the Dioceses.
The Counts of the Markets : —
  In the East and in Egypt.
  In Mœsia, Scythia, and Pontus.
  In Illyricum.
The keepers of the storehouses.
The Counts of the Metals in Illyricum.

The Count and the Accountant of the general tribute of
Egypt.
The accountants of the general tribute.
The masters of the linen vesture.
The procurators of the weaving houses.
The procurators of the mints.
The keepers of the goods dispatch.
The procurators of the linen weavers.

The staff of the aforesaid Count of the Sacred Largesses
includes: —

The chief clerk of the whole staff.
The chief clerk of the bureau of fixed taxes.
The chief clerk of the bureau of accounts.
The clerk of the bureau of gold bullion.
The chief clerk of the bureau of gold for shipment [and
many other clerks, etc.].

[The other great civil ministers have a similar corps of aids and
deputies in the provinces or at the central bureau at Constantinople.]

118. How Theodosius the Great struck awe into the Goths

Jordanes, "History of the Goths," chap. 28. Mierow's Translation

Theodosius I, a clever Spaniard, became Emperor of the East
in 378 A.D. The Visigoths — following the battle of Adrianople,
were overrunning the Balkan peninsula, but he skillfully checked
them, and made a truce. The awe and majesty of the Roman
name was still potent with the Barbarians, and in what manner
they were dazzled by the seeming strength and impregnability of
Constantinople is here explained.

[After the Emperor Theodosius I had made a truce with
the Goths] he gave gifts to their King Athanaric, who had
succeeded King Fritigern, made an alliance with him and in
the most gracious manner invited him to visit him in Con-

stantinople.   Athanaric very gladly consented and as he
entered the royal city exclaimed in wonder, "Lo, now I see
what I have often heard of with unbelieving ears," meaning
the great and famous city.   Turning his eyes hither and
thither, he marveled as he beheld the situation of the city,
the coming and going of the ships, the splendid walls, and
the people of divers nations gathered like a flood of waters
streaming from different regions into one basin.

So too when he saw the [Roman] army in array, he said,
" *Truly the Emperor is a god on earth*, and whoso raises a
hand against him is guilty of his own blood."   In the midst
of his admiration, and the enjoyment of even greater honors
at the hand of the Emperor, he departed this life after a
space of a few months.[1]

The Emperor had such affection for him that he honored
Athanaric even more when he was dead than in his lifetime,
for he not only gave him a worthy burial, but himself
walked before the bier at the funeral.   Now when Athanaric
was dead, his whole army continued in the service of the
Emperor Theodosius and submitted to the Roman rule, forming as it were one body with the imperial soldiery: [and
20,000 Goths served Theodosius valiantly in his successful
war against the rebel Eugenius].

119. The Luxury and Arrogance of the Rich in Rome

Ammianus Marcellinus, History: book XIV, chap. **16**. Bohn
Translation

The following was written only about a generation before Alaric
plundered Rome in 410 A.D.   The emptiness, shallowness, lack of
all real culture that prevailed in the ancient capital, and the disgust that an enforced sojourn in Rome produced on simple and
honest-minded men, is very clearly set forth.   Unless Ammianus

---

[1] No doubt the lavish Roman hospitality told on the good Barbarian's
constitution!

was guilty of gross exaggeration, Rome had in his time ceased to represent anything for the world's betterment.

[Despite the changes of the times] Rome is still looked upon as the queen of the earth, and the name of the Roman people is respected and venerated. But the [magnificence of Rome] is defaced by the inconsiderate levity of a few, who never recollect where they are born, but fall away into error and licentiousness as if a perfect immunity were granted to vice. Of these men, some, thinking that they can be handed down to immortality by means of statues, are eager after them, as if they would obtain a higher reward from brazen figures unendowed with sense than from a consciousness of upright and honorable actions; and they are even anxious to have them plated over with gold !

Others place the summit of glory in having a couch higher than usual, or splendid apparel; and so toil and sweat under a vast burden of cloaks which are fastened to their necks by many clasps, and blow about by the excessive fineness of the material, showing a desire by the continual wriggling of their bodies, and especially by the waving of the left hand, to make more conspicuous their long fringes and tunics, which are embroidered in multiform figures of animals with threads of divers colors.

Others again, put on a feigned severity of countenance, and extol their patrimonial estates in a boundless degree, exaggerating the yearly produce of their fruitful fields, which they boast of possessing in numbers, from east and west, being forsooth ignorant that their ancestors, who won greatness for Rome, were not eminent in riches; but through many a direful war overpowered their foes by valor, though little above the common privates in riches, or luxury, or costliness of garments.

. . . If now you, as an honorable stranger, should enter the house of any passing rich man, you will be hospitably received, as though you were very welcome; and after having had many questions put to you, and having been forced to tell a number of lies, you will wonder — since the gentleman has never seen you before — that a person of high rank should pay such attention to a humble individual like yourself, so that you become exceeding happy, and begin to repent not having come to Rome ten years before. When, however, relying on this affability you do the same thing the next day, you will stand waiting as one utterly unknown and unexpected, while he who yesterday urged you to "come again," counts upon his fingers who you can be, marveling for a long time whence you came, and what you can want. But when at last you are recognized and admitted [again] to his acquaintance, if you should devote yourself to him for three years running, and after that cease with your visits for the same stretch of time, then at last begin them again, you will never be asked about your absence any more than if you had been dead, and you will waste your whole life trying to court the humors of this blockhead.

But when those long and unwholesome banquets, which are indulged in at periodic intervals, begin to be prepared, or the distribution of the usual dole baskets takes place, then it is discussed with anxious care, whether, when those to whom a return is due are to be entertained, it is also proper to ask in a stranger; and if after the question has been duly sifted, it is determined that this may be done, the person preferred is one who hangs around all night before the houses of charioteers, or one who claims to be an expert with dice, or affects to possess some peculiar secrets. For hosts of this stamp avoid all learned and sober men as unprofitable and useless, — with this addition, that the *nomenclators*[1] also, who usually make a market of these invitations and such favors, selling them for

[1] Nomenclators were slaves who always went with a great noble to remind him of the names of people whom he had met before.

bribes, often for a fee thrust into these dinners mean and obscure creatures indeed.

The whirlpool of banquets, and divers other allurements of luxury I omit, lest I grow too prolix. Many people drive on their horses recklessly, as if they were post horses, with a legal right of way, straight down the boulevards of the city, and over the flint-paved streets, dragging behind them huge bodies of slaves, like bands of robbers. And many matrons, imitating these men, gallop over every quarter of the city, with their heads covered, and in closed carriages. And [like skillful generals] so the stewards of these city households [make careful arrangement of the cortege; the stewards themselves being] conspicuous by the wands in their right hands. First of all before the [master's] carriage march all his slaves concerned with spinning and working; next come the blackened crew employed in the kitchen; then the whole body of slaves promiscuously mixed with a gang of idle plebeians; and last of all, the multitude of eunuchs,[1] beginning with the old men and ending with the boys, pale and unsightly from the deformity of their features.

Those few mansions which were once celebrated for the serious cultivation of liberal studies, now are filled with ridiculous amusements of torpid indolence, reëchoing with the sound of singing, and the tinkle of flutes and lyres. You find a singer instead of a philosopher; a teacher of silly arts is summoned in place of an orator, the libraries are shut up like tombs, [but] organs played by water-power are built, and lyres so big that they look like wagons! and flutes, and huge machines suitable for the theater.

[The Romans] have even sunk so far, that not long ago, when a dearth was apprehended, and the foreigners were

[1] This frequent use of eunuchs was an abuse of the later rather than the earlier Empire.

driven from the city,[1] those who practiced liberal accomplishments were expelled instantly, yet the followers of actresses and all their ilk were suffered to stay; and three thousand dancing girls were not even questioned, but remained unmolested along with the members of their choruses, and a corresponding number of dancing masters.

[On account of the frequency of epidemics in Rome, rich men take absurd precautions to avoid contagion, but even] when these rules are observed thus stringently, some persons, if they be invited to a wedding, though the vigor of their limbs be vastly diminished, yet when gold is pressed in their palm [2] they will go with all activity as far as Spoletum! So much for the nobles.

As for the lower and poorer classes some spend the whole night in the wine shops, some lie concealed in the shady arcades of the theaters. They play at dice so eagerly as to quarrel over them, snuffing up their nostrils, and making unseemly noises by drawing back their breath into their noses: — or (and this is their favorite amusement by far) from sunrise till evening, through sunshine or rain, they stay gaping and examining the charioteers and their horses; and their good and bad qualities.

Wonderful indeed it is to see an innumerable multitude of people, with prodigious eagerness, intent upon the events of the chariot race!

[1] To lessen the number of mouths to fill.

[2] It was usual to make a present of a small sum of money on such occasions to each regular guest. Spoletum was a town in Umbria.

CHAPTER X

THE DYING EMPIRE AND THE GERMAN INVADERS

The story of the fall of the Roman Empire is exceedingly hard for young students to understand. This is because the history of the world is losing that unity which it possessed while all political power was centralized on the Tiber, and one becomes highly confused in tracing down the respective advances of the Visigoths, Vandals, Ostrogoths, Burgundians, Franks, Lombards, Angles, and the innumerable lesser tribes which cast themselves upon the dying Empire ; furthermore, the difficulty is increased by the fact that every one of the kingdoms founded by these invaders was presently to be blotted out, saving always the monarchy of the Franks. A source book is no place wherein to develop the story of these kingdoms, but it is possible to give some vivid pictures of the terrible fifth and sixth centuries when Europe was painfully ridding herself of her old government and society and was preparing to assume things new.

Thus we can have excerpts illustrating the state of the Germans while still in "the forest primeval," and others giving effective glimpses of the progress of the invasions, the fearful interposition of the Huns (more inimical to the Germans even than to the Romans) and of the development of the spirit of Christianity — however feeble at first — among the raw Barbarians, who found in the civilized territories of the Empire a perfect wonderland, and who were prepared to accept the institutions of the Church in much the same receptive spirit with which they learned to make use of marble palaces and the delicious southern wines. Again we may cast our eyes upon Constantinople, with its glory, its commerce, and its survival of imperial power — a power not to be despised by the German, as Vandal and Ostrogoth found to their sore cost in the days of Justinian. Finally in Clovis and his Franks can be seen that fraction of the invaders, — cruel, treacherous, almost

310

savages in their habits, and actual pagans when they entered Gaul, — who were destined by a strange Providence to found modern France and Germany, and to affect to a marked degree the history of modern Italy.

The misery and wanton destruction brought to pass during the period of the invasions must not be underestimated. It was an era when any man of refined instincts and a lover of the intellectual life must have despaired of letters, arts, of everything, in short, associated with civilized existence. On the other hand, as Rome was not built in a day, she did not fall in a day. The Barbarians did not always come as devouring conquerors. They were willing to confess the men of the Empire superior to themselves in all human activities save war. Very often they settled beside the Romanized provincials quite peacefully. Above all, they had deep awe for the august shadow of that Empire, which they claimed to wish to share rather than to destroy. And even more than the name of the Empire, they held in reverence the authority of the Church, the " Power not of this World," which was the more terrible, because it fought with unseen weapons, and not with battle-axes. The Roman Emperor vanished ; the Roman Pope remained, and therein lies the interpretation of many chapters of medieval history.

120. THE DEATH AND BURIAL OF ALARIC THE VISIGOTH

Jordanes, " History of the Goths," chap. 30. Mierow's Translation

Alaric died shortly after he had pillaged Rome (410 A.D.). The famous story of his burial is here given, as preserved in the legends of his people. Although not a leader of the very first order, not many generals have been permitted to make a greater impress upon history than this tall, blonde Visigoth who broke the spell of the inviolability of Rome.

[After Alaric's Visigoths had sacked Rome] they departed to bring like ruin upon Campania and Lucania, and then came to Brutii. To this place came Alaric, king of the Visigoths, with the wealth of all Italy which he had taken as spoil, and from there, he intended to cross by way of

Sicily to the quiet land of Africa. But since man is not free to do anything he wishes without the will of God, that dread strait [betwixt Italy and Sicily] sunk several of his ships and threw all into confusion.

Alaric was cast down by the reverse, and while deliberating what he should do, was suddenly overtaken by an untimely death and departed from human cares. His people mourned for him with the uttermost affection. Then turning from its course the river Busentus near the city of Consentia — for the stream flows with its wholesome waters from the foot of a mountain near that city — they led a band of captives into the midst of its bed to dig out a place for his grave. In the depths of this pit they buried Alaric, together with many treasures, and then turned the waters back into their channel. And that none might ever know the place, they put to death all the diggers.

They bestowed the kingdom of the Visigoths on Athavulf, his kinsman, who returned again to Rome, and whatever had escaped the first sack his Goths stripped bare like locusts, not merely despoiling Italy of its private but even of its public resources. [Presently, however, he made peace with the Emperor Honorius, married his sister, and became his ally against the other Barbarians invading the Empire.]

121. DESCRIPTION OF THE EARLY GERMANS

Tacitus, "Germania," chap. 4 ff. to 20. Bohn Translation

About 100 A.D. the Great Latin historian wrote this account of the peoples and manners of Germany. Perhaps his aim was to point a moral, by contrasting the chaste, unaffected forest children, with the artificial, corrupt society of the Empire. In any case, he has left us an invaluable picture of the life of the race that was to possess so much of Europe and America. Tacitus probably had never visited Germany, but he could draw fairly accurate information from Roman traders and soldiers, and possibly from German captives.

I agree in the opinion that the Germans have never inter-married with other nations; but to be a race pure, unmixed, and stamped with a distinct character. Hence a family likeness pervades the whole, though they are so numerous: — eyes stern and blue; ruddy hair; large bodies, power-ful in sudden exertions, but impatient of toil and labor, least of all capable of sustaining thirst and heat. Cold and hunger they are accustomed by their climate and soil to endure.

The land, though varied to a considerable extent in its aspect, is yet universally shagged with forests, or deformed by marshes; moister on the side of Gaul, more bleak on the side of Noricum and Pannonia. It is productive of grain, but unkindly to fruit trees. It abounds in flocks and herds, but generally of a small breed.

[There are very few metals in the country; and coined money is scarce, though not unknown.] Even iron is not plentiful among them, as may be inferred from the nature of their weapons. Swords or broad lances are seldom used; but they generally carry a spear, called in their language *framea,* which has an iron blade, short and narrow, but so sharp and manageable that, as occasion requires, they use it either for close or distant fighting. Few are provided with a coat of mail; and scarcely here and there one with a casque or helmet [though all have shields].

Their line of battle is drawn in wedges. To give ground, provided they rally again, is considered rather as a prudent strategem than cowardice. . . . The greatest disgrace that can befall them is to have abandoned their shields. A per-son branded with this ignominy cannot join in their religious rites, or enter their assemblies; so that many, after escaping from battle, have ended their infamy by the halter.

Political Institutions of the Germans

In election of *kings* they have regard to birth; in that of *generals* to valor. Their kings have not an absolute or unlimited power, and their generals command less through the force of authority than of example. If they are daring, adventurous, and conspicuous in action, they procure obedience from the admiration they inspire. It is a principal incentive to their courage that their squadrons and battalions are not formed by men fortuitously collected, but by the assemblage of families and clans. Their pledges are also near at hand; they have within hearing the yells of the women, and the cries of their children. [The women care for the wounded and boldly] carry food and encouragement to the men who are fighting.

On affairs of small moment the chiefs consult. On those of greater importance, the whole community, yet with the circumstance that what is referred to the decision of the people is first maturely discussed by the chiefs. [At their assemblies] they all sit down armed. Silence is proclaimed by the priests. Then the king, or chief, or such others as are conspicuous for age, birth, military renown, or eloquence are heard; and gain attention rather from their ability to persuade, than their authority to command. If a proposal displeases, the assembly reject it by an inarticulate murmur; if it prove agreeable, they clash their javelins; for the most honorable expression of assent among them is from the sound of arms.

Before this council, too, it is allowed to prosecute capital offenses. Punishments are varied according to the crime. Traitors and deserters are hung upon trees; cowards, renegades, and vile livers are suffocated with mud under a hurdle. [Lesser offenses are punished by fines of] horses and cattle. Part of the mulct goes to the king or state, part to the injured man or his kindred.

In these same assemblies chiefs are also elected to administer justice in the cantons and districts [of the tribe]. A hundred "companions," chosen by the people, attend upon each, to aid them both by their advice and their authority.

German Youths and War-bands

[When a youth is man grown] then in the midst of the assembly, one of the chiefs, or the father, or a relation, equips the youth with a shield and javelin. Before this the lads are counted simply part of a household; afterward part of the state. [Young men are associated as companions of a distinguished chief] and there is great emulation among the "companions" who shall possess the highest place in the favor of their chief; and among the chiefs who shall have the most and the bravest "companions." [The chief with the finest band of "companions" enjoys the highest honor in peace and war.] It is reproach and infamy during a whole succeeding life for "companions" to retreat from the battle surviving him. To aid, to protect him; to place their own gallant actions to the account of his glory, is their first and most sacred engagement. The chief fights for victory; the "companions" for their chief. The "companion" requires from his lord's bounty, the warlike steed, the bloody and conquering spear; in place of pay he expects to be supplied with a table, homely indeed, but plentiful. [These "companions" have to be maintained by constant feuds and booty, else they may desert their chief for another more warlike.]

Domestic Customs of the Germans

It is well known that the Germans do not inhabit cities. They dwell scattered and separate, as a spring, meadow, or grove may chance to invite them. [In their villages] they are not acquainted with the use of mortar and tiles; and for every purpose use rude unshapen timber, fashioned with no view to beauty; but they take great pains to coat parts of their buildings with a kind of earth, so pure and shining that it gives them the appearance of painting. They also dig underground caves, and cover them over with a great quantity of manure. These they use as winter retreats and granaries. . . .

The marriage bond is strict and severe among them; nor are any of their manners more praiseworthy than this. Almost singly among the Barbarians they content themselves with one wife, [though a very few great chiefs are polygamists. When a woman is married] she is admonished by the ceremonial that she comes to her husband as a partner of his toils and dangers, to suffer and to dare equally with him in peace and in war. The women live therefore fenced around with chastity, corrupted by no seductive spectacles, no convivial excitements. Adultery is extremely rare among so numerous a people [and profligate women are outcasts from society]. Every mother suckles her own children and does not deliver them into the hands of servants and nurses [as at Rome]. The young people are equally matched in their marriage, and the children inherit the vigor of their parents.

122. Effect upon the World of the Taking of Rome by Alaric

Dill, " Roman Society in the Last Century of the Western Empire," p. 305

Professor Dill, a well-known writer, has given the following opinion touching the effect produced upon the world of the great deed of Alaric — as the news of the incredible disaster penetrated the remote provinces.

In 410, when after the failure of all negotiations, the city [of Rome] had at last fallen a prey to the army of Alaric, everything was changed. Eight hundred years had passed since Rome had been violated by the Gauls of Brennus. In spite of all the troubles on the frontiers, in spite of the alarms of the great invasions of the second, third, and fourth centuries, the sacred center of government had never realized the possibility that her own stately security would ever be disturbed. Not only had all true sons of Rome a religious faith in her mission and destiny, but they had good reason to rely on the awe which she inspired in the barbarous races who ranged around her frontiers.

But now the spell was broken ; the mystery and awe which surrounded the great city had been pierced and set at nought. The moral force, so much more important in government than the material, had been weakened and desecrated. The shock given by this great catastrophe to old Roman confidence and pride must, for the time, have been overwhelming. We can conjecture the feelings [of men of the time . . .] from the words St. Jerome penned in his cell in Bethlehem in the year 411. Although he had fled from the world, he was still a Roman at heart, steeped in her literary culture, and proud of her great history. When the rumor of the fall of Rome reached him, he broke off his commentary on Ezekiel; his voice was choked with sobs as he thought of the capture of the great city, "which had taken captive all the world."

In an earlier letter, referring to the invasion of the eastern provinces, he says that his soul shudders at the ruin of his time. For twenty years all the lands from Constantinople to the Julian Alps are drenched with Roman blood. The provinces are a prey to Alans, Huns, Vandals, and Marcomanni. Matrons and virgins devoted to God, the noble and the priest, are made a sport of these monsters. The churches are demolished; the bones of the martyrs are dug up; horses are stabled at the altars of Christ. "The Roman world is sinking in ruin, . . . and yet we wish to live, and think that those who have been taken from such a scene are to be mourned rather than deemed happy in their fate. It is through our sins that the barbarians are strong."

[In another letter] he speaks of the countless hordes that have swept from the Rhine to the Pyrenees. Great cities like Mainz, Rheims, and Nantes have been wiped out; the provinces of Aquitaine, Lyons, and Narbonne have been desolated, thousands have been butchered even in the churches, and famine has completed the work of the sword.

[St. Jerome may be overcoloring the extent of the disaster, but] there can be no doubt that the moral effect of the capture was for the moment overwhelming.

123. THE GREATNESS OF ROME EVEN IN THE DAYS OF RUIN

Poem of Rutilius Numantius, " On his Return," book I, ll. 47 ff.

Rutilius Numantius, a native of Gaul, but about 413 A.D. the City Præfect of Rome, wrote this poem in praise of the city that he had seen plundered by Alaric. He was a pagan, one of the circle of literary men who fixed their eyes on the glorious past, and had no pleasure in Christianity. His tribute to the greatness of Rome is clear evidence that even the awful calamities of the reign of Honorius did not shatter men's faith in the abiding majesty and empire of the Eternal City.

Give ear to me, Queen of the world which thou rulest, O Rome, whose place is amongst the stars! Give ear to me, mother of men, and mother of gods!

Through thy temples we draw near to the very heaven. Thee do we sing, yea and while the Fates give us life, thee we *will* sing. For who can live and forget thee ? Before thy image my soul is abased — graceless and sacrilegious, it were better for me to forget the sun, for thy beneficent influence shinest — even as his light — to the limits of the habitable world. Yea the sun himself, in his vast course, seems only to turn in thy behalf.   He riseth upon thy domains; and on thy domains, it is again that he setteth.

As far as from one pole to the other spreadeth the vital power of nature, so far thy virtue hath penetrated over the earth.   For all the scattered nations thou createst one common country.   Those that struggle against thee are constrained to bend to thy yoke; for thou profferest to the conquered the partnership in thy just laws; thou hast made one city what was aforetime the wide world!

O Queen, the remotest regions of the universe join in a hymn to thy glory!   Our heads are raised freely under thy peaceful yoke.   For thee to reign, is less than to have so deserved to reign; the grandeur of thy deeds surpasses even thy might destinies.

124. A Picture of a Visigothic King

A Letter of Sidonius Apollinaris.   Abridged from the Translation in Sheppard, "Fall of Rome," pp. 433–437

Theodoric II reigned over the Visigoths in South Gaul from 453 to 466 A.D.   He was the grandson of Alaric the Conqueror. This picture of him is drawn by a courtly Gallo-Roman bishop who had every reason to flatter this leader of the new lords of the land.   Making ample allowances, however, we can conclude that the Gothic kings soon absorbed a veneer of Roman culture, and liked to keep up the show of a Cæsar, treating the provincials fairly graciously; although at heart they were still crude Barbarians.

"He is a prince well worthy of being known even by those not admitted to his intimate acquaintance, to such a degree have Nature and God, the sovran Arbiter of all things, accumulated in his person gifts of varied excellence. His character is such that even envy itself, that universal accompaniment of all royalty, could not defraud him of his due praise."

"You ask me to describe his daily outdoor life.   Accompanied by a very small suite he attends before daybreak the

services of the Church in his own household; he is careful
in his devotions, but although his tone is suppressed, you
may perceive that this is more a matter of habit with him
than of religious principle. The business of administration
occupies the rest of the morning. An armed aide-de-camp
stands beside his throne; his band of fur-clad bodyguards
is admitted to the Palace in order that they may be near to
the royal presence; while in order that there may not be
too much noise, they are kept out of the room; and so they
talk in murmurs, inside a railing and outside the hangings
[of the hall of audience].

"Envoys from foreign powers are then introduced. The
King listens much and says little. If their business calls
for discussion, he puts it off; if for prompt action, he presses
it forward. At eight o'clock[1] he rises, and proceeds to
examine either his treasures, or his stables. When he goes
to hunt, he does not deem it suitable to the royal dignity
to carry his bow upon his own person; when, however, . . .
any one points out to him a wild animal or bird, he puts
out his hand, and receives his bow unstrung from a page:
for, just as he regards it as an undignified thing to carry
the weapon in its case, so does he deem it unmanly it should
be prepared by another for his use. He selects an arrow
. . . and lets fly, first asking what you wish him to strike.
You make your choice and invariably he hits the mark;
indeed if there is ever any mistake, it is oftener in the sight
of him who points out the object than in the aim of him
who shoots at it.

"His banquets do not differ from those of a private
gentleman. You never see the vulgarity of a vast mass of
tarnished plate, heaped upon a groaning table by a puffing
and perspiring slave. The only thing that is weighty is the
conversation: for either serious subjects are discussed, or

[1] Note how early in the morning formal business is begun and disposed of.

none at all. Sometimes purple, and sometimes fine silk are employed in adorning the furniture of the dining room. The dinner is recommended by the skill of the cookery, not by the costliness of the provisions: — the plate by its brightness, not by its massive weight. The guests are much more frequently called upon to complain of thirst, from finding the goblet too seldom pressed, than to shun ebriety by refusing it. In brief, one sees there the elegance of Greece and promptness of Italy, the splendor of a public along with the personal attention of a private entertainment, likewise the regular order of a royal household. After dinner Theodoric either takes no siesta at all or a very short one. When he feels like it, he picks up the dice quickly, looks at them carefully, shakes them scientifically, throws them at once, jocularly addresses them, and awaits the result with patience. When the cast is a good one he says nothing: when bad, he laughs; good or bad he is never angry, and takes both philosophically. . . .

" About three in the afternoon again come the cares of government, back come the suitors, and back those whose duty it is to keep them at a distance. On all sides is heard a wrangling and intriguing crowd, which, prolonged to the royal dinner hour, then only begins to diminish; after that it disperses, every man to seek his own patron. Occasionally, though not often, jesters are admitted to the royal banquet, without, however, being permitted to vent their malicious raillery upon any persons present.[1] When he has risen from table, the guard of the treasury commences its nightly vigil: armed men take their station at all approaches to the palace, whose duty it will be to watch there during the first hours of the night."

[Despite this eulogy, Theodoric II had climbed to power by the foul murder of his brother, the rightful king.]

---

[1] As was evidently the custom in other great houses.

125. An Account of the Person of Attila

Jordanes, "History of the Goths," chap. 35.   Mierow's Translation

Attila ruled the Huns from 434 to 453 A. D.   During that time the "Scourge of God" held in terror nearly all the known world.   A Gothic chronicler leaves us this account of his personal traits and appearance.   Probably like other savage conquerors of his type Attila was a curious combination of qualities admirable and diabolical.

When Attila's brother Bleda who ruled over a great part of the Huns had been slain by Attila's treachery, the latter united all the people under his own rule.   Gathering also a host of the other tribes which he then held under his sway he sought to subdue the foremost nations of the world — the Romans and the Visigoths.   His army is said to have numbered 500,000 men.   He was a man born into the world to shake the nations, the scourge of all lands, who in some way terrified all mankind by the dreadful rumors noised abroad concerning him.   He was haughty in his walk, rolling his eyes hither and thither, so that the power of his proud spirit appeared in the movement of his body.   He was indeed a lover of war, yet restrained in action, mighty in counsel, gracious to suppliants and lenient to those who were once received into his protection.   He was short of stature, with a broad chest and a large head : his eyes were small, his beard thin and sprinkled with gray : and he had a flat nose and a swarthy complexion showing the evidences of his origin.

126. The Battle of the Catalaunian Plains or of Chalons

Jordanes, "History of the Goths," chap. 38.   Mierow's Translation

In 451 A.D. Attila the Hun with his hordesmen, after having been repulsed before Orleans in Gaul, was brought to bay by Aëtius,

the Roman general, and his allies, the Germanic Visigoths, Burgundians, and Franks. It should be remembered in this connection
that the Huns were, if possible, more hated by the Germans than
by the Romans. The battle represented the first alliance of the
western races against "the yellow peril." Even if Attila had won,
his empire would probably have soon gone to pieces, but not until
an irreparable shock had been given the civilized life of Gaul.

The armies met in the Catalaunian Plains. The battle
field was a plain rising by a sharp slope to a ridge which
both armies sought to gain; for advantage of position is a
great help. The Huns with their forces seized the right
side, the Romans, the Visigoths and their allies the left, and
then began a struggle for the yet untaken crest. Now
Theodorid with his Visigoths held the right wing, and
Aëtius with the Romans the left [of the line against Attila].
On the other side, the battle line of the Huns was so arranged
that Attila and his bravest followers were stationed in the
center. In arranging them thus the king had chiefly
his own safety in view, since by his position in the very
midst of his race, he would be kept out of the way of threatened danger. The innumerable peoples of divers tribes,
which he had subjected to his sway, formed the wings.
Now the crowd of kings — if we may call them so — and the
leaders of various nations hung upon Attila's nod like slaves,
and when he gave a sign even by a glance, without a murmur
each stood forth in fear and trembling, or at all events did
as he was bid. Attila alone was king of kings over all and
concerned for all.

So then the struggle began for the advantage of position
we have mentioned. Attila sent his men to take the summit
of the mountain, but was outstripped by Thorismud [crown
prince of the Visigoths] and Aëtius, who in their effort to
gain the top of the hill reached higher ground, and through
this advantage easily routed the Huns as they came up.

When Attila saw his army was thrown into confusion by

the event he [urged them on with a fiery harangue and . . .] inflamed by his words they all dashed into the battle.

And although the situation was itself fearful, yet the presence of the king dispelled anxiety and hesitation. Hand to hand they clashed in battle, and the fight grew fierce, confused, monstrous, unrelenting — *a fight whose like no ancient time has ever recorded.* There were such deeds done that a brave man who missed this marvelous spectacle could not hope to see anything so wonderful all his life long. For if we may believe our elders a brook flowing between low banks through the plain was greatly increased by blood from the wounds of the slain. Those whose wounds drove them to slake their parching thirst drank water mingled with gore. In their wretched plight they were forced to drink what they thought was the blood they had poured out from their own wounds.

Here King Theodorid [the Visigoth] while riding by to encourage his army, was thrown from his horse and trampled under foot by his own men, thus ending his days at a ripe old age. But others say he was slain by the spear of Andag of the host of the Ostrogoths who were then under the sway of Attila. Then the Visigoths fell on the horde of the Huns and nearly slew Attila. But he prudently took flight and straightway shut himself and his companions within the barriers of the camp which he had fortified with wagons. [The battle now became confused: chieftains became separated from their forces: night fell with the Roman-Gothic army holding the field of combat.]

At dawn on the next day the Romans saw that the fields were piled high with corpses, and that the Huns did not venture forth; they thought that the victory was theirs, but knew that Attila would not flee from battle unless overwhelmed by a great disaster. Yet he did nothing cowardly, like one that is overcome, but with clash of arms sounded the trumpets and threatened an attack. [His enemies] determined to wear him out by a siege. It is said that the king remained supremely brave even in this extremity and had heaped up a funeral pyre of horse trappings, so that if the enemy should attack him he was determined to cast himself into the flames, that none might have the joy of wounding him, and that the lord of so many races might not fall into the hands of his foes.

[However, owing to dissensions between the Romans and Goths he was allowed to escape to his home land, and] in this most famous war of the bravest tribes, 160,000 men are said to have been slain on both sides.

127. The Youth and Rise to Power of Theodoric the Ostrogoth

Jordanes, " History of the Goths," chaps. 52 and 57. Mierow's Translation.

The Ostrogoths had been reduced to vassalage by the Huns. After the breakup of Attila's empire, they recovered their liberty, and entered the Eastern Empire seeking a place of settlement and booty, — something after the manner of their kinsfolk the Visigoths. How they found a king in the semi-Romanized Theodoric, and how he decided to transfer his people from the Balkan peninsula to Italy, is told by the Gothic historian. Despite, however, a show of Roman manners, it is likely that Theodoric always remained at heart a barbarian.

[At the time peace was made between the Ostrogoths and the Romans] the Romans received as a hostage of peace, Theodoric the son of [prince] Thiudimer. He had now attained the age of seven years and was entering upon his eighth [461 A.D.]. While his father hesitated about giving him up, his uncle Valamir, besought him to do it, hoping that peace between the Romans and the Goths might thus be assured. Therefore Theodoric was given as a hostage by the Goths and brought to the city of Constantinople to the

Emperor Leo, and, being a goodly child, deservedly gained the imperial favor.

[After a while Theodoric returned as a young man to his people and became king over them. He was treated with great favor by the Emperor Zeno (474–491) but resolved to go as the Emperor's deputy to Italy, and deliver it from the Rugi and other barbarians oppressing it, saying to Zeno], " If I prevail I shall retain Italy as your grant and gift : if I am conquered Your Piety will lose nothing." So the Emperor sent him forth enriched by great gifts and commended to his charge the Senate and the Roman People.

Therefore Theodoric departed from the royal city and returned to his own people. In company with the whole tribe of the Goths who gave him their unanimous consent he set out for Hesperia. He went in a straight march through Sirmium to the places bordering on Pannonia and, advancing into the territory of Venetia, as far as the bridge of the Sontius, encamped there. When he had halted there for some time to rest the bodies of his men and pack animals, Odoacer sent an armed force against him which he met on the plains of Verona, and destroyed with great slaughter. Then he broke camp and advanced through Italy with greater boldness. Crossing the river Po, he pitched camp near the royal city of Ravenna.

When Odoacer saw this, he fortified himself within the city. He frequently harassed the army of the Goths at night, sallying forth stealthily with his men, and this not once or twice, but often ; and thus he struggled for almost three whole years. But he labored in vain, for all Italy at last called Theodoric its lord and the Empire obeyed his nod.[1] But Odoacer suffered daily from war and famine in Ravenna. Since he accomplished nothing he sent an embassy and

[1] Of course an exaggeration. He had little or no power outside of Italy.

begged for mercy. Theodoric first granted it, then deprived him of his life.[1]

It was in the third year [493 A.D.] after his entrance into Italy that Theodoric, by the advice of the Emperor Zeno, laid aside the garb of a private citizen and the dress of his race, and assumed a costume with a royal mantle, as he had now become a ruler both over Goths and Romans.

128. A DESCRIPTION OF CONSTANTINOPLE UNDER THE EASTERN EMPERORS

Abridged from Bury, " History of the Later Roman Empire," vol. I, pp. 52 ff.

A distinguished English scholar gives us this description of Constantinople in the fifth and sixth centuries A.D., when it was displacing Rome as the greatest city of the world. Thanks to the wholesale plundering of more ancient places, it was probably even more magnificent than " Old Rome " at its best. During much of the subsequent Middle Ages, Constantinople was about the only place in Europe where a modern man could have found quasi civilized conditions of life.

The shape of Constantinople is triangular. It is bounded on two sides by water and on one side by land. At the east corner and on the south side it is washed by the Bosphorus, which flows at first almost from north to south and then takes a southeastern course ; on the north by the inlet of the Bosphorus, which was called the Golden Horn; and on the west by the wall of Constantine, protecting the enlarged city.

A traveler coming [overland from Italy] would enter Constantinople by the " Golden Gate " erected by Theodosius the Great. A long street with covered colonnades — suggesting an eastern town — on either side would lead him in a due easterly direction to the great *Milion*, the milestone

---

[1] Odoacer seems to have been slain most treacherously.

from which all distances were measured. For since Constantinople had become the capital all roads tended thither. But before he saw the Milion, the traveler would be struck by the imposing mass and great dome of the [cathedral of] St. Sophia, the eternal monument of Justinian and his architect Anthemius. As he stood in front of the west entrance of the great church the northern side of the hippodrome would be on his right hand.

Then passing a few steps farther, and standing with his back to St. Sophia he would see stretching before him southward a long rectangular place, bounded on one side by the eastern wall of the hippodrome and on the other by the western wall of the Imperial palace. . . . This place was called the *Augusteum*, that is the place of Augustus. . . . The magnificence of Justinian had paved this piazza with marble, and the southern part was distinguished as the " Marble Place," while the northern part was called Milion from the building of that name close by.

The Milion was not a mere pillar; it was a roofed building open at the sides, supported by seven pillars, and within were to be seen the statues of Constantine the Great [and other imperial personages. Along the eastern side of the Augusteum were some other important buildings, especially a splendid long portico and the baths of Zeuxippus, a magnificent structure, rebuilt after a conflagration by Justinian. Close by it were the elegant Senate House, and Palace of the Patriarch which] contained a splendid hall, called the Thomaites, and also halls of justice for the hearing of ecclesiastical cases.

The Hippodrome was the scene of many important political movements and transactions at Constantinople. Its length from north to south was 639 cubits, its breadth about 158. Its southern end was of crescent shape. The northern end was occupied by a small two-storied palace, and the Emperor beheld the games from a box or *cathisma* which he entered from the palace by a winding stair. Under the palace were porticoes in which horses and chariots were kept. The hippodrome had at least four gates; one to the right of the cathisma through which the "Blue"[1] faction was wont to enter, a second corresponding on the left, which was appropriated by the Greens, [and two others for different purposes]. . . .

[Near the Augusteum rose the main Imperial palace, a magnificent and huge structure, but owing to the rack of time it is impossible to trace out all its wonderful halls of audience, gilded and mosaic-lined chambers, governmental offices, barracks for the guard, gardens, and the like.]

Also from Bury, "History of the Later Roman Empire," vol. II, p. 55

The population of Constantinople at the beginning of the sixth century has been calculated at about 1,000,000. It was full of Gepids, Goths, Lombards, Slaves and Huns as well as Orientals: Abasgian eunuchs and Colchian guards might be seen in the streets. . . .

In the urban arrangements of Constantinople, for the comfort of whose inhabitants the Emperors were always solicitous, the law of Zeno (474–494 A.D.), which provided for a sea prospect, is noteworthy. The height of the houses built on the hills overlooking the sea was regulated in such a way that the buildings in front should not interfere with the view of the houses behind. Besides the corn, imported from Egypt, which was publicly distributed to the citizens in the form of bread, the chief food of the Byzantines was salted provisions of various kinds — fish, cheese, and ham. Wine was grown in the surrounding district, and there was a good vegetable market. Of public amusements there was no lack. As well as horse races in the hippodrome, there

---

[1] The "Blues" and "Greens" were theoretically merely partisans of rival charioteers, but often they developed into downright political factions, whose riotous feuds endangered the thrones of Emperors.

were theatrical representations and ballets; and it is probable that troupes of acrobats and tight-rope dancers often
came over from Asia.   [Combats of men with wild animals
were sometimes allowed, but not old style gladiator fights.]

[The mechanical arts and industries flourished. Constantinople was the chief manufacturing city and commercial center in the world; among other things manufactured
were silk fabrics, glazed pottery, mosaic work to adorn
churches and palaces, crosses and crucifixes for Christian
worship, all kinds of fine jewelry, and all kinds of weapons
and armor.   The city was in short the wealthiest, most civilized, best governed spot in Christendom all through the
earlier Middle Ages.   In it the shipping and caravans of
East and West met for commerce.   There was absolutely
no other city in Europe and very few in Asia that could
rival it, even faintly.]

129. The Title of a Later Roman Emperor

From the Preamble of the "Institutes" of Justinian. Moyle's Translation

Under the later emperors there was not the least abatement in
their claims to universal sovranty. If barbarian kings had
seized certain provinces, their possession was in theory only temporary. Justinian (527 to 565 A.D.) did indeed reconquer many
of the lost lands, but his title would have been no less high-
sounding and grandiloquent if his reign had been disastrous. An
emperor was still a god on earth.

The Emperor Cæsar Flavius Justinianus, conqueror of
the Alemanni, the Goths, the Franks, the Germans, the
Antes, the Alani, the Vandals, the Africans; — pious,
prosperous, renowned, victorious and triumphant, ever
august.

[He asserts in the course of the preamble to his laws:]
The barbarian nations which we have subjugated know our
valor, Africa and other provinces without number being

once more, after so long an interval, reduced beneath the
sway of Rome, by victories granted by Heaven, and themselves bearing witness to our dominion. ALL PEOPLES *likewise are ruled by laws which we have either enacted or arranged.*

130. THE IMPERIAL LAW-MAKING POWER AS DEFINED BY JUSTINIAN

"Institutes" of Justinian, book I, title II. Moyle's Translation

Under the later Empire practically the sole law-making power
lay with the sovereign Augustus. How absolute was his authority
is bluntly stated in the codification of the Roman Law by Justinian
(published in 533 A.D.). The fiction is still preserved, however,
that the emperor does this because he has been commissioned so
to do by the people. He does not claim to rule simply "by the
grace of God"; — that was a later medieval pretension.

What the emperor determines has the force of a statute,
the people having conferred on him all their authority and
power. Consequently, whatever the emperor settles by
rescript, or decides in his judicial capacity, or ordains by
edicts, is clearly a statute; and these are what are called
"constitutions." Some of these of course are personal, and
not to be followed as precedents — since this is not the
emperor's will; but others are general and bind beyond all
doubt.

131. HOW CLOVIS THE FRANK BECAME A CATHOLIC CHRISTIAN

From the "Chronicle of St. Denis," book I, chaps. 18–19

In 496 A.D. Clovis, the founder of the Frankish power which
was to develop into modern France and Germany, was converted
to *Catholic* Christianity from heathenism. This was an event of
high historical importance. If like other Germanic kings he had
become an Arian heretic, he would have been hopelessly estranged
from his subject Roman population. As it was, the Franks and

the provincials coalesced as in none other of the new barbarian kingdoms. The story of Clovis's conversion, of course, gave the pious chroniclers an opening for many edifying anecdotes.

[Clovis having a Catholic wife, Clothilde, was often urged by her to accept Christianity, but long resisted her entreaty.]

At this time the King was yet in the errors of his idolatry [and went to war] with the Alemanni, since he wished to render them tributary. Long was the battle, many were slain on one side or the other, for the Franks fought to win glory and renown, the Alemanni to save life and freedom. When the King at length saw the slaughter of his people and the boldness of his foes, he had greater expectation of disaster than of victory. He looked up to heaven humbly, and spoke thus, " Most mighty God, whom my queen Clothilde worships and adores with heart and soul, I pledge Thee perpetual service unto Thy faith, if only Thou givest me now the victory over mine enemies."

Instantly when he had said this, his men were filled with burning valor, and a great fear smote his enemies, so that they turned the back and fled the battle; and victory remained with the King and with the Franks. The king of the Alemanni was slain; and as for the Alemanni, seeing themselves discomfited, and that their king had fallen, they yielded themselves to Clovis and his Franks and became his tributaries.

The King returned after this victory into Frankland. He went to Reims, and told unto the Queen what had befallen; and they together gave thanks unto Our Lord. The King made his confession of faith from his heart, and with right good will. The Queen, who was wondrously overjoyed at the conversion of her lord, went at once to St. Remi, at that time archbishop of the city.

Straightway he hastened to the palace to teach the King

the way by which he could come unto God, for his mind was
still in doubt about it.   He presented himself boldly before
his face, although a little while before he [the bishop] had
not dared to come before him.

When St. Remi had preached to the King the [Christian]
faith and taught him the way of the Cross, and when the
king had known what the faith was, Clovis promised fer-
vently that he would henceforth never serve any save the
all-powerful God.   After that he said he would put to the
test and try the hearts and wills of his chieftains and lesser
people: for he would convert them more easily if they were
converted by pleasant means and by mild words, than if they
were driven to it by force; and this method seemed best to
St. Remi. The folk and the chieftains were assembled by the
command of the King.   He arose in the midst of them, and
spoke to this effect: —

"Lords of the Franks, it seems to me highly profitable
that ye should know first of all what are those gods which
ye worship.   For we are certain of their falsity: and we
come right freely into the knowledge of Him who is the
true God.   Know of a surety that this same God which I
preach to you has given victory over your enemies in the
recent battle against the Alemanni.   Lift therefore your
hearts in just hope; and ask the Sovran Defender, that He
give to you all, that which ye desire — that He save our
souls and give us victory over our enemies."

When the King full of faith had thus preached to and
admonished his people, one and all banished from their
hearts all unbelief, and recognized their Creator.

[According to the *Chronicle of Frodoard* (13), when
shortly afterward Clovis set out for the Church for baptism,
St. Remi prepared a great procession.   The streets of
Reims were hung with banners and tapestry.]   The church
was decorated.   The baptistery was covered with balsams

and all sorts of perfumes. The people believed they were already breathing the delights of paradise. The cortége set out from the palace, the clergy led the way bearing the holy Gospels, the cross and banners, chanting hymns and psalms. Then came the bishop leading the King by the hand, next the Queen with the multitude. Whilst on the way the King asked of the bishop, "If this was the Kingdom of Heaven which he had promised him." "Not so," replied the prelate; "it is the road that leadeth unto it."

[When in the church, in the act of bestowing baptism] the holy pontiff lifted his eyes to heaven in silent prayer and wept. Straightway a dove, white as snow, descended bearing in his beak a vial of holy oil. A delicious odor exhaled from it: which intoxicated those near by with an inexpressible delight. The holy bishop took the vial, and suddenly the dove vanished. Transported with joy at the sight of this notable miracle, the King renounced Satan, his pomps and his works; and demanded with earnestness the baptism; at the moment when he bent his head over the fountain of life, the eloquent pontiff cried, "*Bow down thine head, fierce Sicambrian!*[1] *Adore that which once thou hast burned: burn that which thou hast adored!*"

After having made his profession of the orthodox faith, the King is plunged thrice in the waters of baptism. Then in the name of the holy and indivisible Trinity, — Father, Son, and Holy Ghost, — the prelate consecrated him with the divine unction. [Two sisters of the King and] 3000 fighting men of the Franks and a great number of women and children were likewise baptized. Thus we may well believe that day was a day of joy in heaven for the holy angels; likewise of rejoicing on earth for devout and faithful men!

[The King showed vast zeal for his new faith. He built a splendid church at Paris, called St. Geneviève, where later he and Clothilde were buried.] Faith and religion

[1] A term practically meaning "Frank."

and zeal for justice were pursued by him all the days of his life.

[Certain Franks still held to paganism, and found a leader in Prince Ragnachairus] but he was presently delivered up in fetters to Clovis who put him to death. Thus all the Frankish people were converted and baptized by the merits of St. Remi.

How Clovis was declared a Roman Patrician (508 A.D.)

Chronicle of St. Denis, I, 23

At this time there came to Clovis messengers from Anastasius, the emperor of Constantinople, who brought him presents from their master, and letters whereof the effect was, that it pleased the emperor and the Senators that he [Clovis] be made a " Friend of the Emperor," and a " Patrician " and " Councilor " of the Romans.

When the King had read these letters, he arrayed himself in the robe of a senator, which the emperor had sent to him. He mounted upon his charger; and thus he went to the public square before the church of S. Martin; and then he gave great gifts to the people. From this day he was always called " Councilor " and "Augustus."[1]

132. How Clovis Disposed of a Rival

Gregory of Tours, "History," book II, chap. 40

Clovis reigned over the Franks from 481 to 511 A.D. Both before and after his nominal conversion to Christianity he showed himself a wholly evil, unscrupulous savage, who prospered by a combination of lionlike bravery and vulpine cunning. Nevertheless, in view of his favoring " Orthodox " Christianity, the churchmen of the age were willing to condone almost all his acts.

---

[1] It is very unlikely that he had any right to the title " Augustus," but it tickled the barbarian's pride to assume it.

While King Clovis dwelt at Paris he sent secretly to Cloderic, son of Sigebert, king of Cologne,[1] and said unto him, "Behold, thy father is old and lame. If he should die, his kingdom would be thine on the strength of our friendship together."

Then it came to pass that Sigebert quitted the city of Cologne and crossed the Rhine to enjoy himself in the forest of Buconia. And as he slept in his tent about noon time, his son sent assassins against him, and caused him to perish, in order to gain his kingdom. The murderer sent messengers to Clovis saying: —

"My father is dead, even as was enjoined, and I have in my possession both his wealth and his kingdom. Send therefore some of thy people, and I will freely commit to them whatever thou wishest of his treasures."

[When Clovis's messengers came] Cloderic opened before them the treasures of his father; but as he thrust his hand deep down in [the chest], one of the messengers raised his "Franciska"[2] and cleft his skull. Then Clovis straightway presented himself at Cologne, assembled the folk [there] and spoke to them: —

"Hear ye what has befallen. Whilst I sailed upon the river Schelde, Cloderic, the son of my kinsman, pursued his father, pretending that I desired him to kill him; and while Sigebert fled across the forest of Buconia, Cloderic compassed his death by brigands. Then he himself, — at the moment he was opening the treasures of his father, — was smitten and slain! — I know not by whom. I am in no way an accomplice in these deeds; for I cannot shed the blood of my kinsfolk — something utterly unlawful! But since the thing is done, I give you council; if you are willing, receive me [as your king]. Have recourse to *me* and put yourselves under *my* protection!"

[1] The ruler of an outlying tribe of the Franks.
[2] Native Frankish battle ax.

The Ripuarian Franks [of Cologne] welcomed these words with loud applause, and with the clashing of their shields. They lifted Clovis upon a shield, and proclaimed him king over them.

[The kind of "Orthodox Christianity." Clovis represented is shown by the following anecdote from the historian, Gregory of Tours (II, 37).]

King Clovis said unto his soldiers [being about to fall upon the Visigoths] : —
"It is with heaviness that I see these Arians [heretics] holding a portion of Gaul. Come now, with the aid of God let us march on them : and when we have conquered them, let us make their country submit to our lordship."

[Again Gregory of Tours (II, 40) says of the piety of this savage :]

"Daily did God cause Clovis's enemies to fall into his hand, and increased his kingdom ; seeing that he went about *with his heart right before the Lord,* and did that which was pleasing in His eyes."

133. TYPICAL PASSAGES FROM THE LAW OF THE SALIAN FRANKS

Henderson, "Select Historical Documents of the Middle Ages," book II, No. 1, pp. 176 ff., extracts

This compilation of the law and customs of the Salian Franks (an important branch of the Frankish people) was made probably about 500 A.D. From it one gets a good idea of the Germanic institution of *Wergeld,* and how a higher price was set on a Frank than on a Roman. Note, too, that this law had to deal with a very primitive society. Most litigation would be over crimes of violence, while cases of broken contracts, nice questions of land title, etc., were far less important.

If any one steal a sucking pig and it be proved against him, he shall be sentenced to 120 denars, which make 3 shillings.

If any one steal a pig that can live without its mother he shall be sentenced to 40 denars — that is, 1 shilling.

If any one steal that bull which rules the herd and has never been yoked, he shall be sentenced to 1800 denars, which make 45 shillings.

If any free man steal, outside the house, something worth 2 denars, he shall be sentenced to 600 denars, which make 15 shillings.

If any slave steal, outside the house, something worth 2 denars, he shall, besides paying the worth of the object and the fines for delay, be stretched out and receive 120 blows.

If any one shall have assaulted and plundered a free man and it be proved against him, he shall be sentenced to 2500 denars, which make 63 shillings.

If a Roman has plundered a Salian Frank, the above law shall be observed.

But if a Frank have plundered a Roman, he shall be sentenced to 35 shillings.

[Under the title " *Concerning Wounds* " there is a carefully graded line of penalties, *e.g.* for] striking another on the head so that the brain appears and the three bones which lie above the brain shall project [penalty 30 shillings].

[Same penalty plus 5 shillings physician's fee] if the wound shall be between the ribs or the stomach so that the wound appears and reaching to the entrails.

If any one shall strike a man so that the blood falls to the floor [penalty 15 shillings].

[For a fist blow] so that the blood does *not* flow, for each blow up to three blows [penalty 3 shillings].

If any one shall have called a woman a " wanton " and shall not be able to prove it, he shall be sentenced to 1800 denars, or 45 shillings.

For calling another " fox " [penalty 3 shillings].

For calling another " hare " [penalty 3 shillings].

If a man shall have charged another with having thrown away his shield,[1] and shall not be able to prove it, he shall be sentenced to 120 denars, or 3 shillings.

If any man have called another " spy," or " perjurer," and shall not be able to prove it, he shall be sentenced to 600 denars, or 15 shillings.

[Among the penalties for murder are] : —

For killing a free Frank, or a barbarian living under the Salic law [penalty 8000 denars].

But if the slayer have cast him into a well, or covered him with branches or anything else to conceal him, then the penalty is 24000 denars, or 600 shillings.

[For killing a Frank in service of the king the penalty is thrice as great.]

If any one have slain a Roman who eats in the king's palace [the penalty is 12000 denars, or 300 shillings].

But if the Roman shall not have been a landed proprietor and table companion of the King [the penalty is 100 shillings].

But if the Roman was obliged to pay tribute [2] [the penalty is 63 shillings].

[Under the title *"Concerning Private Property"* the entries read] : —

If any man die and leave no sons, if the father and mother survive they shall inherit.

If the father and mother do not survive and he leaves brothers or sisters, they shall inherit.

But if there are no sisters of the father, the sisters of the mother shall claim that inheritance.

If there are none of these, the nearest relatives on the father's side shall succeed to that inheritance.

---

[1] Which implied having fled the battle in a cowardly manner.

[2] That is, was a humble plebeian or semi-serf.

But of Salic land no portion of the inheritance shall come to a woman, but the whole inheritance of the land shall come to the male sex.[1]

[Title *Concerning Wergeld.*]

If any one's father have been killed, the sons shall have half of the compounding money (wergeld); and the other half the nearest relatives, as well on the mother's side as on the father's side, shall divide among themselves.

But if there are no relatives, paternal or maternal, that portion shall go to the public treasury.

[1] A law invoked eight odd centuries later to prevent a woman from sitting upon the throne of France. This original law clearly had to do with mere land ownership; there was no question here involved of rights to sovranty. This seems to be, however, the famous *Salic Law* of later history.

CHAPTER XI

THE EARLY MIDDLE AGES AND CHARLEMAGNE

After the first clash and roar and confusion of the downfall of the Western Empire and the coming of the Germans is over, certain definite factors display themselves in Europe. It is evident, *e.g.*, that while the Roman Empire is destroyed, many elements in Roman life and thought are firmly perpetuated within the new kingdoms of the invaders. Especially in Frankland (France plus modern Belgium and a large portion of western Germany) do the Merovingian kings inherit many of the forms of government and traditions of power possessed originally by the Cæsars, and in Frankland especially does the great amalgamating process go on, which ultimately fuses the Romanized provincials and the Teutonic invaders into new races; thus out of the barbarous kingdom of Clovis are born, slowly and painfully, the glorious nation of France, and her mighty compeer, Germany.

Another important phase of this period is the development in the Church of certain factors which become important elements in medieval history — especially the institutions of Monasticism, and the rise of the temporal power of the Papacy; while in the background of the Western Christian world now looms the rival society and religion of Islam, which remains a menace to the very life of Christendom all through the Middle Ages, and which is destined to make important contributions to the sum total of modern civilization.

Last of all, at the end of this first medieval period we have the figure of Charlemagne and his Empire. Roman and Teuton in him seemingly have completed their amalgamation. The old classical civilization and Christianity appear to have entered into permanent alliance. There is again a Western Empire, apparently on a far firmer basis than that of the fifth century. The prospect indeed proves to be delusive. The revived Empire is in

reality the creation of one exceedingly able man and of his immediate predecessors. In less than a century it has fallen again
into numerous contending fragments, while society has lapsed into
the " organized anarchy " of the Feudal System. Nevertheless the
reign of Charlemagne may be fairly considered a turning point in
world history. Before him we still speak of " Gaul " and " Gallo-
Romans"; after him we soon must speak of "France" and "French-
men." In the place of the " vulgar Latin " of the provincials we
soon meet the developing French and German tongues as exemplified in the Oaths of Strassburg (842 A.D.). An entirely new set
of problems confronts the historical student, and " Medieval
History " in the strictest sense of the term may be said to begin.

In this chapter will be found excerpts illustrating typical phases
of this most interesting period, although space limitations compel
the omission of much profitable material, especially that relating
to Charlemagne.

134. MANNERS AND LIFE IN FRANKLAND IN THE MEROVINGIAN PERIOD

Based upon Parmentier, " Album Historique," vol. I, pp. 33 ff.

In Gaul, from the Age of Clovis down to the rise of the Carolingians,
there was terrible confusion, and a setback to all forms of culture
from which it took centuries to recover ; nevertheless the forms of
civilized life were never wholly lost. Parmentier, a modern French
writer, thus summarizes the scanty information as to the manners
and customs of the Frankish conquerors of Gaul drawn from
Gregory of Tours and other contemporary writers.

When the different barbarian peoples were established in
the Empire, they preserved at first their costume and their
manners. But little by little, living among descendants of
the Romans, who had also kept their own customs, they
borrowed a great deal from the conquered population. These
in turn were influenced by their new masters. A new society thus formed itself, which had its manners derived partly
from the Germans, partly from the Romans.

The Merovingian kings gave to their people the example of these changes. They surely distinguished themselves still by their long and carefully dressed hair, from their subjects who clipped their hair short. As formerly, at their accession they were lifted upon a shield: the emblem of their power was always the spear grasped in their hand. But speedily they took over the insignia of the emperors. They are represented on their coins with the consular toga and the imperial diadem. They had a seal. However, the kings did not as a rule live in "palaces"; they preferred to reside in great "villas" in the midst of forests, close by rivers, at Compiègne, Clichy, etc.

In war the king rode on horseback, surrounded by cavaliers with lances, forming a kind of guard of honor. Their barbarian subjects were armed still after the barbarian manner; nevertheless a good many had adopted the Roman military costume. In sieges they made use of machines and of methods which the Romans had utilized. Their wars were usually cruel. They ravaged the country they attacked, and cut down the standing crops, the vines, and the fruit trees. Neither monasteries nor churches were respected. The warriors slew and massacred without pity.

Life in Frankland during Peace

In times of peace the great "Gallo-Roman" and Frankish magnates lived by preference in the open country. But the former, especially in south Gaul, often lived in cities built after the Roman fashion. In the north of Gaul, the rich barbarians resided in great farmsteads, protected by a moat and a palisaded wall, strengthened by towers; or, lacking that, by hedges often as high as a person. These establishments, usually built of wood, contained besides quarters for the master, many buildings for agricultural purposes, storehouses, stables, cowsheds, water wheels, and lodgings for the slaves and serfs who lived near the master. Sometimes could be found near the house a garden, with green turf, flowers, and fruit trees.

The poor folk of the open country lived in mud huts, or in cabins of rough boards, with roofs covered with thatch or with reeds.

In their fine estates the Gallo-Roman nobles devoted their leisure — apart from looking after the upkeep of their estates — to games (among which tennis and dice were the favorites), or to reading, and to efforts at literary composition. Their wives were kept busy spinning wool and embroidering their garments of ceremony. The Gallo-Romans, too, as well as the barbarians, loved the chase. As for the kings, they had still other diversions, *e.g.* King Childebert at his palace in Metz took part in games in which some animal was baited by a pack of hounds.

Eating had a great place in the life of this people, if one may judge from the descriptions of feasts which contemporary authors give us. Meats were much in demand, especially pork. The rich ate wheat bread : the poor, barley bread. The most common beverages were beer, perry (made from pears), cider, and various wines. After dinner the men continued to drink, and we know from Gregory of Tours that neither masters nor varlets drank with moderation.

Cities in Frankland

The rich were all betaking themselves to the country, and the cities dwindled rapidly in importance. Since the last years of the Empire, almost all of these had protected themselves from the barbarians by a circuit of walls. The cities of the south still retained many of the monuments wherewith they had been adorned in Roman times. The northern cities had suffered more from barbarian ravages. Often they had been quickly rebuilt out of wood, and so were frequently the prey of conflagrations. Sometimes the inhabitants simply rebuilt their houses with the wreckage of

the old buildings. These houses, which sometimes rose to
three storeys, were grouped around the basilica, where the
faithful came to participate in the religious services, to take
their oaths upon the altar or tomb of the saints, or, in case
of attack, to hide their movable wealth.

Economic Conditions in Frankland

The agricultural arts were fairly well developed; there
was a certain amount of industry; the slaves in a great
establishment manufactured about all the articles needed in
it; there was considerable commerce still with Constantinople and the East, especially for spices, silks, cotton goods,
jewelers' wares, etc.; colonies of Syrian merchants were
located at Paris and other cities; nevertheless the Merovingian period was a very wretched one. Very often the lands
lay waste, as the result of the continual wars waged by the
princes. Pestilence joined itself to famine, and devastated
whole districts. The rivers, illy guarded in their beds,
produced inundations. Commerce was obstructed by the
bad condition of the roads, which were often infested with
brigands. Let us add to these miseries, the violent deeds
and cruelties of men at once avaricious, ignorant, and brutal,
and there is suggested a picture of the desolation of Gaul in
the days of the Merovingians.

135. Usages of the Church in the Early Middle Ages

Based upon Parmentier, " Album Historique," vol. I, pp. 77 ff.

The usages of the Church at the time that the Empire was dis-
solving, and the new barbarian kingdoms were forming, has been
summarized by a very recent French writer.

Beginning with the fifth century the Church began to
distinguish itself from the lay-society in which it dwelled.
Its members have their own peculiar costume: its build-

ings differ from secular edifices: it gives its special rules to its solemn ceremonies.

At first, the Christian clergy dressed like other men, but from the fifth century onward the laymen, little by little, *abandoned* the old Roman costume, while the clergy *preserved* it, and so separated themselves from the rest of society. Already custom had distinguished the two kinds of clergy — the "Regular Clergy" — monks under a "rule" for their mode of life, and the "Secular Clergy," — who mingled in the doings of the world.

From about 500 A.D. the Pope, and the bishops upon whom he had conferred it, wore, as special insignia, the *pallium*, a long tippet of white wool, draped around the shoulders and the two tips whereof fell one in front, one behind. It was decorated at the ends by little black crosses. The bishops only wore the miter commonly in the eleventh century, but from the eighth century onward the popes wore the tiara. The clergy were already *tonsured*. In Carolingian times they ran to great luxury in their dress. The miniature paintings of this time show us the churchmen wearing red, purple, blue, and green garments. They had embroidered "chasubles"[1] and "dalmatics,"[2] adorned with pearls, laces, and fringes.

Churches were now very numerous. They were of two kinds, — *cathedrals*, where a bishop had his seat, and others built at burial places and used for funeral services, funerary masses, and anniversaries and other commemorations. Often they were built over the tomb of some old-time martyr. To the churches it was needful to join *baptisteries*, erected close by them: these were small structures containing the bathing places into which the new Christians entered to be baptized.

---

[1] Either a circular cloak hung from the shoulders, or a broad back piece and narrower front piece connected over the shoulders only. Worn only by the priest celebrating the Eucharist.

[2] A full-length vestment with closed sleeves, slit at the sides.

The Liturgies of the Church

It was only towards the fourth century that the ceremonies of the Christian worship — the " Liturgy " — became somewhat fixed. But the liturgy varied always according to the different ecclesiastical provinces. Between the fourth and eighth centuries the mass was said after two manners. In the churches of the north of Italy, Gaul, Spain, Britain and Ireland they followed the so-called *Gallican Usage*. This Usage had peculiarities somewhat like the liturgy used in the Orient. At Rome and in Africa they followed a more original usage, — the *Roman Usage*. This liturgy only supplanted the other in the eighth century, at the time of the great reform of the clergy undertaken by the Carolingian princes. In Spain the Gallican Usage held its own down to the eleventh century, and during the whole of the Merovingian epoch mass was thus celebrated in Gaul.

The Church Holidays

It is during this time that the principal holidays of Christianity began to be observed. The "movable feasts" were always borrowed from the Jewish calendar; *e.g. Easter* and *Pentecost :* but the observance of *Lent* did not date back of the fourth century. The celebration of Palm Sunday by a procession with palms was at first peculiar to Jerusalem, and only spread to the West in the eighth and ninth centuries. Among the "fixed feasts" Christmas began to be celebrated in the fourth century. It is also beginning with this period that they began to observe by festivals the different events in the life of the Virgin Mary, the merits of the great saints, the anniversaries of martyrs. Most of the greater feasts were preceded by fasts.

The bishop of Vienne, Mammertius, introduced into Gaul in the fifth century the practise of *Rogations*. These consisted in a procession around the country, accompanied by prayers, chants, and invocations of God, the angels, and the saints. The dedication of churches, the translation of saints' relics, — something held greatly in honor during this period, — were also accompanied by important ceremonies. It was at this time too that the use was established of consecrating by prayer the different hours of the day; and from this period the "holy office" was celebrated daily in the churches at "the canonical hours" with the participation of the clergy and under their direction.

136. St. Simeon Stylites and how he achieved Holiness

Evagrius, "Ecclesiastical History," book I, chap. 13. Bohn Translation

Very early after their inception, the monks of the Greco-Oriental church ran off into practices which the more rational Latin church of the West never imitated. What passed for "extreme holiness" in Syria in the fifth century A.D. is shown by this story of St. Simeon of the Pillar. Attempts in Gaul to imitate this man were wisely frowned upon by the Church authorities.

In these times [about 440 A.D.] flourished and became illustrious, SIMEON, of holy and famous memory, who originated the contrivance of stationing himself on the top of a column, thereby occupying a space of scarce two cubits in circumference. This man, endeavoring to realize in the flesh the existence of the heavenly hosts, lifts himself above the concerns of earth, and overpowering the downward tendency of man's nature, is intent on things above. [He was adored by all the countryside, wrought many miracles, and the Emperor Theodosius II listened to his advice and sought his benediction.]

Simeon prolonged his endurance of this mode of life through 56 years; nine of which he spent in the first monastery where he was instructed in divine knowledge, and

47 in the "Mandra" as it was called; namely, ten in a certain nook; on shorter columns, seven; and *thirty upon one of forty cubits.*[1] After his departure [from this life] his holy body was conveyed to Antioch, escorted by the garrison, and a great concourse guarding the venerable body, lest the inhabitants of the neighboring cities should gather and carry it off. In this manner it was conveyed to Antioch, and attended, during its progress, with extraordinary prodigies.

[The body] has been preserved nearly entire until my time [about 580]; and in company with many priests, I enjoyed a sight of his sacred head, in the episcopate of the famous Gregory, when Philippicus had requested that precious relic of the saints might be sent him for the protection of the Eastern armies. [The head was well preserved save for the teeth] some of which had been violently removed by the hands of the pious [for relics].

[According to another writer, Theodoret, in Simeon's lifetime, he was visited by pilgrims from near and far; Persia, Ethiopia, Spain, and even Britain. To these at times he delivered sermons. He wore on his body a heavy iron chain. In praying, " he bent his body so that his forehead almost touched his feet." A spectator once counted 1244 repetitions of this movement, and then gave up reckoning. Simeon took only one scanty meal per week, and fasted through the season of Lent. It is alleged that the devil having afflicted him with an ulcer in his thigh as reward for a little self-righteousness, Simeon, as penance, never touched the afflicted leg upon the pillar again, and stood for the remaining year of his life upon *one* leg.][2]

[1] Say sixty feet or higher.
[2] Some of these details are, no doubt, exaggerations, but the feats in physical austerity of Simeon hardly surpass those of the sacred fakirs of India.

137. Extracts from the Monastic Rule of St. Benedict

Abridged from Henderson, "Select Historical Documents of the Middle Ages," book III, 1, p. 274 ff.

In 529 A.D. St. Benedict of Nursia founded at Monte Casino in Campania a famous monastery. The "rule," or system of government, which he gave it, became a model for countless other monasteries. Benedict was not a fanatic. He gave no impossible precepts of austerity, like certain monkish leaders in the East. In him again the old *practical* Roman spirit manifested itself. Thousands of men have sought holiness in the Benedictine cloisters, and the system they followed possesses abiding interest.

Prologue. We are about to found *a school for the Lord's service ;* in the organization of which we trust that we shall ordain nothing severe and nothing burdensome. But even if, the demands of justice dictating it, something a little irksome shall be the result . . . thou shalt not therefore, struck by fear, flee the way of salvation. But as one's way of life and one's faith progresses, the heart becomes broadened, and with unutterable sweetness of love, the way of the mandates of the Lord is traversed.

What the Abbot should be like. An abbot who is worthy to preside over a monastery ought always to remember what he is called, and carry out with his deeds the *name* of a " Superior " ; for he is believed to be Christ's representative. And so the abbot should not teach or decree or order anything apart from the precept of the Lord ; but his order or teaching should be sprinkled with the ferment of divine justice in the minds of his disciples. . . . [Only where he has exercised his uttermost care and ability can he be absolved of responsibility to God if his monks go astray.]

Concerning obedience. [The monks are to practice humility by implicitly obeying their superiors.] And in the same moment let command of the master and the perfected work of the disciple — both together in the swiftness of the fear of God — be called into being by those who are possessed with a desire of advancing to eternal salvation. Thus living not according to their own judgment, nor obeying their own desires and commands, let them desire an abbot to rule over them.

Whether the monks should have anything of their own ? More than any other thing is this special vice to be cut off root and branch from the monastery, that one should presume to give or receive *anything* without the order of the abbot, or should have anything of his own. He should have absolutely nothing — neither a book, nor tablets, nor a pen — nothing at all, — for indeed it is not allowable to the monks to have their own bodies or wills in their own power; but all things necessary they must expect of the Father of the monastery.

Concerning the food allowance. We believe that for the daily refection of the sixth as well as of the ninth hour two cooked dishes, on account of the infirmities of the different ones, are enough for all tables ; so that, perchance, whoever cannot eat of one dish may partake of the other. Therefore let two cooked dishes suffice for all the brothers ; if it is possible to obtain apples or growing vegetables, a third may be added. One full pound of bread shall suffice for a day ; and [. . . half a hemina of wine,[1] but care must be taken to prevent overindulgence].

Concerning the daily manual labor. Idleness is the enemy of the soul. And therefore, at fixed times, the brothers ought to be occupied in manual labor ; and again at fixed times in sacred reading. Therefore we believe that both seasons ought to be arranged [so that the time for sleeping, praying, working, eating, and reading be carefully apportioned].

Whether a monk should be allowed to receive letters or any-

[1] About half a pint.

thing ? By no means shall it be allowed to a monk — either from his relatives, or from any man, or from one of his fellows — to receive or give, without order of the abbot, letters, presents, or any gift however small. But even if by his relatives anything has been sent to him, he shall not presume to receive it, unless it has been first shown to the abbot. But if he order it to be received, it shall be in the power of the abbot to give it to whomever he will; and the brother to whom it happened to be sent shall not be chagrined.

[*The Independence of the monastery from the world.*] A monastery ought — if it can be done — to be so arranged that everything necessary, — water, a mill, a garden, a bakery, — may be made use of, and different arts be carried on within the monastery, so that there shall be no need for the monks to wander about outside; for this is not at all good for their souls.

How the monks shall sleep. They shall sleep separately in separate beds. If it can be done, they shall all sleep in one place; [if too numerous] by tens and twenties. A candle shall always be burning in that same cell until early in the morning. They shall sleep clothed, and girt with belts or with ropes, and they shall not have their knives at their sides while they sleep, lest perchance in a dream they should wound the sleepers. And let the monks be always on the alert [to rise with great promptness, without grumbling, upon the signal].

138. Legal Conditions and the Personality of Law during the Barbarian Settlement

Vinogradoff, " Roman Law in Mediæval Europe," pp. 14-18, abridged

The perplexing problems that arose during the death struggle of the Empire and the rise of the new Germanic kingdoms as to the legal systems under which all the heterogeneous peoples — Romans, Franks, Goths, Burgundians, etc. — might dwell, is here stated by a modern writer; there is also given an explanation of the rough-and-ready methods by which a very difficult problem was handled.

It must be noticed that no State of this period was strong enough to enforce a compact legal order of its own, excluding all other laws, or treating them as enactments confined to aliens. Even the most powerful of the barbarian governments . . . such as the Lombard or Frankish, dealt with a state of affairs based on a mixture of legal arrangements. The Carolingian rulers, and especially Charlemagne, introduced some unity in matters of such vital importance to the government, but racial differences were allowed to crop up everywhere. Law became necessarily personal and local in its application.

The forcible entry of the Goths, Lombards, and Franks into the provinces did not in any sense involve the disappearance or denationalization of the Roman inhabitants. The legal status of the latter was allowed to continue. The personality of a Roman was valued in a peculiar way, differing from the barbarians that surrounded him. It cost 200 soldi to atone for the homicide of a Roman in Frankish Gaul. All intercourse between Romans was ruled by the law of their race. When a Roman of Toulouse married a girl of the same race, she brought him a *dos* in accordance with Paulus's *Sententiœ*.[1] He exercised a father's authority over his children, on the strength of the ancient custom of *patria potestas* as modified by the laws of Constantine. [And so Roman law ruled the provincials in matters of wills, property, etc.]

In all these and in many other respects the legal rights of the Roman would be at variance with those of his German neighbors. These again would act differently, each according to his own peculiar nationality, as Salian Franks,

[1] A well-known Roman law book.

or Ripuarian [Franks], Bavarians, or Burgundians, etc.
The position became very intricate when members of different nationalities, living under different laws, were brought
together to transact business with each other. As Bishop
Agobard of Lyons tells us about 850 A.D. it happened constantly that five people meeting in one room, each followed
a law of his own.

The reports of a trial [in Gaul] between the monasteries
of Fleury on the Loire, and St. Denis provides a good illustration of the points raised on such occasions. The case
was brought before the tribunal of the Frankish Court. It
was found necessary to adjourn it, because both [litigants]
were ecclesiastical corporations, and as such entitled to a
judgment according to *Roman* Law, of which none of the
judges was cognizant. Experts in Roman Law are summoned as assessors, and the trial proceeds at the second
meeting of the tribunal. The parties would like to prove
their right by single combat between their witnesses, but
one of the assessors of the court protests against the waging of battle, on the ground that such a mode of proof
would be contrary to Roman Law. The point at issue is
therefore examined and decided according to Roman rules
of procedure, — that is, by the production of witnesses and
documents. . . .

The rules for allowing or disallowing recourse to one or
the other personal law were necessarily rather complicated.
For instance, the payment of fines for crimes was appor-
tioned according to the law of the criminal, and not of the
offended party. As regards contracts, each party was held
bound by the rule of its own law; but if the contract was
accompanied by a wager, it was interpreted according to
the law of the party making the wager. In the case of
a contract corroborated by a deed (*carta*), the legal form
and interpretation depended on the status of the person
executing the deed. Some cases [were still more complex,

e.g.] in an Italian charter of 780, we find that a certain Felix makes a donation to his daughter, and receives of her a *launegild* (a compensation), according to the Lombard Law, although as a clerk he is himself subject to Roman Law. The reason is that, while still a layman, he received the property in question from his wife according to Lombard Law.

139.   MEDIEVAL ORDEAL FORMULAS

Henderson, " Select Historical Documents of the Middle Ages," book III, No. 2, p. 314 ff.

In resorting to the casting of lots or to various forms of ordeals to determine questions of guilt, the churchmen and laity of the Middle Ages found ample authority in the Bible (*e.g.* Jonah, chap. I, vs. 7). Again the whole process of referring a vexed question to an infallible Deity would seem highly satisfactory to a people still in a state of very simple faith. Besides this, it must be remembered that the means of sifting evidence skillfully, according to the methods of modern courts, were very imperfect.

The Judgment of the Glowing Iron

After the accusation has been lawfully made and three days have passed in fasting and prayer, the priest clad in his sacred vestments shall take with the tongs the iron placed before the altar, and singing "The Hymn of the Three Youths,"[1] namely, "Bless Him all His works," he shall bear the iron to the fire and shall say this prayer over the place where the fire is to carry out the judgment: "Bless, O Lord God, this place that there may be for us in it sanctity, chastity, virtue, and victory, and holiness, humility, goodness, gentleness, and plenitude of law and obedience to God the Father and the Son and the Holy Ghost."

[1] The three children of Israel cast into the furnace by Nebuchadnezzar of Babylon.

After this the iron shall be placed in the fire, and shall be sprinkled with holy water; and while it is heating he shall celebrate mass. But when the priest shall have taken the Eucharist, he shall adjure the man who is about to be tried . . . and cause him to take the communion.

Then the priest shall sprinkle holy water above the iron and shall say, "The blessing of God descend upon this iron for the discerning of the right judgment of God." And straightway the accused shall carry the iron to a distance of nine feet. Finally his hand shall be covered under seal for three days, and if festering blood be found in the track of the iron, he shall be judged guilty. But if, however, he shall go forth uninjured, praise shall be rendered to God.

The Judgment of Boiling Water

Having performed the mass the priest shall descend to the place appointed, where the trial itself shall be gone through with; he shall carry with him the book of gospels and a cross and shall chant a moderate litany, and [when finished] he shall exorcise and bless that water before it boils.

After this he shall divest the accused of his garments, and clothe him with clean vestments of the church, that is, with the garment of an exorcist or of a deacon — and shall cause him to kiss the gospel, and the cross of Christ, [and sprinkle him with the water, and cause him to drink thereof]. Then pieces of wood shall be put under the caldron, and the priest shall say prayers when the water itself shall begin to grow warm. . . . And that boiling water shall be put down hastily near the fire, and the judge shall suspend that stone, bound to that measure, within that same water, in the accustomed way.

Thus he who enters to be tried by the judgment shall extract it thence in the name of God Himself. Afterward with great diligence his hand shall be wrapped up, signed with the seal of the judge, until the third day; when it shall be viewed and judged of by suitable men.

[*The Judgment of the Morsel* was another ordeal, when after due prayers and exorcisms all the parties accused of a theft partook of consecrated bread and cheese; the priest saying as he places the morsel in the mouth of each defendant,] "I conjure thee, O man, by God [and all the saints], that if thou werest partner in this theft, or didst know of it, or have any fault in it, that bread and cheese may not pass thy gullet and throat; but that thou mayest tremble like an aspen leaf; and have no rest, O man, until thou dost vomit it forth with blood, if thou hast committed aught in the matter of the aforesaid theft."

140. Typical Passages from the Koran

Rodwell's translation of the Koran by Mohammed

Mohammed was an illiterate man. After he came to have a following, his disciples reduced his utterances to writing, and under the first kalif (Abu-Bekr) they were put in some sort of order, albeit with very slight editing. There are 114 suras (chapters). We find no narrative as in the Bible; the suras are, some of them, religious poems (something like the Hebrew psalms), sometimes lists of formal injunctions and precepts to the prophet's followers. They are in rhythmic prose, and occasionally rise almost to the level of noble poetry. The Koran can best be understood by remembering that it was composed by a Bedouin Arab in Bedouin language and metaphor. With some pains to make out the figures of speech, Mohammed's religious meanings are fairly easy to understand.

The Moslem "Lord's Prayer." [Sura 1]

In the Name of Allah the Compassionate and Merciful.[1]
Praise be to Allah, Lord of the worlds!
The compassionate, the merciful!

[1] All the suras (chapters) of the Koran properly begin with this formula.

King of the day of reckoning!
Thee only do we worship, and to Thee do we cry for help.
Guide Thou us on the straight path,
The path of those to whom Thou art gracious: — with whom
    Thou art not angry, and who go not astray.

The Day of Judgment and the Fate Hereafter.   [*Sura 87*]

Hath the tidings of the day [of judgment] that shall over·
    shadow reached thee?
Downcast on that day shall be the countenances of some,
Travailing and worn,
Burnt at the scorching fire,
Made to drink from a fountain fiercely boiling.
No food shall that have but the fruit of Darih,[1]
Which shall not fatten, nor appease their hunger.

Joyous too on that day, [shall be] the countenances of
    others,
Well pleased with their labors past,
In a lofty garden.
No vain discourse shalt thou hear therein;
Therein shall be raised couches,
And goblets ready placed,
And cushions laid in order,
And carpets spread forth.

Can they not look up to the clouds, how they are created;
And to the heaven how it is upraised;
And to the mountains how they are rooted;
And to the earth, how it is outspread?
Warn them then, for thou[2] art a warner only;
Thou hast no authority over them;
But whoever shall turn back and disbelieve,
Allah shall punish him with greater punishment.

[1] A thorny, bitter shrub.
[2] God is conceived as giving this message to Mohammed.

Verily to Us shall they return ;
Then shall it be Ours to reckon with them.

The Fate of the Righteous and Wicked. [Sura 37]

[As to the righteous] a banquet shall they have,
A banquet of fruits, and honored shall they be,
In the gardens of delight,
Upon couches face to face.
A cup shall be borne round among them from a fountain ;
Limpid, delicious to those who drink :
It shall not oppress the sense, nor shall they therewith be
    drunken.
And with them are the large-eyed ones [the houris] with
    modest, refraining glances. . . .
Truly great is their felicity !
[And the wicked in turn must eat of the tree Ez-
    zakkoum.]
It is a tree that cometh up from the bottom of hell ;
Its fruits are as it were the heads of Satans ;
And lo ! the damned shall surely eat of it, and fill their
    bellies with it.
Then shall they have thereon a mixture of boiling water ;
Then shall they return to hell !

The Mandate of God to Mohammed and his Followers. [Sura 73]

O Thou enfolded in thy mantle :
Stand up . . . for prayer.
For we shall devolve on thee **mighty words** :
Verily at the oncoming of night are devout **impressions**
    strongest, and words are most collected.
But in the day time thou hast continual employ —
And commemorate the name of thy Lord, and devote **thy-**
    self to him with entire devotion.

Lord of the East and of the West! No God is there but
He! Take Him for thy protector!

The day cometh when the earth and the mountains shall be
shaken: and the mountains become a loose heap of
sand.

Verily we have sent you an Apostle to witness against you,
even as we sent an Apostle [Moses] to Pharaoh.

And how if ye believe not, will you screen yourselves
from the day that shall turn children grayheaded?

The very heaven shall be reft asunder by it: this threat
shall be carried into effect.

Lo! this is a warning. Let him who will, take the way to
his Lord.

Of a truth, thy Lord knoweth that thou [O Mohammed]
prayest two thirds, or half, or a third of the night, as
do a part of thy followers. But Allah measureth the
night and the day: — He knoweth that ye cannot count
its hours aright, and therefore, turneth to you merci-
fully. Recite then so much of the Koran as may be
easy to you.[1] He knoweth that there will be some
among you sick, while others travel through the earth
in quest of the bounties of Allah; and others do battle
in His cause. Recite therefore so much of it as may
be easy. And observe the prayers and pay the legal
alms, and lend Allah a liberal loan; for whatever good
works ye send on before for your own behoof, ye shall
find with Allah. This will be best and richest in the
recompense. And seek the forgiveness of Allah; verily
Allah is forgiving [and] merciful!

---

[1] Note the extremely practical and accommodating spirit of these pre-
cepts. There is nothing in them of the Christian doctrines of perfection.
Any man of average zeal and conscientiousness could be a good
Moslem.

Various Passages illustrating Mohammed's Doctrine

On the Unity of God. [*Sura 112.*]

Declare — Allah is God alone :
Allah the Eternal !
He begetteth not, and He is not begotten.
And there is none like unto Him.

On attacking Christians and Jews. [*Sura 9.*]

Make war upon such of those to whom the Scriptures have
been given as believe not in Allah or in the last day, and
who forbid not that which Allah and his Apostle have
forbidden, and who profess not the profession of the
truths, until they pay tribute by right of subjection,
and they be humbled.

On the Mission of Mohammed. [*Sura 33.*]

O Prophet ! we have sent thee to be a witness, and a
herald of glad tidings and a warner !
And one who, through His own permission, summoneth
to Allah and a light giving torch.
Announce therefore to believers, that great boons await
them from Allah !

On The Last Dread Judgment. [*Sura 99.*]

When the Earth with her quakings shall quake,
And the earth shall cast forth her burdens,
And men shall say " What aileth her ? "
On that day shall she tell out her tidings,
Because thy Lord shall have inspired her.
On that day shall men come forward in throngs [from the
dead] to behold their works.
And whosoever shall have wrought an atom's weight of
good — he shall behold it !
And whosoever shall have wrought an atom's weight of
evil — *he* shall behold it !

141. The Opinion of Musa, the Saracen Conqueror of Spain, as to the Franks

From an Arabian Chronicler. Quoted in Zeller, " Rois Faineants et Maires du Palais," p. 120

The following opinion was expressed about the Franks by the emir who conquered Spain, and who — had he not been recalled — might have commanded at Tours. It shows what the Arab leaders thought of the men of the North up to the moment of their great disillusionment by " The Hammer."

[Musa being returned to Damascus, the Kalif Abd-el-Melek asked of him about his conquests,] saying

"Now tell me about these Franks, — what is their nature?"

" They," replied Musa, " are a folk right numerous, and full of might: brave and impetuous in the attack, but cowardly and craven in event of defeat."

" And how has passed the war betwixt them and thyself ? Favorably or the reverse ? "

"The reverse ? No, by Allah and the prophet!" spoke Musa. "Never has a company from my army been beaten. And never have the Moslems hesitated to follow me when I have led them ; though they were twoscore to fourscore."

142. An Early Story of the Battle of Tours or Poitiers

Isidore of Beja's " Chronicle." Quoted in Zeller, " Rois Faineants et Maires du Palais," p. 122

The defeat of the Saracen invaders of Frankland at Tours (more properly Poitiers) in 732 A.D. was a turning point in history. It is not likely the Moslems, if victorious, would have penetrated, at least at once, far into the north, but they would surely have seized South Gaul, and thence readily have crushed the weak Christian powers of Italy. It is very unfortunate that we do not possess scientific accounts of Charles Martel's great victory, instead of the interesting but insufficient stories of the old Christian chroniclers.

Then Abdrahman, [the Moslem emir] seeing the land filled with the multitude of his army, crossed the Pyrenées, and traversed the defiles [in the mountains] and the plains, so that he penetrated ravaging and slaying clear into the lands of the Franks. He gave battle to Duke Eudes (of Aquitaine) beyond the Garonne and the Dordogne, and put him to flight, — so utterly [was he beaten] that God alone knew the number of the slain and wounded. Whereupon Abdrahman set in pursuit of Eudes ; he destroyed palaces, burned churches, and imagined he could pillage the basilica of St. Martin of Tours. It is then that he found himself face to face with the lord of Austrasia, Charles, a mighty warrior from his youth, and trained in all the occasions of arms.

For almost seven days the two armies watched one another, waiting anxiously the moment for joining the struggle. Finally they made ready for combat. And in the shock of the battle the men of the North seemed like unto a sea that cannot be moved.[1] Firmly they stood, one close to another, forming as it were a bulwark of ice ; and with great blows of their swords they hewed down the Arabs. Drawn up in a band around their chief, the people of the Austrasians carried all before them. Their tireless hands drove their swords down to the breasts [of the foe].

At last night sundered the combatants. The Franks with misgivings, lowered their blades, and beholding the numberless tents of the Arabs, prepared themselves for another battle the next day. Very early, when they issued from their retreat, the men of Europe saw the Arab tents ranged still in order, in the same place where they had set up their camp. Unaware that they were utterly empty, and fearful lest within the phalanxes of the Saracens were drawn up

---

[1] The Saracens may be imagined hurling their splendid cavalry all day long in battering charges upon Charles's lines, and being unflinchingly repelled.

for combat, they sent out spies to ascertain the facts.
These spies discovered that all the squadrons of the
" Ishmaelites " had vanished. In fact, during the night
they had fled with the greatest silence, seeking with all
speed their home land. The Europeans, uncertain and fearful, lest they were merely hidden in order to come back [to
fall upon them] by ambushments, sent scouting parties
everywhere, but to their great amazement found nothing.
Then without troubling to pursue the fugitives, they contented themselves with sharing the spoils and returned
right gladly to their own country.

Part of Another Account of the Same Battle by the Chronicle of St. Denis

[The Moslems planned to go to Tours] to destroy the
Church of St. Martin, the city, and the whole country.
Then came against them the glorious Prince Charles, at the
head of his whole force. He drew up his host, and he
fought as fiercely as the hungry wolf falls upon the stag.
By the grace of Our Lord, he wrought a great slaughter
upon the enemies of Christian faith, so that — as history
bears witness — he slew in that battle 300,000 men [!], likewise their " king" [i.e. leader] by name Abdrahman. Then
was he [Charles] first called "Martel," for as a hammer of
iron, of steel, and of every other metal, even so he dashed
and smote in the battle all his enemies. And what was the
greatest marvel of all, he only lost in that battle 1500 men.
The tents and harness [of the enemy] were taken: and
whatever else they possessed became a prey to him and his
followers.

Endes, Duke of Aquitaine, being now reconciled with
Prince Charles Martel, later slew as many of the Saracens
as he could find who had escaped from the battle.

143. BAGDAD UNDER THE ABBASIDE KALIFS

Abridged from Ameer Ali, "History of the Saracens," p. 454

Bagdad "the city of the Arabian nights" was founded in 764 A.D. by the Abbaside Kalif Almansur. It was in its prime about 800 A.D., during the reign of the famous Haroun-al-Raschid. What this city, — which represented the crown of Saracenic civilization, — resembled, is told by a modern and very scholarly Mohammedan writer. He in turn makes a transcription from the medieval "Geographical Encyclopædia" of Yakūt — an author who saw Bagdad in its glory.

The city of Bagdad formed two vast semi-circles on the right and left banks of the Tigris, twelve miles in diameter. The numerous suburbs, covered with parks, gardens, villas and beautiful promenades, and plentifully supplied with rich bazaars, and finely built mosques and baths, stretched for a considerable distance on both sides of the river.

In the days of its prosperity the population of Bagdad and its suburbs amounted to over two millions! The palace of the Kalif stood in the midst of a vast park "several hours in circumference" which beside a menagerie and aviary comprised an inclosure for wild animals reserved for the chase. The palace grounds were laid out with gardens, and adorned with exquisite taste with plants, flowers, and trees, reservoirs and fountains, surrounded by sculptured figures. On this side of the river stood the palaces of the great nobles. Immense streets, none less than forty cubits wide, traversed the city from one end to the other, dividing it into blocks or quarters, each under the control of an overseer or supervisor, who looked after the cleanliness, sanitation and the comfort of the inhabitants.

The water exits both on the north and the south were like the city gates, guarded night and day by relays of soldiers stationed on the watch towers on both sides of the river. Every household was plentifully supplied with water at all seasons by the numerous aqueducts which intersected the town; and the streets, gardens and parks were regularly swept and watered, and no refuse was allowed to remain within the walls.

An immense square in front of the imperial palace was used for reviews, military inspections, tournaments and races; at night the square and the streets were lighted by lamps.

There was also a vast open space where the troops whose barracks lay on the left bank of the river were paraded daily. The long wide estrades at the different gates of the city were used by the citizens for gossip and recreation or for watching the flow of travelers and country folk into the capital. The different nationalities in the capital had each a head officer to represent their interests with the government, and to whom the stranger could appeal for counsel or help.

Bagdad was a veritable City of Palaces, not made of stucco and mortar, but of marble. The buildings were usually of several stories. The palaces and mansions were lavishly gilded and decorated, and hung with beautiful tapestry and hangings of brocade or silk. The rooms were lightly and tastefully furnished with luxurious divans, costly tables, unique Chinese vases and gold and silver ornaments.

Both sides of the river were for miles fronted by the palaces, kiosks, gardens and parks of the grandees and nobles, marble steps led down to the water's edge, and the scene on the river was animated by thousands of gondolas, decked with little flags, dancing like sunbeams on the water, and carrying the pleasure-seeking Bagdad citizens from one part of the city to the other. Along the wide-stretching quays lay whole fleets at anchor, sea and river craft of all kinds, from the Chinese junk to the old Assyrian raft resting on inflated skins.

[The mosques of the city were at once vast in size and remarkably beautiful. There were also in Bagdad numerous colleges of learning, hospitals, infirmaries for both sexes, and lunatic asylums.]

144. How Pope Gregory I made Peace with the Lombards and corresponded with the Lombard Court

Paulus Diaconus, "History of the Langobards," book IV, chaps. 5–9. Abridged

Gregory I (Pope 590 to 604 A.D.) was perhaps the greatest pontiff who ever reigned on the throne of St. Peter. No problem he confronted was more baffling than that of the Lombards, the latest and the fiercest invaders of Italy, who were threatening the very gates of Rome. Although left practically without support by the Eastern Emperor, Gregory by the mingling of a show of authority and of skillful negotiation brought about a tolerable peace, and established friendly relations with the Lombard court at Pavia. Gregory was prince of Rome in all but name, and did much to found the temporal power of the Papacy.

In these days (593 A.D.) the most sage and holy Pope Gregory of Rome, after he had composed many other things for the use of the holy Church, also indicted four books of the Life of the Saints. This writing he called a dialogue, which is a conversation of two persons, because he had produced it in discourse with his deacon Peter. The aforesaid Pope then sent these books to the Queen Theudelinda [of the Lombards], whom he knew to be undoubtedly devoted to the faith of Christ and distinguished in good works.

By means of this queen, too, the church of God procured much that was serviceable. For the Lombards, when they were still bound in the error of heathenism, seized nearly all the property of the churches, but the King [Agilulf, her husband], moved by her wholesome supplications, not only embraced the Catholic faith [1], but also bestowed much wealth upon the church of Christ, and restored to the honor of their accustomed dignity certain bishops who were in a straitened and abject condition.

[Presently resenting some aggressions of the exarch of Ravenna, King Agilulf] straightway marched out of Pavia with a great army and attacked the city of Perusia, [Perugia] and there for some days he besieged Maurisio, the duke of the Lombards who had gone over to the Romans, and speedily took him and slew him. The blessed Pope Gregory was so sorely alarmed at the approach of this king that he ceased from his commentary upon the temple mentioned in Ezekiel, as he himself declares in his homilies.

King Agilulf then, when matters were settled, returned to Pavia, and not long afterward, upon the special instigation of his wife, Queen Theudelinda — since the blessed Pope Gregory had frequently so admonished her in his letters — he concluded a firm peace with the same most holy Pope Gregory and with the Romans, and that venerable prelate dispatched to this queen this letter, as expression of his gratitude : —

Gregory to Theudelinda, Queen of the Lombards : We have learned from the report of our son, the abbot Probus, that your Highness has consecrated yourself, as you are wont, zealously and magnanimously to making peace. Nor was it to be presumed otherwise from your Christianity but that you would show to all men your labor and your goodness in the cause of peace. Wherefore we render thanks to God Almighty, who thus rules your heart by His affection, that He has not only given unto you the true faith, but that He also grants that you devote yourself always to the things which are pleasing to Him. For think not, most noble daughter, that you have obtained but scant reward for

---

[1] Probably this is a mistake. Agilulf seems to have been merely a tolerant heathen, who let his son be baptized.

staying the blood that would otherwise have been poured
out on either side.   On account of this act we return thanks
for your good will, and invoke the mercy of our God that
He may mete out to you a recompense of good things in
body and soul, both here and hereafter.

Do you therefore, according to your wont, ever busy yourself with the things that relate to the welfare of the parties,
and take pains to commend your good actions more fully in
the eyes of God Almighty, wherever an opportunity may be
given to win His reward.

[A similar friendly letter, setting forth the advantages of
peace, is sent to King Agilulf.]

145. How Pepin the Short became King of the Franks

Chronicle of St. Denis, book V, chap. 82

In 752 A.D. Pepin the Short replaced the last "Sluggard
King" of the Merovingian line, as is here related. His appeal
to the Pope for judgment on a purely temporal matter was another act in that process of linking the secular governments with
the Papacy, which plays such an important part in medieval
history. If the Pope could *advise* the deposition of a king, he
would presently be in a fair way to be able to *command* it.

Prince Pepin, when he saw that the King of the Franks
who then was, wrought no profit to the kingdom, sent to
the Pope Zacharias his messengers — Burkart the archbishop of Wurzburg and Fulrad Abbot of St. Denis to ask
advice as to, " Who ought to be the King? — He who had not
the least power in the kingdom, and who bore the *name*
only: or he by whom the kingdom was ruled, and who
had the power and the care over all things?"   And the
Pope replied to them "that he ought to be called king who
ruled the kingdom and who had the sovran power."   Then
he gave sentence that Pepin be crowned as King.

In this same year Pepin was declared King by the decision of Pope Zacharias and by the election of the Franks. He was consecrated in the city of Soissons by the hand of St. Boniface the martyr in the year of the incarnation of Our Lord 752. Childeric [the last Merovingian] who had been called King was shorn and cast into a monastery. Then King Pepin reigned 15 years 4 months and 20 days. He had previously held the lordship over the palace and the kingdom, since the death of Charles Martel his father, for 10 years.

146. Personal Traits of Charlemagne

Eginhard, "Life of Charlemagne," XXII–XXVI

Charles the Great or Charlemagne reigned from 771 to 814 over Frankland. He was in many respects the most notable figure in the Middle Ages. In him the strength of the young Germanic element, and the culture of the old Roman were happily combined. He seemed to reëstablish that Empire of the West, which still gripped the imagination of Latin Christendom, and long after his dynasty had ceased to reign men thought of him as the *ideally* wise, beneficent, and omnipotent Emperor. An intimate sketch of such a person is always interesting.

Charles was large and strong, of lofty stature, though not disproportionately tall (his height, it was well known, was seven times the length of his foot), the upper part of his face round, his eyes notably large and brilliant, his nose in the least long, his hair fair, his features laughing and merry. Thus whether standing or sitting he seemed always stately and dignified, notwithstanding that his neck was thick and rather short, and his belly rather prominent; — the good proportions of the rest of his body covered these defects.

In accordance with the national custom he took frequent exercise riding and in the chase, accomplishments in which the Franks probably excel the world. He enjoyed the exhalations from natural warm springs. Often he practiced swimming, in which art he was surpassingly proficient. Hence he built his palace at Aix-la-Chapelle [where there were warm baths], and lived there constantly during his latter years until his end.

He was wont to wear his national, or Frankish, costume, — next to his skin a linen shirt and linen breeches, and above these a tunic fringed with silk; while hose fastened by bands covered his lower limbs, and shoes his feet, and he shielded his shoulders and chest in winter by a close fitting coat of otter or marten skins. Over all he cast a blue cloak: always too he had a sword girt about him, usually one with a golden or silver hilt and baldric. Sometimes too he carried a jeweled sword, but only on great feast days, or at the reception of foreign envoys. He despised foreign costumes — no matter how elegant. Never did he suffer himself to wear them save twice, in Rome: when he put on the Roman tunic, chlamys[1] and shoes. The first time he did this at the request of Pope Hadrian: the second time to please Leo, Hadrian's successor. On great festivals he used embroidered clothes, and shoes adorned with jewels: a golden buckle would fasten his cloak, and he would appear wearing a gem-set golden diadem. On other days however he dressed practically as did the ordinary [Frankish] people.

Charles was temperate in eating, and particularly so in drinking. Drunkenness he abominated in anybody, much more in himself and in any one of his household.[2] Yet he did not readily go hungry, and he often complained that "the fast-times hurt his health." Rarely did he give large entertainments, except on great feast days, but then to a large number of guests.

[1] An outer cloak.
[2] Drunkenness was a very serious and common failing among the Franks.

While at table he listened to reading or music. The sub-jects of the reading were the stories and deeds of the olden time. St. Augustine's books too he liked, and especially the one called " The City of God." In summer after the mid-day meal he would eat some fruit, drink off a single cup, lay aside his clothes and shoes, just as at night, and for two or three hours take his rest. When he was dressing and putting on his shoes, not merely did he listen to his friends, but if the "Count of the Palace" reported any suit which needed his judgment, at once he would have the parties be-fore him, heard the case, and gave his decision just as if he were sitting on the judgment seat. [And any other neces-sary business he would thus attend to, at these times.]

Charles had the gift of ready and fluent speech, and could express whatever he had to say with the uttermost clearness. He was not satisfied with command of his native tongue alone, but attempted the study of others, especially he gained such control of Latin that he spoke it as well as his own vernacular. Greek however he understood better than he could speak. He possessed such eloquence that he could actually pass for a teacher of oratory. Assiduously too did he cultivate the liberal arts.

He held their teachers in great favor, and on them be-stowed high honors. The deacon Peter of Pisa, an aged man, gave him lessons in grammar.[1] Another deacon Alcuin [of England] who was the greatest scholar of his age, was his teacher in other learned subjects. The King devoted time and labor in abundance, studying with him rhetoric, dialectic and particularly astronomy. He learned to calcu-late, and was wont to investigate the movements of the heavens, with great intelligence. He also endeavored to [learn to] write, and was accustomed to keep tablets and [writing] blanks under his pillow on his bed, so that he

[1] Peter was teaching at Pavia in 774 A.D. when Charles, on taking the city, carried him off to teach at his palace.

could get used to shaping the letters. But he began this attempt too late in life, and it met with poor success.

He cherished with the greatest zeal and devotion the tenets of Christianity, as taught him from his youth. Hence it was he built the elegant basilica at Aix-la-Chapelle. He adorned it with gold and silver, also with lamps, likewise with rails and doors of solid brass. He had the columns and marbles used in it conveyed from Rome and Ravenna, for nowhere else could he find any more suitable. He was a constant worshiper at this church: he [seldom missed attending mass: and gave to both this church, those at Rome, and many others, most valuable treasures and gifts, and did all he could] to defend and protect the Church of St. Peter [at Rome] and to beautify and enrich it.

147. The Wars of Charlemagne

Eginhard, "Life of Charlemagne," V–VIII

Most of Charlemagne's reign was consumed with wars in which he was usually victorious. He never had to confront a first-class enemy in battle, and his martial father and grandfather had transmitted to him the well-trained Frankish army. He cannot therefore be called a distinguished general. His wars, however, were of high importance for history ; especially the conquest of the Saxons and the Lombards implied the bringing of much of Germany and Italy into the circle of " The Holy Roman Empire," and of medieval civilization.

After bringing a war in Aquitania to an end, he was persuaded, by the prayers and promptings of Hadrian, Bishop of Rome, to undertake a war against the Lombards. Already before him his father [Pepin] had assumed this task, at the asking of Pope Stephen, under great difficulties, for certain Frankish chiefs of his very council, had opposed the proposal so vehemently as to threaten to desert their King and go home. Notwithstanding, the war against Astolf,

King of the Lombards, had been undertaken, and promptly brought to an issue. Now [773 A.D.] although Charles had similar, or rather precisely the same grounds for declaring war that his father had, the war differed from the former both in its hardships and its results.

Pepin, to be sure, after a brief siege of King Astolf in Pavia, had compelled him to give hostages, to restore to the people of Rome the cities and castles he had seized, and to swear that he would not try to take them again. Charles, however, did not turn back — once war was declared — until he had exhausted King Desidarius [Astolf's successor], by a prolonged siege; then forced him to surrender unconditionally. He also drove his son Adalgis, the last hope of the Lombards, not only from his kingdom [in the north], but from all Italy. He likewise restored to the Romans all they had lost; crushed Henodgans, Duke of Friuli, who was scheming revolt; reduced all Italy to his sway, and set his son Pepin over it.

The war ended with the subjection of Italy, the banishment of King Desidarius for life, the expulsion of his son Adalgis from Italy and the restoration to Hadrian, Primate of the Roman Church, of all the conquests by the Lombard kings.

The Great Saxon War

[As to the Saxon War] no war ever undertaken by the Franks was waged with such persistence and bitterness, or cost so much labor, because the Saxons, like almost all Germans, were a ferocious folk, given over to devil-worship, hostile to our Faith, and they did not consider it dishonorable to transgress and violate all law — be it human or divine. Then, too, special circumstances caused a breach of the peace daily. [There was no well-defined frontier between Saxony and Frankland, and continual border feuds were raging.]

Accordingly, war was begun against the Saxons and was waged furiously for thirty-three consecutive years [772–804] on the whole to the disadvantage of the Saxons. Much earlier surely it would have terminated but for the perfidy of the Saxons. It is hard to tell how often they were conquered, humbly submitted to the King and promised to do what was commanded, gave the required hostages and received the royal officers. Sometimes they were so abased that they promised to renounce "devil-worship" and adopt Christianity. Nevertheless, they were as prone to repudiate these terms as to accept them. It was actually impossible to tell which came easier for them to do. Hardly a year passed from the beginning of the war without such changes on their part.

[The King, however, pressed them with unvarying purpose despite great difficulties] and either took the field against them himself, or sent his counts against them with a host to wreak vengeance and exact due satisfaction. [Many of the prisoners he settled as colonists in Gaul and the obedient parts of Germany.] The war that had lasted so many years at last terminated when the Saxons gave way to the terms proffered by the King; namely, the renunciation of their native religious cults and devil-worship, the acceptance of the Christian sacraments, and union with the Franks into one people.

The Saxon war began two years before the Italian war, but although it went on continuously, business elsewhere was not neglected, nor did the King hesitate to enter on other equally severe contests. Excelling, as he did, all the princes of his time in wisdom and magnanimity, he did not suffer difficulty to turn him back, nor danger to daunt him, from any task to be assumed or carried to a conclusion.

148. How Charlemagne was crowned Emperor

Eginhard, " Life of Charlemagne," XXVIII

The Coronation of Charlemagne in 800 A.D. and the reëstablish-
ment in name at least of the Western Empire is usually considered as
a cardinal point in history, the practical end of the Greco-Roman
civilization, and the beginning of a new society on foundations
largely Germanic. Of the occasion itself, it is said that Charlemagne afterwards asserted that if he had known what was about
to befall, he would never have gone to St. Peter's Church. He was
probably entirely willing to assume the imperial title, but foresaw
the perils likely to arise from an emperor's reigning, not in his
own right, but because of an apparent grant of the crown by the
Pope.

When Charlemagne made his last journey to Rome he
had other ends [than mere piety] in view. The Romans
had inflicted many injuries upon Pope Leo, tearing out his
eyes and cutting out his tongue, so that he was compelled
to summon help from the King. Therefore Charles repaired
to Rome to regulate the sorely confused affairs of the
Church; and at Rome he passed the whole winter. Then
it was he received the titles of " emperor " and " Augustus."
[Christmas day 800 A.D.] To these titles he had such re-
pugnance at first that he asserted that " he would not have
set foot in the church the day they were conferred, although
it was a great festival day [Christmas]," if he had surmised
the intention of the Pope [then to crown him].

Very patiently he bore the jealousy of the [Eastern]
Roman Emperors, which they showed when he assumed
these titles; for they took this step very ill; and by means
of repeated embassies and letters, in which he saluted them
as his " Brothers "; at length their haughty attitude yielded
to his magnanimity — a quality in which he beyond doubt
far surpassed them.

149. Selections from the Great Capitulary of Charlemagne of 802 A.D.

Henderson, "Select Historical Documents of the Middle Ages," book II, No. 2, pp. 189 ff.

In 802 A.D. Charlemagne issued a great "Capitulary" (decree) covering a vast number of subjects. It is permeated by a manifest desire to establish truth, peace, and justice, and to foster the intellectual and spiritual advancement of both clergy and laity. The few selections here given will convey some idea of the spirit animating this high-minded monarch, representative as he was of both the German and the Roman.

The most serene and noble Christian Emperor did choose from among his nobles the most prudent and the wisest men — archbishops as well as other bishops, and venerable abbots and pious laymen — and did send them over his whole kingdom and did grant through them, by means of all the following provisions, that men should live according to law and right. He did order them moreover, that, where anything is contained in the law that is otherwise than according to right and justice, they should inquire into this most diligently and make it known to him; and he, God granting, hopes to better it. And let the [imperial] messengers investigate diligently all cases where any man claims that injustice has been done to him by any one, according as they themselves hope to retain the grace of omnipotent God.

And he ordained that every man in his whole realm — priest or layman, each according to his vow and calling — who had previously promised fealty to him as *king* should now make this promise to him as *emperor*, and those who had hitherto not made this promise at all, down to those under 12 years of age, do likewise.

[This oath was to be understood not merely as promising

to defend the emperor's life and to resist enemies or traitors, but other points also *e.g.*:]

Every one of his own accord should strive wholly to keep himself in the holy service of God according to the precept of God and to his own promise.

[No one shall conceal any runaway slave of the emperor's.]

No one shall presume through fraud to plunder or do any injury to the holy Churches of God, or to widows, orphans or strangers; for the emperor himself, after God and his saints, has been constituted their protector and defender.

No one dare to devastate a fief of the emperor or to take possession of it.

No one shall presume to neglect a summons to arms of the emperor.

No man shall make a practice of unjustly carrying on the defense of another in court; whether from any cupidity, [the client] being no very great pleader, or in order by the cleverness of his defense, to impede a just judgment; or, his case being a weak one, by a desire of oppressing. But each man with regard to his own case, or tax or debt, must carry on his own defense; unless he be infirm, or ignorant of pleading [in which case the Imperial officers must help him].

[*Rules touching the conduct especially of the clergy.*]

Bishops and priests should live according to the canons and should teach others to do likewise. They should not oppress [the laity] with severe and tyrannous rule, but should carefully guard the flock committed to them, with simple love, with mercy and charity, and by the example of good works.

The abbots should live where the monks are, and wholly with the monks according to the rule: and they should diligently teach and observe the canons, and the abbesses shall do the same.

[The bailiffs of great churchmen must be honest, and refrainers from oppression.]

Bishops, abbots and abbesses and counts [*i.e.* lay magistrates] shall be mutually in accord,[1] agreeing in all charity and unity of peace, in wielding the law and in finding a right judgment. The poor, widows, orphans, and pilgrims shall have consolation and protection from them.

Abbots and all monks shall be subject in all obedience to their bishops as the canons require. . . .

Monasteries for women must be firmly ruled, and the nuns by no means permitted to wander about, but shall be kept in all diligence. [Strict measures shall be taken to prevent vice], drunkenness or cupidity, but in all things the nuns shall live soberly and justly.

No bishops, abbots, priests, deacons, — no one in short belonging to the clergy, — shall presume to have hunting dogs[2] or hawks, falcons, or sparrow-hawks [and violators of this rule are to be unfrocked].

[After enjoining the penalty for many crimes the capitulary adds near its conclusion,] Let no one in our forests dare to rob our game, which we have already many times forbidden to be done. If any count or lower official of ours or any of our serving men shall have stolen our game he shall be brought into our presence and called to account. Any common man so offending shall compound for it to the full extent of the law, and by no means shall any leniency be extended.

[1] The dissensions of the magnates, especially between bishops and lay magistrates, had often been very serious.

[2] " Sporting clergymen," were frequent offenders in Frankish days.

APPENDIX

ROMAN MONEY AND MEASURES

MONEY IN THE AGE OF AUGUSTUS

All values are highly approximate, and differ considerably from preceding and later centuries.

Sesterce [coined both in copper and silver] = 4 cents.
Denarius [silver] = 16 cents.
Aureus [gold] = about $5.
Talent [silver money of account, a variable Oriental unit] = $1000 or more.

Roman writers stated the ordinary money values usually in terms of sesterces, but sometimes as denarii. Before Augustus's day the Romans coined very little gold.

MEASURES OF CAPACITY

Cyathus = $\frac{1}{12}$ pint.
Sextarius = 1 pint.
Modius = 2 gallons.

MEASURES OF LENGTH

Roman foot = 11.65 English inches.
Roman mile = 4854 English feet [*i.e.* about $\frac{1}{10}$ less than an English mile.]

MEASURE OF LAND SURFACE

Jugerum = $\frac{5}{8}$ acre.

MODERN TRANSLATIONS AND OTHER WORKS
DRAWN UPON FOR EXTRACTS

Where no translator is named in the text the author of this book is usually responsible for the translation given; and in many other cases the original translation has been substantially recast. The titles of several books utilized have been omitted here as not readily obtainable by English readers.

Ammianus Marcellinus: *History.* Bohn Library. London.

Appian: *Civil and Foreign Wars.* Dr. Horace White's translation. 2 vols. New York, 1899.

Appuleius: *Works.* Bohn Library. London.

Bury, J. B.: *History of the Later Roman Empire, from Arcadius to Irene.* 2 vols. London, 1889.

Cæsar: *Commentaries.* Bohn Library. London.

Cassius Dio: *History of Rome.* H. B. Foster, translator. 5 vols. Troy, New York.[1]

Cicero: *Letters,* etc. Shuckburgh's translation. 5 vols. London, 1904.

Dill: *Roman Society in the Last Century of the Roman Empire.* London, 1899.

Duruy: *History of the Romans.* 16 "half" volumes. London. (See " Select List of Books.")

Epictetus: *Meditations,* etc. Carter's translation, in Everyman's Library. London. (Satisfactory and inexpensive version.)

Eusebius: *Life of Constantine.* Bagster's translation. London.

Eutropius: *Compendium of Roman History.* Bohn Library. London.

Evagrius: *Ecclesiastical History.* Bohn Library. London.

Heitland: *The Roman Republic.* 3 vols. London, 1910.

---

[1] While this version of Cassius Dio has proved useful, the translations here given have been so substantially recast that the entire responsibility must be assumed by the author of this book.

Henderson, B. W. : *The Life and Principate of the Emperor Nero.* London, 1903.

Henderson : *Select Historical Documents of the Middle Ages.* Bohn Library. London.

Horace : *Poetical Works.* Bohn Library. London. (Use has also been made of De Vere's translations of the Odes.)

Jordanes : *History of the Goths.* Mierow's translation. Princeton, N.J., 1910. (Excellent and highly desirable version of a work hitherto inaccessible to English readers.)

Juvenal : *Satires.* Bohn Library. London.

Koran of Mohammed. Translated by Rodwell. 1871. Reprinted in Everyman's Library. London. (On the whole, the most intelligible translation for English readers. The old Sale version also is not without merit. Various modern translations, *e.g.* Palmer's, are too "scientific" to be useful save to Orientalists.)

Livy : *History of Rome.* Bohn Library. London.[1]

Lucian : *Select Dialogues.* Bohn Library. London.

Marcus Aurelius : *Meditations.* Causabon's translation, Everyman's Library edition. London. (An old but good version : some use has also been made of the translation by George Long.)

Martial : *Epigrams.* Bohn Library. London.

Mau : *Pompeii.* English edition from the German, by Kelsey. New York, 1902.

Milne : *Roman Egypt.* London, 1898.

Nepos, Cornelius : *Lives.* Bohn Library. London.

Ovid : *Fasti.* Bohn Library. London.

Petronius : *Satyricon.* Ryan's translation. London.

Plautus : *Comedies.* Bohn Library. 2 vols. London.

Pliny the Elder : *Natural History.* Bohn Library. 2 vols. London.

Pliny the Younger : *Letters.* Firth's translation. London.

Plutarch : *Lives of Illustrious Men.* Dryden-Clough translation. 4 vols. London and New York. (Many reprints.)

[1] Of relatively little use in preparing this book. Among the poorest of the Bohn translations. A good English version of Livy is sadly needed.

Polybius: *History.* Shuckburgh's translation. 2 vols. London, 1889.

Sallust: *Historical Works.* Bohn Library. London.

Seneca: *On Benefits.* and *Minor Works.* Bohn Library. 2 vols. London.

Sheppard, *The Fall of Rome.* London.

Sozomen: *Ecclesiastical History.* Bohn Library. London.

Statius: *Poems.* Slater's translation. Oxford, 1908. (A good and recent translation.)

Strabo: *Geography.* Bohn Library. 3 vols. London.

Suetonius: *Lives of the Twelve Cæsars.* Bohn Library. London. (Among the most satisfactory of the older Bohn translations.)

Tacitus: *Works.* Translated by Church and Broadrib. 3 vols. London, 1877. (Use has been also made of the Bohn version, which is better for Tacitus than usual.)

Theodoret: *Ecclesiastical History.* Bohn Library. London.

University of Pennsylvania Historical Reprints. A series of pamphlets issued by the History Department. Philadelphia, 1898. (Excerpts here printed by kind permission.)

Velleius Paterculus: *History of Rome.* Bohn Library. London.

Vergil: *Æneid.* Ballard's translation. Boston, 1903. (Extract here printed by translator's kind permission.)

Vinogradoff, Paul: *Roman Law in Medieval Europe.* London, 1909.

Workman, H. B.: *Persecution in the Early Church.* London, 1906. (Contains many valuable excerpts from early Christian writers.)

A SELECT LIST OF BOOKS ON ROMAN HISTORY

No attempt is here made to prepare a complete list of all worthy books on Roman History. The works named are merely those most likely to appeal to the inexperienced student, and no book is mentioned which has not been examined in its entirety with this end in view. A great many important essays, the appreciation whereof would call for considerable previous knowledge, have been omitted. On numerous topics the best treatises in English are inferior to those in French and in German.

General Histories.

Duruy, Victor : *History of Rome.* Translated from the French. 8 vols., each in two parts. London and Boston, 1884. (Out of print, but can be purchased second hand.)

This is practically the only large work that covers the whole scope of Roman history from the founding of the city to the eve of the fall of the Empire. It is the product of distinguished French scholarship, and while here and there it stands in need of correction, in the main it is a safe as well as an inspiring guide. The work is profusely illustrated. The portion dealing with the Empire is on the whole decidedly better than that dealing with the Republic.

Merivale, Charles : *History of Rome.* American Book Company, 1877. (Also in the cheap Everyman's Library, Dutton.)

Published some years ago, and still of considerable value. It is a straightforward narrative of the rise and fall of Rome, with nonessentials omitted, and important things emphasized. It is the only history of Rome in a single volume that rises above the rank of the mere text-book.

The Roman Republic.

Mommsen, Theodor : *History of Rome* (to the time of Cæsar). Translated from the German. 5 vols. (an old edition in 4). Scribner's, 1905.

A remarkable book by a remarkable German scholar. So

385

completely have the theories of this work been accepted that until recently it has been almost heresy for historians to differ from Mommsen in the slightest particular. To-day some of his theories are subject to questioning, but in the main the work stands intact. The reconstruction of early Roman institutions is remarkably ingenious. No seriously minded scholar of Roman history should fail to read the entire work.

Heitland, W. E. : *The Roman Republic* (to the death of Cæsar). 3 vols. The Cambridge Press, 1909. (Also a good abridgment in one volume. The Cambridge Press, 1911.)

A recent English work, summing up the best products of modern investigation. The narrative is easy, the judgments well poised, and the author has shown a happy tendency to reject the often crude and ill-considered attempts of the German followers of Mommsen to elaborate upon the work of their master. While not of the epoch-making class with Mommsen's history, to the inexperienced student Heitland is likely to be far more helpful, merely because it is less learnedly ingenious.

How, W. W., and Leigh, H. D. : *History of Rome.* Longmans, 1907.

Shuckburgh, E. : *History of Rome.* Macmillan, 1894.

These are both well written single volume histories of the Romans down to the fall of the Republic. That by Shuckburgh is more purely narrative, and a recasting of the stories in the ancient historians ; that by How and Leigh is really a clever abridgment of Mommsen, and more purely constitutional. Either is highly useful to a scholar, although How and Leigh is a little better adapted for the student.

Taylor, T M.. : *Constitutional and Political History of Rome.* Methuen, London, 1899.

Extends to the reign of Domitian, thus giving a view of the early Empire. A well written and relatively up-to-date manual of the subjects named in the title.

Granrud, J. E. : *Roman Constitutional History.* Allyn and Bacon, 1902.

An accurate little history, covering the salient points down to the fall of the Roman Republic. Based upon the recent investigations on many debatable matters.

The Roman Empire.

Merivale, C. : *History of the Romans under the Empire.*   8 vols.
(sometimes bound in 4).   Longmans, 1890.

The most extensive piece of work on the early Empire in
the English language, covering from the time of Sulla to the
death of Marcus Aurelius.   Despite the fact that it was
written before use could be made of much inscriptional evidence recently discovered, the scholarship is in the main
sound, and the conclusions may be safely followed.   The
chapters on the reigns of Tiberius, Claudius, and Nero are
very good indeed.   On the whole, however, the second half
of Duruy's masterly work is slightly superior.

Bury, J. B. : *The Roman Empire* (to 180 A.D.).   American Book
Company.
This single volume by a great English scholar covers practically the same ground as Merivale (it begins with 31 A.D.).
The narrative is not so easy and readable as the author's
History of Greece, but the book is eminently useful to the
average student, and it is highly unfortunate that it is not
continued beyond the point where the Empire begins its
decline.

Jones, H. S. : *The Story of the Roman Empire.*   Putnam's, 1908.

A clearly written sketch of the story of the Cæsars, from
Augustus to the downfall.   The scholarship is recent and
excellent, but the slender proportions of the book prevent
it from being a final word on the subject.[1]

Gibbon, Edward : *Decline and Fall of the Roman Empire.*
Many editions, the most valuable being edited by Bury, with
desirable notes, and published in 7 vols. by Macmillan.
This is the most important historical work in the English language, perhaps in any language.   Written in the eighteenth
century, it has never been superseded.   In inimitable stately
Johnsonian prose it tells the story of the slow crumbling of

[1] A still briefer treatment of the subject is by the author of these
"Readings": *An Outline History of the Roman Empire:* Macmillan,
1909   In it especial stress is laid on the political history.

the old Empire from the death of Marcus Aurelius to the
capture of Constantinople by the Turks. Incidentally a
great deal of strictly Medieval history is dealt with. Here
and there recent investigators have been able to correct
Gibbon, or to amplify him, but in the main his work is surprisingly accurate. Two serious criticisms only have to be
made: 1. Scholars are agreed he took an erroneously unfavorable view of the later Roman Empire at Constantinople;
2. He was tinctured by a most obvious prejudice against
Christianity which he knew only in its unspiritual eighteenth-
century garb. But the needful deductions are easily made,
and the work remains a prime essential to every scholar.

Topics Connected with Roman History.

Abbott, F. F.: *Roman Political Institutions.* Ginn and Company,
1907.

An excellent handbook describing the officials and general
government of Rome both under the Republic and the Empire.
There is besides a good outline of Roman constitutional
history, also abundant references to ancient and modern
authorities. A useful book to any student.

Ramsay, Wm., and Lanciani, R.: *Manual of Roman Antiquities.*
Scribner's, 1895.

A rather old book fairly brought up to date. Practically
every subject of Roman antiquities is covered in it, and in a
way making the information very accessible. A most desirable
reference book.

Sandys, John E.: *A Companion to Latin Studies.* Cambridge
Press, 1910.

Corresponds in aim and effectiveness to Whibley's *Companion to Greek Studies* (see note thereon, Vol. I, p. 349).
Almost every topic likely to interest a student in Roman
history has been handled in admirable articles by experts.
An invaluable book.

Arnold, W. T.: *Roman Provincial Administration.* Stechert,
1905: also Macmillan.

A notable monograph on a very important subject. There
is no better treatment anywhere, of how the Romans con-
trolled their vast Empire.

Botsford, G. W.: *Roman Public Assemblies.* Macmillan, 1909.

The most important work on Roman history ever written by an American. The whole problem of the Roman Comitia, how they affected the course of Roman history, their composition, their influence and ultimate decadence is taken up skillfully, and at some points the author has overthrown the long-accepted conclusions of Mommsen. The work is for scholars, however, and not for the merely casual reader.

Bailey, Cyril: *The Religion of Ancient Rome.* Open Court Publishing Company, 1907.

A decidedly short, but highly illuminating discussion of the early Roman religion, which scholars are now realizing was entirely dissimilar from the Greek.

Platner, S. B.: *Topography and Monuments of Ancient Rome.* Allyn and Bacon, 1911.

The best and most recent work in English on the city of Rome in antiquity.

Dill, S.: *Roman Society from Nero to Marcus Aurelius.* Macmillan, 1904.   *Roman Society in the Last Century of the Western Empire.* Macmillan, 1899.

Admirable discussions of the respective periods they cover. They are particularly good as explaining the transition in life, thought, and religion, which prepared the way for Christianity.

Pellisson, M.: *Roman Life in Pliny's Time.* Jacobs, 1901.

Preston, N. W., and Dodge, L.: *Private Life of the Romans.* Leach, Boston, 1893.

Thomas, E.: *Roman Life under the Cæsars.* Putnam's, 1899.

These are all convenient books, presenting in somewhat similar manner the salient phases of Roman private life.[1]

[1] The author of the present volume has attempted his own contribution to the study of Roman life in *The Influence of Wealth in Imperial Rome,* Macmillan, 1910.   In this book such questions as the commerce, economic life, public benefactions, slave system, luxury, etc., of the Romans, are considered.

Friedlænder, **L.** : *Roman Life and Manners under the Early Empire.* 4 vols. Dutton and Company.

A translation of a masterly, exhaustive, and illuminating German work. It has long been the standard work on the subject.

Fowler, **W. W.**: *Social Life at Rome in the Age of Cicero.* Macmillan, 1909.

Interesting pictures of life in the days of Cicero and Cæsar.

Becker, **W. A.**: *Gallus; or Roman Scenes in the Days of Augustus.* Longmans, 1903.

A somewhat wooden novel, yet nevertheless conveying a vast deal of information ; but the valuable part of the work is the Appendix, which really is an elaborate treatise on Roman private life.

Periods of Roman History and Biographies.

Ihne, **Wm.**: *Early Rome.* Longmans.

Smith, **R. B.** : *Rome and Carthage.* Longmans.

Beesly, **A. H.** : *The Gracchi, Marius and Sulla.* Longmans.

Merivale, **C.**: *The Roman Triumvirates.* Longmans.

Capes, **W. W.** : *The Early Roman Empire.* Longmans. — *The Age of the Antonines.* Longmans.

These are small handy books in the " Epochs of History " Series. All are good and useful, but especially the last two, which together constitute a clear and concise account of the great age of the Empire.

Ferrero, **G.**: *The Greatness and Decline of Rome.* 5 vols. Putnam's, 1907–1909.

No work dealing with Roman history has created so great a stir in recent times as this. The author is a well-known Italian scholar, and the work has been satisfactorily translated. The promise of the title is hardly borne out by the volumes so far published ; they merely begin with the decline of the Republic, and end with the death of Augustus. The style is fascinating, and the conclusions frequently so aptly put that the reader is tempted to accept them without sifting the author's evidence. Signor Ferrero is no great admirer of Julius Cæsar, he believes there was little or no romance between Antony and Cleopatra, he takes a most unusual view of the principate of Augustus. These are only samples of his radical attitude. Everywhere great stress is laid upon the economic factor as determining the course of history. But the work is almost hopelessly subjective. In no other extensive modern work is the author's own surmise so often put forward as serious history. A great many of the statements that seem so revolutionary are really without valid authority either ancient or modern. The result is that the set is not a safe guide to the inexperienced student: to the advanced student, however, who is able to check up the evidence, it is highly stimulating, and occasionally informing.

Long, George: *Decline of the Roman Republic.* 5 vols. London, 1864–1874. Out of print.

A standard work, of sound and accurate scholarship and judgment, but rendered repellent to most readers by an almost deliberately heavy style, and the elimination of every literary quality except that of clearness.

Dodge, T. A.: *Hannibal.* Houghton, Mifflin, 1891.
Cæsar. Houghton, Mifflin, 1892.

Exhaustive and well-written biographies of these great men, considering them, however, almost entirely from the military point of view. As a result, the volume on Cæsar is decidedly incomplete for a student of political history: as a picture of the great captain's campaigns, however, it is excellent. The life of Hannibal is also very good.

Froude, James A.: *Cæsar, A Sketch.* Harper's, 1895.

The mere name of the author suggests controversy, and this book has been subject to violent attack. Part of the strife, however, has really arisen out of the fierce personal animosities that have rent English literary circles. This book is not blameless, but its virtues far outweigh its defects. It takes an excessively favorable view of Cæsar, and an unfavorable view of Cicero, but most historical students to-day concur in its general attitude. The method of handling the evidence is not absolutely critical. On the other hand, the book is written with a verve and a literary vivacity that make it a joy to read. It is highly interesting without ceasing to be dignified. It can be read with the same avidity one can read a novel. For a person just beginning the study of Roman history, there is *no* volume more likely to give him a taste for the subject than this.

Henderson, B. W. : *Life and Principate of the Emperor Nero.* Lippincott's, 1903.

An attempt, not entirely successful, to explain away some of the worst iniquities of its very unworthy subject, and to make out that Nero, if not an agreeable personage in his private life, was at least an able ruler. The book is plausible enough to be worth reading, although it is an advocate's plea in behalf of an all but confessed criminal.

Forsyth, Wm. : *Cicero.* Scribner's, 1869.

The standard life of the great orator, — sound, scholarly, and not unduly laudatory.

Strachan-Davidson, J. L. : *Cicero.* " Heroes of the Nations " Series. Putnam's, 1891.

Warde-Fowler, W. : *Julius Cæsar.* Putnam's, 1892.

Firth, J. B. : *Augustus Cæsar.* Putnam's, 1903.

Gardiner : *Julian the Philosopher.* Putnam's, 1895.

Firth, J. B. : *Constantine the Great.* Putnam's, 1905.

These are all worthy biographies in a well-known and on the whole excellent series. The one by J. B. Firth on Augustus Cæsar is a valuable account of the building of the Empire by the great successor of the great Julius : the other volumes are also useful.

Watson, P. B. : *Marcus Aurelius Antoninus.* Harper's, 1884. (Out of print.)

A somewhat discursive biography of the noblest though not the ablest ruler in the whole Imperial line.

The Period from 395 to 800 A.D.

Gibbon : *The Roman Empire.* (See entry on page 387.)

Bury, J. B. : *The Later Roman Empire at Constantinople.* 2 vols. Macmillan, 1889.

The standard work on the subject. Written with a just appreciation of the great work the East Romans did for civilization.

Oman, C. : *The Story of the Byzantine Empire.* Putnam's.

This is an excellent short sketch of the Empire of Constantinople, and the reading of it will prove an excellent antidote to the false estimate Gibbon gives to the later Roman Empire.

Finlay, G. : *Greece under the Romans.* Everyman's Series. Dutton.

This is the first volume of a standard history of Greece since the Roman conquest. Though written many years ago, it is still of very high value. It deals more with the condition of the subject Greek peoples, especially from the time of Constantine onward, than with the doings of Emperors.

The Mohammedans.[1]

Gilman, Arthur : *The Story of the Saracens.* Putnam's, 1887.

A good readable popular account of the rise and decline of the Empire of the Arabs.

Amir Ali : *History of the Saracens.* Macmillan, 1900. (Out of print.)

A most interesting attempt by an educated Mohammedan to tell from a sympathetic standpoint the story of the rise of Islam and to explain away the prejudices of Western readers. In the main the work has been well done, and the attempt has been measurably successful.

Muir, Sir Wm. : *Mohammed.* Scribner's (English edition, 1894).

The standard scholarly life of the founder of Islam.

The Church.[2]

Milman, H. H. : *Latin Christianity.* 8 vols. in 4. Doran (formerly Armstrong), 1872.

A standard scholarly account of the rise and greatness of the Western church as centered about the Papacy.

---

[1] The account given by Gibbon of the rise and progress of Mohammed and his followers is justly celebrated. Gibbon's prejudice against Christianity led him to take extra pains to apologize for Islam.

[2] A compact, readable, and unbiased history of the rise of the Christian Church — telling the story in untechnical language for general readers — is entirely lacking. Only a very few of the vast number of special titles on the subject are here given.

Robertson, J. C. : *History of the Christian Church.* 8 vols. Young Churchman Co., 1875.

This is the best extensive history of Christianity, — at least from the Protestant standpoint. It has the great merit of avoiding for the most part unprofitable ecclesiastical and doctrinal details, and the narrative is readable. It carries the story from the founding of the church down to the age of Martin Luther.

Smith, Philip : *Ecclesiastical History* (to 1000 A.D.). American Book Company, 1888.

A fairly satisfactory attempt at a short history of the progress of Christianity. It is mainly an abridgment of Robertson.

Stanley, Arthur : *Lectures on the Eastern Church.* "Everyman's Library," Dutton.

Charming and informing lectures on the Christianity of the East, — the council of Nicæa, etc.

Alzog, J. : *Church History.* 3 vols. Robert Clark and Company, 1874–1878.

On the whole, the best history giving the story of the church from the Catholic point of view.

The Barbarians and the Frankish Kingdom.[1]

Hodgkin, T. : *Italy and Her Invaders.* 8 vols. Clarendon Press, 1885–1899.

This work, covering the story of the invasions of Italy and incidentally of the rise of the Ostrogothic, Lombard, and Frankish kingdoms (down to Charlemagne), is a narrative of first-class importance to every English reader. The criticism that the author has borrowed rather copiously from the German historian Dahn is probably well founded, but the fact remains that the work is a monument of well-applied learning, and the story is well told, though at points diffuse.

---

[1] For the Barbarian Invasions and the new kingdoms which the Germans founded, Gibbon is of high value : also there are very useful chapters on the Frankish monarchy, etc., in the well-known histories of France by Guizot, Kitchen, Michelet, and others. The first volume of the *Cambridge Medieval History* (Macmillan, 1912) possesses great importance to every student.

It is unfortunate that the work is not published in a cheaper edition.

Hodgkin, T. : *Charles the Great.* Macmillan, 1897.

A well-written biography of the mighty Emperor, by the author last mentioned. Thoroughly useful to the inexperienced student.

Kingsley, Charles : *The Roman and the Teuton.* Macmillan, 1864.

Famous lectures by a famous writer on the downfall of the Empire and the rise of the new nationalities. The treatment of the later Romans is not always fair, and the German invaders are somewhat overglorified, but in the main the book is excellent, and preëminently entertaining.

Emerton, Ephraim : *Introduction to the Middle Ages.* Ginn, 1888.

The work of a distinguished American scholar. It is by all odds the best sketch we possess of the early Middle Ages. Although written as a text-book it can be read with interest merely for its narrative qualities.

Sergeant, L. : *The Story of the Franks.* Putnam's, 1898.

A good account of the only one of the Barbarian invaders that founded a permanent dominion in continental Europe.

Mombert, J. I. : *Charles the Great.* Appleton's, 1888.

This is the standard biography of the personage usually known as "Charlemagne," and on the whole meets every fair requirement. It is much fuller than Hodgkin's sketch.

BIOGRAPHICAL NOTES OF ANCIENT AUTHORS CITED

In this list are included brief notices of most of the regular Greek and Latin authors from whose works excerpts have been taken, but no attempt has been made to include various obscure Christian chroniclers, or to trace the authorships of Oriental inscriptions, etc. Many famous writers are not mentioned because no quotations are made from their writings.

Ammianus Marcellinus (died about 390 A.D.). A native of Antioch. Served in the Roman Imperial bodyguard, but presently retired from the army, and wrote a history that is (so far as the work is preserved) one of our best authorities for the age just before the fall of the Empire. The books remaining to us cover 353 to 378 A.D. He was not the master of a good style, but his story is accurate, faithful, and impartial. Often in his writings is displayed a hatred of the shallow artificial life of his age, a spirit quite worthy of a bluff old soldier.

Appian (an Alexandrian. Greek who lived at Rome during the reigns of Trajan, Hadrian, and Antoninus Pius). He seems to have been an advocate of some consequence, well acquainted with public affairs. His history of the Wars of Rome is extremely unoriginal, but is clearly written, and possesses the great advantage for us of being compiled from reliable contemporary authors whose writings are now lost.

Appuleius (born about 130 A.D.). A native of Africa who traveled extensively in the Roman world, and studied the Platonic philosophy at Athens. His writings reflect pretty clearly what passed for learning and wisdom in his age. He was the author of a curious kind of romance — *The Golden Ass*.

Cæsar (100 to 44 B.C.). Julius Cæsar is, of course, one of the leading figures in history, and only secondarily a man of letters. Yet he was counted among the leading Roman orators, barring only Cicero, and his literary productions are of remarkable merit. In his *Commentaries on the Civil War*, while no doubt he suppresses facts unfavorable to his own cause, he is never-

theless in most instances excellently informed, and certainly he tries hard to convey the impression of being impartial.

Cassius Dio (often called *Dion Cassius:* born 155 A.D., died about 230 A.D.). He was a Bithynian who rose to the consulship, and held various other high offices, especially under Alexander Severus. He wrote, in Greek, a history of Rome from the coming of Æneas down to 229 A.D. Much of this large work is lost, although we possess an inferior abridgment of nearly the whole. The history is of high value, especially for the period of the Empire. Cassius Dio was well acquainted with the routine of the imperial government, and able to describe political movements clearly, although he was by no means a perfect master of a good literary style.

Cicero. Quintus Cicero (102 to 43 B.C.) was a polite literary gentleman, the feebler image of his famous brother Marcus. He rose to the prætorship, and the interesting tract on the " Candidacy for the Consulship " is attributed to him.

Eginhard, or **Einhard** (about 770 to 850 A.D.). He was the secretary and intimate friend of Charlemagne, and held many important church benefices. His fame rests upon his authorship of *The Life of Charlemagne* — " which is generally regarded as the most important historical work of a biographical nature, that has come down to us from the Middle Ages."

Epictetus (lived from reign of Nero to Hadrian). A slave, and later a freedman, who became one of the most famous masters of the later school of Stoics. The *Discourses* and *Handbook* which we have as his, are the compilations of his faithful pupil Arrian, the historian. Epictetus's gospel may be summed up in the words *suffer and abstain*, *i.e.* man should endure all things with noble calmness, confident that a benevolent Providence is ruling everything for an ultimate good end. He was one of the " inspired Pagans " who accomplished an almost indispensable work in preparing the world for the final triumph of Christianity.

Eusebius (about 264 A.D. to about 340 A.D.). A learned Christian writer, who was bishop of Cæsarea, and an intimate friend of Constantine the Great. He was the author of an important

Chronology, a *Life of Constantine* (extremely eulogistic), and an *Ecclesiastical History*, which is an invaluable repository of information about the church during the period of its growth and of its rise to equality with Paganism.

Eutropius (latter part fourth century A.D.). He wrote a concise and clear *Epitome of Roman History* from the founding of the city down to 364 A.D. It shows little original research, but is frequently useful, especially for the history of the Empire.

Evagrius (536 to about 600 A.D.). A Christian Syrian, who wrote an *Ecclesiastical History* which gives much information as to events in the church — and occasionally as to secular matters — between the years 431 and 593 A.D. It is on the whole superior, in accuracy and style, to most histories prepared by churchmen in his age.

Gregory of Tours (540 to 595 A.D.). A learned bishop who kept alive something of the old Gallo-Roman traditions of culture during the wrack and ruin of the Merovingian Frankish period. His *Annals of the Franks* are our main authority for the story of the deeds of Clovis and of his evil sons. Gregory delineates with unsparing hand the iniquities of his age, although he has a marked tendency to excuse the crimes of Clovis and other kings in view of their " Christian Orthodoxy."

Herodianus (late second and early third centuries A.D.). The author of a history in Greek of the Roman Emperors from 180 to 238 A.D. Very little is known of him personally.

Horace (65 to 8 B.C.). Quintus Horatius Flaccus was probably the most distinguished of the Latin poets save only Vergil. He was a native of Venusia in Apulia, but passed most of his life at Rome, where the patronage of Mæcenas — Augustus's prime councilor — gave him a fortune and a distinguished audience. Horace was preëminently " the gentleman in the world." He had abundant common sense, wisdom, and a quick observation of the shams and the true pleasures of life : an admirable and typical versifier for the practical Romans. He never reached the loftiest heights of poetry, but few lyricists have appealed to larger audiences, across longer ages than he.

Probably no Latin writer surpassed Horace in the delicacy and felicity of his language.

Inscriptions. See Note in Vol. I, page 356.

Jordanes, or **Jornandes** (lived in sixth century A.D., during the reign of Justinian). He was a Goth, who finally became a bishop in Italy. His most valuable history is the book *Upon the Origin and Deeds of the Goths.* In it we find the old traditions of his people, as well as an uncritical account, often very prejudiced in favor of the Goths, of the conquests of Alaric, Theodoric, etc. With all its failings, however, the work has a marked value.

Juvenal (about 60 to 130 A.D.). He was the greatest of the Latin satirical poets; perhaps the greatest poet, for his own peculiar field, of all time. He knew to a nicety the vices and foibles of the Rome of Domitian and Trajan, and he declaims against them with the fury of a Hebrew prophet, mingled, however, with much wit and wisdom of a kind that almost makes him seem a "modern" writer. His humor has been likened to that of certain American authors — notably Mark Twain. His sixteen *Satires* are therefore a precious literary treasure, although their effective translation is by no means easy. It ought to be said, however, that Juvenal is prone to exaggerate — to lay undue emphasis upon things evil, and to ignore the good that undoubtedly existed in the Rome of his time.

Livy (59 B.C. to 17 A.D.). Titus Livius a native of Patavium (Padua) is by all odds the leading historian for the Roman Republican period. His entire history in 142 books extended from the foundation of Rome down to 9 B.C. Most unfortunately we possess only 35 of these intact, although *Epitomes* have been preserved of most of the others. A critical and scrupulously impartial historian Livy was not. He often gives us myths that have obviously no factual value, and again he suppresses or colors such evidence as reflects upon the glory of Rome. On the other hand, his style is "clear, animated, and eloquent," and often under the legends a little sifting will bring out valuable data; while no Roman who had read through his long narrative could fail to gain a clear grasp upon the long slow process of war and patriotic sacrifice by which the little city by the Tiber rose to world-wide dominion.

Lucian (active in reign of Marcus Aurelius). A Greek of northern Syria who was first a lawyer at Antioch, then traveled through Greece teaching rhetoric, and later entered the governmental service in Egypt. His *Dialogues* are among the shrewdest, keenest writings of all antiquity. He thrusts the knife of sarcasm into almost all the honored conventionalities of the artificial society of the second century A.D. Some of his scenes are irresistibly comic, and all are witty.

Lucretius (95 B.C. to about 52 B.C.). A Roman Epicurean, whose poem in defense of the Epicurean philosophy (*De Rerum Natura*) is a really noble, readable, and poetical attempt to expound and apologize for a very unworthy system of conduct and ethics. It is one of the most commendable pieces of Latin verse.

Marcus Aurelius (121 to 180 A.D.). He was perhaps the noblest personality who ever sat upon the throne of the Cæsars, although not the ablest in mere governmental ability. He was a Stoic philosopher who endeavored faithfully to carry his stern high doctrines with him into the palace or camp. His *Meditations* — written in Greek — are an excellent presentation of the Stoic ideal, and are incidentally by far the best book ever written by a reigning monarch.

Martial (43 to about 104 A.D.). A Romanized Spaniard, who spent most of his career at Rome. His *Epigrams* are a precious collection of keen and witty comment upon all the mazes of society at the metropolis; the poems are defiled by frequent impurities, but no student of the life of the Empire can dispense with the light they cast on innumerable subjects.

Ovid (43 B.C. to 18 A.D.). A clever and versatile Latin poet, of much talent and little real genius. His *Metamorphoses* preserve to us in their most accepted form the standard stories of Greek mythology, as conventionalized by the first century A.D., but of greater historical value is his *Fasti* — a sort of Roman calendar in verse, describing the various old Latin festivals, the rites proper for each, etc. Only half of this interesting work has been preserved.

Petronius (age of Nero). He was an unprincipled but elegant and clever companion of Nero, for a while a kind of 'master-of-the-revels' (*Elegantiæ arbiter*) of that evil Cæsar's court. He committed suicide on losing the imperial favor. To him is commonly attributed the *Satyricon*, a kind of comic romance, often disgustingly coarse, but written with a lively wit and a cynical insight into all the follies and iniquities of the age. "Trimalchio's Dinner" forms an important episode in the book.

Plautus (about 254 to 184 B.C.). An Umbrian, who after a varied career at Rome undertook to eke out a living by preparing comedies for stage managers. In this way he presently gained fame and a competence. Twenty of his plays have been preserved : they all seem to be founded upon Greek models, but he took greater liberties in adapting them than the rival comedian Terence, and as a rule we may feel we are given the Roman atmosphere of about 200 B.C.

Pliny the Elder (23 to 79 A.D.). He was a distinguished Roman official, and at the time of his death he was admiral of the fleet at Misenum (he perished during the famous eruption of Mt. Vesuvius). His fame rests upon his *Natural History*, a vast compendium in 37 books, containing an enormous deal of varied learning and pseudo-learning, often on historical subjects. The work is very ill arranged, and lacks critical sifting, but to it we owe many of the most interesting items and anecdotes of ancient history.

Pliny the Younger (about 61 A.D. to about 114 A.D.). Nephew and adopted son of the preceding. He held various high governmental posts, *e.g.* the consulship and governorship of Bithynia, and claimed the personal friendship of Trajan. He was the author of a series of *Letters*, which, although tainted by a certain artificiality, are, on the whole, the clearest and most informing documents we have as to life among the polite leisured classes at Rome about 100 A.D. Judging from the tone of the letters, Pliny was an affectionate husband, a kindly master to his servants, and a genial friend: a good example of the *best* in the old society.

Plutarch. See Biographical Note in Vol. I, page 358.

Polybius (about 204 to about 122 B.C.). A Greek nobleman of Megalopolis, who, after taking a leading part in the doings of the Achæan League, was banished to Italy by the Romans in 168 B.C. In 151 B.C. he was released, but in the interval he had won the friendship of the younger Scipio and was present with him at the fall of Carthage. Later he used his influence to mitigate the lot of the Greeks after the destruction of Corinth. Polybius undertook in a long history to explain to his countrymen how it was the Romans were able to conquer them, and to explain the secrets of Roman greatness. His work begins with the outbreak of the First Punic War. His sources of information were ample, and he had a critical faculty and power of philosophic grasp rare in ancient writers. His literary execution is not correspondingly excellent, but his history perhaps — next to Thucydides's — comes nearest of all from Antiquity to satisfying the demands of modern scholarship. It is a great misfortune that the larger part of it is lost.

Prudentius (about 348 to 410 A.D.). A poet who has been called " the Horace and Vergil of the Christians." Little is known about his life. He seems to have held high civil offices under Theodosius and Honorius, but late in life he became weary of worldly honor and turned himself strictly to religion. His religious hymns and versified expositions of Christian doctrines often show very high poetic qualities.

Rutilius Numantianus (wrote about 417 A.D.). A Gaul, who held the city præfectship at Rome about 413 A.D. He described his return to Gaul in a rather long poem, *Upon the Return.* He was a Pagan with little love for Christianity, but he celebrates the praises of old Rome with a truly poetic and admirable fervor.

Sallust (86 B.C. to 34 B.C.). A Roman politician, who, after a decidedly chequered career, threw in his lot with Cæsar and served with him during the Civil War. As governor of Numidia he was charged with gross extortions. Of his historical writings we still have his *Catilina*, and his *Jugurthine War*. These short essays are too rhetorical and often strain the truth for the sake of the literary effect; but they form important links in Roman annals.

Seneca (about 5 B.C. to 65 A.D.). He was born in Spain, of a noble Roman family there settled. After he had won fame as a pleader at Rome, Claudius banished him to Corsica, but Agrippina had him recalled, and as tutor of young Nero he was for a while the most influential man in the government, until Nero degenerated. Seneca then retired from office, and was presently put to death on suspicion of conspiracy. Seneca was the author of treatises on the Stoic philosophy in which he set forth a severe and noble doctrine, — almost unattainable by human virtue. Unfortunately the great riches he amassed did not correspond well with the austerity of his doctrines, yet he died very bravely, in a manner that became a good man and a philosopher.

Sidonius Apollinaris (lived in fifth century A.D.). A native of Lyons (Lugdunum) in Gaul, who became Bishop of Clermont. He played a considerable part in public affairs during the painful period of the Barbarian conquest, and his poems and letters show him to have been a man of genuine literary culture, who did his best to keep alive the old civilization in a very degenerate age.

Sozomen (lived in fifth century A.D.). A Greek ecclesiastical historian, probably born near Gaza in Palestine. His *History of the Church* extends from 323 A.D. to 423 A.D. He wrote in a good style, and his work is useful for secular as well as for merely ecclesiastical history.

Spartianus (lived in reigns of Diocletian and Constantine.) He was said to be the author of the *Life of Hadrian* and several other biographies in the so-called *Augustan History*. These essays have a very unequal value, but they give us much personal information and many anecdotes about the Emperors.

Statius (about 61 to 96 A.D., dates uncertain). He was a clever and versatile Roman poet, who was at his best during the

reign of Domitian. His poems cover a wide variety of subjects, and occasionally show a slight touch of genius; in the
main, however, he may be described as talented, but by no
means great.

Strabo. See Biographical Note in Vol. I, page 358.

Suetonius (lived from reigns of Vespasian to that of Hadrian).
He was an advocate at Rome, and for a while private secretary
of Hadrian, then fell into disgrace. His *Lives of the Twelve
Cæsars* (Julius Cæsar to Domitian inclusive) are a series of
lively biographies in Latin, comparable with the *Lives* (in
Greek) by Plutarch. They give personal sketches, not political histories; but are excellent in style, comparatively careful
in statement, and one of our chief sources for the early Empire.

Tacitus (about 60 A.D. to about 120 A.D.). Next to Livy he was
the greatest Roman historian. He was consul in 97 A.D. and
a valued friend of Pliny the Younger. To him the establishment and continuance of the rule of Cæsars meant the breaking down of the political prestige of the old Roman families
to which his interests were linked. With consummate literary
skill and with great appearance of devotion to truth he wrote
the story of the Emperors from 14 to 96 A.D. Of this great
work we only have fragments known as the *Annals* (Tiberius,
Claudius, and Nero) and the *Histories* (telling of the civil
war following the death of Nero). By a skillful cumulation
of unfavorable evidence Tacitus draws a most damning in-
dictment of the Cæsarian régime. Most of his charges are
probably true; but he does not give the Emperors proper
credit for the good which they undoubtedly wrought in the
provinces. His *Germany* is a valuable separate essay.

Theodoret (about 393 to 457 A.D.). A famous churchman of Antioch who had a prominent part in the ecclesiastical tumults
of the fifth century. His *Ecclesiastical History* (from about
320 to 429 A.D.) is learned and impartial, although often be-
traying extreme credulity. It is only one of his many writings
— mostly theological.

Vellius Paterculus (lived in reign of Augustus and Tiberius). A
Roman historian who served on campaigns in Germany, and

who wrote a short *Compendium of Roman History*, that is especially valuable for the information it gives as to events during the reign of Augustus.

Vergil (70 to 19 B.C.). The greatest poet who ever wrote in Latin. It is here needful only to remark that the *Æneid* was a magnificent attempt to glorify Rome and incidently the Julian house, by means of a poetic adaptation of the old traditions of the founding of the great city by the Tiber.

Vopiscus (lived about 300 A.D.). One of the authors contributing to the *Augustan History;* especially he was the author of the *Life of Aurelian.*

The Ancient World.   Revised Edition

By Professor WILLIS MASON WEST, of the University of Minnesota.

PART ONE, Greece and the East. 12mo, cloth, 324 pages.
PART TWO, Rome and the West. 12mo, cloth, 371 pages.
COMPLETE EDITION. 12mo, cloth, 681 pages.

THE New Ancient World is well within the scope of the abilities of the youngest students in high schools and academies. Its style is simple, direct, vivid, and interesting, and never fails to impress even the most immature reader, who carries away from a study of this book a series of striking pictures of ancient life.

The author emphasizes the unity in historical development; he shows that national life, like individual life, has continuous growth and development, and that a knowledge of the past explains the present. Every experiment in government in ancient times has its lesson; and in the hands of Professor West history becomes an instrument for teaching the duties of modern citizenship.

(1) Most stress is laid on those periods and those persons who contributed most to the development of civilization.

(2) Space is found for the exciting and the picturesque whenever it is matter of historical importance. Narrative and biography abound.

(3) Little weight is given to the legendary periods of Greek and Roman history, and the space thus gained is devoted to the wide-reaching Hellenic world after Alexander, and to the Roman Empire which had so deep an influence on later history.

(4) In every paragraph the leading idea is brought out by italics, and illuminating quotations introduce many chapters.

(5) The book teaches the use of a library by giving specific references to topics for reports.

(6) There are forty-six maps and plans, which are made the basis of study, suggested by questions given in the text. There are also one hundred eighty-one illustrations taken from authentic sources.

The Modern World

By Professor W. M. WEST, 12mo, cloth, 794 pages.

THIS volume, intended as a companion to the author's *Ancient World*, is a revision of his *Modern History*.

As in the Ancient World, there has been a determined effort to make a simple history that can be easily understood by pupils in the early years of the High School. Interesting phases of history are given prominence, difficult ideas have been avoided, the language throughout is simple.

One new feature of the Modern World is five preliminary chapters, giving an outline of history from prehistoric times to the accession of Charlemagne. These chapters serve as an excellent review for a course in Ancient History, or even make it possible to use the Modern World to cover the general history of the world.

The book contains nearly two hundred handsome illustrations and is provided with fifty-three maps, all but five of which are colored.

Like the Modern History the book gives especial prominence to the period since the French Revolution. The author treats with comparative briefness many phases of the history of the Middle Ages in order to gain adequate space for the marvellous nineteenth century, and so for an intelligent introduction to the twentieth.

American Government

By DR. FRANK ABBOTT MAGRUDER, 12mo, cloth, 488 pages.

THE economic element in government is emphasized throughout this book. It has a thorough treatment, not only of theoretical government, but especially of practical politics, caucuses, marking ballots, registration.

The enormous influence of the judiciary is made clear, and it is shown how, through interpretation, they often legislate. It contains a frank discussion of the weaknesses of our government, as well as of its strong points.

American History and Government

By Professor WILLIS MASON WEST. With maps and illustrations. 12mo, cloth, 814 pages.

THIS volume fuses the study of American history with the study of our political institutions in their practical workings — each group of institutions being taken up for complete study where it may best be understood as a product of progressive history. Large place is given to economic and industrial development, as the main explanation of political growth, with clear consciousness of the constant interaction between these mighty forces.

Aside from this combination of "History" and "Civics," the book is unique in three great features: (1) the large place given to the influence of the West; (2) the attention given to the deeply significant labor movements of 1825–1840; (3) and the story of the recent Progressive movement. Indeed, a fourth of the space is given to the last forty years.

The common delusion of a golden age of democracy in the days of Jefferson or of John Winthrop is firmly exposed and corrected, and the student is surely and skilfully led to look forward, not backward. The tremendous problems of to-day, too, are put forward with no shading of their difficulties. The book is in no sense a special plea; but it is written in a sincere conviction that a fair presentation of American history must give to American youth a robust and aggressive faith in democracy.

A Source Book in American History

By Professor WILLIS MASON WEST. 12mo, cloth, 608 pages.

THIS is a companion volume to *American History and Government*. It contains much material never before accessible to young students. No extract has been selected unless it has some definite articulation with the purpose of the main text.

A Short History of England

By Charles M. Andrews, Farnam Professor of History in Yale University. With Maps, Tables, and numerous Illustrations. 12mo, cloth, 473 pages.

THIS history of England aims to present within the compass of about 400 pages the main features of England's story from earliest times to the present day. The book traces in rapid survey the development of the people and institutions of England from Anglo-Saxon times to the close of the year 1911, and shows by what steps the primitive organization of a semi-tribal people has been transformed into the highly complicated political and social structure of the United Kingdom and the British Empire. It retains on a smaller scale the essential characteristics of the larger work by the same author, with some additions, chiefly of a geographical and biographical character, and many omissions of details.

The author tells a clear and simple story, avoiding technical expressions and yet passing over no important feature of the history that is necessary for the proper understanding of the subject.

The aim of the book is to be instructive as well as interesting. The narrative is made as continuous as possible, that the pupil may follow in unbroken sequence the thread of the story. It is accompanied with a large number of newly selected illustrations and an ample supply of maps and chronological tables. The elaborate bibliographies contained in the larger work have been omitted and only a small but selective list of the best books in brief form has been retained. The history has been brought down to date in matters of scholarship as well as chronology, and contains many views and statements not to be found in the larger work. It is designed as a text-book for half-year, or elementary courses, but it might well be used by any reader desiring a brief and suggestive account of the main features of England's history.

History of the United States

By the late CHARLES K. ADAMS, and Professor W. P. TRENT, of Columbia University. 12mo, cloth, 630 pages.

THE authors have laid the stress on the two crises of American history — the Revolutionary War and the Civil War. They have treated both these periods very fully, and have endeavored in the case of the first to present the side of Great Britain with fairness, while, at the same time, bringing out the necessity of the struggle, and the bravery and wisdom of the American patriots. In dealing with the period of the Civil War they have aimed to give the Southern side with sympathy and, while upholding the cause of the Union, have sought to avoid recrimination, and to give each side credit for its sincerity and bravery. The other periods of our history have not been unduly subordinated to the great crises, but have been so treated as to lead up to them. The process of the making of the Constitution and the various developments in its interpretation have been fully studied. While emphasis has necessarily been laid on the political and military features of our history, the social, industrial, scientific, and literary development of the country has been given due space.

The following are some of the special features of the book:

Thirty-six maps, of which nineteen are colored.

Two hundred and three illustrations, reproduced from authentic sources. Especial care has been taken to include the best possible portraits of eminent men. Some of these were taken from private collections and have not been published before.

A full chronological table.

Foot-notes which describe the lives of persons mentioned in the text, in order that the narrative shall not be interrupted at the appearance of each new name.

The great development of the United States during the past decade makes it imperative that an adequate history be kept up to date. The present edition covers the period to March, 1913, and contains a full account of the chief events of President Taft's administration.

A Day in Old Athens

By Professor WILLIAM STEARNS DAVIS, of the University of Minnesota. 12mo, cloth, 254 pages.

THIS book offers a vivid picture of the most important phases of Athenian life in the fourth century B.C. The fascinating word pictures of the author, together with the numerous illustrations from drawings based on vase paintings of ancient Greek life, make the book particularly desirable for supplementary reading.

Ancient History

By Professor WILLIS MASON WEST, of the University of Minnesota. 12mo, cloth, 606 pages.

THIS book is in complete harmony with the report of the Committee of Seven of the American Historical Association. It deals with the Eastern nations and with the Greeks, Romans, and Teutons, the elements from which the modern world has grown. Its aim is to show the continuity of history. Little space is given to legends, or to anecdotes, or to wars; attention is directed to the growth of society, to the development of institutions, to the fusion of peoples.

Ancient Greece

From the earliest times down to 146 B.C. By ROBERT F. PENNELL. Revised Edition with Plans and Colored Maps. 16mo, cloth, 193 pages.

Ancient Rome

From the earliest times down to 476 A.D. By ROBERT F. PENNELL. Revised Edition with Plans and Colored Maps. 16mo, cloth, 284 pages.

IN Ancient Greece and Ancient Rome the leading facts are presented in a concise and readable form. Minor details and unimportant names are omitted. The maps and plans have been drawn and engraved especially for the books, and contain all the data, and only the data, necessary for following the story.